Thomas Mitchell

Conflict of the Nineteenth Century

The Bible and free thought; Ingersoll's lecture on the gods dissected, its charges a

combine of misconception and reckless assertion

Thomas Mitchell

Conflict of the Nineteenth Century
The Bible and free thought; Ingersoll's lecture on the gods dissected, its charges a combine of misconception and reckless assertion

ISBN/EAN: 9783337099749

Printed in Europe, USA, Canada, Australia, Japan

Cover: Foto ©Lupo / pixelio.de

More available books at **www.hansebooks.com**

CONFLICT OF THE NINETEENTH CENTURY—THE BIBLE AND FREE THOUGHT

INGERSOLL'S LECTURE ON THE GODS DISSECTED ITS CHARGES A COMBINE OF MISCONCEPTION AND RECKLESS ASSERTION

BIBLICAL RELIGION THE EXACT COUNTERPART DEMANDED BY THE MENTAL, MORAL, SOCIAL, AND PHYSICAL NATURE OF MAN ; MAN FOR GOD, AND GOD FOR MAN

"Fool to think how vain against
The Omnipotent to rise in arms!"

BY

REV. THOMAS MITCHELL

AUTHOR OF "COSMOGONY," "THE LATTER DAY GLORY," "THE HOUSE WITHOUT
A FOUNDATION: ROMANISM THE ANTITHESIS OF CHRISTIANITY"

"VOICES FROM PARADISE"
A Poem
AND OTHER WORKS

"Buy the truth and sell it not."—*Prov.*

NEW YORK
THE UNIVERSAL BOOK COMPANY
1893

TROW DIRECTORY
PRINTING AND BOOKBINDING COMPANY
NEW YORK

PREFACE.

THIS book, and the four others mentioned on the title page, comprise the results of more than a half century of impartial and independent investigation of the works and words of God. When commencing a religious life, which was at the age of eighteen years, I caught a new inspiration for acquiring knowledge. My parents were natives of Scotland, and I was born in the city of New York, 1818. My mother was religious and a great reader, especially a student of Scripture. My father was not religious, but a philosophic thinker and reader of scientific works, and would converse with me when a mere child, upon scientific and historic subjects. I inherited and thus acquired a passion for original investigation. This rendered it impossible for me to accept or believe anything upon mere authority, no matter from what source it professed to have come, or the range of thought to be circumscribed within the boundaries of human opinion; in religion the product of creeds, and in science the hypothesis of men, it may be of high titles and educational position, who generally seem to be perfectly contented by becoming masters of the text-books, many of whom look upon original ideas as innovations, just as though there was nothing more to be learned from Scripture and Nature, the two great books of the Creator.

In a short time I was advised to enter the ministry, which, being congenial to my own mind, I did. It was but a few years before I learned to my utter astonishment my great ignorance, and lost all confidence in attempting to teach what I did not understand, and this was the most important lesson of my life; to know that I did not know.   Up to this time I had studied the standard works of my own denomination, the M. E. Church, and by their controversies with other Protestant denominations, discovered wide differences of doctrinal opinion among men equally learned and honest, all claiming to have the Bible for their bases.   These observations led me into a complete state of mental confusion.   To solve such a question it was necessary to begin at the foundation of such relations.   Here was man possessing the organic elements of devotion and reasoning faculties, which led him from effects to causes and to a single first and only cause, thus arriving at the existence of the Creator and object of the devotion, and that the Creator must have given His creature, with such endowments, a written revelation in correspondence with such a nature.

In view of all this I came substantially to the following conclusions :

1st.   That if the Scriptures are what they purport to be, the inspired words of God, those words must be in harmony with themselves.

2d.   As these words of prophesy not only claim to foretell events, but those developed by the march and connection of the great universal dynasties connected with the Church, either corrupting it by their fostering care, or attempting its destruction by the bloody sword of persecution, running the prehistoric record down to the very end of the world itself, and that if these events can be understood, then they constitute a chronological chart by which the age of the world itself may be measured, the fulfilment of each in the succession approximates so much nearer the last.   And the events thus passed form the history of the world ; to understand and know the one is equally to know the other.

3d.   If the statements of Scripture touching the origin of the world and its inhabitants are true. they cannot be in conflict with the logical deductions of the works of the same Being—properly called philosophical science.

4th.   If the Creator is the author of a book claiming to be for the enlightenment of His creatures, involving their duties and destiny, He must have been capable of making its teachings intelligible to all of such creatures ranking high enough in the scale of being to know right from wrong, providing they study those revelations according to their own prescribed rules.

Thus, was the almost appalling task before my mind; but, in self-defence as against infidelity, I was obliged to master these great questions, though comprehending the solid literature of the ages.

The first questions which arose were: What was taught in the prophetic Scriptures in regard to the design and destiny of the world and man, and the events through which both must pass in order to complete those designs? This I accomplished, at least to my own satisfaction.

The second question was: Have those prophetic events been fulfilled, and in the predicted order and according to the predicted periods of time covering them? Of course this task necessitated a knowledge of the history of all nations. We not only accomplished this, but found the historic to be the complement of the prehistoric, or prophetic, and which admitted of no other conclusion than that the Creator of the world was the author of Scripture.

About this time what was called the science of evolution and the geological chronology of the world came prominently before the people, claiming that man did not originate at the time nor in the manner stated in the Bible. This involved as the third part of our task a philosophical knowledge of all the facts and phenomena of natural science bearing upon these questions, many of which could not be found in books, and by which false science could be exposed. Again did we master this part of our task, demonstrating that the account of creation given in the book of Genesis, if not thus written, could have been written by a man who had acquired a correct knowledge of the science of nature, which comprehends the reciprocal interdependence of intelligent being and lifeless matter, the whole involving a complete system of philosophic necessities—thus vindicating the writing to have originated in the mind of the Creator himself. The results of this part of the investigation are published in the first of the series of the five herein mentioned, and entitled Cosmogony, and we appeal to literary observers of the ten years, since its publication, whether the arguments have not nearly put to silence the defenders of the pretentious science of evolution and the geological age of the world, inconsistent with its chronology as given in the Bible, unmasking the atheistic deception of sailing under the false colors of "free thought."

TABLE OF CONTENTS.

INTRODUCTION.

CHAPTER I.

CHAPTER II.

CHAPTER III.

CHAPTER IV.

CHAPTER V.

CHAPTER VI.

CHAPTER VII.

CHAPTER VIII.

CHAPTER IX.

INTRODUCTION.

THE conflict of the nineteenth century is between Atheists, Agnostics, Astrologists, and Freethinkers, on the one side, and believers in revealed religion and sacred Scripture, on the other.

As Ingersoll's lecture on "The Gods," delivered in Booth's Theatre, New York, a few years since, repeats all the skeptical sentiments of the past, involving the question of God—or no God ; if, therefore, we refute these, it leaves the whole crowd without the show of honest defence, and any attempted effort to repeat the exposed errors, will only manifest a dogged morosity and an obstinate resolution becoming only the wilful destroyers of all good, and the propagators of all evil.

"When the enemy shall come in like a flood, the Spirit of the Lord shall lift up a standard against him." (Isa. 59 : 19.)

The Standard of Truth Defined.

When measured by truth, there are but two standards —in science, philosophy, morality, or religion. Each of these divisions of human knowledge—and they comprehend its totality—has its standard of truth and its negative standard of error, that which distinguishes one from the other. Between these there is no philosophical agreement, no community, no harmony. They may seem to run into each other at such nice shades of blending that to the superficial observer there may appear no important difference ; but this is only for the want of discriminating ability to perceive the point where the truth ends and the error begins. If this proposition be correct in regard to either of these grand divisions of human knowledge, it must be equally so of the others; and therefore involves the question of the existence of a living God, the history and character of Christ, and the truth of the Christian religion.

This postulate also necessitates the conclusion that if any of these departments of human knowledge, or any of the ideas they include are established by logical argument, and more especially by one or more syllogisms, then there can be no real evidence against it; and that which appears to be such, must have its foundation in sophistry and vain speculation, leaving the truth all on one side and the error all on the other, as well as the evidence leading up to it. For example: If the logical teaching of natural existence and phenomena prove the existence of a living Creator, then there can be no logical argument against such existence. If science, therefore, proves the existence of a personal cause upon which the origin of its own existence depends, then there can be no scientific evidence against the conclusion; for true science cannot teach contradictions, and erroneous science is no science at all!

The Events Through which Christ Passed—Foretold by Prophets.

Take another example: We find that the history of Christ, from his birth to his ascension, was foretold by prophets and written in the Scriptures; and it is another fact that the writings were in the exclusive possession, except a single copy, of his bitterest enemies and crucifiers —the Jewish priests; and furthermore, that their treatment of him constituted a very large part of the fulfilment of those prophesies, showing the record to be true; for it cannot be supposed that those enemies would write such prophesies after the fulfilment of the events, and pretend they were written before.

A truth established by such a chain of facts and events admits of no evidence against it; and if such is the record

of Christ in prophetic Scripture, its author must have
been he who not only saw the future, but the *end* from
the beginning, and the question as to who were the mere
penmen has absolutely no place in the controversy. And
when it is also found that this prophetic account describes
the leading events of the most prominent nations of the
world which have flourished since the predictions were
known to have been written, its author must have been
the living Creator who inspired the writings !

The events to which we refer are those changes which
have grown out of the connection of the nations of the
world with the true and false church, describing its corrupt, fostering care, or cruel persecution. In addition to
this, when it is found that prophetic Scripture contains an
accurate description of the present peculiar civil, social,
and religious condition of the world, and that it has been
developed in the lifetime of the men now living, as well
as the chronological order of the record, then again it
must be true, and no one could have been its author but
a being who foresaw the history ; and the possession of
such knowledge implies the ability to inspire men to
write it in advance ; of which no being would be able
were he not capable of weighing the reciprocal influences
existing among men, or which would exist and actuate
those concerned in the development of the events described. Furthermore, if our knowledge of philosophical
science demonstrates that the world and its organic inhabitants must have originated in exact accordance with
the statements in the account of creation given in the
book of Genesis, both as to time and manner, then the
Maker of the world must have been the author of those
statements ; or that they were made by a better scientist
than has ever lived, or does live at the present day !

The Nature and Object of Giving Prophetic Events.

These prophetic events are divided into those which
God foresaw would take place in the natural course of
things among men, and those which He determined to
accomplish by direct interference ; and a miracle is that of

which nature was and is incapable, and toward many of
these events nature is repugnant.   Such, for instance, as
the conditions of friendship with the Maker.

Neither could there have been the slightest object in
giving a record to men of prophetic events were they not
susceptible of being understood, at least about the time
of their fulfilment.   There was a first human event, and
there will be a last, and each of the succession measured
its time in passing, and made the world so much older
and nearer its end.   These events are the burden of
prophecy; of course those living near the end of the
record, if biblical and historic students, behold their passage or existence as ominous of the end !—impressing them
as likely to come at any day, and this we may add, instead of setting days and hours for the end, is the only
knowledge that can be obtained regarding it !

Speaking prophetically to those living near the end,
Christ says : "When therefore ye see all these things come
to pass, then know that he is near, even at the door—
then lift up your heads and rejoice, for your redemption
draweth nigh !"

Events Christ Promised to Execute at His Return.

Concerning Christ's promised return, the Apostle Peter
speaks thus : "Knowing this first, that there shall come
in the last days, scoffers, walking after their own lusts
(the strongest expression of desire) saying, Where is the
promise of his coming ?—for since the fathers fell asleep all
things continue as they were since the beginning of the
creation !   (2 Pet. 3 : 3.)   That we have come into the
days here predicted is evinced by the existence of this
significant event, led on by the career of Ingersoll.
While those who study the record rejoice that their redemption draweth near, the others scoff at the idea of
Christ's being near, and act as though their wilful ignorance and unbelief would prevent his coming.

Christ repeated the promise for the last time—in the
last book of the Bible—the last chapter of that book, thus :
"Behold ! I come and my reward is with me and my

work before me to give to every man according to his works! He that testifieth these things saith, Surely I come quickly! Amen!—even so. Come, Lord Jesus!" To show that prevailing ignorance and aversion in our day to have Christ come according to his promise, we may ask how many would give such a response to the announcement as that here given by John? Upon this question, and according to the same record, the sentiment of the world will always remain the same as divided by the two classes; hence, we also read: "But the day of the Lord so cometh as a thief in the night: for when they shall say peace and safety, then sudden destruction cometh upon them!" "But ye brethren are not in darkness, that that day shall overtake you as a thief. Ye are all the children of light and the children of day!" The greatest advantage, therefore, in revelling these events, is to give men a broader foundation for their faith, thus enabling them to look with greater confidence for the events of the future part of the record; especially those promises and threatenings concerning the future world.

Now, if this world-long line of facts and events have been revelled and recorded—and by the study of Scripture —natural science, and history, may be understood, does it not demonstrate the author to have been the creator Himself? This proposition being established, then, no pretended testimony of religious history, or of philosophical science, can disturb it. That such are shown by the Scriptures to be the essential relation between their statements—facts of history and those of natural science, it follows that there can be no evidence in defence of atheism, whatever its seeming, or of any other form of skepticism or infidelity, however plausible its appearance or attractive its guise!

Why Has Skepticism Increased in Our Day?

Why, then, it may be asked, has skepticism or infidelity so increased, especially in our day? The answer is implied in the above argument, namely, as the knowledge of these sources of information which establish the truth must be had, as the remedy, so general ignorance of them must be the cause of the skepticism : false science, false philosophy, and false religion, in theory and practice, flourish because of the prevailing ignorance concerning them. For example, ignorance of the divine authenticity of Scripture results from ignorance of its prophetic teaching and historic record of its fulfilment ; and ignorance of true science results from the adoption of the conclusions of the so-called modern scientists, or its authors, all of whom admit that its basis is only hypothesis, and therefore without evidence. Hence, the only course to be pursued against the skeptics, or to prevent others from becoming such, is the presentation to their minds of the true teaching of Scripture, and philosophical science.

If, therefore, the flood of skepticism is ever to be restrained, such knowledge must be obtained at whatever cost, or however arduous the task of acquiring it ; and this book will do precisely the desired work ! The question is not whether unbelief is to become general and Christianity destroyed ; for it is the same as though destroyed to every lost man ! Our work is to enlighten and save individuals, and not to have Christ professed by nations or generations, for that would make it popular, and popular Christianity begets formalists, bigots, and hypocrites—always bearing these marks.

Thomas Paine and Robert G. Ingersoll's Coming.

That the enemy has come in like a flood, no observing mind will deny ; and there appears to be no effectual standard lifted against him, and if we have been unable to prevent his coming, and poisonous work, how can we be expected, without other weapons, to beat him back and counteract his work ? It is true the " Spirit of the Lord will lift up a standard against him ; " but who will be the standard-bearer ? The plan of God is to save men from error by men. He, therefore, holds every man reciprocally responsible for the discharge of his personal duty toward his fellow-man. It will be no excuse that he is not qualified to extract the poison from the mind of his neighbor, if the antidote in the shape of a book is within his reach to put into his hands by a gift or recommendation; for it is written, and by the coming judge himself: "And that servant which knew his Lord's will, and *prepared not himself*, neither did according to his will, shall be beaten with many stripes." (Luke 12 : 47.)

The wonderful progress of skepticism in modern times cannot be better illustrated than by considering the facts attending the appearance of two notable characters in our country, one of them about seventy-five years ago, and the other at the present day—Thomas Paine and Robert G. Ingersoll.

After publishing his "Age of Reason," Paine came to this country. Here he was looked upon by the people with utter contempt, who in derision they called "Tom Paine!" No periodical of that day condescended to do him honor, or publish his infidel sentiments, and a public delivery of them would have been suppressed by violence. In fact, there was no city in the civilized world in which the people would have permitted him to publicly repeat the blasphemies and vulgarisms of his "Age of Reason;" not even Paris, except during the short period of the "Reign of Terror," which was itself the culmination of the progress of atheism!

But in our day, Paine has his thousands of admirers, who build monuments over his ashes, around which large assemblies gather to do him honor; and men stand up in what are called Christian pulpits, and pronounce encomiums upon his character. It must also be remembered that Paine was only a deist, and in his "Age of Reason" presents conclusive arguments from nature in proof of the existence of a personal God as the creator of the world, which we have elsewhere quoted against the atheists.

But in our day Ingersoll, an atheist, makes his appearance, and is elected to the Congress of the United States; and in the House of Representatives makes allusions to his Godless sentiments, without evoking a rebuke. He is hailed as the interpreter of liberty, and of the glorious progress of the age; and if a judge passes sentence on him for the violation of the laws against blasphemy, he goes about the country abusing him and the laws, as being behind the age; and for doing which his audiences vociferously applaud him. He is interviewed by newspaper reporters, even for his opinions about the state of Christianity, whether it was almost dead, the replies to which the press spreads before the people as its choicest reading matter, and the people endorse its action by their enlarged patronage.

In contrast to his public reception and in cities where Paine was repudiated, Ingersoll's audiences have packed the largest houses from pit to dome, and paid fabulous prices to hear his iconoclastic tirades against all the gods, among whom he most blasphemously ranks the living God that made him; and his impious bravado against God Almighty, evokes the loudest applause. The secular press re-echoes his harangues throughout the length and breadth of the land, and indeed of the civilized world, while many of the papers refuse to publish the most conclusive arguments in opposition to his illogical and unphilosophical fallacies.

When a similar effort was made a century ago by deism and atheism combined, it was met by the Christian ministry of Europe and the managers of the periodical press of that day because they were diligent students of the Scriptures and of philosophical science, and with such weapons its unfounded and blasphemous assumptions were beaten back for nearly a century; nor would it ever have gained its present popularity had the religious ministry of the present day been as well qualified to meet it as then, or had it not been aided by Lyell's skeptical geology, Darwin's Godless evolution, and Proctor's atheistic astronomy; all of which teach that the world and its inhabitants came into existence without miraculous interference. By degrees these sentiments have insinuated themselves even into the schools of the prophets, from which ministers of religion graduate; and how can they be supposed capable of exposing these errors? Instead of studying to be better acquainted with natural science than these authors, they seem to have contented themselves by giving Ingersollism and all other skeptical isms a "wide birth," as they express it; as if, by letting error alone, it would die of itself.

They have, however, pursued this policy until it has become evident that in their hands the Gospel has almost utterly failed to reach and convert the men of our age, most of whom have heard or read Ingersoll. Not that they profess skepticism, or that they even desire it to be true; but the poison of it and that of evolution, is in their mind, and must be extracted. The deceptive reasoning must be exposed by true reasoning, and the teaching claimed for the so-called facts of science must be shown to be without logical force or defence.

The so-called theological dogmas which rest solely on human authority must be so far abandoned that the Bible will not be held responsible for any sentiment which cannot be vindicated by its entire harmony; and that, too, when interpreted by itself. Who, then, will comply with the injunction, "Lift ye up a standard for the people?" and report, "Here am I, send me!"

Limit of Mental Conception—Philosophy of Creation.

If nature as a whole came into existence of herself, then each particular part did so as well, and which would have been as true of man, the highest of her intelligencies. The opposite hypothesis involves the absurdity that the weakest and most helpless was the most capable of self-existence. If nature thus originated, then those things which manifest the greatest degree of mechanical skill in their construction would be the work of the greatest mechanical ability. As man himself is the most distinguished part of nature, and could create, or develop every lower part, and could not create himself, he must have been the work of an intelligent being as much higher in the scale as to qualify him to have been man's creator; and the power is in the degree of its manifestation.

The word "create," as used in the Bible, is synonymous with "make" and "form," and expresses the idea of changing one form of matter into another, and never in the sense of making things out of nothing—"The Lord God formed,—created,—made man out of the dust of the earth," not out of nothing ! The creations of man are limited to those of art. Select the most intelligent botanist, and ask him to ascertain all the chemical properties contained in a stem of the simplest moss—supposing it to be the simplest plant, and combine them in the proportions to form a stem which, when set in soil, would grow and produce the spore or function of seed, and which would reproduce its kind ; and would he not be as incompetent to the task as to make the world itself? But such incompetency by no means proves him to have less creative skill than nature ; for he can create such things as steam-engines, electric telegraphs, phonographic speaking machines, etc., while nature can create nothing, can originate nothing. The skill and power she manifests is wholly involuntary—evolving that which was involved in her by the knowledge and power of her Creator. In fact, nature has not as much ability to perform the least act as that possessed by the minutest animalcule which swims in a drop of bog-water ; for it moves in any direction, or ceases to move at pleasure, while helpless—lifeless nature can only act or move in fixed grooves, according to the power imposed upon her, and cannot deviate from the course marked out for her, or cease to act under it. Which, then, is the greater, the lifeless solar system, which cannot originate the least possible phenomenon, or the insect that moves or stops at will ? Hence the superiority of man to lifeless nature, and that of man's Maker, to man himself. How, then, could nature have brought herself into existence ? The very question shocks the simplest degree of reason, and intensifies it as the reason grows profound. With greater propriety can it be said that man originated himself, and still greater that God originated himself, than that the insect caused its own existence ; for the greater the work, the greater the workman, is an unanswerable postulate.

Although to trained thinkers no argument can make the axiom, " From nothing, nothing comes," more conclusive ; yet the popular mind may be aided by a few remarks upon the most important facts thus comprehended. For example, if God is nothing, He did not bring Himself into existence ; for, from nothing, nothing comes. The converse of this is, that if God exists, He is something. As God exists, and is something, He did always exist ; as something cannot come from nothing. Space is that in which things exist, but of itself is nothing and always was nothing, and always will be nothing, as from nothing, nothing comes ! As God exists, He must have dimensions, and a location in space.

Matter, in its homogeneous or heterogeneous particles, exists, and did not come from nothing ; for from nothing, nothing comes ; therefore matter always was. Here, then is space, matter, and God, existing as philosophical and scientific necessities, rendering the idea of bringing things from nothing or its opposite—annihilation, impossible. It may be objected that this gives us two eternities— which is absurd ; but it does no such thing. This is evident from the fact that the term " eternity " means simply duration, or unmeasured time ; but God, and everything else are things existing in duration, which are no more parts of the duration than that when the thing, man, is a hundred years old, he is the hundred years itself ! Whoever, therefore, denies the eternity of homogeneous matter, puts himself in contradiction to this self-evident truth, and declares that from nothing, something comes ; or that something may become nothing, or be annihilated.

Such a sentiment would no more be true, though taught in the Bible, and claimed God as its author, than that truth can contradict itself, or that natural impossibilities may become possible !

It is not, however, taught in that book ; in every instance where the creation or formation of things are described, the process is by changing one thing into another; it is simply transformation.

To say that the Creator is the God of the pantheist, in nowise effects the fact of his personality; indeed, it asserts it, by making him a part of every person and thing existing. Its absurdity, however, consists in confounding him with the world he made, thereby making him his own creator.

According to human conception, if a compound substance or an organic being exists, it, or he, must have been made into that form, implying the prior existence of the maker. But it may be contended that this maker must also have had a maker, and so on, without the least prospect of arriving at the first; but this is on the supposition that human conception is without limit. And it is just herein lies the error; but to deny there was a first, is as absurd as to deny there is a second, and that there is either no God, or there has been an endless succession of gods, as well as things.

The fact of the succession of organic—living things, is, that they begin and end—are born and die, either as generations or individuals. It is another fact that if we begin at the last and count back, we come to the first, and this demonstrates there was a first.

These existences are in lines, and not in circles. To be in a circle which has no beginning or end, would require that the whole number of living beings and things must have existed simultaneously without increase or diminution; that in all history such should have been the condition of things and of the inhabitants of the world. From such a state of facts the conclusion of no beginning and no end would have been legitimate; but as the reverse of this is true, therefore the world and its inhabitants owe their origin to a prior existing being, and of sufficient mechanical skill and power, to have been the Creator of all.

Let us suppose that a man is the most perfect piece of workmanship which his Maker is capable of constructing, and that the construction of a steam-engine is the most perfect piece of mechanism of which man is capable of producing ; do we not see that there is just as great a difference between the mechanic who made the steam-engine and himself as between himself and the mechanic who made him, and that it would be just as absurd for the man-mechanic to deny the existence of his Maker, or that he was made, as for the steam-engine to deny the existence of its maker, or to say to another such engine, unless you can give me a clear conception of the mechanic who made you, and also of Him who made him, I will not believe a man made you, or that there is any such being as man existing ? The natural principle is, that no being is capable of conceiving or comprehending the mechanical principles involved in his own organization, infinitely less the history and greatness of his Maker.

In fact the power of any mind or being is limited to the greatest and most complicated piece of work he can conceive and construct, or have constructed under his dictation ! Is it not, therefore, just as reasonable for any piece of man's work to deny the existence of its maker because it cannot conceive his greatness and origin, as for the creature, man, to pursue the same course of skepticism in regard to his Maker ?

It is not that there are no beings higher in the scale, but that a conception of them, in the sense of comprehension as to their nature and origin, is beyond ; not contrary or repugnant to the capacity of all grades of organism below them ; and the folly lies in the assumption and presumption that, as a comprehensive answer cannot be given to the question, Whence came this superior being ? —and as I know not, none such exists ! Up to this point all is resonable, philosophical, scientific, and logical, and the skeptic may have a very large amount of knowledge ; but because he is incapable with all others of knowing one thing more, he therefore knows nothing ; and as he is too proud to stand alone in total ignorance, he declares all other men equally ignorant, and would acknowledge it if they were not superstitious : this is good agnosticism ! It knows nothing.

If measured by such a standard, each lower being or

thing in the scale is atheistic to everyone of a higher degree. A man may know nothing of the mechanical organization or chemical properties of the sun, or of its origin; but would that prove its non-existence, or that all vegetable and plant life on our planet did not depend upon it for continued existence?

" I am that I am!" is what the Creator knows of himself, and declares: " This is my memorial forever; " and no words could convey to man a clearer conception of his origin than this declaration! If the mechanic should say to the machine he made, " You owe to me your existence, as I owe mine to my Maker," would the machine be enlightened? Would it not have been just as much so as if he had said: " I am that I am! "

Philosophy of Cause and Effect—Its Sequence—Creation.

The only correct definition which it seems to us can be given to " Cause," is to ascribe its source to mind, or to that alone which is in some degree intelligent; and this includes everything endowed with voluntary motion. Every species of living beings, from the lowest up to the Creator himself, possesses the power of causation; each being able to produce effects greater or less, according to its own order. No existence or phenomena are better, or more universally known, or can be depended upon with as much certainty as that of cause and effect.

An effect is that which invariably follows a certain combination of things, or elements, while that which has the power of causation may act within the same sphere an indefinite number of times, and each time differently. The mind that caused the man unwittingly to walk into the snare laid for him, causes him to avoid it the second time it is presented; while the great sun, shining in her strength, must suffer eclipse every time the little moon presents its sombre intervening disc. We speak of second causes in the movements of inorganic nature; but if in any other sense than that of accommodation, it is an incorrect expression; for all of these are themselves effects, and these in turn are effects of effects. And this being the quality of all the phenomena, from that of the small-est atom of matter possessing chemical affinity or electri-cal endowment, up to every member of the solar system —each has the quality to effect another ; but all is the work of compulsion. Within the telescopic or micro-scopic range of vision, or within the electrical or chemi-cal laboratory of lifeless nature, not the smallest cause exists.

We may state the argument thus : All nature is effect ; effect must have cause ; cause can only reside in the mind of a living person ; every such person may act, or not act as he pleases, at any given time ; for if he must act, he is an effect of that which compels him. But as man is a common part of nature itself, not being the cause of his own existence, he is the effect of a prior cause.

Still every branch of nature had a cause who must have been her intelligent Creator, free to act—to make or not make the world as he pleased and in the fashion he pleased. Therefore, all nature being effect, her cause must have been prior and superior to nature, therefore, supernatural. It is immaterial so far as the science of nature is concerned by what name this being may be known. He is the living, thinking, personal Creator of the world ; consequently the proprietor of its living, thinking inhabitants, who, because of this relation, owe him supreme allegiance ; which they must pay, or forfeit their right to citizenship in His coming new world !

Why We Make Ingersoll Our Target.

This conclusion simplifies our work to that of exposing the sophistry and false pretension repeated by its mouth-piece, Robert G. Ingersoll, around whom in our day the defence of freethinkerism (which embodies every form of skepticism and unbelief) centres, and this because all others concede him to be its ablest defender ; and this, too, is the reason why we make him our target !

*The Power of Truth — An Example — A Colloquial
Spar with a Skeptic.*

This man was Mr. Charles Hunt, who was employed
eighteen years on the New York *Tribune,* and part of the
time on the editorial staff.

By request Mr. Hunt carefully read the manuscript of
this book, after which the author said: "Mr. H., how
much do we differ in sentiment upon the fundamental
principles of this manuscript?" "Well," he replied,
"I do not know." "Will you please to answer me a few
questions that we may know, and first do you now know,
just as you know anything else which you have not tested
by your senses, that there is a personal, living God?"
"Yes, I cannot avoid that conclusion which these facts
and arguments seem to establish." "For the same reasons, do you accept the conclusion that this God was the
Creator of the world and its inhabitants, and that, therefore, they did not come into existence by what is called
evolution?" "Yes, I do; but now I do not know any
more, I do not know where this God is, or how He came
to exist." I replied: "Well, Mr. H., does that which
you do not know militate against or destroy that which
you do know?" To this he replied, "No, it does not."

But do not these admissions involve more knowledge
than this? For example, would a being with the wisdom nature manifests in every part of the creation, and
in the utmost detailed interdependence, and all governed
by inherent laws with penalties annexed, which execute
themselves, have left man, the highest in the scale without law for his government, and especially relative to his
mental and moral constitution; besides, would he not
desire this highest part of his work to please and obey
him?" "To these questions," he said, "Affirmative
answers must be given according to the common principles of mental and moral philosophy." "Well, if the
man was capable of obeying and pleasing his Creator,
would he not be capable of disobeying and displeasing
him; does not the one imply the other, or would it not

be a natural impossibility to make a being who could obey and could not disobey; and can any being make an impossibility possible?" Mr. H. replied: "These principles seem to imply each other and render such conclusions unanswerable." Another question is: "Would the man have known what acts would have been pleasing and obedience, and what displeasing and disobedience, had not the Creator have said to him what things he might do and what he might not, toward himself and his fellow-men?" The answer was: "He could not otherwise have known."

Question: "Could a being thus endowed be forced to perform a mental or moral act which would have virtuous or vicious character, or be praise or blameworthy; but which character must have been attributed to him who exerted the force?" "This seems to be logical reasoning," was the reply. Question: "After creating a being thus high in the scale, can he be governed in any other manner than by inducement; the promise of possession, or fear of loss?" Answer: "There does not seem to be any other." "Let me ask one more question: "Would it not be a greater pleasure to the Creator to receive the hearty devotion and loyal obedience of one such being than that derived from the fixed involuntary movements of all the creation besides?" Answer: "It would."

"Now, Mr. Hunt, as it is the highest duty of man prescribed in revealed Christianity to please and obey his Creator, involving everything of a lesser nature, and as you have admitted the existence, imposition, and discharge of these to be philosophic and scientific reasoning, without the least reference to anything taught in the Bible, must not its revealed system have originated and been revealed to mankind by the Creator himself?" To which Mr. H. replied: "I cannot conceive that any other answer to such a conclusion can be given."

ZOROASTER A THEIST.

CHAPTER I.

IT is historic that the great philosophers and reformers of the nations and generations of antiquity believed in one God as the Creator of the world, and considered man-made gods merely as symbolic representatives of the supreme God, as Plato and others called Him. There are three of the wisest of these ancient men who were at once philosophers, statesmen, philanthropists, and religious reformers, and who were most prominent in moulding the civil, social, and religious heathen world, and whose writings have come down to us. Some of these flourished at such early periods that the traditional history of the world's origin had not become very much corrupted from the account of its creation recorded in the book of Genesis. We refer to Zoroaster, the Persian ; Confucius, the Chinaman, and Buddha, of India.

According to the best evidence, Zoroaster was a native of Media, in Persia, and lived under the reign of Hystaspes, the father of Darius, about six hundred years B. C. He was one of the greatest men of all time. His work was twofold—to win the people back to the worship of one God, and to develop them into the higher phase of agriculturists ; and as the sun was the great instrument of vegetable life upon our planet, as the blessed symbol of its Maker, to teach that the natural work of man was the cultivation of earthly products.

He was a reformer and a protester against polytheism and nomadism (wandering shepherds, feeding their flocks wherever they could find pasture growing without cultivation). To the Supreme Being whom his predecessors had worshipped, he applies the name Ah-u-ro; and as Lord, God, and Almighty, Ma-zad-o. This name denotes a conception of the Deity almost identical with Elohim, or Jehovah—of course derived from the Scripture! This title or name was first announced by God to Moses in the year of the world one thousand four hundred and sixty-six, which proves that Zoroaster flourished at a later period.

Zoroaster was the author of the original Zendavesta, very much of which has been lost. The following are said to be two of its most important passages—the one a metrical speech, delivered by Za-ra-thus-tra Spi-ta-ma himself (who was one of Zoroaster's disciples and greatest preachers) when standing before the sacred fire, to a numerously attended meeting of his countrymen. The chief tendency of this speech is to induce them to leave the worship of the Deva, or gods—polytheism—and bow only before Ah-u-ro Ma-zad-o! and to separate themselves entirely from idolaters. He says: "I will now repeat to you who are assembled here, the sayings of the most wise, and the praises of the living God, the songs of the good spirit, the sublime truth which I see arising out of these sacred flames. You shall hearken therefore to the soul of nature, that is, to plough and cultivate the earth. Contemplate the beams of fire with a pious mind! Every-one, both men and women, ought to-day to choose their religion between the Deva and the Ah-u-ro. Ye offspring of renowned ancestors, awake! with me to approve the object of my love, whom I present before you at this moment, the Ah-u-ro Ma-zad-o!"

After declaring the existence of a good and bad spirit, a God and devil, he thus speaks of immortality: "Let us be such as to hope for the life of the future. The prudent man wishes only to be there, where wisdom is at home. (It was about this time that Job, of the same country, was in doubt about his immortality, and asked:

"If a man die, shall he live again?" and was delivered from it by a clear revelation of the resurrection of the dead at the end of the world, when he also would be home with his Ah-u-ro Ma-zad-o! who, in Scripture, is often personified by Wisdom," another title of God.)

Our next extract is from Agatha, and is declared to be the most important piece of literature in the whole Zend-avesta, from which to learn Spitama's exposition of the doctrine of Zoroaster. "Blessed be he, blessed are all men, to whom the living Wise, of his own command, should grant these two everlasting favors—wholesomeness and immortality—for this very good I beseech thee, Ah-u-ro Ma-zad-o! through thy angel of piety, Ar-ma-i-ti, give me happiness, the good, true things, and the posses-sion of the good mind! (How much like—"Let this mind be in you which was also in Christ Jesus our Lord!") I believe thee to be the best being of all; the source of light for the world. Everybody shall choose thee, thou holiest spirit, Ah-u-ro Ma-zad-o! Thou createst all good, true things by thy good mind, and promisest us, who believe in thee, a long life (everlasting life). Thus I believe in thee as the holy God—thou living Wise! I believe thee to be the primeval cause of life in the crea-tion. Thou hast made holy customs and words. (Here, one thousand two hundred and sixty-eight years before Christ, did Zoroaster know that the words of God were written, from which he had learned about the creation.) Thou hast given a bad fortune—emptiness to the base, and a good one to the good man. I will believe in thee, thou glorious God! and in the last future period of cre-ation." This shows that his hope centred in the re-creation of the world—the new heavens and new earth which are to succeed the destruction of the present crea-tion in the last period of time, and which is clearly con-firmed in the Zend literature.

The following shows the sage, searching after light and truth: "What I will ask tell me, thou living Wise! who was in the beginning, the father of truth, and the Creator! Who made the sun and stars! Who causes the moon to increase and wane, if not thee? Who is holding the earth and the skies above us? Who is in the winds and storms, that they so quickly run? Who is the Creator of the good-minded beings, thou Wise? Who made the light of good effect and darkness? Who made the sleep of good effect and activity? Who made the morning, noon and night, reminding the priest of his duties (the Scripture offerings—the morning and evening sacrifice)? To become acquainted with these things I approach thee, thou Wise, holy spirit—Creator of all things and beings!" —("Encyclopedia Britannica.")

Philosophy of Confucius—He a Theist.

According to Memceus, one of his distinguished followers, Confucius appeared from 371 to 288 B.C.

He held that the first thing to be done by a state, was the rectification of names; and his whole social and political system was wrapped up in the sayings: "Good government obtained when the ruler was ruler, the minister—minister; when the father was father, and the son—son. Society, he considered, was made up of five relationships — ruler and subject, husband and wife, father and son, elder brothers and younger, and friends. There was rule on the part of the four first, and submission on that of the others. The rule should be in righteousness and sincerity." "Not more surely," he said, "does the grass bend before the wind, than do the masses yield to the will of those above them. Give the model ruler, and the model people will forthwith appear, and the common people could make the model ruler. They could tell the princes of the states what they ought to be; and they could point them to examples of perfect virtue in former times; to grand sages who lived in a more distant golden age."

Foremost among the duties and relations of human society, says this writer, "We must rank his distinct enunciation of the golden rule, deduced by him from the study of man's mental constitution. Several times he gave that rule in these words: 'What you do not like when done to yourself, do not do to others.'"

A few of his more characteristic sayings may be given, the pith and point of which attest his discrimination of character, and show the tendency of his views: "What the superior man seeks, is himself; what the small man seeks, is in others. The superior man is dignified, but does not wrangle; social, but not a partisan. He does not promote a man simply because of his words, nor does he put good words aside because of the man. A poor man who does not flatter, and a rich man who is not proud, are passable characters; but they are not equal to the poor who are yet cheerful, and the rich who yet love the rules of propriety. Learning, undignified, is perilous. In style all that is required is that it convey the meaning. Extravagance leads to insubordination, and parsimony to meanness. It is better to be mean than insubordinate. A man can enlarge his principles; principles do not enlarge the man. The cautious seldom err."

Sententious sayings like these have gone far to form the ordinary Chinese character. Hundreds and thousands of the literati can repeat every sentence in the classical books; the masses of the people have scores of the Confucian maxims, and little else of an ethical nature in their memories, and with good effect. Confucius laid no claim to divine revelation. Twice or thrice he intimated that he had a mission from heaven, and until it was accomplished he was safe against all attempts to injure him. But his teachings (says the writer) were singularly devoid of reference to anything but what was seen—and temporal. Man, as he is, and the duties belonging to him in society, were what he concerned himself about. He held, however, that man's nature was from God; harmonious acting out of it was obedience to the will of God; and the violation of it was disobedience. But there was a striking difference between his language in affirming this and that of his own ancient models. In the King the references to the Supreme Being are abundant; there is an exulting, awfully sublime recognition of him as the Almighty, personal ruler, who orders the course of nature and providence. With Confucius, the vague, impersonal term—

heaven, took the place of the divine name—but meant the same.

To the inquiry of Tze-lu, he replied : " While you cannot serve men, how can you serve God ? " which is nothing more than is expressed by John, thus : " He that loveth not his brother, whom he hath seen, how can he love God whom he hath not seen ? To the inquiry, " What becomes of a man's self, when he has passed from the stage of life ? " the oracle of Confucius was dumb ; and why should it not be dumb, when the question is answered by the questioner ? When a man's own self passes from the stage of life, why, then, his own self has passed from the stage of life, and his own self is dead and will so remain until the resurrection at the last day, then as it is written, " Thy dead men (addressing the graves of time) shall live, together with my dead body shall they arise—awake and sing ye that dwell in the dust, and the earth shall cast out her dead." " He will swallow up death in victory." (Isaiah.) " While you do not know life," said Confucius, " how can you know death ? "

Doubts as to the continued existences of the departed were manifested by many men of China, before the era of Confucius. " But we see that he did believe in a future existence, and, with Job, that the transition into it was the resurrection of the dead, though not so clearly as he did after the destined redeemer's revelation to him upon the subject." (" Encyclopedia-Britannica.")

Buddhist Creed not Atheistic.

There are two hundred and twenty-two millions of the human family (about one-fourth of mankind) whose religion is Buddhism.

Buddha died B.C. 543. In Ceylon there is a foot-mark, on a rock called Adam's Peak, which has been the object of pilgrimage for ages, which Buddhists ascribe to Buddha, and Mohammedans to Adam. Such beliefs of the human family are strong corroborations of the biblical account of its origin.

In Thibet, the Buddhist creed is thus stated by Cosma de Koros: "To take refuge only with Buddha. To form in the mind the resolution to aim at the highest degree of perfection, and so to be united with the Supreme Intelligence. (God said to Abraham, "Walk before me and be thou perfect.") To humble one's self before Buddha, and adore him. (It is evident that the Buddhist viewed Buddha only as the symbol of the Supreme Intelligence, and the best human model for them to follow in aiming at the highest perfection—that of the Supreme Being, as they called him. If, therefore, from the lesser light of tradition and the revelations of nature, manifesting the goodness of God lead these people to repentance—to humble themselves before him whom Buddha adored—then they obey and please the Supreme Being, to whom Buddha pointed them, both by precept and example, and, with Abraham, share the approval of the great Supreme.) To make offering of things pleasing to the senses, the sixth being the moral sense. (Like Abel, who offered the first mature lamb of his flock, and of the fat thereof, and that every spring. Because it was pleasing to his appetite, it had sacrificial value, and was pleasing in the sight of the Lord his maker, and which must have been so while beholding the sacrificial offerings of the adoring Buddhist, in the estimation of him who respects not persons.

"To glorify Buddha by music and hymns, in praise of his person, doctrine, and love of mankind, his perfection of attributes, and for his acts for the benefit of animated human beings. To confess one's sins with a contrite heart, to ask forgiveness of them, and to repent truly, with a resolution not to commit such afterward. To rejoice in the moral merit of perfection of animated beings, and to wish that they may obtain beatitude. To pray and exhort existing holy men to turn the wheel of religion, that the world may long benefit by their teaching."

This creed is signed, "Prinsep's Thibet—Tartary and Mongolia."

The Buddhist priests in the present century are actively diffusing a knowledge of their creed, as they interpret and expound it. They have printing presses from which tracts and pamphlets issue in great numbers. Some of these contain defiant and blasphemous expressions, like those of Ingersoll, against the name of Jehovah. In consequence of these bad teachers many Buddhists have become atheistic materialists. But it is evident that the doctrines of Buddha contained in the above creed are not only free from atheism, but the nearest in experimental and practical religion to that revealed in the Bible, of any other outside of it, including many of those of Christendom.

Nothing is more obvious from these records of antiquity than that all those nations and generations believed in one personal, living God as the Creator of the world, and acknowledged their obligation to love, serve, and obey Him. Indeed, it seems incomprehensible that however rude in form or grand in construction were the gods the worshippers made (and the very fact of making proves the superiority of the maker) they were regarded in no other light than as symbolic representations, or memory — prompters of the only true and living God, and this worship was as sure to elevate the worshipper as that, by the law of assimilation, man becomes like those with whom he communes, associates, and studies. According to this principle of moral philosophy an atheist, repudiating the existence of any being higher or greater than himself, is not only unable to make the least shade of moral advancement, but must gravitate toward the morose, unlovely, and base. Hence Ingersoll's iconoclastic warfare upon all the gods, if at all successful, only serves to destroy the restraint there is upon the votary of evil inclination, and render human society anarchical and intolerable ; and were these confederates equal to the task of scoffing away the belief in the existence of God, and the authority of the Bible, the whole world would have a short reign of terror, followed by the extinction of everything which makes human life tolerable.

Freethinkerism Degeneracy, not Progress.

The fact that all these great men of antiquity were reformers, proves that, in their days, human society had degenerated. They could point their people to remote golden ages and to ancestors of perfect virtue, and their standard of virtue embraced the belief in God, and heart-devotion to His righteous laws, loving Him, and their brothers also. This shows that the human family had degenerated from the earliest times, and contradicts the lying oracles of the skeptical, so-called progressionists, that there has been continual progress and development from a rude and savage beginning. These facts of profane history corresponds with the biblical history of the nations and generations of mankind, and is corroborated by the common observation of moral science.

Light of Nature and Providence Lead Men to Love the Creator.

He who reads the Scripture revelations of the will and purpose of God, and does not understand the fundamental principle to be met by any man, in any age or country, who is induced to love and adore his Creator, thus reciprocating the prior love of God for him, reads them to very little purpose. Whatever manifestation God has made, even the involvement in human form and the sacrificial offering of Himself, was to induce His creatures to love Him with all their heart ; and if they do this, whether induced to it by the light of nature, the goodness, wisdom, and power in giving them being, and the bountiful provisions surrounding them in nature to meet their necessities and enhance their happiness, it is equally effective, and equally meets the approving smile and benediction of his Lord and Creator ; and in the end, whether called Buddhists, Confucians, or Christians, shall share the resurrection to eternal life and an inheritance in the kingdom of the new earth "wherein dwelleth righteousness," which they had tried to make their own country in the old world.

It is in accordance with another principle of the written revelation, that those who are led to love God (and if they love Him they obey Him), under the less light, are more prominently approved by Him, and will be so distinguished in the promised rewards in the judgment at the end of the world. As an example, said the great teacher : " The men of Nineveh (and they were heathen Gentiles) shall rise up in the judgment, with this generation, and condemn it : for they repented at the preaching of Jonah ; and behold, a greater than Jonah is here." (Luke 11 : 32.) The only question is, do they love God with all their heart, and, as a sequence, their neighbor as themselves ?

The Creator Cannot be Indifferent to the Character of Man.

It is simply preposterous to hold the Scriptures responsible for any sentiment or practice which is not taught and enforced by its entire instruction upon the subject, and for wresting its records, in order to make them appear to approve wicked acts simply because they are written in them ; and that this is the work of Ingersoll, we shall show by the reports of his public discourses after having been submitted to his own revision, which will also show his ignorance of Scripture, not a doctrine of which is he capable of expounding. That he unjustly passes for a man of science we shall also show by what he accepts as science, and with his accustomed arrogance and puffed up conceit supposes the book of Genesis, as to the origin of the world and its inhabitants, to be the " Mistakes of Moses."

The scoffer says : " God demands man's obedience and love, to yield which degrades his manhood." This is without regard as to whether God is his maker or not. Did he know of a single argument of logical force to disprove this relation he would not appear so ridiculous.

Had he charged that to yield this love and obedience, would have humbled his arrogant and indefencible pride and put restraint upon his self-will, which, were it equal to its animus, would not only asperse and slander the character of God his maker, but rather than submit he would hurl him from his throne, and in his proud tyranny trample upon the Omnipotent, who, he complains, "is watching him"—and become so puffed at his victory that he would demand the obedience of every man, every angel, and even that of God himself! In the very nature and constitution of things, such demands must be imposed upon man by his Maker.

As man is endowed with the power of volition—it renders him capable of obedience; and of philosophical necessity this carries with it the power of disobedience. The conception is impossible and absurd that God should have made beings capable of loving and obeying him, and yet not require their love and obedience, and much less that he had no right to demand either. That God is the Creator, and therefore the owner of man's being, settles this question.

To the question, is it best for man to thus love and obey?—the wisdom capable of such a work, and which belongs to him who makes the demand gives an affirmative answer; even though to yield is contrary to man's will and propensities. His ignorance of what is best for him in the end precludes any justification for refusing to yield. Has the father a right to command the love and obedience of his children, when he, too, is only their temporary superior?—and is it for them to ask the question whether it is right and proper to yield to the claim of God? But the claim of God is that of absolute ownership, which lasts as long as the man has reason and conscious being.

Was there ever a rational human father who took no interest in his children, and was totally indifferent to their conduct toward himself and others? And can the father of mankind be thus indifferent? Was there ever a sane human parent against the waywardness and disobedience of his children, who issued no law or penalty?—and can

the supreme owner of man impose no law, or penalty for
the regulation of the conduct of his children ?   The very
question shocks every sensibility of reflecting minds, and
puts the audacious questioner out of court.   Furthermore,
was there ever a human father who did not desire his
children should please him ?—and how infinitely more preposterous the supposition that God should have created
the family of man, and not desire they should have
such characters, and perform such acts as would be pleasing to him ; and, we may add, how could his children
know what kind of character or deeds would be pleasing
or displeasing unless the father should have made a revelation containing the instruction ?   And these are the
Scriptures of truth.

The fact that the Creator provides laws and penalties in
the smallest details for the government of all other animate and inanimate things and creatures, precludes the
possibility of indifference to such provisions for the government of the only moral being upon our globe who is
capable of reasoning up to his existence, or of forming the
least appreciation of his character.   As, therefore, man
must be a subject of moral law and government, his
Maker must offer him reward to induce obedience, and
threaten punishment to restrain him from disobedience, in
mercy giving him the double motive of hope and fear.
Had either of these been omitted, the finally disobedient
might charge his Maker with not having made the inducement to yield obedience as effective as possible !

Ingersoll's Objection to Sacrifices Answered.

The arch-scoffer says : " Most of the gods were pleased
with sacrifice, and the smell of innocent blood has ever
been considered a divine perfume."   Nothing is more
universally acknowledged and practiced in the intercourse
of mankind than the principle of sacrifice, and which is
the exact opposite of selfishness.   The degree of love and
respect one being has for another is more surely measured
and made manifest by the amount of sacrifice made and
suffered for another than by any other test.   The sacri-

fices may consist in money, goods, reputation, or life.
The sacrifice of life implies the shedding of life-blood, as
that of the blood of Christ, to show to mankind the boundless love of God for man, by which in turn He might win
their love for Himself; and this is the whole doctrine of
atonement, or reconciliation, as taught in the Bible.

The shedding of the blood of the lambs ordered at the
beginning of the world, revealed this great truth. The
animal sacrifices of all heathen religions are corruptions
of this institution. All these sacrifices have been laid
upon the altar of devotion for friends. It is admitted
that any of these sacrifices, except that of life, may be
prompted by the hope of receiving from the same friends
increased favors. But he who perils and loses his life for
his friend shows the strongest possible attachment and
degree of love for that friend; and performs an act as
unselfish as it is possible for an act to be ! Men may
make professions and protestations of love and friendship,
but their sincerity can only be evinced by the value of the
sacrifices the professed friends will make when opportunity offers, and when those friends need help.

Unselfish humanity constitutes the bond and bases of
the highest human society. The general acknowledgment
of the efficacy of sacrificial offerings from the most ancient times prove they originated in the mind of the great
Creator himself, and founder of human society, and the
whole sociological philosophy is comprehended and expressed in the golden rule of its author: "All things
whatsoever ye would that men should do to you, do ye
even so to them : for this is the law and the prophets."
That is, this was, and is the doctrine taught in the laws of
Moses and by the prophets, and from which Christ deduced it in this form.

This reciprocity of kind and pleasing acts between all
intelligent beings is that of sacrifice, and is that at which
Ingersoll scoffs.

In all the relations of society it is a recognized principle that the first obligation is due to proprietors ; and
what kind of reasoning is that which denies its extension
to the great proprietor and maker of the man ? This being

inadmissible, we are forced to the conclusion that the first
and absorbing obligation is to love, honor, and worship
the Creator !   Indeed, loving and honoring Him is the
highest worship He demands.   The evidence to the individual himself, as well as to others, whether he is such a
worshipper, possessing and manifesting this large, unselfish spirit toward God and man, is answered by the sacrifices he will make as opportunity presents itself.   " Pure
and undefiled religion before God and the Father is this,
To visit the fatherless and widows in their affliction, and
keep himself unspotted from the world." (James 1 : 27.)
This requires a life of self-denial and crucifixion : " Whosoever hath this world's goods and seeth his brother hath
need, and shutteth up his bowels of compassion from him,
how dwelleth the love of God in him ? " (1 John 3 : 17.)
" Thou shalt love the Lord thy God with all thy heart,
and thy neighbor as thyself," are the two great commandments covering all the reciprocal duties of man with man,
and man with his Maker.

God Taught Cain and Abel the Nature and Object of Sacrifice.

To love God and his neighbor, as here enjoined, and to
render the sacrificial duties growing out of such a state of
heart to both is the height, length, breadth, and depth of
revealed religion and worship, alike in all ages of the
world ; and which justice and mercy demanded should
have been revealed as fully and clearly to the first generation of men born into the world as to any subsequent
one.   It seems that there can be but two reasons assigned
why this was not done, if it was not.   First, the Creator was unable to conceive such a system at that time ; or,
secondly, he was indifferent to the destiny of the men first
brought into the world, both of which are too absurd
to merit reply.   The conclusion, therefore, is that the
Maker must have planned and preached the gospel of
such a salvation to the first generation of men, and before
any death occurred ; and so we find that sacrificial offerings, which typically conveyed this information, was

revealed to the first generation of men born into the world ; and this originated the Christian church.

Nor can it be said that the conditions of such salvation might not have been the same, or as high as in after ages. This is obvious from two facts of these conditions, namely, that the hearts of these men must be brought to love their Creator, and believe His words, and that nothing but this can fit them to obey and please Him.

God Preached the First Gospel-Sermon to Cain and Abel.

That we may understand the lessons and their biblical signification, we read : " In process of time it came to pass that Cain brought of the fruit of the ground an offering unto the Lord.   And Abel, he also brought of the firstlings of his flock and of the fat thereof, and the Lord had respect unto Abel and to his offering ; but unto Cain and to his offering he had not respect. And Cain was very wroth and his countenance fell.   And the Lord said unto Cain, Why art thou wroth ? and why is thy coun- tenance fallen ?   If thou doest well shalt thou not be accepted ? and if thou doest not well, sin lieth at the door. (A lamb for a sin offering lay at his door, so that he was not required to offer as sacrifice that which he did not possess ; nor does he make the excuse that he had no flock or firstling), and unto thee shall be his (Abel's) desire, and thou shalt reign over him.''

(As the oldest son, it was Cain's birthright to be the patriarch of the first generation of men, which made him prophet, priest, and civil ruler as long as he lived.) '' And it came to pass when they were in the field that Cain rose up against Abel his brother, and slew him.   And the Lord said unto Cain, Where is Abel thy brother ? and he said I know not ; am I my brother's keeper ?   And He said, What hast thou done ? the voice of thy brother's blood crieth unto me from the ground, and now thou art cursed from the earth, which hath opened her mouth to receive thy brother's blood from thy hand ; when thou tillest the ground it shall not henceforth yield unto thee her strength ; a fugitive and a vagabond shalt thou be in the earth. And Cain said unto the Lord, My punishment is greater than I can bear. Behold! thou hast driven me out this day from the face of the earth; and from thy face shall I be hid; and it shall come to pass that every one that findeth Cain shall slay him. And the Lord said unto him, Therefore whosoever slayeth Cain, vengeance shall be taken of him sevenfold." (Gen. 4: 1–15.)

In this record we have the history of the foundation of the Christian church, and that of revealed religion; the fundamental doctrines of the gospel of Christ's death and resurrection, and which was here preached by God himself to the first two men born into the world. They were required to sacrifice that which they esteemed valuable, thereby showing their loyalty and obedience. Secondly, that the slaying of the lamb was the typical representation of the future slaying of Christ, "The Lamb of God!" Hence we read of him as the "Lamb slain from the foundation of the world." (Rev. 13 : 8.) And at that time also of the Lamb's book of life being opened and names written therein. Abel was the first member of the church, and the first martyr for his faith in Christ, whose resurrection was taught by the offering of the first-fruits of the harvest.

The Humility of Christ Submitting to be Slain, Humbles Men.

Cain and Abel, as well as all men, were proud. In order to humble them to that state of submissiveness to God's righteous government, necessary to become its loyal subjects, he informed them that although he was their Maker, he intended to become embodied in a human form like themselves; and in this act to be born of a woman—have a human life; and thus becoming subject to death; and that proud, self-willed men would slay him, by spilling his blood.

And now, Cain and Abel, I want you to understand that when you slay this lamb, so will I consent to be slain to show my love for you in order to win you to

love me; that the virtue in the blood is simply because
its loss is death. I will therefore have it written, " Without the shedding of blood there is no remission of sins."
" Hereby perceive we the love of God, because he laid
down his life for us: and we ought to lay down our lives
for the brethren." (1 John 3 : 16.)

" Other sheep have I which are not of this fold ; them
also I must bring. I lay down my life for the sheep." " I
have power to lay it down and take it again ! " Here
was Christ a lamb slain from the foundation of the world.

But, Cain and Abel, you must also understand that I
am not going to remain dead ; and as it is in the human
form I am to be your Saviour, and the salvation includes
your resurrection from the dead, therefore the offering of
a sheaf of the first ripe fruits, and that repeated every
spring, signifies my resurrection, which is to take place
on the third day from my crucifixion.

Cain is willing to offer the first-fruits and have part in
the resurrection, so that he, too, shall not remain perished
in death ; but he is too proud and self-willed to be
humbled even by my death for him, and the sacrifice will
fail to win him to love and please me !

The following is one of the prophetic records of the
great sacrificial transaction : " He was oppressed and
afflicted, yet he opened not his mouth. He was brought
as a lamb to the slaughter, and as a sheep before her
shearer is dumb, so he openeth not his mouth. He was
taken from prison and from judgment ; and who shall
declare his generation ? for he was cut off out of the land
of the living ; for the transgression of my people was he
stricken. And he made his grave with the wicked and
the rich in his death." (Isa. 53.)

These types were afterward incorporated in the laws of
Moses, enlarging the instruction to the Hebrew nation
and according to the design, through it to thus instruct
the world. That in relation to the first-fruits is recorded
thus : " Speak unto the children of Israel, and say,
when ye come into the land I give unto you, and shall
reap the harvest thereof, then ye shall bring a sheaf of
the first ripe fruits, and the priest shall wave the sheaf

before the Lord, to be accepted for you ; on the morrow after the Sabbath the priest shall wave it." (Lev. 23 : 10, 11.)

The crucifixion was on Friday, the day before the Sabbath, which was also the day the Passover Lamb was slain. Christ lay in the grave the remainder of that day, and rose the next—the third day—the morrow after the Sabbath : fulfilling the prophetic type both as to the nature and time of the oblation.

After his resurrection, Christ discoursed to some of his disciples, thus : " These are the words which I spake unto you, while I was yet with you, that all things must be fulfilled, which were written in the law of Moses, and in the prophets, and in the Psalms, concerning me. Then opened he their understanding [by thus expounding them] that they might understand the Scriptures. And he said unto them : Thus it is written, and thus it behoved Christ to suffer, and to rise the third day." (Luke 24 : 44–46.) Therefore, in the lamb Abel slew he saw in typic perspective Christ the Lamb of God being slain, and in the wave-sheaf the resurrection of Christ— " The first-fruits of the resurrection and pledge of that of all his people at the last day."

That it was to this event Abel's faith looked for his salvation, and as the model for that of Christians, we have the following testimony of God himself: " By faith Abel offered unto God a more excellent sacrifice than Cain, by which he obtained witness that he was righteous, God testifying of his gifts [both the lamb and the first - fruits] : and that he pleased God and being dead he yet speaketh." (Heb. 11.)

The Principle of Sacrifice Humbles those it Favors.

The philosophy of sacrifice, without regard to its typical teaching, lies in its power to rebuke and humble the proud—implying ability on the part of the benefactor, which they themselves do not possess. Contact with superiority always has the tendency to produce humiliation. A man may think himself wise ; but beholding a

wiser, he is humbled. A man may think himself the
most honorable; but contact with a more honorable,
humiliates him. A man supposes himself the highest
model of virtue; but seeing a more excellent example, he
is humbled. Christ so manifested his mercy in forgiving offences, that his disciples wanted to know if there
was any limit, and they said to him, " If my brother sin
against me seven times, shall I forgive him?" and he said,
"Not only seven times, but until seventy times seven,
if he say I repent, forgive him." This answer humbled
them, and they said, "Lord increase our faith!" The
limit was not in the number or turpitude of a man's
sins; but in his persistent impenitency like Cain, who
did not say, "I repent."

The spirit and wisdom of Christ's words and example
humbled those with whom he came in contact; and while
some became his humble disciples, others, like Cain and
Ingersoll, were and are maddened at the rebuke of their
pride, and give it vent in the slander of Christ and the
Bible !

We need scarcely say that this great principle of religious sacrifice, established by the great Creator at the
foundation of the world, has been corrupted to the use of
all the idolatries of the world—and to confound it with
these, as Ingersoll and the freethinkers do, exemplifies the
most profound ignorance of the whole subject, as well as
their gross perversion of the associated philosophy of
historic facts and phenomenal teaching in nature. Hence
the slanderous remark, flowing—" Blood has ever been
a sweet perfume to the gods ! ''

Ingersoll's Wanton and Ignorant Attack upon Priesthood.

The arch-scoffer next attacks the priests of religion,
and hurls his weapons against the true and false, those of
Christ and antichrist, the persecuted and the persecutors,
indiscriminately.

"All these gods have insisted upon having a vast
number of priests, and the priests have always insisted
upon being supported by the people."

God established the patriarchal system of religious and civil government in the first generation of mankind. This made the oldest son of a certain genealogical line the prophet, priest, and civil ruler of the generation. This was the order of worship and government until the year two thousand six hundred and seventy-four of the world; at which time it was superseded by the establishment of the Hebrew nation in the land of Palestine. In the division of the land among the twelve tribes, that of Levi had no inheritance given it; for the reason that the males of that tribe were to be the priests and religious teachers of the nation. Having no land from which to obtain a livelihood, and no time to work it if they had—the work of the ministry demanding their whole attention, other provision for their maintenance was a necessity, and which was enacted as follows: "Only unto the tribe of Levi he gave none inheritance; the sacrifices of the Lord God of Israel made by fire is their inheritance, as he said unto them, Unto the tribe of Levi Moses gave not any inheritance." (Joshua 13: 14, 33.)

Here we have the system. God owned the land because he made it, and, being the proprietor, his right cannot be disputed to demand not only recognition, but supreme honor by his creatures, who are tenants at will upon his domain.

In order to test their loyalty to him and make it manifest to others, he commands them to make sacrifices, and which can only be of such things as they esteemed valuable. To offer the sacrifices there must be priests; and as the work must occupy their time, renders their support by the people a necessity. One of these little tenants by the name of Ingersoll rebels against this most lawful and righteous claim, and obtains large pay for attempting to seduce others to join in the conspiracy to defy and tyrannize over his Maker; calling this independency—dignity—standing upright like a man!

Here, early in the world, God established and revealed the great system of religious worship with its sacrifices and priesthood absolutely essential not only to the development of the best citizens of human government, but to citizenship in an endless world ; for this whole question is simply one of permanent, universal, and righteous government. To confound this intelligent and philosophical worship of the living God with its corruptions by the priests of idolatry, is the blundering error repeated by Ingersoll. But even the corrupt forms of idolatrous sacrifices, priests, and their worship, are vastly superior and beneficial to mankind than atheism, which offers in the place of future hope, nothing but blank annihilation.

He must have read history to little purpose who has not discovered the fact that it was the religious element, though idolatrous, which distinguished the civilized from the barbarous and semi-barbarous nations of the ages. Nineveh, Babylon, Persia, Greece, Egypt, and Rome, each of whom had its gods and costly priesthood, and all of those gods symbolized a being superior to man ; thereby throwing a restraining influence around the bad passions of their devotees, the result of which was civilization. Even Troy, for a long time mistress of all Asia, owed her advancement in the arts and sciences, as well as her superior system of government, to her religious standard. When Troy was taken by the Greeks, and Priam, her king, was pursued and overtaken by Pyrrhus, the son of Achilles, who ran a sword through the body of the king's son in the presence of his father, Priam addressed him in these words :

> " The gods," said he, " requite thy brutal rage—
> As sure they will, as sure they must—
> If there be gods in heaven, and gods be just ! "

The reverence in which Socrates, the reputable father of moral philosophy, held the gods, may be seen by his last words. After he drank the hemlock, the instrument of his execution, he gently reproved his friends for weeping in these words : " I have always heard say that we ought to die in peace, and blessing the gods. Crito," said he, and these were his last words, " we owe a fowl to Esculapius ; discharge that vow for me, and pray do not forget it."

But it is useless to select single cases, for there never was an atheistic philosopher which requires a man to be so devoid of reason that he can believe an effect can be produced without a cause, which also exemplifies a blind credulity, more marvellous than a belief in all the miracles the Bible claims for its author. Strange infatuation that such minds should claim to be guided by reason, truth-seekers, freethinkers, etc. To assume any such epithet, to say the least, is a gross misnomer. They may appropriately be designated not as—"fear-thinkers; but free-talkers!"

CHAPTER II.

ANOTHER of the scoffer's repeated objections to expose the ignorance of the gods, including the living God, is this : " These gods did not know the shape of the worlds they created, but supposed them to be perfectly flat." In reply we say that the God of the Scriptures was not thus ignorant, and he is the only God we propose to defend against the would - be cunning flings of the archscoffer.

The world is not only never once declared to be flat in the Scriptures, but clearly taught to be globular in form, and that by very strong arguments shown to have been the source from whence heathen astronomy derived its information that such was its shape ! As it is not the purpose of the Bible to teach natural science, all allusions to it are incidental as statements of fact, without attempting argument, illustration, or verification. It must, however, be conceded that if the statements are true they will be sustained ultimately by the deductions of nature, as philosophical science, and from thenceforth and for all coming time, constitute the standard of philosophical science.

In relation to the circular form of the world, we may remark that this scoffer is too ignorant of the language of the Bible to discriminate between its statements and those of heathen scientists, shown by this sarcasm ; as there is not a sentence in that book which makes the world flat, and this information began to be given at its creation. One very comprehensive account of the work is brought out by a comparison between it and the pre-existence of God, in anticipation of his own Immanuelization, prophetically speaking of it as already accomplished, thus : " When he prepared the heavens, I was there : when he set a compass upon the face of the depth [the great deep of Genesis—the original matter out of which the world was made] : when he established the clouds : when he strengthened the fountains of the deep : when he gave to the sea his commandment : when he appointed the foundations of the earth." (Prov. 8 : 27-30.)

Here are the globular dimensions of the earth described. It would have added nothing to this had it been said, it was a circle every way, for this is implied in not asserting the circle to be flat, and by what follows upon the subject. " God walketh in the circuit of heaven." (Job 22 : 14.) A circuit means a space inclosed in a circle. The atmospheric heaven, or firmament—meaning the same in the Scriptures, and being a circle, it follows that the earth thus inclosed is also a globe. " It is he that sitteth upon the circle of the earth that stretcheth out the heavens as a curtain, and spreadeth them out as a tent to dwell in." (Isa. 40 : 22.) Here, then, God struck out the globular form of the world at its creation—encompassed it within a circling atmosphere. None of the conditions here mentioned admit the idea of a flat circle, as walking, sitting, or dwelling upon a sharp edge ; but all clearly indicate the heaven and the earth to be circles every way, thereby making the world a globe.

The Bible Teaches the World's Suspension.

" He stretcheth out the north over the empty place, and hangeth the earth upon nothing." (Job 26 : 7.) The facts here stated present us with the philosophical astronomy of the suspension of the earth : First—It is hung. Second—It is hung upon nothing. Third—It is hung over empty space. Here is described, in the most positive manner, and by the use of the most unambiguous language, all the essential principles of natural science upon which heavenly bodies and systems are suspended, involving the law of universal gravity. Create a star, or a sun of whatever size or ponderosity, and place it in empty space, which means a perfect vacuum—for if it contained any form of matter, however subtle or sublimated, which, as such must have specific gravity, it would not be empty, and that body would remain fixed—suspended and motionless. No matter how many such stars there are in space, as long as they are beyond the attractive or repellent force of each other, supposing all to be thus endowed, which is more than should be claimed or admitted, as they do not constitute a system, still, all would be hung in their individual localities, and which would also preserve their unchangeable distances from each other. So, also, would it be with planetary systems ; the reciprocal attractive and repellent forces would be limited to the sun and planets composing them ; each being beyond the force emanating from another, would remain suspended in the precise locality of "empty space," where its Creator placed it.

That space is empty, is demonstrated by the fact that the annual motion of the earth is invariable ; but which would be retarded even in passing through the most sublimated ether, and in the degree of its density, being that also of its friction. Instead, therefore, of Ingersoll's objection that God did not know the form of the earth or world he made, having any force or foundation in Scripture teaching, it inculcates more instruction upon the subject than what is now or ever has been known of the philosophic science of astronomy, and yet is perfect science.

Heathen Astronomy Learned from Scripture.

In support of the hypothesis that heathen astronomers learned the suspension and globular form of the earth from the Scriptures of the Old Testament, we introduce the following history :

"The first translation of the Scriptures from the Hebrew into Greek was made by seventy-two interpreters, and by the order of Ptolemy Philadelphus, king of Egypt ; which is hence called the Septuagint, and was completed in seventy-two days, at Alexandria, in Egypt, B.C. 277."

(Josephus.) It was commenced B.C. 284, according to Langlet ; in 283, according to Blair. "The Jewish Sanhedrim consisted of seventy members ; and hence, probably, this number of translators as mentioned by Josephus." (Hewlett.) "The seventy were shut up in thirty-six cells, and each pair translated the whole; and on subsequent comparison, it was found that the thirty-five copies did not vary by a word or a letter." (Justin Martyr.)

"Euclid was a native of Alexandria, and was born about 300 B.C." ("World's Progress," p. 315.) Here is Euclid, the great mathematician, flourishing at Alexandria, thirty years after that city had thirty-five copies of the Scriptures, and in his own language; with which fact he must have been perfectly familiar, as well as all the other Greek philosophers of that day, as all were students of that school.

While Euclid was teaching at the great Alexandrian Institute, a pupil who had come from Scythia to attend his school on one occasion said, "After so long travelling in the sky, we returned to the earth ; " and observed to Euclid, "We have not brought back many important truths, after so long a journey. We shall be more fortunate, no doubt, by confining ourselves to the earth ! "

Euclid asked how so ponderous a mass as the earth could maintain its equilibrium in the air. It is the same with the earth, perhaps, as with the fixed planets and stars. But, said he, precautions have been taken to hinder their falling by attaching them to spheres, extremely solid, but transparent ; these spheres turn, and the heavenly bodies revolve with them, but we see nothing around us by which the earth can be suspended ; why, therefore, does it not plunge into the depth of surrounding fluid ? Some say the reason is because it is on every side environed by air ; the earth is a mountain, the foundations or roots of which extend themselves into the infinite profundity of space. We occupy the summit of this mountain, and may sleep in safety upon it.

Others flatten the under part of it (here was taught the flat earth which Ingersoll designedly or ignorantly attributed to the Scriptures), that it may rest on a greater number of columns of air, or float upon the waters. But, if we make choice of air to sustain it, that is too weak; if of water, it may be asked, what does that rest upon? But our natural philosophers have almost proved the earth to be of a spherical form, and have *lately* discovered a more simple method of calming our apprehensions. By virtue of a general law, say they, all heavenly bodies tend toward one great point which is the centre of the universe, and which is the centre of the earth. All the constituent parts of the earth, therefore, instead of flying off from the centre, are continually pressing against it.

It is said that Thales of Miletus, in Ionia, one of the seven sages of Greece, who lived about two hundred years before, had made this discovery; but, had he done so, is it not unaccountable that a man of such learning and reputation as Euclid should have publicly taught that it was but *lately* discovered, and that, too, by their own Alexandrian philosophers? Up to his day, therefore, it had been taught that the earth was shaped like a cone, the vertex of which we inhabited, while the bottom was flat and supported upon columns of air, and that nothing was known about its suspension, or motion.

The natural solution of this discovery is to be found in the facts that as the globular form of the world and its suspension were taught, as we have seen in the Scriptures, and as there was at least one copy in this school in which it was translated, Euclid and his contemporary philosophers made the discovery of these great truths of natural science from these writings—thus again exposing the wantonness, ignorance, perversity, and blasphemy of the arch-scoffer!

"Thou Sun Stand Still!"—The End must be Known to Justify the Means.

The scoffer says: "Some of the gods thought the day could be lengthened by stopping the sun." This is evidently aimed at the command of Joshua to the sun to stand still; and as it is held by the skeptics to be one of the most inconsistent things recorded in the Bible, we propose to examine it somewhat extensively.

It must be remembered that the other members of the solar system—sun, moon, and stars (planets), were made to subserve the purposes of our earth and its inhabitants, and we have shown in "Cosmogony" that all of them, with all their motions, are essential to the production of vegetables upon our earth.   A slight reference to it is as follows :

"And God said, Let there be lights in the firmament of heaven to divide the day from the night [this implies the motion of the earth on its axis] ; and let them be for signs, and for seasons [this implies the ecliptic motion of the earth ; as it is this which produces the seasons] and for days [this implies the earth's motion on its axis— as it is this which produces the days] and for years [this implies the annual motion of the earth around the sun, as it is this motion which produces the year ; therefore are these the signs of all the phenomenal motions of the members of the solar system] ; let them be for lights in the firmament of heaven to give light upon earth [not that these bodies were placed within the limits of the atmosphere, or firmament ; but that their rays, coming in contact and passing through the air to the earth, sets its oxygen on fire by the friction, and thus they give light upon earth and in or within the firmament of heaven, and which only extends forty-five miles from the surface of the earth to its outer verge.   Hence, also, we have the fact here taught that every object on, or above the surface of the earth are in heaven, properly speaking, which firmament God named heaven at the creation], the greater light to rule the day, and the lesser light to rule the night : he made the stars also."

The waxing and waning of the moon divides the year into thirteen equal parts—in astronomy called "Lunar months," signified by that number of revolutions the moon makes around the earth in a year ; hence it is the sign of these months.   The changes of the moon produces other important effects upon the earth besides this, which is indicated by the expression, "It shall be for signs."

The tides are so accurately ruled—produced by the changing phases of the moon, that the highest tide at New York is invariably at nine o'clock, A.M., on the day of full moon. And so it is at any given point on the face of the globe, at a certain day and hour, each month. Hence, as our knowledge of philosophical science increases, we discover that all its essential facts were indicated in the statements of Genesis, and that just such an origin and constitution of the world were philosophic and scientific necessities, and therefore the account could only have been dictated by an astronomer advanced even beyond any of our day, who was the Creator himself.

If we would understand the superiority of the world, composed of heaven and earth, in comparison with all other bodies in space, we must remember that the Creator's revealed purpose is its re-creation into a new heaven and a new earth, constituting a new world—" The world to come "—in which he himself with his angels and resurrected immortal people, are eternally to reside—" World without end."

It is equally the revealed purpose to keep the present world in existence long enough to induce the desired and determined number by the offer and promise of such an inheritance and nature from among the inhabitants of the present nations and generations, to accept the conditions and become his loving, loyal people, and willing subjects of that coming world and kingdom; consequently, that day upon which the complement is full, will be the last day of the present world, and the first day of the world to come. Everything between the creation of the present world and the destined re-creation is, of course, temporal, while all beyond is changeless immortality. While skeptical, speculative, and false science seeks to belittle the world by making comparisons between it and the stars of space, God's great revelation gives it infinite importance to any and all other bodies of space.

It must be obvious to every intelligent mind, that without taking this revealed end into the account which gives the reasons for the present existence of things, all must be involved in mystery; and as this design and philosophy is only written in the Scriptures, its teaching alone can solve the mystery. Whatever is found here taught conducive to the accomplishment of the proposed end, must be consistent for the Creator to do or have done; consequently, when any man or body of men refuse to become such loyal subjects, and combine for the purpose of preventing others from doing so, they have not only failed of the purpose of their being, but array themselves against the Creator's carrying out his purposes for which he made man and the world.

For one of such characters to remonstrate with the Creator for the execution of whatever he does, manifests the presumption that the owner of the world has no right to establish a universal government of loyal subjects and righteous men, because it involves the necessary destruction of his enemies, who have refused to become such subjects.

Land of Canaan Promised to the Hebrews.

In the accomplishment of his plan with man and the world, and within a certain period, God considered it necessary, or to the best advantage, to raise up a certain nation and place them in a certain country, giving them a written law for their government. He announced this purpose to Abraham, at which time every nation in the world worshipped idol-gods, and of course dishonored the living God and their rightful sovereign. "And God said unto Abraham, Know of a surety that thy seed shall be a stranger in a land that is not their's, and shall serve them; and they shall afflict them four hundred years: and also that nation, whom they shall serve, will I judge; and afterward shall they come out with great substance. In the fourth generation they shall come hither; for the iniquity of the Amorites is not yet full." (Gen. 15.)

Here we have the prediction and promise of a covenant that of Abraham's seed God was to make a great nation, but this seed was first to be in bondage to a strange nation, four hundred years. Of course this was the Egyptian bondage, which took place exactly according to these facts and figures.   It is important to understand that this affliction had culminated in the destruction of the Hebrew nation in a single coming generation.   Pharaoh had made a decree, and was executing it, by which every male Hebrew child that was born, should be killed.   God must therefore deliver his people immediately from Egypt, or suffer the defeat of his purpose.

God told Abraham at the time he made this covenant that the Amorites were then in the land of Canaan, but were not so universally idolatrous that he could induce none of them to become his loyal subjects and candidates for his new world;   hence he would not then dispossess them;   and these were the very people with whom Joshua had the battle when he commanded the sun to stand still, but which was more than four hundred years afterward.   During this period the Hebrews were reared from the family of Jacob, and in the land of Egypt, whom God was to separate from all the idolatrous nations, the time having come for him to put them in possession of the promised land, whose inhabitants— the Amorites—having now filled up the measure of their iniquity;   that is, none of them from this time could be induced to become candidates for his new world.

The sin of idolatry is such as a child may commit against his father by bestowing his love and obedience upon another.   Nay, infinitely worse; for it is the thing made that turns against its Maker.

The law against this sin was given from Mount Sinai while these people were journeying to the promised land, and which show its hateful character in the sight of God, and his desire for its suppression.   "Take heed unto yourselves, lest ye forget the covenant of the Lord your God, which he made with you, and make you a graven image, or the likeness of anything which the Lord thy God hath forbidden thee; for the Lord thy God is a consuming fire, even a jealous God.   When thou shalt beget children, and children's children, and ye shall have remained long in the land, and shall corrupt yourselves, and make a graven image, or the likeness of anything, and shall do evil in the sight of the Lord thy God, to provoke him to anger, I call heaven and earth to witness against you this day, that ye shall utterly perish from off the land whereunto you go over Jordan to possess it ; and the Lord shall scatter you among the nations, and ye shall be left few in number, among the heathen. There ye shall serve gods, the work of men's hands, wood and stone, which neither see, nor hear, nor eat, nor smell. I am the Lord your God, which brought you up out of the land of Egypt, from the house of bondage. Thou shalt have none other God before me. Thou shalt not make unto thee any graven image, or any likeness of anything that is in heaven above, or that is in the earth beneath, or that is in the waters under the earth. Thou shalt not bow down thyself unto them : for I the Lord thy God am a jealous God, visiting the iniquity of the fathers upon the children unto the third and fourth generation of them that hate me, and showing mercy unto thousands of them that love me and keep my commandments.''

Was the Object Important Enough to Arrest the Sun in its Course ?

For these reasons we can understand that the establishment of the Hebrew nation was indispensable in carrying out God's purpose with the world, and, if prevented, would defeat that object. If we now turn to the record about Joshua commanding the sun to stand still, we shall find that the Amorites refused to let Joshua lead the Hebrews through their land. Not only so, but a confederation of five nations made war upon one nation, because it had made friends with the Hebrews. The question therefore was, whether the Creator and owner of the world should abandon his project with it and his kingdom, or those Amorites be destroyed who had made war upon him and his servants.

The history is written thus : " Now it came to pass, when Adonizedec, King of Jerusalem, had heard how Joshua had taken Ai, and had utterly destroyed it ; as he had done to Jericho and her king also; and how the inhabitants of Gibeon had made peace with Israel, and were among them, that they greatly feared, because Gibeon was a great city, one of the royal cities, and greater than Ai, and all the men thereof were mighty, wherefor Adon-i-zed-ic, King of Jerusalem, sent unto Ho-ham, King of Hedron, and unto Pi-ram, King of Jar-muth, and unto Japh-i-a, King of Lach-ish, and unto Derby, King of Eg-lon, saying, come up unto me, and help me, that we may smite Gibeon: for it hath made peace with Joshua and with the children of Israel. Therefore the five kings of the Amorites gathered themselves together, and went up and encamped before Gibeon, and made war against it. And the men of Gibeon sent unto Joshua to the camp of Gilgal, saying, Slack not thy hand from thy servants; come up quickly, and save us: for all the kings of the Amorites that dwell in the mountains are gathered together against us.

"So Joshua and all the people of war, and all the mighty men with him ascended up from Gilgal. And the Lord said unto Joshua, Fear them not: for I have delivered them into thine hand; there shall not a man of them stand before thee. Joshua therefore went up all night and came unto them suddenly and the Lord discomfited them before Israel, and slew them with a great slaughter at Gideon, and chased them along the way that goeth up to Beth-horan, and smote them to A-ze-kah, and unto Mak-ke-dah. And it came to pass, as they fled from before Israel, and were in the going down to Beth-horan, that the Lord cast down great stones from heaven upon them unto A-ze-kah, and they were more which died with the hailstones than they whom the children of Israel slew with the sword.

"Then spake Joshua to the Lord [regretting that the sun was going down] in the day when the Lord delivered up the Amorites before the children of Israel, and said, Thou sun, stand still upon Gibeon; and thou moon, in the valley of Ajalon! And the sun stood still, and the moon stayed, until the people had avenged themselves upon their enemies. So the sun stood still in the

midst of heaven, and hasted not to go down about a
whole day. And there was no day like that before and
the Lord hearkened unto the voice of a man : for the Lord
fought for Israel.'' (Joshua 10.)

That it was the Lord, and not Joshua who obtained
this victory, is certain, from the fact that more were killed
by the hailstones God rained down from heaven upon
the Amorites than by the arms of the Israelites, and that,
too, while they were in full flight. They saw the battle
was going against them, and chose flight that they might
increase their allies and renew the contest at some future
day. To prevent the success of this stratagem the hailstones were brought into requisition. But it was plain
to see that still a great number of the Amorites were
about to make good their escape. The sun was going
down, and, covered by the darkness of the night, many
of them would have escaped, but by this prayer and its
answer they were so completely destroyed that they gave
the Hebrews no further trouble ; and God fulfilled his
word to Joshua : '' Not a man of them shall stand before thee ! ''

Astronomical Objection Answered.

As to the objection of Ingersoll that Joshua was ignorant of astronomy, supposing the day could be lengthened
by the sun standing still when it does not move, we
think for the same reason the ignorance is on the other
side. As it is not the object of the Scriptures to teach
the science of modern astronomy, they do not use its
technical phrases, but discourse about the heavenly bodies
as their phenomena appears to us. We have already
shown that the signs for days, months, seasons, and years,
taught their motions, and that of the earth on its axis produces the day and night, and which no Scripture statement attributes to the sun alone for the division of the
light from the darkness. Having, therefore, once in its
history of creation explained these phenomena, they afterward speak of day and night as they appear, and say the
sun rises and sets, or at sunrise and sunset, or sundown.

Ingersoll would have appeared just as ridiculously ignorant were he to have declared that Sir Isaac Newton was so ignorant of astronomy that he supposed the sun revolved around the earth because he used the phrases, " The sun rose and the sun went down, and that he did not know but that the day was lengthened by the use of such expressions." In a class-book of " Newton's Astronomy," by Elijah H. Burriett, A.M., we read these words : " Now, when the sun or moon is just emerging above the eastern horizon, or sinking beneath the western."

As a consequence of the day being lengthened twenty-four hours where this battle was fought, the night was lengthened equally on the opposite side of the earth ; and as nothing was ever known of such a night, therefore it never occurred, say the skeptics. In answer, we may remind the scoffers that it was only eleven hundred and eighteen years after the flood to the days of Joshua, at which time the repopulation of the earth commenced, and with but eight human beings, and, with their means and motives for travel, had not spread to the Feejee Islands, the opposite side of the globe from Jerusalem, or far enough from that centre to make a perceptible difference in the length of the night. Besides this, the pendulum had not been invented, and there were no timepieces ; and it was long before the period of reliable history—except that of the sacred Scriptures.

The effort to belittle the earth by drawing invidious comparisons between it and the many fixed stars of space, about which there is absolutely nothing known, except their existence, originates in mere atheistic ignorance, and a desire to have it so : for the purpose of creating prejudice against the Bible, as it gives the world more importance than all the material universe besides !

Objections to the Flood Answered.

Another of these skeptical objections to the Creator being the author of the Bible, relates to its record of the flood ; and it is asked where did the water come from, and where did it go ? These objectors generally adopt the views of Professor Agassiz and Sir Charles Lyell, who claim that since men were upon earth, and during what is called "The glacier period, there was a greater deluge of water upon earth than that of the flood, in the days of Noah. The only cause assigned by Agassiz for the deluge of water and ice was the sudden elevation of the European continent, five thousand feet, and that of the American, eight thousand feet." Such an elevation would bring them to a level with the top of those mountains covered with perpetual ice and snow. According to this authority the continents thus elevated were covered with ice hundreds of feet in thickness — great icebergs were formed and floated over the Rocky Mountains, from the Pacific to the Atlantic Oceans, carrying with them bowlders from one section of the earth to another. Agassiz says : "He had seen traces upon the rocks worn by these fields of floating ice at these thousands of feet above the present level of the sea."

It must be remembered that floating ice is about nine-tenths under water ; the water, therefore, must have been hundreds of feet deep upon these land elevations, in order to float the icebergs.

The inventors of this theory and those who adopt it, do not give us the duration of the glacier period, but talk about it as one of the "geological periods ;" and everyone knows the enormous length and indefiniteness of such periods ; but if the continents of Europe and America were thus covered with water for the space of only one year upon that part of the world, the whole earth would be equally covered, as certainly as that water seeks its level. Now let the skeptics, Professor Agassiz and Sir Charles Lyell, tell us where the water came from to thus flood the continents of the world, and where did it subside, and the scientific answer will dispose of the objection of the scoffers as to the biblical flood. Nor did he who produced this flood perform the wonderful miracle (a work of which nature is incapable) of suddenly elevating the surface of the round world thousands of feet every way from its centre and then of covering its surface to the depth of hundreds of feet with water and floating ice ; for the account states that the highest mountains were covered fifteen cubits—twenty-eight feet only. And it must also be remembered that the extreme depressions and elevations upon the surface of the present earth were the results of the flood. " And the fountains of the great deep were broken up : " the crust of the earth which had inclosed these fountains from the creation, permitting the waters to belch forth and cover the earth.

That Agassiz was a skeptic, is certain from what he said in the introduction of a lecture delivered to the students and professors of a New England college, thus : " If any of my listeners believe in the Book of Moses, he had better not hear me." Now, in the name of science, let us ask whether the account of the flood of Agassiz, or that of Genesis, is the most consistent ?

We have every reason to believe that up to the time of the flood, the whole surface of the earth was a beautiful rolling prairie, of gently rising hills, among which ran streams and rivers, with here and there a beautiful lake, all of which were destroyed by the breaking up of the earth's crust by the Creator himself, to use the waters buried within for the purpose of flooding the world, leaving more than two-thirds of its surface covered with briny oceans. Up to that catastrophe there was probably not a mountain higher than thirty feet above the lowest depression of a lake or sea, upon the whole face of the earth. If, therefore, the water had risen fifty feet, it would have covered the highest mountain fifteen cubits.

The ordinary swelling of the oceans by the influence of the sun and moon, sets the waters back on the shores in some places as high as twenty feet in six hours. It is a fact of science that atomic motion, whether of solids or fluids, create heat by their friction against each other. The aqueous motion of this great fountain composed of these atoms and bursting forth upon the earth, would itself have expanded these mighty waters sufficiently to have produced the rise to the extent described, the cessation of which would have condensed it again to the subsequent level of the sea. Hence, according to the well-known facts of science, this universal aqueous tumult was suscept-

ible of producing the flood in the days of Noah. The
catastrophe of Agassiz in breaking up the crust of the
earth—throwing continents thousands of feet high on
every side and piling hundreds of feet of water and ice
upon them, presents a convulsion of nature in comparison
with which that of Noah's day sinks into insignificance !
If, therefore, nature herself produced such a gigantic up-
heaval and flood, could not the God of nature have produced the lesser one? And if that never occurred, could
not he who formed the waters with their inherent laws,
have increased their temperature fifteen degrees, which
would have swollen them to the height demanded for the
purpose, and the very friction of the tumult would have
produced this?   No ! gentlemen, skeptical scientists, you
must bring more formidable objections against Scripture
statements than these, and after having them thus exposed there will not be the least danger of your producing
skeptical impressions upon minds of even ordinary intelligence, and the further demand for such superficial and
cunning sayings as those of Ingersoll's will be taken at
very great discount, if there will be any market whatever
for them, and your craft of money making by slandering
God and the Bible, will be gone.

The Arch-scoffer Sneers at the Little Ark.

" There was not room enough in the ark to accommodate the animals and their food. The wood would rot in
the one hundred and twenty years, the time the ark was
in building. The wild and domestic animals could not
live together."

It would be reasonable to suppose, and so we find it in
Scripture record, that the Creator would employ ordinary
means as far as they were available and adequate for the
execution of any purpose, and afterward any act of creation or destruction, either of individuals or generations,
cities, or worlds.   In a word, the suspension or reversion
of any and every law of nature—cannot the proprietor do
as he pleases with his own? The great miracle of the
world's creation is not a mere matter of faith, but estab-

lished upon the logic of a score of syllogisms which are
no more assailable than are the facts that the sun produces light and heat upon our planet.   This renders the
conclusion inevitable that any and every subsequent interference of the Creator, and of course upon a lesser
scale, is also consistent, because a lesser miracle than that
of the original creation.

The following is the record of the facts of the ark :

" And God looked upon the earth, and behold ! it was
corrupt: all flesh had corrupted their way upon the
earth.   And God said unto Noah, the end of all flesh is
come before me ; for the earth is filled with violence, and,
behold, I will destroy them with the earth.   Make thee
an ark of gopher wood ; rooms shalt thou make in the
ark, and shall pitch it within and without with pitch.
[If the parts were pitched as soon as they were finished
they would not have decayed in a hundred and twenty
years, whether in air or water ; and this answers one of
the scoffer's objections.   He can believe that unconscious
nature could have been engaged an indefinite period of
thousands of years in making the first animals which
necessitated the preservation of the fleshly parts made
first, from decay, during these thousands of years ; but the
God of nature could not keep pitched wood a hundred
and twenty years from decay.   Who cannot see this man's
wickedness and ignorant blunders ?]   And the length of
the Ark shall be three hundred cubits [550 feet], and
the breadth of it fifty cubits [91 feet], and the height of
it thirty cubits [55 feet].

" A window shalt thou make in the ark [so ignorant of
the record itself are these freethinkers, that they publicly
deny there was any ventilation in the ark, when here it
is stated that a window was to be made—a place for the
wind : bad air to escape] and in a cubit shalt thou finish
it above [above is the place for ventilators] ; and a door
of the Ark shall be set in the side thereof : with lower,
second, and third stories shalt thou make it.   And behold ! I, even I, do bring a flood of waters upon the
earth, to destroy all flesh, wherein is the breath of life,
from under heaven ; every thing that is in the dry land

shall die.   And thou and thy sons, and thy wife and thy
sons' wives shall come with thee into the ark, and every
living thing of all flesh, two of every sort [kind—species]
shalt thou bring into the ark, to keep alive with thee;
they shall be male and female.   Of fowls after their kind,
and of cattle after their kind, of every creeping thing of
the earth after his kind.   And take unto thee of all food
that is eaten, and thou shalt gather it to thee and it shall
be for food for thee and for them.   Of every clean beast
thou shalt take to thee by sevens, the male and his
female : of fowls also of the air by sevens, the male and
female ; to keep seed alive upon the earth.   And Noah
went in and his sons, and his wife, and his sons' wives
with him, into the ark, of clean beasts, and of beasts
that are not clean, and of fowls, and of every thing that
creepeth upon the earth.   These went in two and two
unto Noah into the ark, the male and female, as God
had commanded Noah.   And the Lord shut him in.

"And the waters increased greatly upon the earth and
bear up the ark, and the ark went upon the face of the
waters, and all the high hills, that were under the whole
heaven were covered, fifteen cubits [28 feet] upward did
the waters prevail ; and the mountains were covered.
And all flesh died that moved upon the earth, both of
fowls and cattle, and of beast, and of every creeping
thing that creepeth upon the earth, and every man ; all
in whose nostrils was the breath of life, of all that was
in the dry land, died.   Noah only remained alive, and
they that were with him in the ark.   And the waters
prevailed upon the earth one hundred and fifty days."
(Gen. 6 and 7.)

In order to ascertain whether the dimensions of the
ark were sufficient to accommodate the male and female
of each species of animals and fowls living upon earth of
those unclean, and seven pairs of clean beasts and fowls
(the clean beasts were those used for food and sacrifice,
and were a very small part of living creatures or their
species).

The ark was five hundred and fifty feet long, ninety-
one feet wide, and fifty-five high, divided into three

stories, which gives about eighteen feet between the floors; making in all 180,150 square feet of floor surface.

The most celebrated authors of the natural history of animals, such as Buffon, Lennaus, and Cuvier, give classifications founded upon physiological structure and qualities, and not so much upon the definition and identity of species. Of course they did not deem this question of the importance it has assumed in our day by the theory of Darwin's evolution, commenced by Lennaus, which blots out the plurality of species by the unfounded speculation that all the varieties of living things and beings upon our globe, evolved from a single one, and that from lifeless matter. If this theory had been true, an ark, to save life or seed, was wholly unnecessary, as the earth would have evolved all living creatures the second time, just as it did the first, from a single living thing. The true and only scientific test of species, is, that species by crossing will not reproduce; while races will produce generation after generation indefinitely. This fact reduces all the varieties, or races of dogs, for instance, to a single pair; and so it is with all other living creatures.

We do not think the evidence is sufficient to prove that there are or ever have been three hundred species of animals in size between the mouse and elephant, or mastodon, including these. If we give each of these pairs— 600 in all—20 square feet on an average, it would take 12,000 feet. If there were one million insects of less size than the mouse, including male and female, and give each pair one fourth of a square foot, it would take 25,-000 feet more—and ten times the number could live in such a space—it leaves 143,150 feet of floor surface still to be appropriated. Now, give the fowls and birds an equal number of feet—and there are not one quarter as many species of them, nor will they occupy one fourth of the space, and it still leaves 100,000 square feet of floor room for food, which could be piled 18 feet high. We put these facts and figures against the laughs and scoffs of Ingersoll, relating to the little ark of God's design, to meet the necessities of the case.

This disposes of all the infidel objections to the ark and flood, except that relating to the alleged impossibility of the wild and domestic animals living together in peace one hundred and fifty days. It is unaccountable how often it is necessary to remind these gentlemen skeptics that it is not their god, nature, who is doing this business ; so conscious they seem to be that he is a mere slave to himself (nature), and can do nothing requiring will and intelligence, or even to start in a new track, not even the simplest thing of volition, of which they themselves are capable. Now, cannot the Maker of man, as easily send the animals tame and docile to Noah, into the ark, and keep them in such a condition, a hundred and fifty days, as to have made their disposition as a part of their nature ? Thus at every step we find the freethinkers to be no thinkers, but free talkers !

Division of Light on the First Three Days of Creation.

Another astronomical blunder of Ingersoll, and not Moses, relates to the light on the first three days of creation, before the sun was made. As a rule the greater the astronomer, the more blunders he is able to discover in the writings and teachings of science, by mere pretenders of a knowledge of it. In this case Ingersoll makes three blunders, and Moses none : First, in misstating the facts. Second, his ignorance of the essential philosophy involved in the creation of light. Third, in supposing the knowledge and power of God was limited to a single method in the division of light and darkness. In order to vindicate Genesis and expose the ignorance and presumption of the so-called scientific skeptics, we must introduce the history of the transaction, substantially as follows : " In the beginning God created the heaven and the earth. And the earth was without form and void [void of the forms it was now to receive] and darkness was upon the face of the great deep. And God said, Let there be light, and there was light. And God divided the light from the darkness, and the light he called day and the darkness he called night. And the evening and

the morning were the first day.   And God said, Let there
be lights in the firmament of heaven to divide the day
from the night ; and let them be for signs, and for
seasons, and for days, and for years : and let them be
for lights in the firmament of heaven to give light upon
earth ; and it was so.   And God made two great lights ;
the greater light to rule the day and the lesser light to
rule the night : he made the stars also [planets].   And God
set them in the firmament of heaven to give light upon
the earth, and to rule over the day and over the night,
and to divide the light from the darkness : and the evening and the morning were the fourth day." (Gen. 1 :
1–5 and 14–18.)

Here we have the great deep, of the matter called water,
but devoid of the forms it was made to assume during the
work of the six days.   It was not pure water, as we read
afterward of the dry land being separated from it, which
was then called earth ; its particles, therefore, had none of
the properties which identifies them as earth, in contrast
to water or air.   Without these being endowed with adhesive attraction—electrical, or thermo-electricity, not a
particle of it could have moved—as it is these which give
the atoms inclination to move, and this motion displaces
other atoms, and such displacement is disorganization, and
other formation which implies prior organization and formation ; but this matter was without form, and, therefore,
the susceptibility of motion.   As oxygen is essential to
light, and as this is a chemical formation, it did not exist
in the homogeneous, chaotic mass.   The Creator must
therefore have endowed some of those atoms with the
quality which forms the flammable gas we call oxygen ; in
fact the endowment was the formation, and thereby communicated the natural susceptibility of motion to the
atoms.   The motion of the atoms of oxygen produced
heat by the friction in passing other atoms, or those of
themselves, and a certain rapidity of the atoms thus moving produced light, or, by contact with electricity, ignited
the oxygen, and light was the result.

It is an established physiological fact that electricity in
the form of animal magnetism is the agent of the mind,

by which we make voluntary motions and perform intelligent action. Reasoning by analogy, so it is with all orders of mind, especially with that of the Creator, who made man in his own image. It is not simply that God said, "Let there be light;" for if nothing else had been done no effect upon senseless matter would have resulted; but it is added, "And the spirit of God *moved* upon the face of the waters, and there was light." This mental agent was something that moved, which nothing could not do. Here, in the creation of the world, we have the conditions of light, and the same as our well-known science at the present day requires to produce it. First, the prior formation of oxygen. Second, the electric motion of the mind and will. Third, atomic friction, the result of which is light. For the first three days the light was equally divided from the darkness—twelve hours of light, and its absence leaving twelve hours of darkness, darkness being the normal condition of all matter. But what was more simple than that the Being who thus caused light to shine should have continued it twelve hours each of those three days, as typic of the coming day and night during the age of the world? On the fourth day the natural law for the division of light and darkness was made, which was to be perpetual. But now for the production of the light of the three days, the same spirit agency, moved by the mind of the Creator, the solar, electric, oxygenized clouds were sent into the same space they occupy to-day, forming the sun; there being as yet no gravity, or atmospheric pressure, it would stand just where it was placed: the starry planets, each of which are magnets, being essential to the completion of the great law of universal gravity, were also, by the same power, sent into their respective orbits. The motion of these on their axis give day and night to each, including that of the earth; as it is also written, "By his spirit he garnished the heavens," making the lights to shine in the vault of heaven.

In their pride of opinion the scoffers talk as though the Maker could not do that of which they themselves are capable, or of conceiving how it was done; that because the lovers of darkness do not understand how the Creator could light up the solar clouds twelve hours out of twenty-four, for three successive days, therefore it was not done ; and instead of confessing this ignorance, they use the more respectable phrase, " We do not believe it." Let us ask them : Have you not seen the aurora borealis, popularly called northern lights, produce the abnormal illumination of the whole hemisphere ? which, without the direct intervention of the Creator, gives a good illustration of the three days' light—the direct act of his. Could not God have thus lighted cloudy lamps to burn twelve hours of the twenty-four, as man can do on a small scale during the darkness of the night ? You see, we talk about the existence of God, the Creator, just as we do about that of our own, as the one implies the other, and not as a matter of mere belief or faith, but of logical knowledge, just as the arguments in this book compels you to do ; and the only apparent escape from the duty is to denounce free-thought —all thought, all reason, in which you pretend to glory, thus closing your eyes to all evidence—stand out the pitiful objects of apparent demented human kind, afraid to think, afraid to reason, apprehensive of being driven to the knowledge of the existence of God your maker, and as a consequence your responsibility to him. It was in view of this attitude of some of his creatures that he caused it to be written, " The fool hath said in his heart there is no God." Though we have elsewhere shown that the sun has no motion on its axis, yet we may remind the skeptics that their own modern astronomers assume and teach that the sun does revolve, as well as the whole solar system, with all other systems around a common centre, just as our planets revolve around the sun. Hence the sun might have stood still ; though such a theory is as far from being astronomical science as that of Proctor's fiery origin of the world and solar system.

False Skeptical Astronomy Degrades the Earth.

The fact is, the teachers of this modern astronomy have by their groundless speculations degraded the grand science to the level of evolution, both classes of whom now claim that the solar system came into existence without the intervention of God—a creation without a Creator !   Here we see Ingersoll's foolish objection to the command of Joshua, and its sequence, and which would confound him were he possessed of the ordinary fear of having his ignorance exposed.   This standing still of the sun is considered by the scoffers as the most formidable objection to the Bible ; it is the miracle of miracles, as the scoffer with all his sympathetic adherents have learned to repeat like as many parrots, and with about as much sense, at least evincing no more thought or reason.

The Doctrine of Miracles.

The objection to the doctrine of miracles may be exposed and their scientific philosophy established by numerous syllogisms.   For example, a miracle is a work of which nature is incapable ; nature is incapable of causing her own existence ; therefore, her origin was miraculous.   As all shades of skeptics agree in rejecting the occurrence of miracles as they are recorded in the Scriptures, and if we succeed in establishing the fact and necessity for their existence, it will be their universal defeat.   We read, " And the Lord God created every plant of the field before it was in the ground, and every herb of the field before it grew." (Gen. 2 : 4, 5.) " And God said, behold ! I have given you every herb bearing seed, and every tree, in the which is the fruit of a tree yielding seed ; whose seed is in itself." (Gen. 1 : 29.)   Here we have the miraculous work stated. First, the progenitors of each species were created before they were in the ground—before they grew ; and therefore each was mature and perfect, or none would have grown if placed in the ground.   Second, each had involved in it a mechanical department for the production of seed after their kind, or they could not have produced subsequent generations.   They were then planted in the earth for this purpose.   Each of these statements we find to be scientific and philosophic necessities, and therefore true.   Huxley says, "That

during the whole process of these living, moving phenomena, there is no point at which we can say, this
is a natural process and that is not a natural process: "
meaning that everything, from no seed to seed, and to
a perfect plant involving seed after its kind, is the work
of lifeless nature itself; but the exact opposite to the
truth and everything in the process from no seed to
seed and the perfect plant is miraculous work. This is
demonstrated by the fact that the embryonical conditions and products of everything which, by any possibility can evolve or be evolved from another must have
been first involved in it, and therefore each of the successive generations coming out from, or evolving, is the
unfolding of the miracle which the Creator enfolded in
it. He not only made the mature plant, but equally
all the elements and conditions essential to its reproduction—sunlight, moisture, soil, etc. This involvement
was nature, and thus was plant-nature born. To attribute any of the work to it is as absurd as to say the
new-born babe gave itself birth! Therefore there is
no point at which we can say in fact, " This is a natural
process;" for all is the coming out—the unfolding of
the great miracle of the six days' work of the great
Creator.

But it will be seen that the miraculous provisions
are limited to the present temporary necessities of mankind, whose animal existence ends with the present
life. But as the Creator designed man's re-creation, and
that also of the world itself, both of which from that
event are without end, he is therefore to be the adopted
inhabitant of that world, provided he meets the conditions demanded by the Creator, which gives the essential qualification for the society and employment of that
world.

This fitness necessitates another class of miracles, consisting of the provisions for the accomplishment of that
end. These miracles are those which the Creator has
made in the incarnation of himself—the inspiration of
the Scriptures containing the Gospel—the good news,
or the instruction concerning that coming life and world,

that being the object and end for which the present
world was created. This shows the transcendent importance of the present world ; and to set aside any of
the miracles of the temporary world, is to destroy those
essential to its re-creation, involving the objects of that
work. It is as though a beautiful mansion was to be
erected, preparatory to which a temporary workshop
for the workmen and tools was first to be built. Suppose
the shop occupied part of the plot the owner designed
for the garden to the mansion, and when it was finished
he should remove the shop, would it be an inconsistency ?
Or suppose the proprietor should interfere and build the
shop before the mansion, assigning as a reason, it was to
facilitate this object ? In view of which the skeptics say,
O no! you made that shop, and if you destroy it, that
will show you had changed your mind, which, as God,
you could not do. Besides, it would show you had not
made the best possible mansion at first, which, as God,
you must have done, otherwise it would show your ignorance by trying experiments ! Behold ! how these created
things aspire to wisdom above their Maker—how, with
their little conceptions and absurdities, they enslave him ?

CHAPTER III.

ORIGINAL SOIL AN ACT OF CREATION

THE fact is, the whole phraseology, which attributes work to nature, requiring economy and ability, is a gross error without the least defence. In the light of philosophical science, every development nature manifests, from the rolling of the planets to the smallest detail, either of existence or motion, are but the necessary working out of her miraculous creation—it is the running of the machine. The original soil was necessarily a miraculous formation, as it was composed of all the vegetable properties of every plant which will grow therein. There was not even sand or gravel in existence, as these are the results of the aqueous wear and tear of the rocks; in fact, each is a small bowlder itself; and only permitted to enter into the formation of soil to as limited an extent as ashes are to the tree; and unless mixed with a large amount of vegetable decomposition, soil, capable of growing plants, is an impossibility, and as yet there was not a vegetable to decompose. Not even a particle of moss existed upon the mineral rocky surface of the earth; for its seed-dust, carried by the winds of heaven, is as much vegetable-decomposed matter as that of the peat-bogs of the earth. Here is nature with her solar system finished and complete, but without the least ability to prepare the earth for plant and animal life, not having the material of which its soil is composed; and if unable to do this simpler work, how could she have formed the planetary system itself? From this inability of nature are we not forced to the conclusion that the entire work of bringing her into existence is supernatural, and, therefore, miraculous work?

Here, then, we have the demonstration, based upon

philosophic and scientific necessity, the fact that God made the soil of the earth, and sat therein every species of plant existence which have ever lived, constructing and involving in each the faculty of producing and reproducing all future generations. When thus endowed and planted, all commenced unfolding—evolving their wonderful complications, and to continue during the ages of the world. Now, at what particular point could any of these phenomena be said to be the work of nature? "This is a natural process," as Huxley says. He who made the machine, endowed it with all its wonderful possibilities, leaving not the most insignificant thing to be performed. Instead, therefore, of there being any reason for declaiming against miracles, we are called upon by the universal voice of science and observation to proclaim all nature, without omitting the least thing, to be the unfoldment of the one vast, complicated miracle of the Creator! Take another illustration. Suppose a locomotive engine was so constructed that within its parts the entire material and tools were involved and arranged, and in such a manner that when the locomotive was set in motion and doing its ordinary work, it should turn out another locomotive precisely like itself, and this again another, and so on, each successor endowed with the requisite material and mechanism to thus reproduce its kind. Now, what would be thought of the mental calibre of the beholder, who should declare the first engine to be a work of art, but the successors, the children, to be the work of the engine itself? Suppose still further, that the beholder should say, Inasmuch as the engines reproduce each other, the first one also came into existence by the same process ; or, more absurd still, if that can be, that there never was a first ! Or, while beholding these successors thus coming into existence and perceiving that each was superior to its immediate predecessor, should declare the first came from no engine, instead of appreciating the fact that the phenomena showed all the greater mechanical skill was involved in the first locomotive—the involvement was creation, while the running and reproduction was evolution.

But the locomotive, with whatever susceptibilities it was possessed, was one of man's miracles, and it was a miracle because a work of which nature was incapable. The difference between the miracles of man and those of his Creator, are not in kind, but degree, and those of the Creator are as superior to those of man, as the Creator is superior to the creature. But the guidance and cultivation of God's miracles in vegetable nature as much depend upon the miracles of man, as the perpetuity of his existence depends upon food. Let all men cease to till the soil, and plant seed, how long would it be ere they would become extinct? Nature's spontaneous productions would not sustain the life of the present inhabitants of the earth a single year, with all the fowl and fish of the sea which could be caught and gathered. Let the most beautifully cultivated farm, with its fruit orchards, lie untouched by the hand of man for the space of twenty-five years, would it not degenerate to a mere patch of weeds, thistles, thorns, briers and wild-wood? This also shows, that the work of nature is not improved development, but the most rapid degeneracy, even to the extinguishment of man himself, most completely reversing the absurd theory of evolution. Thus has God interwoven his miracles of nature, and of which man himself forms the most distinguishing part; with those of art the man is able to perform, making his existence and the Creator's purposes dependent upon each other.

Is Ingersoll an Atheist?

In regard to the existence of God, and the effects for evil his opinions and sophisms produce upon mankind, the arch-scoffer is so explicit in his lecture on the gods, that misunderstanding upon the question seems impossible. Says he, "If by any possibility it is demonstrated that there is a Being above us, it will be time enough for us to kneel; until then, let us stand upright. He is equally clear upon the existence of any authoritative religion. Hear him: "There is an irrepressible conflict between religion and science, and they cannot peaceably occupy the same brain, nor the same world." True science could no more dwell in peace in his brain, than can true religion. It is the Godless, foolish thing called evolution his discordant brain accepts for science and against which he wages no war. That there is a Being above us, we have demonstrated by forty syllogisms ; consequently the time has come for the arch-scoffer to kneel—it may be he may find mercy at the hand of him he has so slandered. Do this, Mr. Ingersoll, and devote the remainder of your life in earnest effort to neutralize the deadly poison you have infused into the hearts and minds of the young men of our country. But if you attempt to treat these arguments, not one of which are you able to answer with your weapons of flippant speech and ridiculous representation, as you do the Bible, your public and private efforts will be laughed to scorn, as the mere verbiage of an errant braggart. And while we are dealing with you personally, we would say that we dare you to meet us in public discussion, or through the press.

The Scoffer's Specious Sympathy for the Deluded.

Says he : " While utterly discarding all creeds, and denying the truth of all religions, there is neither in my heart, nor upon my lips a sneer for the hopeful, loving, and tender souls who believe that from all this discord will result a perfect harmony ; that every evil will in some mysterious way become a good. [It will be a very mysterious metamorphosis, to make an evil a good—make eternal opposites, harmony ; it is, however, the only process which offers him and his deluded followers the least hope for the harvest of tares they are sowing in vain—hope that tares will become wheat—a miracle which neither God nor man are capable of performing. It is impossible for God to lie.] And that above and over all, there is a Being who in some way, will reclaim and glorify everyone of the children of men ; but for those who heartlessly try to prove that salvation is almost impossible, and damnation almost certain ; that the highway of the universe leads to hell ; who fill life with fear, and death with horror ; who curse

the cradle and mock the tomb, it is impossible to entertain other than feelings of pity, contempt, and scorn."
That this talk about a Being above and over all, who
may reclaim and glorify everyone of the children of
men, is wholly heartless, is shown by the fact that through
his whole lecture he ridicules the very idea of the existence of such a Being. If his existence is admitted, it is
only to compare him with the devil, giving the latter
superior virtue and intelligence; and while thus presuming upon the simplicity of his hearers, tells them there
may be a God, and such a good God, that he will never
hurt even such an implacable enemy as this scoffer; and
yet there is no God. He encourages all to hope for
glorification at the hands of the Being above us, and yet
there is no such Being. But of what avail are any of his
sayings, or of what worth are his shallow religious
opinions? Christ tells us of the broad way that leads to
death, and many there be that walk therein; they choose
the way regardless of his admonition, "Why will ye
die?" "While straight is the gate and narrow is the way
that leads to life, and few there be that find it." This is
the Being who declares damnation general, and salvation
so difficult that "few there be that find it." It is Christ,
therefore, who has the "scorn of the scoffer's heart. This
is not as Christ would have it, but who declares the fact
as it is, and which is confirmed by common observation.
The many refuse the conditions upon which life is offered,
and choose death as a consequence. The probable reason
why the scoffer denounces those who warn the people
against taking his advice, as walking in the broad way, is
because it makes his career in slandering God, and the
Bible, for money, a poor speculation. Let us inquire what
has been the character of the two hundred generations of
mankind, including the present, in relation to a fitness
for future glorification. If there be no Being to glorify
them, they must glorify themselves, but how many among
the masses evince any such disposition in the present life,
and what hope have they for future glorification? If
mankind were tested by their own acknowledged standard of virtue and unselfish benevolence, and hell and

heaven awarded each class, which would be the most crowded? Besides, the atheists believe death to be eternal sleep, among whom our scoffing hero, in opaque mendacity, is most conspicuous. "He has no sneer for any but those who believe the words of Christ;" but of what consequence are his foolish sneers? only as the expression (SNEER) conveys a true idea of the composition of his public lectures, instead of argument. For our part we would prefer his "sneers" to words of praise, as in such a case there would be no fear of identification with him or his cause. Said a very high authority, "Woe unto you when all men speak well of you."

The multitudes who rebel against their Maker, necessitates the highway that leads to death and hell. It is the hatred of God and his holiness that characterizes the throng and fills the broad way with travellers. It is the effect of atheistic sneers which fill life with fear, and death with horror! The work of the scoffer is to relieve the life of the wicked of these fears, by cruelly telling them there is no God to fear; they may commit all the damning deeds their nature prompts, and have "no fear of God before their eyes," and no horrors in their death. It is Ingersoll and his scoffing fellows who fit men for damnation. How can men who join the tirade against their Maker expect any other death or resurrection than that written in the book of truth: that of shame, contempt, and horror? In the very nature of things they must reap the harvest they have sown, which, by giving heed to the arch-scoffer, can only be described by the terrible word, "damnation," the meaning of which they will not realize until the judgment at the last day. Christ said, "Marvel not at this, for the hour is coming in the which all that are in their graves shall hear the voice of the Son of God, and shall come forth, they that have done good, unto the resurrection of life, and they that have done evil, unto the resurrection of damnation." (John 5: 28, 29.)

The Seed and Harvest of Ingersollism.

The seed the scoffer and his confederates are sowing, which induce men to turn against their Maker, dishonoring and trampling upon his laws, on the pretentious ground that there is no God, put themselves in a position wherein they are held in contempt by all good men, and their notoriety is simply that of infamy; but how will the shame and contempt be increased when they come to reap the harvest they have sown, at the judgment-seat of Christ, with whom all will be confronted in person, and when such as he will be surrounded by the victims of his scoffing blasphemy?   Such a career comprehends all the elements of contempt.   If Ingersoll is honest, and does not know there is a God, then he merits the contempt of ignorance, heightened by surroundings of the most favorable opportunities to obtain such knowledge. If he knows there is a God, the proprietor of his being, and yet tries to induce others to ignore the restraint of his laws and refuse obedience to his righteous claims, then he adds to the contempt the arrogance of the thing that is made, warring against the Maker, of course, with the certainty of defeat.   If the power, goodness, and loveliness of God, and the fear of threatened punishment fails now to subdue such a rebel spirit, and reclaim him to loving obedience, will God ever be more just, merciful, powerful, loving, and good?—or will he change his purposes to suit his implacable enemies?   When thus confronted, will God acknowledge to such sinners that he had exaggerated the damnation in order to frighten them into obedience? Such conceptions evince mere childish thoughts and estimates of the character of God, right and wrong, justice and injustice, rewards and punishment.   The scoffer says: "This horror of damnation curses the cradle and mocks the tomb."   As to mocking the tomb, it is a fancy expression without meaning, and about the cradle being horrified, supposes the infants who lie therein are able to understand about damnation, and become horrified at the contemplation—wonderful sagacity !   No!   It is the

ignorant, laughing sayings of the scoffer, covered with
his own chosen contempt, who fills the grave with horror
by making it the bed of eternal sleep, and from which
none but Christ, " the resurrection and the life," can deliver him, and not he unless the scoffer repents, loves,
and obeys his God and Creator. To glorify him upon
any other condition would make Christ a liar, and im-
plicate him with conniving at all the wrong of the universe, and be willing to live in the eternal company of
his bitter enemies—in perpetual warfare.

Christian Religious System the Highest Social Standard.

Ingersoll says: " We are laying the foundation of the
grand temple of the future—not the temple of the gods,
but of all the people—wherein, with appropriate rites,
will be celebrated the religion of humanity. We are doing what we can to hasten the coming of the day when
society will cease producing millionaires and mendicants
—gorged indolence and famished industry, truth in rags,
and superstition crowned. We are looking for the time
when the useful shall be the honorable, and when reason,
enthroned upon the world's brain, shall be the king of
kings, and god of gods." These are the sentiments of
the Anarchists, which, since Ingersoll's career, the chief
Anarch, has grown rampant in this country. The scho-
lastic skepticism of Germany and France, emanating from
the Leipsic University, and the French Academy, for the
last half century, have developed the Nihilism of Europe
—the assassins of statesmen and kings, as impediments in
their way of stealing the property of the wealthy, and to
live in gorged indolence, which, if realized to the degree
Ingersoll here depicts, will render human society an impossibility. It is seen by such men as he and the late
Charles Bradlaugh, that men to any great extent cannot be
induced to commit such crime who believe in the existence of God and future punishment ; hence their hatred
of hell, and atheistic warfare against God and church society.

At the head of this gigantic scheme Ingersoll, in this

country, arms himself with an iconoclastic club and goes
forth to kill all the gods, and yet he has not advanced
far enough to distinguish between the living and dead
gods.   Indeed, he only discovers enough of the evidence
of the existence of God to madden him into the furore of
a pitched battle with whatever of a living God there may
be.   When the chief Anarchist is dead, those who come
after are to build on his foundation the " religion of humanity "—a kind, humane religion, one for the poor and
oppressed.

Ingersoll says : " To read the Bible is to reject it,"
and yet he is so ignorant of it that he thinks he has discovered an improved religion, while that revealed in the
Bible is so absolutely perfect and adapted to exalt man
physically, morally, mentally, and religiously, and therefore to the highest standard of social citizenship, that it
becomes simply absurd to attempt its improvement.   For
the enlightenment of those upon whose ignorance the
scoffer thus presumes, we will transcribe enough of it to
vindicate our position as to the nature of its religion.
The first passage we introduce defines the religion by the
nature of the duties it enjoins, thus : " Pure religion and
undefiled before God and the Father is this, To visit the
fatherless and the widows in their affliction, and keep
himself unspotted from the world."   (James 1 : 27.)   Is
there any higher regard for humanity than this ?   The
following shows in what esteem the poor are held by this
religion, and that no preference is to be shown to robed
and decorated superstition and millionaires :   " My brethren have not the faith of our Lord Jesus Christ, the Lord
of glory, with respect of persons ; for if there come into
your assembly a man with a gold ring, in goodly apparel,
and there come in also a poor man, in vile raiment, and
ye have respect unto him that weareth the gay clothing,
and say unto him, sit thou here in a good place, and say
unto the poor, stand thou there, or sit here under my
foot-stool, are ye not partial in yourselves, and are become judges of evil thoughts ?   Hearken, my beloved
brethren : hath not God chosen the poor of this world
rich in faith, and heirs of the kingdom which he hath

promised to them that love him? But ye have despised
the poor. Do not rich men oppress you, and draw you
before the judgment seats? Do they not blaspheme that
worthy name by which ye are called? If ye fulfil the
royal law according to the Scriptures, thou shalt love thy
neighbor as thyself, ye do well, but if ye have respect to
persons, ye commit sin, and are convinced of the law as
transgressors.'' (James 2 : 5–9.) It is also the religion
of mercy for the oppressed : '' For he shall have judgment without mercy, that hath showed no mercy.''

It is the religion of works as well as faith, neither of
which can take the place of the other ; one practices un-
selfishness and is kept poor by the sacrifices it makes for
the poor and needy, in hope of the promised riches of endless being in an endless world, and faith in its fulfilment
makes its possessors happy in the present world of poverty. '' What doth it profit a man, my brethren, though
a man hath faith, and hath not works? can faith save
him? If a brother or a sister be naked, and destitute of
food, and one of you say unto them, depart in peace, be
ye warmed and filled, notwithstanding ye give them not
those things needful to the body ; what doth it profit?
Even so faith, if it hath not works, is dead, being alone.
Yea ! a man may say, thou hast faith, and I have works ;
show me thy faith without thy works, and I will show
thee my faith by my works. Thou believest that there
is one God ; thou doest well ; the devils also believe and
tremble.'' (James 2.) As Ingersoll does not know or
believe in one God, he is not as worthy, in the estimation
of God, as a devil !

It is the Religion of Principle—Reason—Motive.

Here is a religion of equality, especially adapted for
the protection and comfort of the poor, whose laws command those who have the means to supply the want of
the poor. Its founder said: '' Give to him that asketh
thee, and from him that would borrow of thee turn not
thou away.'' (Matt. 5 : 42.) '' Thou shalt not harden
thine heart, nor shut thine hand from thy poor brother ;

but shalt open it wide unto him, and shalt surely lend him sufficient for his need. And thine heart shall not be grieved when thou givest unto him." (Deut. 15 : 7–10.)

It is a rational religion because it recognizes an authority higher than its subjects, who made the laws and of right imposed the obligations, without which there can be no religion, as religion implies worship, and worship implies the recognition and belief in a God of some form. In order to show the spirit and motives which prompt these acts of kindness, benevolence, and mercy, we have such instruction as the following : "Hereby perceive we the love of God, because he laid down his life for us ; and we ought to lay down our lives for the brethren." "But whoso hath this world's goods, and seeth his brother have need, and shutteth his bowels of compassion from him, how dwelleth the love of God in him?" "My little children, let us not love in word, neither in tongue ; [merely] but in deed and in truth." (1 John 3 : 16–18.) "Let brotherly love continue." "Be not forgetful to entertain strangers." "Remember them that are in bonds as bound with them and them that suffer adversity." "Let your conversation be without covetousness ; and be content with such things as ye have ; for he hath said I will never leave nor forsake thee." (Heb. 13.) "And he lifted up his eyes on his disciples, and said, Blessed be ye poor ; for your's is the kingdom of heaven." (Luke 6 : 20.) "And he said unto him, When thou makest a dinner or a supper, call not thy friends, nor thy brethren, neither thy kinsmen, nor thy rich neighbors ; lest they also bid thee again, and a recompense be made thee ; but when thou makest a feast, call the poor, the maimed, the lame, the blind ; and thou shalt be blessed ; for they cannot recompense thee ; but thou shalt be recompensed at the resurrection of the just." (Luke 14 : 12–16.) "Therefore all things whatsoever ye would that men should do unto you, do ye even so unto them ; for this is the law and the prophets." (This doctrine is not new, but is taught both in the law and in the prophets.)

"Enter ye in at the strait gate ; for wide is the

gate, and broad is the way that leadeth unto destruction, and many there be which go in thereat ; because strait is the gate, and narrow is the way, which leadeth unto life, and few there be that find it." (Matt. 7 : 12–14.) Here is a reciprocal system of religious laws and rules which, if obeyed by a community or state, would be a perfect society, and impossible of improvement. To leave out the religious element would destroy the system by taking away the motive for the discharge of the duties, as they are to be done by the able to the unable. "They cannot recompense thee, but thou shalt be recompensed at the resurrection of the just." This principle recognizes the most complete mental, moral, religious, and physical law, written alike in the constitution of man and his external necessities, which is that he cannot act without motive, and that motive must propose immediate or remote happiness as compensation for the present sacrifice. God himself acts upon this principle in everything he has done or proposes to do for mankind ; all is conducive to his own eventual glory. Paul says of Christ : "Who for the joy that was set before him, endured the cross and despised the shame," etc. The fact that atheists cannot act upon this principle, accounts for the other fact that they stand aloof from all benevolent societies or philanthropic enterprises for the assistance and comfort of the poor. There is not a paragraph in the Scriptures which, in the least, lowers this high reciprocal standard of human obligation ! Atheists put themselves in the incongruous position of denouncing the Bible and its author, simply because men profess belief in both, and yet do not obey its principles ; as though a principle was bad, because men do not like, or obey it.

How the Christian Religion Views Oppressors of the Poor.

Let us hear some of the Lord's complaints against millionaires, and the oppressive monopolies of the poor, and their coming doom : "Go to, now, ye rich men ; weep and howl for the miseries that shall come upon you. Your riches are corrupted, and your garments are moth-eaten. Your gold and silver are cankered ; and the rust of them shall be a witness against you, and shall eat your flesh as it were fire. Ye have heaped treasure together for the last days. Behold, the hire of the laborers who have reaped down your fields, which is of you kept back by fraud, crieth : and the cries of them have entered into the ears of the Lord of Sabaoth. Ye have lived in pleasure on the earth, and been wanton ; ye have nourished your hearts, as in the day of slaughter. Ye have condemned and killed the just [by your combines, have starved them] ; and he doth not resist you. Be patient, therefore, brethren, unto the coming of the Lord.'' (James 5 : 1–7.) This system of religious doctrine did not teach the unphilosophic notion of Ingersoll that there is coming a time when there will be no rich and no poor —in other words, when there will be no selfish, avaricious and oppressive men—a perfect equality—but he did not teach the poor to assassinate the rich, and oppress and rob him ; but refers his suffering brethren to the coming of the Lord, at the last day, when he will meet out retributive justice to all, whether they had been poor murderers and thieves, or selfish, rich oppressors of the poor. The hope that the religion of the Bible holds out for the encouragement of Christians, when such a state of things exists, is the coming of their Lord to put them in possession of an endless kingdom—a government of universal righteousness in the new world he is then to create from the dissolved elements of the present world. But Ingersoll, in his profound ignorance of this most prominent Scripture doctrine, becomes a false prophet, and tells us that this same selfish, oppressive human nature is going to work a most wonderful miracle for its own destruction, converting themselves (its victims) into the highest type of the religion of the Bible—obedience to its two great principles : '' Thou shalt love the Lord thy God with all thy heart, and thy neighbor as thyself;'' but no philosophy, or any other religion, ever changed the heart or character of a rich oppressor of the poor into such a model of unselfish righteousness without being induced by the promise of future reward, yet the atheistic religion of humanity, built upon the ruins of the Church of Christ, is going to do it. Wonderful credulity!

Christ said, "Lay not up for yourselves treasures upon earth, where moth and rust doth corrupt, and where thieves break through and steal; for where your treasure is there will your heart be also." As an example of this love of riches, if possessed, and of the disposition Christ taught should be made of it, we have the following: "Behold, one came and said unto him, Good Master, what good thing shall I do, that I may have eternal life? And he said, If thou wilt enter into life, keep the commandments. He said, Which? And Jesus said, Thou shalt do no murder. Thou shalt not commit adultery. Thou shalt not steal. Thou shalt not bear false witness. Honor thy father and thy mother; and thou shalt love thy neighbor as thyself. The young man said, All these have I kept from my youth; what lack I yet? Jesus said unto him, If thou wilt be perfect, go and sell that thou hast, and give to the poor, and thou shalt have treasure in heaven [the new heaven]: and come and follow me. But when the young man heard that saying, he went away sorrowful; for he had great possessions. Then said Jesus unto his disciples, Verily, I say unto you, that a rich man shall hardly enter into the kingdom of heaven. And again I say unto you, It is easier for a camel to go through the eye of a needle, than for a rich man to enter into the kingdom of God." (Matt. 19: 16–24.)

Who cannot see that if these laws of Christ were obeyed, it would develop the most perfect human society —just, loving, pure, sympathetic, benevolent, unproscriptive in feeling and motive, always actuated to please and honor their Creator, and by faith in his word of promise, look for the possession of the endless world, through the resurrection at the last day, for their reward. As there cannot be a higher religion than this, that which Ingersoll calls the "religion of humanity" must be a lower one, which is but one of its principles; the attempt, therefore, is, to destroy a whole religious system by the substitution of one of its elements. He says, "This chimerical religion is not that of *reason*, but an appeal to superstition and credulity." What are the facts, supposing these to be two religions? which is no more so than a single element of a system, is another system. Both have to deal with the same human nature—man as he is. Some of man's natural characteristics are: First, a disposition to be rich. Second, a desire for self-gratification. Third, a disposition to live without labor, such as personally tilling the soil, manufacturing the implements or clothing for those who do the work; hence, each is striving to live on the labor of another. Fourth, it is as natural for man to demand compensation for his labor as it is to be able to act from motive; and Fifth, man cannot perform the least voluntary act without faith, which is some confidence of success, or without hope of accomplishing that which will be for his interest in the present or future, and which will, in some measure, and at some time, be conducive to his happiness. Sixth, it is a fact of common observation, that hope of reward, and fear of punishment, which fear may consist of loss, are the strongest motives to induce human action, and such motives, relating to future reward or punishment, are impossibilities in the absence of faith, hope, or a natural, or written law, offering reward and threatening punishment. Seventh, it is a fact that no rational man has ever found in the resources of the present world that condition of things which has freed him from apprehension of coming evil, and, therefore, that which has made him permanently happy. Eighth, it is a fact that human society cannot exist without civil law, or that such law can equalize the sources of happiness among men; there must, therefore, be a higher law, with provisions, and revealing them to meet these necessities of his higher nature. Ninth, as man is an imitative being, he must become like those with whom he associates or communes. As a consequence, he cannot rise higher in the scale of intellectual or moral worth, but under the conviction that there is a Being above him of greater virtue, wisdom, and power than himself; and this compels atheists to go downward.

Revealed Religion founded upon a Philosophic Basis.

Founded upon these facts and principles of nature, man being its chiefest work, is the philosophy as well as the highest science of revealed religion ; not an element of which can be left out, without weakening the motives for the elevation of man, as an intellectual, moral, social, and religious being ; and he is no more one of these than he is every other. It is within the structure and functions of these fundamental truths that the enthronement of reason is to be found, not a substitute for God, but an emanation of his ordained and revealed plan for the creation and re-creation of man as an inhabitant of his eternal world. In view of which we have such instructions as the following : " I beseech you therefore, brethren, by the mercies of God, that ye present your bodies a living sacrifice, holy and acceptable unto God, which is your *reasonable* service. " (Rom. 12 : 1.) " Be ready always to give an answer to every man that asketh you a reason of the hope that is in you with meekness and fear." (1 Pet. 3 : 15.) " Come now, and let us reason together, saith the Lord : though your sins be as scarlet, they shall be white as snow ; though they be red like crimson, they shall be as wool." (Isa. 1 : 18.) Thus does God appeal to man as a reasoning being, and asking him whether the service he demands is not that of reason ?

Ingersoll says, " We are looking for the time when *reason*, enthroned upon the world's brain, shall be king of kings, and god of gods." Here is the absurd notion that the King of kings and Lord of lords, the source of all created things and beings, who endowed men with reasoning faculties, is to be superseded ; the faculties are to rise up and unseat the God that made them, and the abstract things enthrone themselves. This is about as good logic and reason as that sung by a socialistic club to a golden calf, as a god. " These be thy gods, O Israel, that brought thee up out of the land of Egypt ! " Is it reason that if a religion with God the Creator as its author, fails to convert men to its practice and spirit, and induce

loyal obedience to its laws : that one can succeed which
has no God to say, " Ye shall, and ye shall not "—" Do
this and live "—do that and die !   Or which will be the
most likely to induce obedience, one which offers endless
life in an endless world, or one which threatens eternal
annihilation at death ?   We are not entirely without examples of what this godless religion develops.   There
stands the ever memorable and ever fearful French Revolution—the proceedings of the Court of St. Cloud ! There
stands the " reign of terror," to warn the world against the
repetition of the experiment of such a religion—the (so
called) " enthronement of reason."   Is it reason to claim
that men will be more unselfish and sacrifice their own
interests for the good of others, without law, which they
will not do with it ?   Is it reason that men would be
more restrained from the perpetration of evil deeds and
sins against society, if they believed there was no God to
call them to account at a coming judgment, than though
they did believe this ?   Is it not more unreasonable and
superstitious to believe that mankind, as well as the world
itself, came into existence without the hand of a Creator,
than with it ?

If the greatness and severity of God as revealed in natural laws, of which he is the author, executing themselves
and inexorably punishing every offender, and for every
offence, fails to make atheists, such as Ingersoll, afraid,
how can we expect the obliteration of all this to succeed ?
But the scoffer says, " I don't believe in the existence of
any God."   Well, we do not respect what a man says
who has no respect for what he says himself, or what he
says he believes or disbelieves : it is not worth the breath
spent in repeating it ; and did he not sophistically attempt to make a show of argument in its defence, well
calculated to deceive the superficial, we would not attempt a line of exposure ; but that he may know there is
a God who created the world and inspired the Scriptures,
we refer him to the forty syllogisms in this book, accommodating the arguments to his easy comprehension ; hoping he may thus have a better idea of the composition of
a syllogism than that of the atheist—Thaddeus B. Wake-

man, who, in his attempted answer to our address—
"Christianity Defended," delivered before the Freethinkers' Convention, assembled at Rochester, N. Y.,
August, 1883, by saying that "Syllogisms cannot weigh
against facts"—not knowing that the first two members
of a syllogism are statements of fact, and the third, the
conclusion which they necessitate—escape from which is
only by showing the assumed facts are not such. For example, " It is a fact that a plant has not the power of locomotion. It is another fact that an oak is a plant. It is a
fact, therefore, that an oak has no power of locomotion."
Here we have the reasoning knowledge of the existence
of the Creator, and that he is the author of the revealed
religion of the Scriptures, confirmed and corroborated by
the moral and religious constitution of man ; and knowledge leaves no room for belief, nor demonstration for
doubt. Study these, Mr. Ingersoll, until you have become
alarmed at your foolish and wicked hostility and abuse of
your Maker, and not only repent with Godly sorrow, but
no more manifest the audacity of a coward, but the learning of a man whom the truth always humbles and makes
free !

The Scoffer's Socialistic Communism.

Though he may not be publicly identified with com-
munism, yet it is easy to see that the arch-skeptic is one
of the most advanced among its leaders in this country, as
Charles Bradlaugh was in England, whose principles are
educating and organizing the people for a repetition of
the French revolution of the last century. With the general conviction of the existence of God, this would be
impossible in any country or age. Hence the popular
career of these two men in their attempts to dissipate
this conviction from the minds of the people of the two
most civilized nations of the world. Not by argument,
for this is impossible in defence of error, but by recourse
to sarcasm and ridicule of their Maker. One of these
atheists has been a member of the Congress of the United
States, and the other of Parliament. Although revealed
religion is opposed to the oppression of the poor by the

rich, it is equally opposed to any combination of the poor against the rich, in a spirit of revenge, or any act to seize their property by force. These, as we have seen, are to be patient in their sufferings, until their Lord comes to judge the oppressor and reward the righteous oppressed "Vengeance is mine, I will repay, saith the Lord." These reformers have the same old selfish nature, which nothing but the gospel of Jesus Christ can change for the better, and which the gospel of humanity (so-called), has and must change for the worse. It is suscept-ible of every possible interpretation, so long as it rejects the idea of a living God, watching the spirit, actions, and motives of men.

Ingersoll's Contumelious Treatment of the Scriptures.

"One of the gods," says the scoffer, "and one who demands our love, our admiration and worship, gave to his chosen people for their guidance the following laws of war: 'When thou comest nigh unto a city to fight against it, then proclaim peace unto it. And it shall be if it make peace with thee and open unto thee, then it shall be that all the people found therein, shall be tribu-taries unto thee, and shall serve thee, and if it will make no peace with thee, but will make war against thee, then thou shalt besiege it. And when the Lord thy God hath delivered it unto thy hands, thou shalt smite every male with the sword, but the women, and the little ones, and the cattle, and all that is in the city, even all the spoil thereof, shalt thou take unto thyself. Thus shalt thou do unto all cities of these nations. But of the cities of these people which the Lord thy God doth give thee for an in-heritance, thou shalt save alive nothing that breatheth.'" (Deut. 20: 10–16.) Here the scoffer stops, while the next two verses introduce the reason for the extermina-tion commanded. In thus quoting Scripture he mis-quotes it by omitting the qualification, and evidently that he may have something to say against it. Of such it is said, "They handle the word of God deceitfully, and wrest the Scriptures to their own destruction." The

3

verses read thus : " But thou shalt utterly destroy them ; namely, the Hittites, the Amorites, Canaanites, Perizzites, Hivites, and the Jebusites ; as the Lord thy God hath commanded thee : that they teach not my people to do after their abominations, which they have done unto their gods ; so should ye sin against the Lord your God."

Now hear the blasphemer : " Is it possible for man to conceive of anything more perfectly infamous ? Can you believe that such directions were given by any being, except an infinite fiend ? Remember that the army receiving the instructions was one of invasion. Peace was offered upon condition that the people submitting should be slaves of the invader [to reduce a conquered people to be tributary, Ingersoll understands to make slaves of them, and he an ex-colonel], but if any should have the courage to defend their homes, to fight for the love of wife, and child, then the sword was to spare none, not even the prattling dimpled-chinned babe." That we may dispose of this sickish cant and scoffing against God and the Bible, we quote another passage ; showing that after the Amorites had fitted themselves for destruction, contemning their Maker by constructing effigies of him, and calling them gods, and making warfare against him and his people, just as Ingersoll is doing ; and this accounts for his expressions of sympathy for the Amorites. The passage is this : " Joshua made war a long time with all those kings. There was not a city that made peace with the children of Israel, save the Hivites—the inhabitants of Gibeon ; all others they took in battle : for it was of the Lord to harden their hearts, that they should come against Israel, that he might destroy them utterly, as the Lord commanded Moses." (Joshua 11.) This battle was that which was fought at the time Joshua commanded the sun to stand still, which we have already considered.

It was the insults offered to the living God and his worship, and by which they would be likely to teach his people, that led to their extermination, just as it led him to destroy the antediluvian generation of men, having utterly failed to answer the purpose for which God made them. To dishonor him even to defiance, they made effi-

gies and mocking likenesses, and worshipped them in derision of his person and worship.   One of these they called
Moloch, a brazen image surrounded by fires which they
kept burning, and caused their children to pass through
the fires to the image, though they were burned to death.
The Lord had said to Israel, "Thou shalt not do so
unto the Lord thy God : for every abomination which
the Lord thy God hateth, have they done to their gods :
for even their sons and their daughters they have burned
in the fires to their gods." (Deut. 2.)   There was
none but the Gibeonites, who had made peace with
Joshua ; all the others worshipped the fire-god Moloch,
sacrificing to him their children.   Here are the loving
fathers and mothers of those nations of Ingersoll's sympathy, burning their prattling, dimpled - chinned little
ones in the fire, to show their hatred and defiance of
their Maker.   Was it not more merciful to kill these little ones by the sword of Joshua, or the hailstones from
heaven, than to leave them for their loving fathers and
mothers to burn in the fires of Moloch?   .

The Laws of God Must be Against Image-worship.

"And the Lord descended in a cloud, and stood with
Moses, and proclaimed the name of the Lord : the Lord
God, merciful and gracious, long-suffering, and abundant in goodness and truth, keeping mercy for thousands,
forgiving iniquity, transgression and sin, and that will by
no means clear the guilty ; visiting the iniquity of the
fathers upon the children, unto the third and fourth generation " ("of them that hate me," is added in the
commandment).   "Thou shalt not make unto thee any
graven image, or any likeness of any thing that is in
heaven above, or that is in the earth beneath, or that is
in the water under the earth :   Thou shalt not bow down
thyself to them, nor serve them : for the Lord thy God
is a jealous God, visiting the iniquity of the fathers upon the children unto the third and fourth generation of
them that hate me ; and showing mercy unto thousands
of them that love me, and keep my commandments."

(Deut. 20 : 4–6). "And Moses bowed his head and worshipped. And he said, Behold ! I make a covenant before all the people, I will do miracles, such as have not been done in all the earth, nor in any nation : and all the people among which thou art shall see the work of the Lord : for it is a terrible thing that I will do for thee. Observe thou that which I command thee this day : Behold ! I drive out before thee the Amorite, the Canaanite, the Hittite, the Perizzite, the Hivite and the Jebusite. Take heed to thyself, lest thou make a covenant with the inhabitants of the land whither thou goest, lest it be a snare in the midst of thee : but ye shall destroy their altars, break down their images, and cut down their groves : for the Lord's name is a jealous God." Ingersoll says, " The army of Joshua was one of invasion ; " this supposes the people in possession had a good title to the land. The only title nations have to land, is one of war : of conquest, the stronger taking it from the weaker, the latter being invaders or revolutionists ; while the Creator is the only real owner, and this particular piece of land God deeded to these descendants of Abraham more than four hundred years before this event, and that seed had now come to take possession of their own land, under the visible direction of Joshua ; but really under the unseen hand of God, the owner and proprietor of the universe.

The Maker of the world is merciful and long-suffering with even his contemners who make effigies in derision of his righteous authority, ascribing to them the honor due alone to him. The work of Ingersoll and his sympathizers have no visible symbols ; but in spirit and purpose manifest the same hatred and dishonor to their Creator, as that of the Amorites. They contemptuously confound him with the things he has made. They have constructed a lifeless image, and call it EVOLUTION ! and blasphemously ascribe to it their creation. They do not burn their living children and friends in the fires of Moloch, as the civil laws would not allow ; but they build cremation ovens, as the same haters of God did of old, in which they burn their children and friends after

they are dead.   Even the disgraceful fiery furnaces are
allowed to be built in our popular cemeteries : shame on
men running into heathenism !   The heathens burned the
Christians because they believed and hoped the Creator
would re-create or raise them from the dead, at the last
day, supposing that as they scattered the ashes of the
martyred saints into the seas and rivers, God could not
resurrect them ; and it is reasonable to suppose that these
evolution-atheists who practice cremation, entertain the
same feeling of defeating their own resurrection, dreading
the personal contact with their Maker at his judgment.
The same class of people under the reign of the Emperor
Adrian, seeing that the Christians were not afraid to die
because they believed God would raise them to life again
at the last day, constructed cremation ovens and burned
the martyrs' bodies to ashes, and then said, "Now let us
see if their God is able to raise them again to life ?"
Thus do these conspirators against God become the modern Amorites.   And because God does not visit immediately upon the scoffers the due penalty of their unholy
deeds, they presume upon his mercy to sin against him.
In view of which he thus remonstrates : "Because sentence against an evil work is not executed speedily, therefore the heart of the sons of men is fully set in them to
do evil." (Ecc. 8 : 11.)   As illustrating this principle
of God's administration, we have such Scripture as the
following : "For the Scripture saith unto Pharaoh, even
for this same purpose have I raised thee up, that I might
show my power in thee, and that my name might be declared throughout all the earth.   Therefore hath he mercy
on whom he will have mercy [and we have seen, these are
they who love him and keep his commandments], and
whom he will he hardeneth [as he did Pharaoh and the
Amorites, who made war against the execution of his
purposes that they might, under the delusion, force themselves against his instruments of destruction—the armies
of the Israelites and the hailstones from heaven].   Thou
wilt say, then, why doth he yet find fault ? for who hath
resisted his will [who hath done this successfully in these
national affairs] ?   Nay, but, O man ! who art thou that

repliest against God ?—shall the thing formed say to him that formed it, Why hast thou made me thus?

" What if God, willing to show his wrath, and make his power known, endured with much long-suffering the vessels of wrath fitted to destruction: that he might make known the riches of his glory on the vessels of mercy." (Rom. 9 : 17–22.) " Behold therefore the goodness and severity of God : on them that fell, severity ; but toward thee, goodness, if thou continue in his goodness : otherwise thou shalt be cut off." (Rom. 11 : 12.) Let us sum up a few of the facts taught in these Scriptures. First, God had endured and suffered the insults and abuses of the Amorites four hundred years, while they had been filling up the cup of their iniquity, which had now culminated in a confederacy to wage a war of extermination against his people ; thus had they made themselves vessels of wrath fitted to destruction. God owned the land of the Amorites, and had promised to give it to this people : the seed of Abraham, four hundred years before. The issue was made by these people, and the question was, whether they or God, their maker, should succeed in the war of extermination. Ingersoll naturally takes sides with the Amorites in the iconoclastic war. During the same four hundred years, the Pharaohs of Egypt were also fitting themselves for the same destruction. All the male children of God's people were killed, which would have exterminated them in one generation, and this necessitated the Red Sea catastrophe. It is when nations and generations thus array themselves against the purposes of God, that he makes examples of them, as in these two instances, that others may be warned, and fear. Hence, in mercy, he makes the wrath of man praise him, restraining the remainder by their destruction.

The Creator Must Manifest His Interest in National Affairs.

So far as the Amoritish mothers were concerned, everybody knows it is the mothers who teach their children religion, whether true or false. Had these mothers been kept alive, the sons and daughters of the next generation would have been just as malignant haters of God as were their fathers. And had they married Hebrew husbands (and this was the danger), they would have succeeded in converting the coming generation into image - worshippers, and haters of the true and living God. It is also the women who generally convert their husbands, either to good or bad religion. Now, what an imbecile would God have been, to have commanded Moses and Joshua to have kept these loving mothers alive whose practice was to offer their own children, while alive, burnt sacrifices to the brazen Moloch : perfect monsters of inhumanity ! As to the prattling, dimpled-chinned babes, as Ingersoll describes them, thinking to enhance the atrocity of exterminating them, by sympathetic expression, that was an act in the line of the purpose for which God made man and the world, securing these innocent infants for his kingdom. Christ said, " Suffer the little children to come unto me, for of such is the kingdom of heaven." Had these children lived to maturity, in all human probability they would have learned about their ancestors ; and though among the Israelites, who themselves were bred among Egyptian idolatry, and therefore inclined to its practice, would have only repeated the experience of their parents, and shared their fate.

All Rational Beings Jealous of their Rights and Honor.

The fact that all rational beings are jealous of their rights and honor, especially that of their veracity, leaves no other conclusion than that such is the character of the Creator himself. As, therefore, no man will submit to their infringement, who has the power to defend them, such must be the character and practice of the Maker himself. It is also a fact that men do not always resent an injury when first committed, but wait—in mercy, hoping that the wrongdoer will repent and repair the evil. So we must infer it is with God, had he not revealed the fact ; but for man or his Maker never to vindicate his character, and defend his rights, shows not only weakness, but a want of self-respect, and common honor. It is another law of mind, to love them that love us. So it is with God, who says, " I love them that love me." It is also a law of natural rights, that proprietors have the first and highest claim. For example, upon tenants, and the discharge of every reciprocal obligation among their fellows in nowise affects their common obligation to owners. All men are God's tenants at will ; and whether he be merciful or implacable, just or unjust, good or bad, loving or a tyrant, makes no difference as to his right to demand the obedience of his creatures, even if he is, as Ingersoll represents him, " A fiend." Even in such a case it appeals to the motive of self-interest to obey him. The answer of Christ to the charge of the unfaithful steward in the parable of the talents, " That he was a hard master, reaping where he had not sown, and gathering where he had not strown," illustrates this principle. " Thou knewest that I was an hard man, thou oughtest therefore to have let out my money to the exchangers, that at my coming I might receive my own with interest."

We expect to be present and hear the arch-scoffer, while surrounded by the willing dupes of his art, interrogated by Christ the judge, who, if he is as bold then as now, will answer after this manner : " I did not think you existed at all, and if you did, you had let me go on so long in defying your authority, and insulting you by ranking you as one of the gods, and being so indulgent, I thought you would never hurt anyone ; and so long as I could make money by my lectures, why, I went on. And if you was so cruel as to burn up your enemies with fire and brimstone, then I would not obey you at all ! " To this we expect to hear the reply : " Then you would not obey me because I was a tyrant, as you called me, and that because I demanded the obedience of my creatures ; but you, as one of those creatures, have tyrannized over me and my laws, and even now it is in your heart to dethrone me, and would do it if you had the power ; consequently you are one of the most arrogant usurpers and malignant tyrants standing in all this ' Court of the gospel,' as you, sneeringly called it, ' A vessel of wrath fitted for destruction.' '' It is clear that this man has not the faintest conception of the character of God, as the Scriptures reveal him, or as he is revealed in the common philosophy of human kind, or of his wisdom, power, and goodness revealed in nature and providence, and that he is equally ignorant concerning his plan and design with man and the world ; and therefore utterly incompetent to discuss a single doctrine or sentiment the Scriptures reveal.   That others understand these with no better natural, intellectual faculties than those he possesses, proves his ignorance to be without excuse.   Therefore, in selecting certain passages descriptive of things God directed to be done, or approved of when done, and holding them up to ridicule, and God's mistakes, he is covering himself with infamy in the eyes of all good men, especially in the estimation of those who understand the revelation of this being, contained alike in the works of Nature, Providence, and Scripture.   There are facts connected with the administration of every civil ruler which, if selected and separated from the legitimate connection explaining them, and if held up to ridicule by a hater of that ruler, would bring him into contempt, at least in the estimation of those unacquainted with that history.   There never was a constitution or code of laws but which contained provisions, if taken alone and handled by an artful enemy, might not be made to appear inconsistent and ridiculous.

CHAPTER IV.

The most fruitful source of error is the supposition that the inhabitants, or any of them, of the present world are the subjects of God's government. The Scriptures represent them naturally as being in a state of rebellion and hostile to his authority. God has revealed no thought or design of establishing a government in this world, and only keeps it in existence in order to induce a sufficient number of its inhabitants to become reconciled to his righteous and endless reign in the world to come—this world re-created and these subjects resurrected or re-created into immortal men and women. It is the promise of this as reward, the glad tidings of which is the gospel God has ordained to be the inducement for men to become those subjects; and we venture the remark, that if Ingersoll was interrogated as to his views upon this only object and revealed design of the creation of the world and man, he would not only show profound ignorance upon the subject, but would be unable to point out an intelligent passage concerning it published in any paper or book of which he was the author. This is our charge for his blunders and foolish talk about God and the Bible.

In further confirmation of this, let us hear him again: " And we are called upon to worship such a God ; to get upon our knees and tell him he is good, merciful, and just —that he is love. We are asked to stifle every noble sentiment of the soul, and to trample under foot all the sweet charities of the heart, because we refuse to stultify ourselves—refuse to become liars. We are denounced, hated, traduced, and ostracized here, and this same God threatens to torment us in eternal fire the moment death allows him to fiercely clutch our naked, helpless souls. Let the people hate, let the God threaten; we will educate them, and we will despise and defy him. The book called the Bible is filled with passages equally horrible, unjust, and atrocious. This is the book to be read in schools in order to make our children loving, kind, and gentle! This is the book to be recognized in our Constitution as the source of all authority and justice!" Here we have an illustration of the scoffer's frenzied metamorphism. First, there is no God; second, if there is, then we should kneel before him; third, if there is such a God as the Bible describes, then we should not kneel before him, but despise, hate, and defy him. This is the standard to which the scoffer and his admirers hope to educate the people. These are the fundamental doctrines in his creed and the purpose of the heart of the man who refuses to stultify himself. (To stultify is to make a man appear foolish. How can a man be more foolish than to defy the God with all wisdom and all power, even if he is a fiend.) A beautiful mind to see faults in God and inconsistencies of dealing with his creatures!

The effect of Ingersoll's war with God, and that of those he induces to join his atheistic conspiracy, must result, as it should, in the endless loss of themselves. They fail in the end of answering the purpose of becoming loyal subjects of God's proposed righteous government, for which they were made; they can, therefore, hope for no place in it. But by such influences the Creator is subjected to a longer state of suffering than he would otherwise have been, as it has taken him a longer time to obtain others to take their place and crown; but all this was taken into the account in appointing the day for the execution of the work, and the whole calamity and loss will fall upon the scoffing seducers and seduced victims of their artful hate. Not that God is unmerciful or unforgiving, but by this despicable habit of rebellion they have disqualified themselves for repentance and compliance with the conditions necessary to become loyal subjects to the rightful ruler of the anticipated eternal government! This result, therefore, is the profoundest natural and moral philosophy of the system, and in itself unanswerable.

The fear of such an end may have the effect of deterring men from the cultivation of such a disposition, which grows more despotic over them with every repeated act of rebellion; but from the very moment the punishment begins to be felt, it is as impossible to make the sufferer love him who inflicts it as to make a man love his fellow-man who subjects him to punishment. One being may induce another to thus obey him in outward acts, as painful as the torments may be; but it is unnatural and impossible that such means can beget love. The opinion of Ingersoll is that men cannot love the God of the Bible —and this expresses his own experience, which must be common to all who are still rebellious; for how can such love a being against whom they are prosecuting a relentless warfare? Nor can such have the least conception how anyone else can love him. But how many millions of men with hostile feelings and views of God have been induced by the Bible revelation of his love for them, manifested by the sacrifice of his life, and the reward promised those who love and obey, to cease the unequal and unnatural warfare, and not only become reconciled to his propositions and way of doing things, but so to love him that they have laid and will lay down their lives rather than thereafter offend him !

The testimony of Ingersoll is but negative—what he does not know; and correctly enough, because still on the rebellious side, waring against God and his laws. On the other hand, we have the testimony of the millions of those who love him and all he says in his word, and heartily approve of everything he professes in the Bible to have done and proposes to do. These also testify that once they had the feelings of the rebellious, and now of the loving and loyal. In view of this, we would ask which of these classes is it reasonable to credit?—which are to be believed, those who had a knowledge of one class of facts, or those who had that of both? In the total ignorance of the latter experience, the scoffer says, "We are called on to stifle every noble sentiment, tram-

ple on charity, and stultify—make fools of—ourselves."
But what would a court say and do with Ingersoll if,
when called as a witness to tell what he knew about a
certain case, he should persist in talking about it in the
most positive manner, and yet knew nothing about it?
Would they not put the audicious fool out of court?
Thus does he stultify himself!

Doctrine of Devils—The Scoffer's Preference for Them.

Says he: "Our ancestors not only had their godfath-
ers, but they made devils as well. These devils were
generally disgraced and fallen gods. [This is not true of
the devils brought to view in the Bible, for they were
fallen angels—creatures. Nor have Freethinkers thrown
such light upon the subject that leads intelligent Christians to be caught in the devil's last snare, with which he
has captured Ingersoll—namely, that there is no devil;
that he himself does not exist—nor was he cunning
enough to make our ancestors believe the lie.] Some had
headed successful revolts. [This is not true of the devil
or devils in biblical history; but this man does not know
the difference between its statements and those of John
Milton. Nor has the devil's opposition to the will of
God proved in the least successful against the accomplishment of his purposes, and he himself is yet reserved unto
the judgment of the last day to be punished, in common
with all his human dupes, who might have been coro-
nated in the coming kingdom of God had they been wise
enough to have discovered Satan's devices.] Some had
been caught sweetly reclining in the shadowy folds of a
fleecy cloud, kissing the wife of the god of gods. [There
is not only nothing like this account in the Bible, nor in
Homer, that a devil kissed the wife of the god of gods,
and we hold Ingersoll responsible for its origin.] These
devils generally sympathized with man." [This is a fact,
and is explained by the other fact that men, especially
such as Ingersoll, always sympathized with their father,
the devil, in their hatred of God and his cause. It is
also explained by the adage, "Misery loves company,"

and by the philosophic words of Burns, "Like draws like to like." Said one of these devils to Christ, his destined destroyer, "Art thou come to destroy us before the time?" It is another historic fact contained in the Bible, that when any man forsook the friendship and service of the devil, and he failed to seduce him back, that he did his best to torment and kill him, as in the case of Job. So that the extent of the devil's sympathy is limited to the circle of his friends.] He further says, "There is in regard to devils a most wonderful fact: in nearly all the theologies, mythologies, and religions, the devils have been much more merciful and humane than the gods." [All this general talk about devils by Ingersoll means those of the Bible, who wickedly brings in the fabled legends to disparage those of the sacred book, in which there is not a humane act a devil ever did recorded.] "No devil ever gave one of his generals an order to kill the children, and rip open the bodies of pregnant women." This is another of his lying slanders against God and the Bible.

As to the devils having generals, this is one of Ingersoll's funny sayings which makes him popular with like shallow-brains; and that God ever gave this order to kill the women is another of his lies and blasphemies, for which he should be hissed out of the society of all but devils. That our readers may see the scoffer's mixture of hatred, ignorance, and lies, we will examine the passage about killing the women and children.

"And Elisha came to Damascus; and Ben-hadad, the king of Syria, was sick: and it was told him the man of God was come. And the king said unto Hazael, Take a present in thy hand, and go, meet the man of God, and inquire of the Lord by him, saying, Shall I recover of the disease? So Hazael went, with a present of every good thing of Damascus, forty camels' burden, and said, Thy son Ben-hadad, king of Syria, hath sent me, saying, Shall I recover of this disease? And Elisha said, Go, say unto him, Thou mayest certainly recover; howbeit the Lord hath showed me he shall surely die. And the prophet settled his countenance steadfastly upon Hazael until he

was ashamed ; and the man of God wept. And Hazael said,
Why weepeth my lord ?   And he answered, I know the
evil that thou wilt do unto the children of Israel ; their
strongholds wilt thou set on fire, and their young men
wilt thou slay with the sword, and wilt dash their children, and rip up their women with child.   And Hazael
said, But what ! is thy servant a dog, that he should
do this great thing?   And Elisha answered, The Lord
hath showed me that thou shalt be king over Syria.
[The Lord saw the fact in advance, and inspired the prophet to see it as he did ; but the Lord had no hand in
making this murderer king.]   So he departed from Elisha,
and came to his master ; and he said, What said Elisha?
And he answered, He told me that thou shouldest surely
recover.   [This was a lie Hazael told.]   And it came
to pass on the morrow, that Hazael took a thick cloth,
and dipped it in water, and spread it on his face, so he
died.''   (2 Kings 8 : 7–15.)

The history of the fulfilment of this prediction is as
follows :   '' Then Menahem smote Tiphsha, and all that
were therein, and the coasts thereof from Tizah, because
they opened not unto him ; and all the women therein
that were with child he ripped up.   And Pul the king of
Assyria came against the land.   And Menahem gave
Pul a thousand talents of silver, that his hand might be
with him to confirm the kingdom in his hand.   And
Menahem exacted the money of Israel.   So the king of
Assyria stayed not then in the land.''   '' In the nine and
thirtieth year of Azariah king of Judah began Menahem
the son of Gadi to reign over Israel, and he reigned ten
years in Samaria.   And he did that which was evil in
the sight of the Lord.   He departed not all his days
from the sins of Jeroboam the son of Nebat, who made
Israel to sin.''   (2 Kings.)   Here is Menahem king of
Israel, in Samaria, whose whole career was evil in the
sight of the Lord, but it was not even he who killed the
women and children in this manner, but Pul, the king
of heathen Assyria.   This is the man who Ingersoll says
was one of God's generals, and whom he ordered to commit this horrible deed.   Thus does this dutiful child of

his father, the devil, charge his lies, slanders, and blas-phemies against God and the Bible for money.

Another False Charge Refuted.

If Ingersoll had the least desire to establish right and punish wrong, could he charge upon God the work for sending one of his prophets to hew an inhuman king in pieces who had killed the children of Hebrew mothers, and pervert Scripture history by substituting lies for facts? He says, "One of the prophets of one of these gods, having in his power a captured king, hewed him in pieces in the sight of all the people: was ever any imp of any devil guilty of such savagery?" The account of this act is as follows: "Then said Samuel, Bring ye hither to me Agag the king of the Amorites. And Agag said, Surely the bitterness of death is past. And Samuel said, As thy sword hath made women childless, so shall thy mother be childless among women. And Samuel hewed Agag in pieces before the Lord in Gilgal" (1 Sam. 15 : 32, 33.) Here was a man waging a war of ex-termination against the people of God and his righteous purposes. He had ordered king Saul to slay king Agag, and he disobeyed ; and now he sent his prophet to execute the judgment. It was done in sight of all the people, that they might fear and obey their God and Creator. The scoffer has no word of rebuke for the savage war of Agag in defence of his gods and in derision of his Crea-tor ; no word of protest against the heathen king for mercilessly killing all the children of mothers in Israel, which he had been savagely prosecuting; but when God orders him to be hewn in pieces, why, it is a more atro-cious deed of savagery than that of which any imp of any devil was ever guilty. If the living God will only submit to let the angel and human devils, who fight him and try to induce his own children to turn against him, and never show any disposition of defence or resentment, why, then they would let him alone in pitiable contempt. What stirs the wrath of Ingersoll and animates his savage elo-quence is, by beholding such a fate as that of Agag, as in it he sees his own approaching doom. This God who can order his prophets to hew men in pieces, and his angels to bind the finally rebellious and cast them into a lake of fire and brimstone, bewilders him and his atheistic sympathizers so that they seem to act as though, if they did not believe it, it would not take place. And then that this God never changes his purposes calls forth the most boisterous protestations, while upon all the other gods only funny jokes are passed at the expense of the worshippers.

The Scoffer's Sentimentalism to Awaken Sympathy.

The scoffer says: " The pestilences were sent by the most merciful gods. The frightful famine, during which the dying child with pallid lips sucked the withered bosom of a dead mother, was sent by the loving gods. No devil was ever charged with such fiendish brutality. The devils were always on our side." In answer to the first charge, we may say that this man professes to believe in and honors modern science, which exalts Nature herself to be the author of his being ; it is therefore his god, and yet in every age this god has afflicted the old and young with cruel famine, pestilence, and earthquakes. Now, why does he worship such a god ? Was any devil ever charged with such fiendish brutality ? There are two reasons why the devils were not thus charged. One is that their own children, having the family agreement and sympathy, would not charge such an act on their devil-parents, but, like Ingersoll, would rather charge it on God, their Maker, with whom they are at terrible enmity. The other reason is that none of God's children, consequently the devil's enemies, were ever foolish enough to suppose any devil ever had power to make a famine or a pestilence, which implies control of atmospheric elements.

It is true the devil once stirred up the wind so that it blew down the house wherein Job's children were feasting ; but this was by an especial permit of his Maker. But was it ever written that God sent a famine or pestilence upon a people for their loving obedience to his will and commands? The lesson taught by famine is the same as that taught to a prodigal son who has squandered his father's bounties in selfish gratification until he is reduced to gnawing of husks, the tendency of which is to bring him to repentance and reformation. It is true Ingersoll does not attempt to show the injustice of sending these upon the adult rebels, though it is evident this is what maddens him; but because it falls equally upon the little children. The answer to this we have already given, namely, that all the little children, even those of idolators who thus die, not being mature enough to make the sins of their parents their own, Christ has pledged his word to redeem from death, and ransom from the grave, and to introduce them immortal subjects of his endless world. To the old sinners, their parents, he said, "Except ye be converted and become as this little child, ye can in no case enter into the kingdom of God." Was it an act of cruelty to take these little children thus, rather than let them live, if they did not starve by the famine, in communities where they would have been taught the God dishonoring and degrading worship of gods of wood and stone, causing them to fail of this grand object of their being? Die they must at some time; and about one-third of the human family die in infancy in any case.

The Blasphemy Against the Holy Ghost—What is it?

"The devils," says Ingersoll, "have always been on our side." This is a remarkable confession, and, from comparisons he makes, he seems to glory in the family relationship; and he certainly renders well his part of the service to the common devildom, thus unwittingly acknowledging the Scripture philosophy, "Know ye not that to whom ye yield yourselves servants to obey, his servants ye are." Christ said to the Jews who were blaspheming, by ascribing his miracles to the devil, "Ye are of your father, the devil, and the lusts of your father ye will do. He was a murderer from the beginning and abode not in the truth. When he speaketh a lie, he speaketh of his own: for he is a liar, and the father of it"

(John 8 : 44, 45.)   Some of the Pharisees attributed the
power by which Christ cast out devils, to Beelzebub, the
prince of devils.   They said to him, " Thou art a Sam-
aritan and hast a devil."   For this manifestation of despicable hate they were told that there..was no forgiveness, neither in this world nor in that which is to come.
Not that the sin in itself was so atrocious that by complying with the conditions of repentance it could not be
pardoned ; but the heart from whence it emanated had
reached such an adamantine devil-likeness of hatred to
Christ, that it despised him for his goodness, and to ever
be brought to reverence him as God and the only Saviour
was a moral impossibility, and without such repentance
and reverence the sin must remain.   The expression is,
" It *hath never forgiveness.*"   If these Jews thus committed the sin against the Holy Ghost, how shall that of
Ingersoll be measured ?   Hear him : " No devil was ever
charged with such fiendish brutality as the living God,
and the barbarities of the good God."   It seems as though
all the mythological and theological devils of the world
must have acknowledged themselves outdone by this their
human brother.   Had they all been in Booth's Theatre
and heard these ebullitions, and could have spoken with
audible voice, a yell of all devildom would have rent the
air in praise of their eloquent military chieftain.   It is
natural that there should be common agreement among
the whole family of devils, parents and children, both of
angelic and Adamic origin.   Of course all would be fault-
finders with the Bible and its Author, especially that part
which threatens them with punishment for their opposition to their Creator and his righteous government.
Nothing would more irritate them than the accounts of
its severe execution in the present world, of which there
is no other reasonable solution than that of fearful apprehension.

" Conscience does make cowards of us all."

It is utterly unreasonable to suppose that a man should
be so excited against God if he had no conviction of his
existence, or that he would some day vindicate himself

and his word. No! take this language out of the Bible, and Ingersoll's venom and craft would both vanish at once; and not a devil would find a flaw in the book. But even the father-devil himself is the victim of this conviction, and understands Christ to be the awarder at the coming punishment. On one occasion a devil said to him, "Art thou come to torment us before the time?" not knowing but that it was his intention to execute this work at his first instead of his second visit to the world. It must not be thought objectionable that we should thus use the word devil to designate men who have this scoffer's character. We have seen that Christ called his opposers and traducers the "children of their father, the devil." He said once to Peter, "Get thee behind me, Satan," because he contradicted and opposed his words. All such are entitled to the ancestral name. This whole family are haters of true religion, and would exterminate it if they had the power. Christ's example and doctrine are their standing condemnation. All agree in attempts to degrade Christ to the level of a mere man. Especially are the human part of his opposers conspicuous in this phase of the work, as in that case they have none but an equal to fear. Not one of the human devils was ever heard to speak well of faith in God or of the truth of the Scriptures. In every one of these particulars is Christ in disagreement with all the devils. Here is the irrepressible conflict, and it must go on until the end of the world, at which the loss and punishment is appointed to be executed upon the whole devilhood, and when truth and righteousness will prevail over the whole face of the new-made world, and without the existence of a will hostile to that of God!

The Scoffer Exalts the Devil's Virtue above his Lord's.

Says he: "One of these gods, according to the account, drowned the entire world by a flood, with the exception of eight persons: the old, the young, the beautiful, and the helpless, were remorselessly devoured by the shoreless sea. This, the most fearful tragedy that the

.imagination of ignorant priests ever conceived, was the
act, not of a devil, but of a god, so-called, whom men
worship unto this day.   What a stain would such an act
have been upon the character of a devil ! ''   Hear how
the blaspheming scoffer praises the good devil, when the
same book contains the account of the introduction by
the devil of the death, not only of a single generation,
alive at the flood, but of the two hundred generations of
mankind—men, women, old and young, the beautiful
and fair, the innocent and the guilty alike.   He introduced sin, and death came in consequence, and the only
way in which God could keep them alive was by performing a perpetual miracle and to be abused by them
while in the service of the devil, and which would have
subjected them to six thousand years of pain and suffering, but which, by depriving them of the means of perpetuating their life, cut the suffering down to three score
and ten years.   Thus they obeyed the devil and received
the pay—"The wages of sin is death.''   This is the
only wages the devil could pay, and the scoffer praises
the devil-murderer of the whole generations of men, and
abuses God for prematurely cutting short the life of a single generation.   This is another example of the scoffer's
ignorance of God and the Bible.   He has well learned
the " subtle,'' thin, and lying arts of his devil-father, to
whom he pays all the honor in his power and commits
the same degree of detraction from the character of God
his Maker.

No doubt the oldest devil of the family smiles in his
sleeve at the childishness and devotion of this, his youngest grandson.   But now let us hear God's accusation and
complaint of the antediluvian generation of men who
perished by the flood, and we shall see whether it was not
just to destroy it, and whether the transaction cannot be
vindicated.   " And it came to pass, when men began to
multiply on the face of the earth, and daughters were
born unto them, that the sons of God saw the daughters
of men, that they were fair ; and they took them wives of
all which they chose. [It was Utah.] And the Lord said,
My Spirit shall not always strive with men, yet his days

shall be [but] an hundred and twenty years. And God saw that the wickedness of man was great in the earth, and that every imagination of the thoughts of his heart was only evil, and that continually. And it repented the Lord that he had made man on the earth, and it grieved him at his heart. And the Lord said, I will destroy man, whom I have created, from the face of the earth. The earth also was corrupt before God, and filled with violence ; for all flesh had corrupted his way before God." [Such was the character of those whom Ingersoll calls the innocent women—the fair and the beautiful.] " And God said unto Noah, The end of all flesh is come before me ; for the earth is filled with violence through them." [There have been outbursts of violence at times in all generations, but among this generation it was universal— " every imagination of their hearts was continually evil."] " And, behold, I, even I, do bring a flood upon the earth, to destroy all flesh, wherein is the breath of life, from under heaven ; and all flesh died that moved upon the earth, every man, in whose nostrils was the breath of life, all that was in the dry land, died." (Gen. 6 and 7.)

In the New Testament we have such references to the character of these people as the following : " For if God spared not the old world, but saved Noah the eighth person, a preacher of righteousness, bringing in the flood upon the world of the ungodly " (2 Pet. 2 : 5)—" which sometime were disobedient, when once the long-suffering of God waited in the days of Noah, while the ark was preparing, wherein few, that is, eight souls, were saved." (1 Pet. 3 : 20.) " For as the days of Noah were, so shall also the days of the coming of the Son of man be. They were eating and drinking, marrying and giving in marriage, until the day that Noah entered into the ark, and knew not " [because they did not take heed to the preaching of Noah] " until the flood came, and took them all away ; so shall also the coming of the Son of man be." (Matt. 24 : 37–39.) Here we have the evidence, showing a condition of universal disobedience and heartfelt hatred of God by his creatures. God had given them a hundred and twenty years' probation after he had determined on their destruction, during which he had sent the only preacher of righteousness in all the earth, to give the warning of the coming destruction ; but in all that time the warning did not induce a single man or woman to repent—universal unbelief and infidelity prevailed, in addition to universal corruption.

The Wickedness of the Antediluvians Necessitated their Destruction.

God had created these people to please and obey him, which power carried with it the power to disobey and displease ; consequently their very existence put him to grief.   Not another loving, loyal subject for his immortal world could he induce to become such from among that generation ; and how would such teach future generations what they did not know and hated themselves ?—the eventful object for which he had created mankind, being a universal and endless government of righteous men and women covering the face of the world.   But the continuation of this state of things rendered the accomplishment of that end an impossibility.   He must, therefore, abandon the sole purpose for which he made the world, or destroy the whole generation, and commence anew with eight righteous people.

God must be true to his Friends and Promises.

As long as a nation or world of men are mixed, the good mingling with the bad — occasionally the good inducing one of the bad to become reconciled to the disposition and laws of God—he spares that people, because they serve to answer the purpose of obtaining loving, loyal subjects for his projected universal, endless empire.   But when all become evil, then he must destroy them by some catastrophe equal to the emergency ; and this must be executed in the present world as exemplary, although it involves the whole of mankind.   Not to

do it would subject himself and his loyal people to the
tyrannical rule of, and extinguishment by, his and their
enemies, thus also exhibiting a pusillanimity degrading
in an ordinary ruler, and utterly incompatible with the
Rightful Ruler of the universe.   Not to do it he must
prove false to his solemn engagements and promises to
his faithful and loving children.   In a word, not to
bring the wickedness of the wicked to an end, whether
of angelic or human origin, would be to fail in his
revealed purpose for which he made the world and
man, falsifying himself in the sight of all his faithful
saints and angels ; rendering it thereafter impossible
that he should be trusted, venerated, loved, or obeyed
from the heart.

But had we not one of these arguments of defence
for the act of flooding the world, it would be enough
to know of the fact that it was done ; and to question
the right or motive of him who did it, is to assume
that an absolute owner and proprietor may not do as
he pleases with his own, at least so long as he does
not violate any promise or obligation to another.   It
is true that the rebels thus to be disposed of may
complain and threaten vengeance, just as the antediluvians did when the flood came, and while its waters
were covering them, after climbing the tallest trees and
highest mountains ; but the waters rose just the same,
and instead of the Creator suffering by the flood, he
was at once delivered of the long-suffering to which
the wicked had subjected him.   " Well," says Ingersoll,
and the rest of his self-chosen devil companions, " I will
not serve such a God."   Then you must take the alternative, hate on, and perish !   Others will serve, love, and
obey him, with the utmost confidence that righteousness,
justice, and truth shall triumph in precisely the same
perfection and universality as though a sinner never had
lived.

Universal Belief in Devils Argues their Existence.

Says Ingersoll: "All ages and nations supposed that the sick and insane were possessed of evil spirits. For thousands of ages the practice of medicine consisted in frightening these spirits away." [This is a fair sample of this man's exaggeration. As to its chronology, there have existed but two hundred ages of men, instead of thousands, taking the average life as defining the term, which is not more than thirty years. To call the practice of medicine the frightening away of evil spirits shows ignorance of the subject. In the history of the healing art, such things were only the exceptions, and then but among the rudest tribes; and this is the reason why they found place in mythological narration. There never was a nation or tribe so ignorant or rude that they did not use roots and herbs as medicine; especially was this true of the nations of biblical record. So common was it, that it is made a symbol of backsliding Israel, thus: "Is there no balm in Gilead? is there no physician there? why then is the health of the daughter of my people not recovered?" (Jer. 8 : 22.) "Usually," says the scoffer, " the priests would make the loudest and most discordant noises possible. They would blow horns, beat upon rude drums, clash cymbals, and in the meantime utter the most unearthly yells. If the noise remedy failed, they would implore the aid of some more powerful spirits. To pacify these spirits was considered of infinite importance. The poor barbarian, knowing that men could be softened by gifts, gave the spirits that which seemed to him of great value. With bursting heart he would offer the blood of his dearest child." [Who supposes that this man ever read such a nonsensical story as this, that the heart-bursting father, on account of having a sick member in his family, had called his priest to heal him, and that the priest should demand, as the price for healing the sick one, the blood (death) of his dearest child, and that the thoughtless Ingersoll should have told the foolish story in public?] "It was impossible for him to conceive of a God utterly unlike himself." [In harmony with this, we may say that the God the Bible reveals is the very image of man's person, and it is only the atheists who try to conjure an impersonality so unlike everything in nature, or conceivable, that it is superstition to believe and worship him. Of course it is an easy victory to cast down the straw god they have erected.] "And he naturally supposed that these powers of the air would be affected at the sight of so great and deep a sorrow." One of the meanest things about Ingersoll is, that when talking of heathen gods and barbarian practices of relig- ion, he uses Scripture expressions, as here (Christ called Satan "the prince of the power of the air"), his object evidently being to degrade Scripture and Christianity by confounding them with the lowest forms of heathen- ism. To expose and counteract the injury of the satanic scheme, it is only necessary to refer to the historic fact that the worship of God, with its ministers, sacrifices, objects, and conditions, was established at the foundation of the world, and when there were only three men living; and that Abel had as clear conceptions of the Christian religion and its salvation as did Paul; consequently all other forms and elements of worship are corruptions of the original. This, having been taught to Cain and Abel by the Creator himself, is the genuine, while all others are counterfeits. Their existence, however, demonstrates that of the original, and their universality also proves the original to have been designed for all mankind.

Remember these things, and the efforts of the scoffer will not only be destroyed for evil, but will furnish unan- swerable argument in defence of revealed religion, which he hopes to degrade, and of the existence and doom of all the human and angelic devils, whose only happiness con- sists in their opposition to God and his worship. The scoffer says: "It was with the barbarian then as with the civilized now; one class lived upon and made mer- chandize of the fears of another." [Just as you are making money by your professed attempts to deliver others from the fear of God.] "Certain persons took it upon themselves to appease the gods, and to instruct the people in their duties to these unseen powers. This was the origin of the priesthood." [No, sir! here is your ignorance manifest again, both in history and common sense. The principal office of a priest is to offer sacrifice, and God himself originated the priesthood when he instructed Cain and Abel to offer the sacrificial lamb, the firstling of his flock—the typic Christ thus virtually and in revelation slain from the foundation of the world ; this with the oblation of the first-fruits of the harvest, the type of his resurrection—" Christ the first-fruits of them that slept." (1 Cor. 15 : 23.)] "The priest pretended to stand between the wrath of the gods and helpless man. He carried to the invisible world a flag of truce, a protest and a request." [This is the corruption which the corrupt scoffer always sees because he desires it—the wish is father to the thought. The true, pure, and original is that "God so loved the world" of mankind, and to make it manifest to them assumed human form, in which to be born and in which to die by the cross, a living sacrifice, and which has won millions of men to love him in turn, and to sacrifice their lives rather than offend him : hence we read, "Hereby perceive we the love of God, because he laid down his life for us : and we ought to lay down our lives for the brethren." (1 John 3 : 16.) "We love him, because he first loved us." (1 John 4 : 19.) Here we see how the scoffer burlesques the great truth of Christ's love and sacrifice, and its perfect success in the accomplishment of the designed and revealed purpose : "To wit, that God was in Christ, reconciling the world unto himself." (2 Cor. 5 : 19.) Not two parties, one with a flag of truce, reconciling a third ; not that Christ went into another world to appease the wrath of another God, but came into this world and sacrificed his life to show the love of the only God for man, and for the purpose of winning him in turn to love him. Behold how Ingersoll requites it ! See how he confounds the corrupt with the incorrupt, the lie with the truth.] "He came back with a command, authority, and power. Man fell upon his knees before his own servant, and the priest, taking the

advantage of the awe inspired by his supposed influence
with the gods, made of his fellow-man a cringing hypocrite and a slave." [Such is the man's conception of
liberty—that freedom from guilt makes a man a slave.]
"Even Christ, the supposed Son of God, taught that
persons were possessed of evil spirits." [If the scoffer did
not give false glossary he would have nothing to say upon
these subjects. Christ found people thus possessed, and
cast the devils out, as matters of fact. It is not necessary
to argue that men are even now possessed of evil spirits,
for if they hear or read Ingersoll's blasphemy about
Christ, they would have abundant evidence to show the
fact.] "According to the account, Christ gave proof of his
divine origin and mission by frightening droves of devils
out of his unfortunate countrymen. Casting out devils
was his principal employment, and the devils thus banished took occasion to acknowledge him as the Messiah." [That Christ made casting out devils a test of his
divine mission is lie No. 1. That casting out devils was
his principal employment is lie No. 2. That the devils
generally acknowledged him to be the Messiah is lie No.
3. Never did any but one do this. We learn from such
statements that when Ingersoll says "generally" it may
mean but a single case, and this is the estimate we must
put upon his pretended historic references.] "The religious people have always regarded the testimony of
devils as perfectly conclusive ; and the writers of the New
Testament quote the words of these imps of darkness
with great satisfaction." [Here are more glossary lies.
The New Testament writers quote them but as historic
statements, and Christian people believe the testimony
concerning devils, as Christ speaks of them thus : "The
devil was a murderer from the beginning, and abode not
in the truth, because there is no truth in him. When he
speaketh a lie, he speaketh of his own : for he is a liar,
and the father of it." (John 8 : 44.) If Ingersoll had
said the human servants of the devil always believe and
obey him, it would have been conclusive at least so far as
he is concerned.] "The fact that Christ could with-
stand the temptation of the devil was considered conclu-

sive evidence that he was assisted by some god, at least by some being superior to man." [Here he attempts to confound God with the devil, but nothing is too scurrilous for him to attempt.] " St. Matthew gives an account of an attempt made by the devil to tempt the supposed Son of God ; and it has always excited the wonder of Christians that the temptation was so nobly and heroically withstood."

[This is another misrepresentation ; for no Christian writer can be produced who believed it was possible that Christ could have committed the sin of yielding to the temptation ; but as the lie subserves his devil-purpose of degrading Christ, the Son of God, he tells it.] " In the olden times the existence of devils was universally admitted." [There are as many people who believe in the existence of evil spirits at the present day as ever before. The reason, it seems, why he makes such an allusion is to put a high estimate upon his efforts in banishing the belief, that his admirers may not suppose the money they pay him for doing the missionary work is misspent.]

" The people had no doubt upon the subject. From such belief it follows, as a matter of course, that a person, in order to vanquish these devils, had either to be a god or assisted by one. All forms of religion have established their claims to divine origin by controlling evil spirits, and suspending the laws of nature. Casting out devils was a certificate of divinity." [So far as the Christian religion is concerned, this is untrue, for it was founded by God himself in the Eden world ; and when Christ came he established his claim to divinity by the facts that his birth, life, death, and resurrection was each associated with such peculiar and concurring events that characterized those of no other man, and all of which were of prehistoric or prophetic record. Nothing is more evident than that Ingersoll makes history and facts to suit his satanic purposes.]

" A prophet unable to cope with the powers of darkness was regarded with contempt." [Another false slander upon the holy prophets of Scripture, not one of whom ever attempted to cope with anyone in the work of casting out devils—indeed, an archangel dared not railingly accuse the devil. "Yet Michael, the archangel, when contending with the devil about the body of Moses, durst not bring against him a railing accusation, but said, The Lord rebuke thee." (Jude 9.)] He says, "The utterance of the highest and noblest sentiments, the most blameless and holy life, commanded but little respect unless accompanied by the power to work miracles and command spirits." [Here we have a general misrepresentation and effusion of biographical ignorance, the fact being that Ingersoll knows of no idolatrous prophet in history, even mythological, whose life was blameless and holy, and who was but little respected because not having the power to command spirits, as there are none; and he must refer to the prophets whom God selected and inspired to write the Holy Scriptures—and this is what made them prophets—all of whom were men of blameless and holy character, and whose record shows they never had, nor claimed to have, the power to command spirits or work miracles, or even to cast out devils—running all the way back to Enoch, God's first prophet, and the seventh person born into the world from Adam. There is but one period of mythological record or reliable history, during the whole of which the Pagan priests and prophets, without exception, were lying deceivers, imposing alike on kings and subjects. Failing to make the distinction between them and the prophets of biblical record which the facts of history and common honesty required, Ingersoll identifies himself with the lying priests of heathenism. Were this done, not a shadow of reflection would have attached to the records of Holy Scripture touching the character of God's prophets; but to have done this would have destroyed his craft. Take away his lies and false glossary of sacred Scripture and its approved characters, the scoffer would be as dumb as a mute for harm, and no sensible man or woman would allow him to prejudice their minds against the Bible, and would leave him ranked, as he merits, among the lying wonders of devildom.]

Ingersoll's Rant about Prayer.

The scoffer says, "The foolish doctrine that all phenomena can be traced to the interference of good and bad spirits, has been, and still is, almost universally entertained. That people still believe in some spirit that can change the natural order of events, is proven by the fact that nearly all resort to prayer. Thousands at this very moment are probably imploring some supposed power to interfere in their behalf. Some want health restored ; some ask that the loved and absent be watched over and protected ; some pray for riches ; some for rain ; some vainly ask for food ; some ask for revivals ; a few ask for more wisdom ; and now and then one tells the Lord to do as he may think best. Thousands ask to be protected from the devil ; some, like David, pray for revenge ; and some implore even God not to lead them into temptation. All these prayers rest upon, and are produced, by the idea that some power not only can, but probably will, change the order of things in the universe. This belief has been among the great majority of tribes and nations. All sacred books are filled with accounts of such interferences, and our own Bible is not an exception to the rule."

Thus, in his ignorant conceit and silly freethought has Ingersoll demolished the whole subject of God's providence ! When John Milton was about to write upon the subject, and feeling his inability to do it justice, he uttered the following prayer : " What in me is dark, illumine ; what is low, raise and support ; that to the height of this great argument, I may assert eternal Providence, and justify the ways of God to man." Here the scoffer confounds the Bible with other religious books ; and were it not his hatred to this, not a word of protest would he have uttered against any other so-called sacred book. The scoffer had no right to say, " *Nearly* all the tribes and nations believed in a power above man to whom all might apply for help," for there is no authentic record of any tribe of men, however rude, who did not believe thus, and thus pray.

It is a philosophical necessity that some power equal to the creation of the world must have interfered to do the work of establishing its working order. As man is the superior department of nature, and as he is not finished, but according to the order of nature demands a re-creation ; and that re-creation contemplates this change to be wrought in the nature of each individual while living on the earth, beginning with the first and ending with the last, and is a work which none but the Creator is able to perform, demands his direct interference in each case. It is described in Scripture by the use of such language as this : "For we are his workmanship, created in Christ Jesus unto good works, which God hath before ordained." Thus was it in his plan as a part, and the most important part, of the creation of the world. The condition upon which God proposes to do this work in the nature of any man, is humble, penitent prayer. If, therefore, God should not thus interfere, this fundamental work of creation would never be accomplished, and he would not have a subject in his kingdom, heartily sympathizing with his will and manner of work.

Do Personal Devils Exist?

In the first place, we argue the existence of a personal devil, and devilish interference with men, from the fact of its universal belief. It is a principle in mental philosophy, that if a thing be a fact at all, it is a universal fact. Another principle of science is that belief is the result of conviction—conviction of conception, and conception presupposes the possible existence of the thing conceived, or that which is essentially like it. According to these laws and their application to the case in hand, the devil must exist, in order to make a conception of him possible. Such a conception must exist in order to have produced the conviction of such existence. The conviction must have existed in order to have rendered the belief possible. These interdepending factors in the process of reasoning force the evidence for the belief, and demonstrate the fact that the belief is and must be founded upon evidence ; of course, unbelief is the absence of evidence, and is equivalent to total ignorance upon the subject.   If, therefore, a man says, I do not believe in the existence of a personal God, he virtually admits entire ignorance upon the subject.   Hence his opinion concerning it, or whatever he says about it, is worthless. If he says, I do not believe in the existence of a personal devil, for the same reason he admits total ignorance upon the subject.   In both cases, and every similar one, he should have said, I do not know ; I am entirely ignorant concerning the matter, and therefore have no belief or unbelief about it.   This philosophy involves the following conclusions : First : If a thing, or a discourse relating to a thing, is believed, it is upon that which appears to be evidence at the time ; but this evidence may subsequently be found to have no true foundation, and, this being gone, the belief goes with it.   Now the man is ignorant of that which he supposed to be a fact of existence.

Every sane man and woman has the conviction, from experience and observation, that all are guilty of acts which cannot be justified by any standard of which they have any knowledge, or defended by any process of reasoning.   This would seem to imply that they were moved to the commission of such acts by some unseen power. The goodness of God as read in the endowments of our being for happiness, enhanced by the surrounding bounties of nature, cannot have originated from the same source which prompted the acts of violence against ourselves and society, and which only conduce to shame and misery.

In order to defend the position of the non-existence of the devil, it would be necessary to have such a comprehensive knowledge of demonology that would enable its possessor to account for every phase of its phenomena upon reasonable grounds—such as the origin of evil without the existence of an evil being ; that the Scriptures are not true which teach the existence of a personal devil ; that the statements of the Bible upon the subject of sin do not corroborate those of observation and experience, concerning the nature of evil and temptation.

4

Biblical History of the Devil.

But as to the history and power of the devil, and his personality as a sequence, we propose to expound the Scriptures upon the subject, and with the reasonable expectation of benefiting those who desire to know the truth. The first we hear of the devil is in the garden of Eden, and the account was written thousands of years before any other book existed, consequently every other subsequent account is an exact copy or a corrupt one, either as a whole or a part; consequently all devilism must be corrected by this first account. " Now the serpent was more subtle than any beast of the field which the Lord God had made; and he said unto the woman, Yea! hath God said, ye shall not eat of every tree of the garden? And the woman said unto the serpent, We may eat of the trees of the garden; but of the fruit of the tree which is in the midst of the garden, God hath said, Ye shall not eat of it, neither shall ye touch it, lest ye die. And the serpent said unto the woman, Ye shall not surely die: for God doth know that in the day ye eat thereof, then your eyes shall be opened, and ye shall be as gods, knowing good and evil. And when the woman saw that the tree was good for food, and that it was pleasant to the eyes, and a tree to be desired to make one wise, she took of the fruit thereof, and did eat; and gave also unto her husband with her; and he did eat. And the eyes of them both were opened, and they knew that they were naked. [Here was shame, the result of sin and of the devil's lie, realized—they were covered with shame instead of becoming gods.] And they sewed fig-leaves together, and made them aprons. And they heard the voice of the Lord God walking in the garden in the cool of the day [as he was walking thus]: and Adam and his wife hid themselves from the presence of the Lord God amongst the trees of the garden. [Here was the effect of the second lie of the devil—that they would become wise by obeying him, instead of which they immediately lost so much of the knowledge of God, that they thought they could hide from his presence among the trees.] And the Lord God called unto Adam, and said, Where art thou? And he said, I heard thy voice in the garden, and I was afraid, because I was naked; and hid myself. And he said, Who told thee that thou wast naked? Hast thou eaten of the tree, whereof I commanded thee that thou shouldest not eat? And the man said, The woman whom thou gavest me to be with me, she gave me of the tree, and I did eat. And the Lord God said unto the woman, What is this that thou hast done? and the woman said, The serpent beguiled me, and I did eat. [Now she saw, when it was too late to avert the calamity, the deception of the lying serpent, and began to experience its sad effects.] And the Lord God said unto the serpent, Because thou hast done this, thou art cursed above all cattle, and above every beast of the field; upon thy belly shalt thou go, and dust shalt thou eat all the days of thy life, and I will put enmity between thy seed and her seed; it shall bruise thy head, and thou shalt bruise his heel." (Gen. 3 : 1–15.)

What was the Serpent?

We remark, in the first place, that the serpent was not what we call a snake. He is here ranked among the cattle and beasts of the field, which we always contrast with crawling and creeping things. As an illustration, we read: "Every kind of beasts, and of birds, and of serpents," etc. The serpent was one of the beasts which God had made. There are two facts here taught, which furnish very strong evidence to show that this beast was one of the monkey tribes or species. That he was thenceforth to go upon his belly shows that, before this, he must have walked upright; which a snake could not do. The physiological structure of the monkey shows that his natural locomotion was upright. Indeed, the quadruped motion of the monkey appears as awkward and unnatural as for man to go on his all-fours, as we say of the creeping of babes; like man it has long legs, shorter arms or fore-legs, large thighs, and slender shoulders, all of which fit it for upright gait. The pronounced doom, changing this attitude, was not On thy belly shalt thou crawl (as a snake), but shalt go (as we say of a man when thus moving). The expression, " Dust shall be thy meat," comprehends the chemical properties composing vegetable soil. Adam was made out of this: " And the Lord God formed man of the dust of the ground." The serpent's diet, being thus extensive, admits of no objection as to what the monkey eats, because it is identical with the meat of snakes and men.

Wisdom of the Serpent and Faculty of Speech.

The distinguishing feature of the wisdom of man is shown in his faculty of speech, and this implies that of forming abstract ideas—both of which this beast possessed. It is well known, from the anatomical structure of the mouth, jaws, tongue, throat, etc., that the monkey possesses the organs and power of human speech. His reasoning faculties, however, but poorly compare with those of man, nor did he manifest profound reasoning on this occasion, and before his degradation. The expression is, " The serpent was *more subtle* than any of the beasts of the field." Subtle means, thin—not dense ; as subtle air, subtle vapor, subtle medium, etc. This kind of wisdom, is the contrivance of cunning, mischievous speech, with but little regard to consequences. All of which are here apparent and attributed to the beast himself ; and he was cursed for its employment, or yielding to be thus used : " And the Lord God said unto the serpent, because *thou* hast done this thou art cursed above all cattle, and above every beast of the field." All the beasts of the earth were involved in the general curse now about to fall, in consequence of man's disobedience of his Maker's command—extending to the very ground itself ; but among the cattle and beasts of the field, that which fell upon the serpent was the heaviest. He lost his faculty of speech, and this implied the degradation of the mental power of forming ideas, which reduced him to the intellectual level of brute knowledge, besides degrading him from the erect gait with which, among all the other animals, he was honored as the sole associate and principal servant of man.

It must be remembered that this monkey and his mate were the primordial of the whole species, and therefore the inherited loss was transmitted to all succeeding generations.   It is also easy to conceive how great the loss was which thus fell upon man himself.   The fleet-footed monkey, his physical strength and power of out-door exposure and endurance, with his knowledge and faculty of speech, and yet an animal servant over whom man was given dominion, would have been of incalculable benefit to mankind in the business relations of life.   Here, then, we have the beast of the field—the serpent, as God made him, before and after his curse.

Who was the Devil?

We come now to the consideration of the question, Who was the devil, and whence his origin ?   That there is one prominent, personal devil, and that he was once an angel, is as clearly taught in the Scriptures as that there are angels at all, and that they are of a higher order than man, and somewhat of a different being.   Some of these facts are stated thus : " And the angels which kept not their first estate, but left their own habitation, he hath reserved in everlasting chains under darkness unto the judgment of the great day." (Jude 6.) Here we see that there was a plurality involved in this leaving, and there is no distinction mentioned as existing among them ; but that they are all reserved unto the judgment of the great day.   We have seen that Christ refers to him as being a liar from the beginning, and who abode not in the truth. We turn now to a passage which describes the execution of the destined punishment of the devil at the judgment of the great day, and which distinguishes one of them as the leader : " Then shall he [the Son of man and Judge of quick and dead] say unto them on his left hand, depart from me, ye cursed, into everlasting fire, prepared for the devil and his angels." (Matt. 25 : 41.) From the time, therefore, that these angels left their own former abode and chose the earth in preference, contrary to the will of God—and this is what made them devils—there has been a devil, who is a fallen angel, having other angel-devils under him, and who are to continue to live until the day of judgment appointed to take place at the end of the world; and the appointment was made at its very beginning.

The Location of the Devil.

The location of the devil and his work is on the earth. This is clearly shown by the following Scripture : " Then Jesus sent the multitude away, and went into the house : and his disciples came unto him, saying, Declare unto us the parable of the tares of the field. He answered and said unto him, He that soweth the good seed is the Son of man ; the field is the world ; the good seed are the children of the kingdom : but the tares are the children of the wicked one ; the enemy that sowed them is the devil ; the harvest is the end of the world ; and the reapers are the angels. [These are the angels who continued to abide in the truth, and did not leave their own habitation.] As, therefore, the tares are gathered and burned in the fire ; so shall it be in the end of this world. The Son of man shall send forth his angels, and they shall gather *out of his kingdom all things* that offend, and them which do iniquity, and shall cast them into a furnace of fire : there shall be wailing and gnashing of teeth. Then shall the righteous shine forth as the sun in the kingdom of their father [the same kingdom]. Who hath ears to hear, let him hear." (Matt. 13 : 36–43.) This is Christ's interpretation of his own parable, and therefore leaves nothing for conjecture, and it was given to show what the kingdom of God was like, and shows that the destined kingdom is the world, in which all the devils and offensive things of iniquity exist, and out of which, at the end of this world, the Son of man, by his faithful angels, is to gather all the wicked, devils and men, out of the field—

out of the world, out of his kingdom—and then kindle a furnace-lake of fire and brimstone, which is to be on the earth and in the land of Idomea, and burn them up, just as the husbandman gathers the tares out of his field and burns them in the fire.

By this parable Christ, the great teacher, condenses the whole subject as taught in the Scriptures, and in so clear a manner that leaves no room for honest misunderstanding. " The earth being now cleansed of all offensive things, Christ takes possession and sets up his kingdom under the whole heavens — the new heavens and new earth wherein dwelleth righteousness." (2 Pet. 3 : 13.) Now the immortal saints of all ages shine forth in the kingdom of their Father. Because Ingersoll cannot find hell existing now, he makes merry over the discovery; but let him be a little patient, and he will very likely find it, to his sorrow.

The devil is sometimes called Satan, which means an opposer of the words of God and the objects he seeks to accomplish with man and the world. The title Satan is not confined to the devil, but designates men and all systems of religious persecution of his people. For opposing his words, Jesus said to Peter, " Get thee behind me, Satan : thou art an offense unto me : for thou sayest not the things that be of God, but those that be of men." (Matt. 16 : 23.) The false, persecuting church of the Revelation is called the " place where Satan's seat is." That the theatre of the devil's locality and action is on the earth, is also shown by the following : " Now there was a day when the sons of God came to present themselves before the Lord, that Satan came also among them. And the Lord said unto Satan, whence comest thou? Then Satan answered the Lord, and said, from going to and fro *in the earth* [not yet in hell], and from walking up and down in it." (Job 6 : 7.) Here is the devil doing his work on the earth. But as he is a liar, especially when he speaketh of himself, we cannot trust him unless his words are confirmed by a better witness, and this we have thus : " Be sober, be vigilant ; because your adversary the devil, as a roaring lion, walketh about, seeking whom he may devour : whom resist steadfast in the faith, knowing that the same afflictions are accomplished in your brethren that are in the world." (1 Pet. 5 : 8.) The expression, "in the world," shows the place of the devil's action, and the whole passage declares the work of the devil is to afflict the saints of God in the world.

"And the Lord said, Simon, Simon, behold ! Satan hath desired to have you, that he might sift you as wheat." (Luke 22: 31.) "Wherein in time past ye walked according to the course of this world, according to the prince of the power of the air, the spirit that now worketh in the children of disobedience." (Eph. 2 : 2.) Here the devil is called "the prince of the power of the air ; Beelzebub the prince of devils." In the days of Job the devil had power over atmospheric elements, as he went into the wilderness and raised a hurricane, with which he killed all Job's children, by blowing down the house wherein they were assembled. He also once, in common with all the angels, had the mental power over the gravity of atmospheric pressure ; by an act of will he could decrease that which was above him and increase it beneath, and thus descend and ascend into it at pleasure. At his first coming Christ deprived Satan of this power over inanimate elements, so that he was no longer prince of the power of the air ; no longer could he wield the winds of heaven for any purpose then, he fell from heaven, about which Christ speaks thus : "And the seventy returned again with joy, saying, Lord, even the devils are subject unto us through thy name. And he said unto them, I beheld Satan as lightning fall from heaven. Behold ! I give unto you power to tread on serpents and scorpions, and over all the power of the enemy : and nothing shall by any means hurt you. Notwithstanding in this rejoice not, that the spirits are subject unto you ; but rather rejoice, because your names are written in heaven." (Luke 10: 17–20).

Since this the power of Satan is confined to the earth, and, in his broken yet wrathful pride, labors under the re-

strictions—the chains of darkness ; hopeless dispair.   In
this condition will he remain, until the judgment of the
great day, for destruction.

The Devil Awaiting his Destruction.

The doom of the devil, as we have seen, is entirely
different from that of the serpent—the beast of the field,
and, upon whom the punishment fell in the present world,
and was that of physical degradation.   It is evident that
the devil is a fallen angel, and of so superior natural structure that age makes no mark of decay on it ; and having
lived six thousand years of health, what knowledge he
must have acquired ! He has power to control the speech
of man so as to speak through his organs, for the accomplishment of any purpose of deception.   If the devil has
such power over the human mind, he had it over the
mind of the serpent, a weaker animal, and used it in the
garden of Eden, and spake through the organs of the serpent.   In this transaction the following passage and its
Scriptural connections indicate the contest, contestants,
and final triumph of the one and destruction of the other :
" And I [the Lord] will put enmity between thee [the
serpent] and the woman, and between thy seed and her
seed ; it shall bruise thy head, and thou shalt bruise his
heel.''   (Gen. 3 : 15.) Christ is the seed of the woman,
as well as the Son of man—not by any natural generation,
for this he did not have ; he was the natural Son of no
man or woman ; but the birth was that of miraculously
forming—making and creating of a woman, by the Creator himself, a body for himself like that of man. " The
Word was God, and the Word was made flesh ; and that
which was made flesh was the Son of God, and by whom
were all things made that was made.''   " Christ made
of a woman,'' and, therefore, " The seed of the woman
and the Son of Man.''

The seed of the serpent was not the generations of the
beast of the field, whose progenitor the devil tempted in
beguiling Eve ; but the devil with his subordinate angels,
whose instruments are also the children of men—" Led

captive by Satan at his will." These shall bruise the heel of Christ—make war against him and his church in his absence, behind his back; bruise his heel, but Christ shall bruise Satan's head at his return. Speaking of this, Paul says: "And the God of peace shall bruise Satan under your feet shortly." (Rom. 16 : 20.) Of this destruction and by whom it is to be executed, Paul also speaks thus : " Forasmuch as the children are made partakers of flesh and blood [our nature] he also himself took part of the same ; that through death [Christ passing through his death and resurrection] he might destroy him that had the power of death, that is, the devil ; and deliver them who through fear of death were all their lifetime subject to bondage." (Heb. 2 : 14, 15.) As sure, therefore, as Christ died and did not remain dead, so sure will he destroy the devil—so sure will the seed of the woman bruise his head.

That the devil had the power of death is explained thus : " Wherefore, as by one man sin entered into the world, and death by sin ; so death passed upon all men, for all have sinned." (Rom. 5 : 12.) The devil used the serpent as his willing instrument, and led Adam and Eve into sin. Up to this time they had access to the fruit of the tree of life, which God had endowed with the chemical properties of keeping men always youthful, thereby perpetuating human life indefinitely. But now, lest he should live thus in sin, he saw fit to deprive him of the antidote for the ravages of age ; and immediately, in that very day, he died—died by the loss of the means for preserving life. " In the day thou eatest thereof thou shalt surely die." " And the Lord God said, Behold ! the man is become as one of us [us means, not two gods, but one God with the two titles, Lord God], to know good and evil. And now, lest he put forth his hand, and take also of the tree of life, and eat, and live forever : therefore the Lord sent him forth from the Garden of Eden, to till the ground from whence he was taken." By this exclusion, of course, death passed upon all men : " For as in Adam all die [because none since have had access to the tree of life, and immortality is thenceforth only to be obtained through Christ, the second Adam, and to be conferred upon the saints in the resurrection at the last day]—as in Adam all die, even so in Christ shall all be made alive.'' But to be in Christ is to be a new creature; to become like him in spirit, disposition; to believe his words, love his doctrines, and follow his example in working righteousness.

CHAPTER V.

WE have said angels were a higher order of beings than man. This is shown in such passages as the following. " Bless the Lord, ye his angels, that *excel in strength*, and do his commandments, hearkening unto the voice of his words, bless ye the Lord, all ye his hosts ; ye ministers of his, that do his pleasure. Praise ye him, all ye his angels. Man did eat angels' food. And the angel answering, said unto him, I am Gabriel that stand in the presence of God ; and am sent to speak unto thee, and to show thee these glad tidings." (Luke 1 : 19.) " And I heard a man's voice [then angels speak like men] between the banks of Ulai, which called and said, Gabriel, make this man to understand the vision." (Dan. 8 : 16.) " Yea ! while I was speaking in prayer, even the man Gabriel [Gabriel was so much like a man that the prophet thus names him], whom I had seen in the vision at the beginning, being caused to fly swiftly [to go quickly], touched me about the time of the evening oblation." (Dan. 9 : 21.)

" Who maketh his angels spirits " [sends them with spiritual messages]. (Heb. 1 : 7.) The angel of Jesus carried his spirit-messages to the seven churches. " Verily, he took not on him the nature of angels, but the seed of Abraham." (Heb. 2 : 10.) Here angels are natural beings. " But we see Jesus, who was made a little lower than the angels for the suffering of death, crowned with glory and honor ; that he by the grace of God should taste death for every man." (Heb. 2.) The human-Immanuel nature was lower than the nature of angels, since they have lived out their probation, and cannot suffer the death penalty, which is the result of sin.

" The wages of sin is death." But God, who took this
nature on himself, was higher than the angels. " Being
made so much better than the angels, as he hath by inheritance obtained a more excellent name than they ; for
unto which of the angels said he at any time, Thou art my
Son, this day have I begotten thee? And again, I will
be to him a Father, and he shall be to me a Son? And
again, when he bringeth in the first-begotten into the
world, he saith, And let all the angels of God worship him ; and of the angels he saith, Who maketh his
angels spirits, and his ministers a flame of fire ; but unto
the Son he saith, Thy throne, O God, is forever and ever :
a sceptre of righteousness is the sceptre of thy kingdom."
(Heb. 1 : 4–8.)

The Angels of the Sepulchre.

"And entering into the sepulchre, they saw a young man
sitting on the right side, clothed in a long white garment ; and they were affrighted. And he saith unto
them, Be not affrighted : ye seek Jesus of Nazareth,
which was crucified : he is not here ; he is risen : behold the place where they laid him." (Mark 16 : 5, 6.)
Matthew says they said, " Come, see the place where
the Lord lay." (28 : 6.) This angel appeared to be a
young man, and yet he was more than four thousand
years old ; showing that time makes no impression on
immortal beings. This was the first time Mary Magdalene
went to the sepulchre, and she was the first of the friends
of Jesus, with the other Marys, who went there. " Now
when Jesus was risen, early the first day of the week he
appeared first to Mary Magdalene, and she went and told
them that had been with him, as they mourned and wept."
John gives more particulars, thus : " Then she runneth to
Simon Peter, and to the other disciple whom Jesus loved
[John thus modestly speaks of himself, not even mention-
ing his own name], and saith unto them, They have taken
away the Lord out of the sepulchre, and we know not
where they have laid him. So they ran both together ;
and the other disciple did outrun Peter, and came first to

the sepulchre. And he, stooping down and looking in, saw the linen clothes lying; yet went he not in. Then cometh Simon Peter, and went into sepulchre, and seeth the linen clothes lie; and the napkin, that was about his head, not lying with the linen clothes, wrapped together in a place by itself. Then went in also the other disciple which came first to the sepulchre, and he saw and believed. For yet they knew not the Scripture, that he must rise from the dead. Then the disciples went away again unto their own home. But Mary stood without at the sepulchre weeping [she had returned again], and as she wept, she stooped down, and looked into the sepulchre, and seeth two angels in white, sitting, the one at the head, and the other at the feet, where the body of Jesus had lain. And they said unto her, Woman, why weepest thou? She saith, Because they have taken away my Lord, and I know not where they have laid him." (John 20 : 2–13.)

This was Mary's second visit to the sepulchre. The first time she saw one angel in the sepulchre, but the second time she saw two. We quote this so particularly to brush away another mistake of Ingersoll's about the disagreement in the account, as seeing one and two angels in the sepulchre. Matthew records the scene of rolling away the stone thus: " And behold ! there was a great earthquake : for the angel of the Lord descended from heaven, and rolled back the stone from the door of the sepulchre, and sat upon it. His countenance was like lightning, and his raiment white as snow ; and for fear of him the keepers did shake, and became as dead men." (28 : 2.)

This angel had gone into the sepulchre, where Mary saw him, and veiling his glory from her, which had driven the Roman soldiers from the grave.

Christ not a Spirit in the Sense of a Ghost.

In this account, as well as generally in Scripture, there are three distinct orders of persons—Christ, angels, and men ; and so much resembling each other that one is taken for the other, and all are so much like men that they are thus named. We quote the following, to show that Christ used his power to hold the eyes of men that they might not know him, whenever he pleased so to do, and which explains the saying, "He vanished out of their sight, the doors being shut." He thus held their eyes until he made himself known, and then again until he opened the door and went out. This fact removes the scoffer's objection to the effect that it was not possible a man with a body of flesh and bones could go through a shut door. "And behold, two of them went that same day [two of his disciples on the day of the resurrection] to a village called Emmaus, which was from Jerusalem about three score furlongs. And they talked together of all these things which had happened. And it came to pass that, while they communed together, and reasoned, Jesus himself drew near, and went with them, but *their eyes were holden that they should not know him.* And he said unto them, What manner of communications are these that ye have one with another, as ye walk, and are sad? And one of them, whose name was Cleopas, answering, said unto him, Art thou only a stranger in Jerusalem, and hast not known the things which are come to pass in these days? And he said, What things? And they said, Concerning Jesus of Nazareth, which was a prophet mighty in deed and word, before God and all the people. And how the chief priests and our rulers delivered him to be condemned to death, and have crucified him. But we trusted that it had been he which should have redeemed Israel, and besides all this, to-day is the third day since these things were done. Yea! and certain women of our company made us astonished, which were early at the sepulchre; and when they found not his body, they came, saying that they had seen a vision of angels, which said that he was alive. And certain of them that were with us went to the sepulchre, and found it even so as the women had said: but him they saw not." (Luke 24: 13–24.)

During all this conversation the eyes of the disciples with whom he had familiarly mingled for more than three years, were so holden by him that they did not know him.

Angel-Escort at the Ascension and Return of Christ.

" And when he had spoken these things, while they beheld, he was taken up, and a cloud received him out of their sight. And while they looked steadfastly toward heaven as he went up, behold ! two men stood by them in white apparel ; which also said, Ye men of Galilee, why stand ye gazing up into heaven ? this same Jesus, which is taken up from you into heaven, shall so come in like manner as ye have seen him go into heaven." (Acts 1 : 9–11.) Here are probably the same two angels who had been seen in the sepulchre forty days before, and they are called two men. This event fulfilled the prediction of Christ, thus : " Hereafter ye shall see heaven open, and the angels of God ascending and descending upon [with] the Son of Man." (John 1 : 51.) This is a quotation from the prophecy of Jacob, thus : " And he dreamed, and behold ! a ladder set up on the earth, and the top of it reached to heaven, and the angels of God ascending and descending on it." (Gen. 28 : 12.) The first part of the prediction was fulfilled when Christ ascended, as above accompanied by angels, and the second part will be fulfilled thus : " When the Son of Man shall come with all his holy angels, in the glory of his Father." Two angels only accompanied Christ at his ascension ; but at his return, in the clouds of heaven, he is to be accompanied thus : " And they shall see the Son of Man coming in the clouds of heaven, with power and great glory." " And he shall send his angels with a great sound of a trumpet, and they shall gather together his elect from the four winds of heaven, from one end of heaven to the other." (Matt. 24.)

Scripture Prophecy of the Event.

" He maketh the clouds his chariots." " He rode upon the wings of the wind." " For behold ! the Lord will come with fire, and with his chariots like a whirlwind." " The chariots of God are thousands of angels." " The

Lord thundered in the heavens, and came down; he
bowed the heavens, and came down; and the earth
was lighted with his glory." "And Jesus, answering,
said unto them, The children of this world marry and
are given in marriage, but they which shall be counted
worthy to obtain that world, and the resurrection from
the dead, neither marry nor are given in marriage;
neither can they die any more; for they are equal unto
the angels, and are the children of God, being the
children of the resurrection." (Luke 20 : 34–36.) Here
are the resurrected saints: the re-created world, restored
to its original perfection: the endless abode of God:
Immanuelized: angels, and immortal men. The devil
and his works are no more, and the eternal reign of
righteousness and peace covers the new-made world.

When and How the Angel-devil Became a Devil.

It is certain that at some period before the creation of
the world, and up to that time, the angels were on trial
and were susceptible of death, because of sin, as "the
wages of sin is death." Some had stood the test, and
remained obedient to the restrictions and commands of
their Maker; who consequently became exempt from all
future liability. Others had failed, and incurred the
death penalty, and yet await its execution, to be awarded
at the judgment in the last day; hence we read: "For
if God spare not the angels that sinned; but cast them
down to hell." (2 Pet. 2 : 5.) The Scripture explanation
is, that they are to be cast into hell at the end of the
world; using the present for the future tense, so common
in Scripture. Now, these fallen angels having no hope
of happiness or immortality themselves, they are confined
to the animosity and sweet morsel of revenge in seeking
to make every one else unhappy and hopeless like themselves, and whom God desires to be happy and live forever. It is easy to see how the devil can enjoy such
acts. Hence his implacability in attempts to baffle the
plans and delay the purposes of God in the salvation of
his children to life and immortality, as that will be the

time for the destruction of every living devil. The common complaint of the wicked against God is for having made any tests, or laws requiring obedience. What they wish is, the liberty to do as they please with impunity: be unlike their Maker and displease him to any degree and all their days, and yet wish to be rewarded with eternal life in his kingdom, just as those who had served him. The gratification of such a course is thrown into the form of a question God inspired the prophet to write, thus: "Why do the heathen rage, and the people imagine a vain thing? The kings of the earth set themselves, and the rulers take counsel together, against the Lord, and against his Anointed [Christ], saying, Let us break their bands asunder, and cast away their cords from us.

"He that sitteth in the heavens shall laugh : the Lord shall have them in derision. Then shall he speak unto them in his wrath, and vex them in his sore displeasure. Thou shalt break them with a rod of iron ; thou shalt dash them in pieces like a potter's vessel. Be wise now, therefore, O ye kings: be instructed, ye judges of the earth. Kiss the Son, less he be angry, and ye perish when his wrath is kindled but a little." Second Psalm.

It was the will of God that the angels and their leader, who became devils, should have continued to inhabit his abode, which is not in this world, until its re-creation— the world to come ; but they desired to change their estate for the Eden world as soon as they saw it finished. It was a world of such beauty and charming delight that called forth the highest joy of the angels, of which Job speaks thus : "The morning stars sang together, and all the sons of God shouted for joy." (Job 38 : 7.) Of course there was nothing wrong in such a desire, and which every angel of heaven indulged ; but being informed by the Creator that the earth was to be their final abode ; yet not to commence then, as it was to pass through a terrible history, and of such derangement that would render its re-creation a necessity. While such an explanation was satisfactory to some of the angels, it was not to others ; and these determined to make the change at once and immediately; "and they kept not their first estate, but left their own habitation" for that of the world. This self-will of the angels, in opposition to the plan and will of God, made them devils. That no provision has been made for their recovery and salvation, seems to leave no other inference than that, in the estimation and providence of God their Creator, there was none available for the purpose.

Personality of Angels, and therefore of Devils.

The biblical history of angels shows them to be so much like men, that they can eat the same food, and were always taken for men. There is, however, no intimation that they are male and female. From which fact it would follow that, like Adam, each was a distinct creation; and that they sang the world's dedicatory hymn shows their creation to have been prior to the creation of the world. When they come to men they are God's messengers, and are recognized as such by the Lord himself, and receive his titles without crime. Some of these visits are recorded as follows: "And the Lord appeared unto Abraham in the plains of Mamre: as he sat in the tent door in the heat of the day; and he looked, and lo! three men stood by him: and he bowed himself to the ground, and said, My Lord, if now I have found favor in thy sight, pass not away, I pray thee, from thy servant: let a little water be fetched, and wash your feet, and rest yourselves under the tree: and I will fetch a morsel of bread, and comfort your hearts; after that ye shall pass on: for therefore are ye come to your servant. And he said, So do as thou hast said. [Here we see that even among these three angels, one was the leader, and decided for the rest.] And Abraham said unto Sarah, Make ready quickly three measures of fine meal; knead it, and make cakes upon the hearth. And Abraham ran unto the herd, and fetched a calf tender and good, and gave it to a young man; and he hasted to dress it. And he took butter, and milk, and of the calf which he had dressed, and set it before them ; and he stood by them under the tree, and *they did eat.*

" And the men rose up from thence, and looked toward Sodom ; and Abraham went with them on the way. And the Lord said, Shall I hide from Abraham that thing which I do ; seeing that Abraham shall surely become a great and mighty nation, and all the nations of the earth shall be blessed in him ? And the Lord said, Because the cry of Sodom and Gomorrah is great, and because their sin is very grievous, therefore I am come to destroy them. [Then came the noble prayer of Abraham's for the cities and people, which exhibited the highest order of humanity and great breadth of mental discernment ; but so bad were the inhabitants of those cities that Abraham, after using every form of prayer and ground of plea, was forced to acquiesce in the decision of his merciful Lord.] " And the men turned their faces from thence, and went toward Sodom." (Gen. 18.)

Angels at the Burning of Sodom and Gomorrah.

Two of these angels arrived at Sodom that evening, the other having left them : " And there came two angels to Sodom at even ; and Lot sat in the gate, and he rose up to meet them, and bowed himself, and said, Behold ! now, my Lords, turn in, I pray you, into your servant's house, and wash your feet, and ye shall rise up early and go on your way. And they said, Nay ! but we will abide in the street all night. And he pressed them greatly ; and they turned in unto him, into his house, and he made them a feast, and did bake unleavened bread, and *they did eat.* But before they lay down, the men of Sodom compassed the house round, both old and young, from every quarter ; and they called unto Lot., and said, Where are the men which came in to thee ? bring them out unto us, that we may know them. And Lot went out at the door and shut the door after him, and said, I pray you, brethren, do not so wickedly. And they said, Stand back. And they said again, This one fellow came in to sojourn, and he will needs be a judge ; now will we deal worse with thee, than with them. And they pressed sore upon Lot, and came near to break the door; but the men from within put forth their hand and pulled Lot into the house, and shut the door, but smote the men that were at the door with blindness, both small and great, so that they wearied themselves to find the door. And the men said unto Lot, Hast thou here any besides son-in-law, and sons, and thy daughters, and whatsoever thou hast in the city, bring them out, for we will destroy this place, because the cry of them is waxen great before the face of the Lord; and the Lord hath sent us to destroy it." (Gen. 19.) In referring to these angel-visits, Paul speaks thus: "Be not forgetful to entertain strangers, for thereby some have entertained angels unawares." (Heb. 13 : 2.) So much were angels like men in appearance, speech, and appetite, that as intelligent men as Abraham and Lot could discover no difference. The fact here stated, that the angels at Lot's house had the power to smite men with blindness without touching them, implies the possession of the lesser power of holding human eyes from seeing themselves if they pleased. The devil, being a fallen angel, has also the same power. Neither Adam nor Eve saw the devil, and if he was as close to them as the serpent, he might have held their eyes from seeing him. And so also may it be with the devil in relation to men ever since, and everywhere. So also may it be with the holy angels; were they near us, we might not see them, though they are as palpable to our senses as our fellow-men to each other.

The Angel Gabriel and the Prophets.

Gabriel was once detained twenty-one days from reaching the prophet Daniel, by the king of Persia. The account is as follows: "Then he [Gabriel] said unto me, Fear not, Daniel; for from the first day that thou didst set thy heart to understand, and to chasten thyself before thy God, thy words were heard, and I am come for thy words. But the Prince of the kingdom of Persia withstood me one and twenty days; but, lo,

Michael, one of the chief princes, came to help me ; and I remained there with the kings of Persia." (Daniel 10: 12, 13.) Here Gabriel has been transacting national business with the king of Persia, and for the King of kings, one and twenty days; but the king of Persia did not see him, and the power was psychologic, turning him aside from one purpose to another as best he might, by mental impression produced by his will upon the mind of the king and his court; so his brother fallen angel was, in the court of Eden, also by psychologic power quickening the mind and controlling the organs of the serpent's speech in beguiling the woman into disobedience. When Gabriel came, Daniel was thrown into holy vision, in which state he was made to see and understand events to come, just as God saw they would be, and communicated that knowledge to the prophet. Hence it is said that revelations of God were sometimes given "by the disposition of angels." In relation to these psychologic phenomena, we have ourselves, by mere acts of will, without speaking a word, controlled the will and mental power of others, and in the presence of hundreds of people, so that they were made to see, hear, feel, taste, and smell just as we willed they should; drinking, as they supposed, tea, coffee, milk, and wine, while none of these things were real! Nor could they perform a voluntary act without the consent of our will, and only in the direction of such will; the eyes of a half-dozen men were held and blinded, in an instant, or made to see some persons, and not others equally near. In this manner they were made to steal, and manifest hatred to religion, and violence upon others, contrary to the commands of God ; and yet these persons were Christians.

Now, if the mind of one man possesses this wonderful will-power over his fellow-man, and that of angels also over men, as we have seen, may not the devil exert the same power over men, and if done only to this extent, does it not account for all his acts in the garden of Eden? That this psychologic or mesmeric power has been exerted over horses, cats, and other animals, is equally a matter of fact. It is true, there are comparatively few men susceptible of such influence by his fellow-men ; but may not the mind of a devil, whose natural powers excel those of men, and having had six thousand years' experience, so seduce every man ?   In fact, we have no evidence that the devil possesses as great psychologic power, except in its extension to all men, as that now possessed by man over his fellow-man.

Psychologic Power and Devil Possession.

By these experiments we may say that there is not a case recorded in the New Testament of a devil-posses-sion but which could be produced upon individuals by this human psychologic power. Suppose, then, that a man had an envious, revengeful neighbor, and that he him-self was susceptible of this peculiar animal-magnetic in-fluence, and that the enemy should produce upon his mind the conviction that he was a witch, or was possessed of the devil, and that he must live the rest of his life among the tombs of the dead—be wild, and fiercely attack every traveller passing that way : here is the devil tempt-ing one of his own servants to commit this terrible crime of tormenting his neighbor !   Suppose, further, that the man is made to believe and feel that he is possessed of a legion of devils, and that they could, by controlling the victim's organs of speech, in answer to the question, " What is thy name ? " reply, " My name is legion "— all of which can certainly be done in this manner by the power of a human enemy, and if so done, would it not be the work of the devil? and would he not as really be possessed of the devil as though the devil had done it all directly?   Therefore, by the instrumentality of his human servants, "led captive by Satan at his will," can one original devil tempt the whole fallen human family ; lead men into crime, and then upbraid and torment them for yielding.   And this is the philosophy and work popularly known as spiritualism, which degrades the Bible and blas-phemes its Author by declaring all superseded by these psychologic impressions reciprocally produced, and read from each other's mind !

Suppose, still further, that Jesus Christ, the Maker and Owner of the angel-devils, had met this man, and being about to dispossess him, the devil—anxious to do all the evil he could, as in the case of Job's person and cattle—should have asked to be permitted to go into a herd of swine feeding close by, and was so permitted, would it not have been possible, and in this case consistent also? It is in the history of witchcraft that cattle were possessed by witch-devil influence. In order to vindicate the act of Jesus giving the devils permission to destroy the swine, about which Ingersoll scoffs, it must be remembered that the law of Moses forbade eating swines' flesh, and that these swine were raised by the Gadarenes, the tribe of Gad, for the Jewish market. This case illustrates all other similar ones recorded of devil-possession in the Testament, and shows them to have been of psychologic character, or what in our day is called animal-magnetism and known as modern spiritualism.

But there is another class of devil-possession, which was physical diseases themselves. As an illustration we have the following account: "And when he came to his disciples, he saw a great multitude about them, and the scribes questioning with them. And straightway all the people, when they beheld him, were greatly amazed, and running to him, saluted him. And he asked the scribes, What question ye with them? And one of the multitude answered, and said, Master! I have brought unto thee my son, which hath a dumb spirit; and wherever he taketh him he teareth him, and he foameth, and gnasheth with his teeth, and he pineth away; and I spake to thy disciples that they should cast him out, and they could not. He answereth him, and saith, O faithless generation, how long shall I be with you? how long shall I suffer you? Bring him unto me. And they brought him: and when he saw him, straightway the spirit tare him, and he fell on the ground, and wallowed foaming. And he asked his father, How long is it ago since this came unto him? And he said, Of a child, and oft-times it hath cast him into the fire, and into the waters, to destroy him; but if thou canst do anything, have compassion on us. Jesus said unto him, If thou canst believe, all things are possible to him that believeth. And the father of the child cried out and said, with tears, I believe ; help thou mine unbelief! When Jesus saw that the people came running together, he rebuked the foul spirit, saying unto him, Thou dumb and deaf spirit, I charge thee, come out of him, and enter no more into him. And the spirit cried and rent him sore, and came out of him ; and he seemed as one dead ; inasmuch as many said, He is dead. But Jesus took him by the hand and lifted him up ; and he arose.'' (Mark 9 : 14–27.)

It may be said, that the young man had what is popularly called '' falling fits,'' a predisposition to which he inherited from his parents, or grandparents, or by degrees of development further back still ; as the symptoms described are the same. In reply we may say, had there been no other influence back of that, why was it that the man did not instantly become vigorous, and which physiological law would have required ; instead of which he became almost lifeless. Indeed, Jesus had to take him by the hand and lift him up ; which would seem to show that it was the foul spirit of the devil, instead of natural vigor, which so powerfully animated him a few moments before. This, however, is of but little importance, because every physical derangement is either the direct or indirect work of the devil. He induced Adam and Eve to obey him and disobey their Maker ; and thus sin entered into the world, and death as a consequence. This being the greatest physical derangement, necessarily includes all forms and lesser degrees of disease ; some one of which must precede and accompany death, though it may only be the hardening process of the physiological system we call age, which sometimes reaches ossification of vital organs before death, beginning with our first breath and steadily advancing until a rigidity of them is reached, which the nutritious forces fail to move ; and this is death. If, therefore, there had been no sin, there had been no death, with its concomitants of pain and disease ; and lastly, had not our first parents, or one of their succeeding generations, obeyed the devil and disobeyed their Creator, the human family

would still have had access to the tree of life, the antidote for ossification, and consequently have lived forever.
Hence all possible forms and phrases of physical derangement among mankind are the work of the devil and that
of devil-possession, now its natural development. In
harmony with this natural philosophy is the Scriptural
doctrine which attributes the power of death to the devil.
This, being the culmination of physical derangement, carries with it the power of disease, its forerunner and accom-
paniment. It in nowise alters the case if any or all the
satanic possessions and powers have been transmitted
through every one of the two hundred generations of
mankind : if the devil introduced them, then they are his
inheritance, and to cure any of them, according to Scripture, is to cast out devils. Hence Christ gives us a general declaration of the nature of the work, by whomsoever
performed, thus : " The same day there came certain of
the Pharisees, saying unto him, Get thee out, and depart
thee hence ; for Herod will kill thee. And he said unto
them, Go, tell that fox, Behold ! I cast out devils, and
do cures to-day and to-morrow, and the third day I shall
be perfected." (Luke 13 : 31, 32.)

We have produced the evidence in another place to
show that the six days of creation were symbols of six
thousand years of the world's existence, and the seventh,
that of the rest of another thousand : the seventh of
the seven millenniums. Christ was on earth in the fifth
thousand (the fifth day) : He must cast out devils and do
cures the remainder of that day—that thousand ; all the
next day—the sixth thousand—the second day ; and the
third thousand from his own, and seventh of the world,
he would be perfected—glorified by entering upon the
millennial rest, which had remained a matter of promise up
to that time : " If we suffer with him, we shall also reign
with him." "And if children, then heirs : heirs of God,
and joint-heirs with Christ ; if so be that we suffer with
him, that we may be *glorified together*." (Rom. 8 : 17.)
The work of casting out devils and doing cures was to
accompany the gospel down to the end of the world, and
he himself is credited with whatever is done in his name;

therefore Christ casts out devils and does cures as long as the world stands. It is easy to see from these well-known reciprocal influences of mind upon mind, will upon will, and mind and will upon inorganic matter, that the transactions recorded in Scripture as having taken place in the garden of Eden are in perfect accord with the philosophic and psychologic power of all sentient beings. God made the devil an angel, but he made himself a devil, by violent opposition to the will of his Creator. This first devil had the power to conceal himself from Eve, Adam, and all other men, by holding their eyes from seeing him. By his will he also had the power to use the organs of speech belonging to the serpent, and which were quickened into higher capability for the purpose of artful deception. It is thus that mystery vanishes by knowledge, unbelief by evidence, producing intelligent confidence, or faith, as the rational result, and vindicating Scripture record free from incongruity. Without a knowledge of these facts and principles, as well as the design of an author, every book is filled with apparent contradictions and irreconcilable theories ; and there is not one which may not be made to appear in some of its features contemptible, in the hands of a skilful enemy.

CHAPTER VI.

WHAT IS A MIRACLE?

To investigate any subject satisfactorily it must be treated in a philosophic manner, and this supposes accurate definition to be of pre-eminent importance. Truth courts definition, while error fears and abhors it. A very large proportion of the controversies among men arise from no definition, or an incorrect one; while true definition and clear statement of any subject requires little else in its settlement than illustration. We may also remark that a true definition commends itself to the understanding of all who are seeking for truth. We may say, *a miracle is that of which nature is incapable.* To make a thing out of nothing, of course would be a miracle; but as it involves natural impossibility it cannot be done, and if the Bible declares it was done, then it would be open to philosophic and scientific objection. But the Bible nowhere claims that even God ever made anything out of nothing; on the contrary, its terms, Create, Made, and Formed—words used as equivalents in describing the great work of bringing the world and its inhabitants into existence, and which is its method of defining the terms it uses—show that the great miracle of creation consisted in changing one form of matter into another. For example, "The Lord God formed man of the dust of the ground," not out of nothing. "And the rib, which the Lord God had taken from man, *made* he a woman." Here the woman was made out of a rib of Adam, and not out of *nothing!* And the work is described by the word *made*, which therefore means the same as *create*, and which is also used in the work of bringing her into existence, thus: "So God created man in his own image, in the image of God created he him; male and female created he them." "And God formed man out of the dust of the ground." "And out of the ground the Lord God formed every beast of the field and every fowl of the air." In a word, all nature was created out of what is called "the great deep"—the mass of chaotic matter formed at the "beginning," collected and condensed from the more diffuse matter of space for the purpose—but which work was no part of that of the creation, or of that of the six days, the work of each of which being subsequently and particularly described and defined. The question, therefore, Whence came the matter, devoid of any of the forms its parts were made to assume during the six days? has no relevancy to the subject; and to make the Scriptures responsible for the interpretation of the Roman priests, that God made it out of nothing, is simply absurd, and has no more foundation in the Bible than in science, not once intimated in the sacred book.

Philosophy of Miracles.

As it requires an intelligent cause to do an act of which nature is incapable, it must be one of mind; for there is no cause but in mind. A miracle requires origination; but to originate is the exclusive work of mind, demanding intelligence to conceive and construct, as well as will to perform: from which it follows that all beings possessed of mind are creators, and the comparative greatness of the miracles is according to the order or grade of the mind performing them. The mind of the man qualifies him to make a vessel by which he is able to cross the ocean, and thus indirectly to overcome the law of gravity. This is the miracle of a man, because it is a work of which nature is incapable. By mental effort an angel is able directly to overcome gravity, so as to walk upon the water or mount into the air, simply by controlling the atmospheric pressure with his will; the philosophy and science of which we have illustrated in the discussion of mental-magnetic power. This is the miracle of an angel. Both orders of mind are causes; but, properly speaking, they are second causes, as the actors themselves are effects—creatures of the first cause—and their creation was God's miracle. To this great mind, therefore, according to the stern conclusions of philosophic science, logic, and fact, must be attributed the existence of the world and everything, of whatever form or nature, it contains, as well as that of the angels of his immediate habitation. Here is the original mind—the first cause of all things—whose personality is inseparable from intelligent existence, as the one implies the other. Such an existence no more depends upon faith or belief than does the existence and personality of man to his fellow-man or to himself, but is absolute knowledge; and the vessel made by the man, and by which he crossed the ocean, no more demonstrates his personal and intellectual existence than does the existence of the man himself, as well as all other things which men, angels, or nature cannot make, demonstrate the existence, personality, and intellectuality of God the Creator himself. Here, in the necessity of things, we find the absolute cause and only cause of all causes, proclaimed alike by the harmonious voice of organic and inorganic nature.

The only second causes, as connected with this world, are men endowed with faculties enabling them to cause things to exist of which nature is incapable, including all their contrivances. A surgeon sets the bones of a broken limb, so that it regains its ordinary strength and performs its functions as before. This is a miracle of man. A physician cures a patient of a disease of which he would otherwise have died. This is also a miracle of man—a work of which nature was incapable. It is admitted that both of the recoveries took place in accordance with the laws of nature; but the skill and interference of the surgeon and physician was the miraculous part of the work, while nature was incapable of effecting either. If a man has fixed upon himself a disease, or a supposed one, by simply a morbid, mental impression, called "imagination," which if not removed would prove fatal—(such as the following, which happened but a little time ago: A woman in Massachusetts imagined she had an internal cancer, and held to the conviction in spite of positive denial by reputable physicians; and she died of cancer, when an autopsy disclosed the fact that she had no disease whatever)—another succeeds in removing it by a counter impression of greater strength, either by reasoning or administering some simple substance having no curative properties, but which he was induced to believe was a sure remedy, and the patient recovered. Here was a miracle; because a process of which nature was incapable —one of supernatural power, and yet it was in accordance with the natural law between mind and vitality. It is within these limits that men with their natural powers are able to perform miracles.

The Conditions upon which Men may Work Christ's Miracles.

Let us now bring Christ into the work. Here is a man by the name of Lazarus, who had died and had been buried four days : " I say unto you plainly, Lazarus is dead." This man died of some vital disease, and never could have lived again, unless the vital parts were restored, so that they would again perform their part in the vital economy. It is evident that to do this demands the same degree of knowledge and skill as that displayed in making the vital organs of the first living man; and as this is the greatest manifestation of skill and power the universe manifests, none but the Creator could have performed it. But Christ did the work, and the dead man lived. It is also evident that, if this being should choose so to do, he could say to a man, I am going to leave the world personally, and I desire still to manifest this power in it, and if you will follow my example and directions, you may do just such acts as this. I do not propose to delegate to you my knowledge or power, to be permanently used as your own; but when you desire to cast out devils, cure diseases, and even to raise the dead to life, and will call on my name, I will know it, and if your motive is my honor, my glory, and in every case which will subserve my cause, I will do the work : thus may men work the works of God. In such a work there is no more mystery than that God or man lives, and he who cannot conceive such a philosophy can scarcely be considered an accountable being ;—not able to reason from effects to causes, or comprehend the necessary superiority and priority of the cause.

To understand nature, involving her interdependent relations, any man would know that, aside from mind, there was nothing but effects—not a phenomenon in the unknowing universe, even of the most simple form, but which is the direct or remote effect, and therefore the effect of an effect, and so on endlessly, until philosophic and mathematical inquiry is exhausted ; and yet the cause lies beyond, above, and prior to the living, moving universe of effect—consequently supernatural. This involves the conclusion that, instead of there being no miracles, everything, as the effect of mind, is miraculous, because nature is, and always was, incapable of bringing one of the least of these into existence.

The Scoffer's Superficial Ideas.

Ingersoll says : " If we believe in a power superior to nature, it is perfectly natural that such a power can and will interfere in the affairs of the world. If there is no interference, of what practical use can such a power be ? " Here the absurdity is implied that the existence or non-existence of such a power depends upon whether men believe it or not. In the estimation of such a mind, what a powerful thing is belief or unbelief? It may be of no practical use to the assassin that the officers of the law should interfere in his affairs ; but they interfere just the same. It is of no practical use to mankind that such a power did interfere and make this boasting piece of humanity, nor that he should ever interfere to dispossess his enemies, and give the inheritance to his own loving, loyal subjects ; but he will interfere just the same. Had he qualified " mankind," to whom such interference was of no use, to mean those who hated God and his proposed universal government of righteousness, we agree with him that to such it will be of no practical use ; but

he will interfere just the same, and without consulting
their wishes, and to the infinite advantage of his people.
But as Ingersoll is totally ignorant of the existence of a
Being superior to nature, he must also be of the purposes
for which he has interfered, and proposes to interfere, in
the affairs of men. Hence, as we see, he is unable to
talk about the subject with the least sense or dignity, but
plays with the words concerning it, as a child does with
his toys.

He says: "The Scriptures give us the most wonderful
accounts of divine interference: Animals talk like men"
[but is it not more consistent for an ass to talk like a
man than for a man to talk like an ass?]; "springs gurgle
from dry bones" [how funny that seems to be to his sagacious mind]; "the sun and moon stop in the heavens,
in order to give General Joshua more time to murder"
[the scoffer seems never to tire in repeating this stale
slander]; "the shadow on a dial goes back ten degrees,
to convince a petty king of a barbarous people that he is
not going to die of a boil." [Here our truth-seeker tells
several lies. It was not a petty king, but Hezekiah king
of Judah; and not of a barbarous people, but the most
enlightened and civilized people of the world up to that
period, and having the best code of laws for the development of virtue and knowledge that has ever existed, and
whose provisions were formulated by Christ into the
golden rule.] "All other nations, even the civilized and
learned Grecian, with her seven wise men, taught the
people to make gods with their own hands, and that these
were so superior to themselves that they were to fall down
and worship before their shrines."

In view of which, why does not this abusive slanderer
of God and his people stigmatize all the other nations of
the world barbarous? The answer is, the God of the
Bible is the only one who has issued laws to restrain his
heart and will, and lives to execute their penalty; but
he seems to act upon the fool-hardy theory that if he
does not believe it, he will escape justice being done him.
"Fires refuse to burn." [Yes, but an angel was in the
flaming furnace with the servants of the Lord, into which

5

they had been cast for refusing to imitate the barbarous worshippers of a brazen image the king had set up, and who commanded all men to prostrate themselves before it ; and an angel has the power, when sent by God for the purpose, to deprive fire of its power to burn, and by a reversion to cause the heavens to rain fire and brimstone to consume the cities of the plains.]   "Water positively declines to seek its level." [Could not the God who made the waters, and carries them into the heavens that they may rain down again, by a change of their temperature, have carried them up a hill not as high as heaven, and let them run down on the other side?   The trouble with the scoffer is, that he has got in his head the fool's thought of no God, which prevents anything unperverted from entering its dark chambers relating to these subjects.] "Grains of sand become lice." [Lice exist, and God made them ; and certain grains of sand, or other dirt, in children's heads, become lice.   Do you say this is the work of nature?   Well, is nature greater than the Maker of nature?   But nature makes nothing, and is wholly the work of God.   In view of which, the only force there is in the scoffer's lying relates to the number of the lice God sent to plague a proud king for making war upon his people, who, like Ingersoll, defied him ; but he perished in the end, as all such do or will.]

"Common walking sticks, to gratify a mere freak, twist themselves into serpents, and swallow each other by way of exercise." [This is funny, yet studied blasphemy, committed to gratify the sordid purpose of making fools laugh to get their money.   Instead of this being a common walking stick, when in the hand of the servant of God it embodied almighty power, and was the most dreadful instrument that ever scourged a nation of God's enemies.   Before it Red Seas and mighty kings and their armies are as the dust of the balance !   Ask Pharaoh and his extinct army, whose dead carcasses sank like lead in the mighty waters and were dashed against their rocky shores, about this rod ; and, could they answer, O what an expression of horror would be heard !   But how inadequate is the mental conception of the slanderer of God's mighty acts to comprehend these things! He interprets this childish mentality to be progress, and whatever phase of the subject he contemplates, it diminishes to microscopic littleness and gross absurdity.] "Prophecy becomes altogether easier than history." [Here his mind, little as it is, seemed to have stopped working altogether while the talking-machine went on, uttering the absurdity of quoting history and declaring it prophecy!] "The sons of God became enamoured of the world's girls." [We wonder if it was news to the crowd in Booth's Theatre, that only the antediluvians became enamoured with the girls of the world?] "Women are changed into salt, for the purpose of keeping a great event fresh in the minds of men." [Another scoffing lie; it was because she disobeyed the command of God's angel-servant and looked doubtingly back, that she was thus changed.]

"An excellent article of brimstone is imported from heaven free of duty." [He seems to think that if he makes fun of the fire and brimstone, it won't burn him. About the Sodomites he does not seem to be very curious. Their doom, however, is set forth as the example of all such scoffers. "Even as Sodom and Gomorrah, and the cities about them, are set forth for an example, suffering the vengeance of eternal fire."] Here is the doom of all who speak evil of those things which they know not (and the history of the world does not furnish a more striking example of this ignorant speaking than Ingersoll himself); but what they know as natural brute beasts, in those things they corrupt themselves. "Woe unto them! they have gone in the way of Cain, and ran greedily after the error of Balaam for reward." (Jude.)

Balaam was willing to curse the children of God for money; but Ingersoll, an advanced son of the false prophet, not only delights in the cursing and bitterness against the servants of God, the holy of the ages, but blasphemes God himself, his word, and his angels, and for the low gratification of exciting a laugh and, lower still, for making money—the wages of unrighteousness; which wages is death. "Clothes refuse to wear out for forty years." [This philosophic scientist cannot conceive how God, in order to make wool for clothing, could make the sheep first—the indirect method; how much less that he should have made the wool directly of the elements of which he formed the sheep, causing their chemical atoms, floating in surrounding nature, to adhere to a man's coat, in order to restore the ordinary wear or decay, although it is a fact that he is thus clothing and restoring all the organic things of nature. According to Ingersoll, God is a very poor and inconsistent mechanic; he can make things on a large scale, but cannot on a small one; he can make them in an indirect manner, but cannot do it directly, as in the case of the wool, by making the sheep-machines first. He can make a series of coats for forty years indirectly to clothe his enemy, Ingersoll; but he cannot directly restore the clothing of his friends, and that, too, after he had brought them into an emergency where their clothing and shoes wore out and they had no material of which to make more. But Ingersoll does not know that there is a God, and this makes his sayings still more absurd as to what he is able or unable to do, or whether it is consistent for him to do it.]

" Besides keeping restaurants to feed wandering prophets free of expense." [Why not feed his own holy prophets, who flee into the wilderness from the face of such hating slanderers, and with whom he declares he cannot live in peace in the same world, as to feed him with the money he gets for abusing them and their Lord at expensive hotels and restaurants? Yes! feed them with flocks of live birds from heaven; as him with dead birds washed down with costly wine and other stronger drinks.]

" Bears tear children in pieces for laughing at old men without wigs." [God made the law of humanity:] "Thou shalt rise up before the hoary head, and honor the face of an old man" (Lev. 19 : 23), and at which Ingersoll thus scoffs; but the children with whom he naturally takes side, had been taught and had learned to despise this law and mock God's holy prophet: "And as Elisha was going up to Beth-el [to worship] there came forth little children out of the city, and mocked him, and said, Go up, thou bald head ; go up, thou bald head. And he turned back, and cursed them, in the name of the Lord. And there came forth two she bears out of the wood, and tare forty and two children of them." (2 Kings 2 : 23, 24.)

If these little children had been taught thus early to mock God's aged and honored prophet, they would have all become Ingersolls when grown to maturity, and, like their antitype, would have scoffed at and mocked, not only his prophets, but God himself. It seems natural that the scoffer should dislike to hear about God's tearing people to pieces for irreverence toward his servants and himself, as it indicates his own coming doom written in advance, thus : " Now consider this, ye that forget God, lest I tear you in pieces, and there be none to deliver." (Ps. 50 : 22.) " Muscular development depends upon the length of one's hair." [This is a cunning saying, and is meant for a pun upon Samson, one of the judges of Israel ; but as usual, it is a lying misrepresentation, for the strength of Samson was a direct inspiration of God, given at every time of need, and not his normal condition.] " Dead people come to life simply to get a joke on their enemies." [As there is no such record in the Bible, it must be put down to the scoffer's credit of becoming exhausted for things to ridicule, which obliges him to stop, or make facts for the purpose.] " Witches and wizards converse freely with the souls of the departed." [We suppose this allusion is intended for the account relating to the witch of Endor and the prophet Samuel ; but there was no communication or conversation between the witch and the prophet, and, as usual, the scorner misunderstands and misquotes the record. This we have shown in another place.] " God himself becomes a stone-cutter and engraver, after having been a tailor and dressmaker." Here the scoffer's slanders and blasphemies reach their climax, and we only ask our readers to behold the silly braggart !

Shallow Thinking of Freethinkers.

Ingersoll says, " The people are beginning to think, reason, and investigate. . The first doubt was the want and cradle of progress. Don't keep back your doubts; cherish them, they are the sources of all your knowledge. Slowly, patiently, but surely, the gods are being driven from the earth." [Exactly the reverse of this, as we have shown is true. It is a law of mind that evidence compels belief, and belief removes doubt; the doubt exists for the want of evidence to remove it; and this is ignorance instead of knowledge: therefore, to cherish doubts is to cherish ignorance.] " The first doubt was the cradle of progress." No sir! it was the cradle of blind ignorance, and the first evidence—the precursor of belief— banished it; so that he virtually says, what he is too proud to acknowledge if he conceives it: " Don't keep back your doubts; they are the cradle of your ignorance." Doubts have no evidence as their bases, produce no conviction, beget no conception of the existence of things or beings, or ideas of their qualities, and therefore engender no knowledge; for knowledge is the result of conception, conception of conviction, conviction of evidence; and evidence is the result of intelligent existence, as you can have no evidence of non-existence. This is knowledge; to obtain which is to think, to reason, and investigate.

The Knowledge which Expelled the Doubt.

To illustrate still further this fundamental law of intelligence, of knowledge, let us suppose that I am told for the first time the world and everything it contains evolved out of its own resources, and was not created; that there is nothing superior to nature itself, and no supernatural being in existence, or one who had anything to do with the world or its inhabitants. Up to this time I had an opinion of these existences, but had never investigated the subject; but now I begin to think, to reason, to investigate the new proposition. In the first place, I observe that I have a father and a mother, and by observing others born into the world, as well as the remembrance of my own childhood, that I was also born. My observing and association extends back three generations to my great-grandparents, and forward to my own children, and I see that each child during these generations had two progenitors—parents. From these facts I conclude that such must have been true of every generation of mankind. Another fact of existence forces itself upon my mind ; which is, that one generation succeeds another in coming into existence. I think and reason upon the subject ; I commence at the last generation and count back until I come to the first, which forces me to the conclusion that there was a first generation, and that its parentage consisted of a single man and woman—a male and female.

All Mankind Created in Adam and Eve.

It is a fact that the first man and woman was not a generation, as they were not generated ; for had they been generated they must have had parental generators, and therefore could not have been the first generation ; and as they were the first they must have been created progenitors. It is a fact that the first generation did evolve from the first progenitors, and so down the succession of the two hundred generations of mankind who have lived and died during the ages of the world. By thus thinking, reasoning, and investigating, I discover another fact, namely, that a thing cannot evolve or come out of that which did not possess it, at least in embryonical, rudimental form, as seed, and therefore that the evolution necessitated prior involution. This being a fact of all the generations which come within our experience and observation, as well as being corroborated by universal history, demonstrates it to be as true of every generation from the first as of the last one born into the world. Therefore the evolution of each generation was preceded by the embryonic involution of each ; and as the evolution of the last generation did not take place until the prior involution, neither could this have been true of any succeeding the first ; but as the first parents had no parents, they did not evolve, and were therefore created. We also observe that through all these phenomena nature has worked with constant and undeviating uniformity, proclaimed by the universal voice of organic being, "everything after its kind." A created thing involves the necessity of a Creator, and the whole creation that of his interference with mankind and the world, and of course which makes him absolute owner—universal proprietor. We also see by these facts of philosophic science, attested by universal observation and experience, that nature originated nothing in the whole process ; which had she done, it would have contradicted her uniformity. Here we have the conclusion that, instead of nature having done all the work she manifests, as the self-styled freethinkers (a gross misnomer) suppose and claim, God the Creator was the only original cause, which idea is irreconcilable with himself being any part of nature. He made the first pair, male and female, and in that act involved all future generations, or, properly speaking, created all in the one pair and at once, superseding all further interference in running the great machine of human existence ; and in antithesis to your advice, " cherish your doubts," we put Paul's emphatic words, " He that doubteth is damned." (Rom. 14 : 23.) So surely will this be the doom, unless the doubter repents, that it is expressed as already done.

Here, Mr. Ingersoll, is what we have discovered by thinking, reasoning, and investigation. Your doctrine, that there was no living God, or God-interference in the affairs of mankind, made me doubt ; and the doubt destroyed the opinion to the contrary, and the little knowledge had upon the subject ; but by thought, reason, and patient investigation, slowly but surely we have arrived at positive knowledge upon all these questions, with not a doubt remaining such as you in ignorance advise your hearers to cherish as the cradle of progress—sources of knowledge. O what a state of mind to be in ! We have heard of men selling themselves to the devil ; but if this arrogant scoffer has not brought about such a trade, it would seem as though he has so disgraced the work of his master by overdoing it, that the devil would give nothing for him. It is evident from Ingersoll's hard speeches and crude sayings, that they are founded upon the theory of no God-interference with man and the world; but as this is the doubting of ignorance, it follows that there is not the least force or truth in his godless lecture on the gods. But as we intend to give his *ism* a full and public exposure, we must continue to pursue him and the lecture, the master-piece of his publications; and to omit any of his objections to the Bible or its author might leave ground for his friends to claim them to be unanswerable, which we cannot afford to do. "Only upon rare occasions are the gods, even by the most religious, supposed to interfere now in the affairs of men." [This is not true, even of a single idolatrous religion; the history of each shows that their most intelligent expounders hold that the gods do interfere in the affairs of each individual, even to take notice of the motives which actuate them. The reason why Christians do not so much believe in the interference of God in their affairs in the present life, is because they understand the Scriptures, which teach that the present world is one of probation and trial, and that the future, from the judgment onward, is that of retribution, when God is to take the affairs of every man into his own hands, rewarding or punishing each according to what had been his belief, and obedience, at the time he left the mortal world.] "In most matters, at least, we are supposed to be free." [Just as though it had been taught, by the most religious people, that the interference of God in their affairs made them slaves, whereas a Christian is the only man free from the slavery of his own passions, free from the conviction of having his maker his enemy, and free from the apprehension of the loss of eternal life, and the endless gain of the kingdom of God. Ingersoll's conception of freedom seems to be that of an anarchist, unrestrained by any law; an outlaw, free to do as he pleases, without regard to God or man, especially as it relates to the coming word.]

The Scoffer's Ignorance of Christian Faith.

He says: "The doctrine that future happiness depends upon belief is monstrous: it is the infamy of infamies. The notion that faith in Christ is to be rewarded by an eternity of bliss, while a dependence upon reason, observation, and experience merits everlasting pain, is too absurd for refutation, and can only be relieved by that happy mixture of insanity and ignorance, called faith." The doctrine of faith is not only taught in Scripture, but is a principle of universal practice in all the reciprocities of human society and commerce, and is the very basis of moral philosophy, conceded and acted upon by the great mass of the most virtuous and intelligent of mankind; and is composed of the same elements or principles, whether the faith is between man and man, or between man and his Maker; the fundamental principles of which are trust, promise, and veracity! That faith should be characterized as being too absurd for refutation, shows the boundless egotism, arrogance, and ignorance of this man. Could a man have a friend whom he did not believe existed? If not, then unbelief buries the friendship of the world. If we did not have faith in the veracity of others, how could the ordinary business transactions of life be carried on? If we did not believe in the promises of reward for service rendered, could society exist? Unbelief insults all who thus promise; for what greater insult can be committed against one who has pledged his word to reward another, to whom he would reply, "I do not believe one word you say, not even your oath." Could or would God or man do the least act of kindness for such a man, without repentance? If God made faith in him—which implies confidence in his existence, reliance upon his word of promise and oath, and that he had the ability to read the heart as to its existence—would it not be the surest test of honest loyalty, the highest of virtues? as everything else might be deceptive and false. In view of which, what could equally manifest the low thoughts of Ingersoll as to stigmatize faith as the infamy of infamies, because God promises to honor it with the gift of eternal life? His hatred of the doctrine he thus stigmatizes shows he has some apprehension of the consequences of unbelief, as an absurdity, or that which is conceived so to be, never calls forth such bitter expression. Here, in gross violation of truth and fair dealing, he separates works from faith, which are indissolubly connected, as the fruit to the tree and streams to the fountain, thus changing the condition of salvation; and denounces his own work as the infamy of infamies. By a sentence in this manner does Ingersoll destroy the foundations of revealed religion in the minds of those ignorant of the Scriptures, and which obliges us to refute by presenting the doctrine as taught therein. The Scripture teaching upon the subject is that God is jealous of his word and honor, whether it relates to belief or action. It is the Creator who makes the demand upon the creatures of his handy-work, which fact vindicates its righteousness! Man is proud and self-willed, and for a time all resist God's commands and demands. Here is antagonism, rendering it necessary that one party shall yield in order that they may live together in peace; consequently, if ever, there will be universal peace between God and his living creatures, which, foreseeing he will be able to bring about, has pledged his word, oath, and honor to establish. To such a state of atonement or reconciliation, one of the parties must yield to the will of the other; the creature or the Creator must triumph, and, in that case, God or the finally impenitent must perish. This includes every hostile will, whether of man or devil, or wherever existing in the universe of the Creator, which universal peace renders a philosophic necessity.

God does not make demands of submission simply as sovereign; but reasons with his enemies to induce them to yield by promising them an endless inheritance in the re-creation of the present world—"the world to come," in which they will no more be subject to suffering or death, thus elevated to the enjoyment of eternal bliss. "And Jesus, answering, said unto them, The children of this world marry and are given in marriage; but they which shall be counted worthy to obtain *that world*, and the resurrection from the dead, neither marry nor are given in marriage ; *neither can they die any more :* for they are equal unto the angels [in this respect], and are the children of God, being the children of the resurrection." (Luke 20 : 34–36.) "Jesus said unto her, I am the resurrection, and the life : he that believeth in me, though he were dead, yet shall he live." (John 11 : 25.) "Marvel not at this : for the hour is coming, in the which all that are in the graves shall hear the voice of the Son of God, and shall come forth ; they that have done good, unto the resurrection of life ; and they that have done evil, unto the resurrection of damnation." (John 5 : 28– 29.) This testimony also settles the question that some had died and were raised from the dead at the end of the world, with wills still antagonistic to the will of God, and that this is the time appointed for their destruction, and which is corroborated by scores of passages such as this : "Who shall be punished with everlasting *destruction* from the presence of the Lord, and from the glory of his power; when he shall come to be glorified in his saints, and to be admired in all them that believe." (2 Thess. 1 : 9, 10.)

Re-creation—the World Without End.

Christ gave John a revelation of the present world after it had been destroyed by fire, about which he wrote thus : "And I saw a new heaven and a new earth : for the first heaven and the first earth were passed away ; and there was no more sea. And I, John, saw the holy city, new Jerusalem, coming down from God out of heaven, prepared as a bride adorned for her husband. And I heard a great voice out of heaven saying, Behold, the tabernacle of God is with men, and he will dwell with them, and they shall be his people, and God himself [not merely by his Spirit, as at present] shall be with them, and be their God." (Rev. 21 : 1–4.) In answer to the scoffers, all that is necessary to say in regard to the execution of this work is, that he who made the present world to answer a temporary purpose is able to remake it to sub-

serve an endless purpose. He who created man susceptible of temporal life, is able to re-create, resurrect him,
to be the immortal inhabitant of the world without end.
He who built the solar system, drew the plan and gave
it to David of the temple built in the city of the old Jerusalem, as grand Master-Builder, is able to build the im-
perishable, golden, jeweled city, the antitypic Jerusalem,
" which hath foundations [twelve] eternal in the heavens
[new heavens], and without human hands," as the Jerusalem and temple which came to an end was.

Faith is to Believe God will Keep his Promise.

We have now considered faith as a philosophic principle and of universal acceptation and practice, founded
upon the most profound reasoning; and if the Scripture
record of its nature be true, it must accord with that thus
established, and the question is, What saith the Scriptures
upon the subject? We may remark that biblical faith is
to believe with the heart, to love the things promised
and the conditions upon which they are to be conferred ;
in a word, believe that God tells the truth. And this is
what Ingersoll calls absurd, even infamous ! As the faith
of Abraham is the model of both Testaments, and of all
time, all nations, all the families of the earth, it becomes
necessary to have clear ideas of its revelation. God
promised Abraham and his seed (and his seed were to be
those of all nations, generations, and families of the world,
the individuals—males and females—who believed the
words, loved him who made them, and were obedient to
all his instructions)—to the effect that Abraham personally, in common with this innumerable seed, should have
an everlasting inheritance in the land of the new earth.
Abraham died in this faith and hope, looking to the resurrection of the dead at the end of this world through which
to be brought into the possession.

A condensed history of the engagement is as follows:
" And the Lord brought Abraham forth abroad, and said,
Look now toward heaven, and tell the stars, if thou be
able to number them : so shall thy seed be. And he be-

lieved in the Lord ; and he counted it to him for righteousness." (Gen. 15 : 5, 6.) Abraham did right in believing the promise of his Creator, and it pleased his Lord ;
and he counted, or imputed, it to him for righteousness.

Paul discusses the revelation thus : " For the promise,
that Abraham should be *heir of the world*, was not to him,
or to his seed, through the law, but through the righteousness of faith ; therefore it is by faith, that it might be by
grace ; and grace is the gift of God." Had the inheritance been promised upon the condition of obedience to the law, or those of the Mosaic code which
constituted the Jewish national government, Judaism,
which proud men as well as the humble might perform,
then could they have demanded equally with Abraham
heirship to the inheritance of the coming new world.
Men like Ingersoll, proud, self-willed, and defiant, could
walk into the kingdom of God and take legal possession.
But grace changes all this, and says to the proud, You
have nothing I want but your hearts, and these I cannot receive so long as they are proud ! It is this that
makes the estrangement between God and man. The
great Proprietor says to his creatures, " Study my revealed propositions until you see and feel the reasonable-
ness of them, and that you cannot change or overthrow
my purposes, or subdue my will. This will humble you,
if anything, and will be evidence of your faith in my veracity. Now in your humility come to me, and I will
accept you and in due time exalt you to be my sons and
daughters, the immortal subjects of my kingdom, my
new coming world." " He that exalteth himself shall be
abased ; but he that humbleth himself shall be exalted."
" The proud he knoweth afar off, but giveth grace to the
humble." Paul continues the argument thus : " To the
end that the promise might be sure to all the seed : not
to that only which is of the law, but to that which is of
the faith of Abraham, who is the father of us all. As it
is written, I have made thee a father of many nations before God, who quickeneth the dead, and calleth those
things which be not, as though they were [for God uses
the present for the future tense when speaking of things

of prophetic prediction which are to take place in the future]. He staggered not at the promise of God through unbelief; but was strong in faith, giving glory to God [it was honoring, glorifying God, by believing he would keep his word of promise] and being fully persuaded he was able to perform, therefore, his faith was imputed to him for righteousness. Now it was not written for his [Abraham's] sake alone, that it was imputed to him; but for us also, to whom it shall be imputed, if we believe on him that raised up Jesus our Lord from the dead." (Rom. 4: 13-25.) "Know ye therefore that they which are of faith, the same are the children of Abraham: for ye are all the children of God by faith in Christ Jesus, there is neither Jew nor Greek, bond nor free, male nor female: for ye are all one in Christ Jesus, and if ye be Christ's, then are ye Abraham's seed, and heirs according to the promise." (Gal. 4: 26-29.)

"And the Scripture, foreseeing that God would justify the heathen [Gentile] through faith, preached the gospel unto Abraham, saying, In thee shall all nations be blessed. [Here was the gospel preached, and by God himself, which was the glad tidings of the possession of the immortal kingdom beyond the resurrection of the dead, and was in about the two thousandth year of the world, and six hundred years before the Jewish nation had an existence, and we see that it was the same gospel re-preached by Paul.] So then they which be of faith are blessed with faithful Abraham. And this I say, that the covenant [this new covenant, the promise of which was made to Abraham], confirmed before of God in Christ [here also it is or was the gospel of Christ thus preached to Abraham], the law [which was four hundred and thirty years after] cannot disannul, that it should make the promise of God of none effect; for if the inheritance be of the law [the Jewish national law], it is no more of promise; but God gave it to Abraham by promise." [If it had been given to Abraham while living, faith would have been impossible; the fulfilment would destroy the promise.] (Gal. 3.) But what saith it? "The word is nigh thee, even, in thy mouth and in thy heart: that is, the word of faith,

which we preach: that if thou shalt confess with thy
mouth the Lord Jesus, and shalt believe in thy heart that
God hath raised him from the dead, thou shalt be served:
for with the heart man believeth unto righteousness ; and
with the mouth confession is made unto salvation. ''(Rom.
10 : 2–8.) Here is the faith of the gospel, and there is but
one : '' One Lord, one faith, one baptism, one God and
Father of all.'' (Eph. 4 : 6.) Therefore, no more two or
more faiths than there are two Lords, two Gods, or two
Fathers, etc. This is the faith of all ages. Abel had it,
and by which he pleased God and was righteous, to
which God himself testified ; and without faith it is impossible to please him. It is the faith of all ages, the
faith of the gospel revealed to the saints at the very
foundation of the world. Of the faith it is also written :
'' Beloved, I write unto you of the common salvation, and
exhort you that ye should earnestly contend for the faith,
which was once delivered unto the saints.'' (Jude 3.)
Here are the Christians exhorted, not to adopt a new
faith, but to contend for that of the earliest saints ; and it
was the faith of the gospel which God himself preached
to Abel and Abraham.

It is clear from this record that belief—faith—is not
simply an intellectual process, or an indifferent assent of
the mind to these promises of God ; but a heartfelt
desire for their fulfilment—the possession of the eternal
inheritance to which the faithful of all ages had been
heirs, and who looked to the resurrection of the dead
through which to come into it. Of the father of the
faithful we read : '' By faith Abraham, when he was
called to go out into a place which he should after receive for an inheritance, obeyed ; and he went out, not
knowing whither he went. By faith he sojourned in the
land of promise [not of possession, for that was the new
world], as in a strange country, dwelling in tabernacles
with Isaac and Jacob [son and grandson], heirs with
him to the same promise: for he looked for a city which
hath foundations, whose builder and maker is God
[the new Jerusalem city, with its twelve foundations—
twelve stories—mansions—a foundation to each, which is

to be the capital city of the antitypic land of the new heaven and the new earth—the heavenly country—the world to come, lying beyond the resurrection]. These all died in faith, not having received the [the possession of the things embraced in the] promises; but having seen them afar off [at the end of the world], and were persuaded of them [persuaded that God would keep his word; they therefore, while living, received the salvation and inheritance *by faith*], and embraced them [I loved them], and confessed that they were strangers and pilgrims on the earth: for they that say such things declare plainly that they seek a country. And truly, if they had been mindful of the country from whence they came out, they might have had opportunity to have returned; but they desired a better country, that is, an heavenly [the country of the new heaven and new earth]. Wherefore God is not ashamed to be called their God: for he hath prepared for them a city." ["I go to prepare a place for you; and if I go and prepare a place for you, I will come again and receive you unto myself, that where I am, there ye may be also." (John 14.)] The account goes on to tell how this whole household of faith had suffered the loss of all things, rather than forfeit the heirship to the promised inheritance. They were subjected to every form of torture, not accepting deliverance upon the condition of abandoning their faith; and the reason is added, "that they might obtain a better resurrection"—not that to shame and everlasting contempt.

CHAPTER VII.

OBEDIENT WORKS ESSENTIAL TO SALVATION.

Faith and works stand in the same relation to each other, and to salvation, as lungs and air to vitality, or as trees, moisture, and sunlight to fruit. The good tree is the heart acting with motives to please its Creator, and which becomes thus pure by believing the words of promise revealed in the Scriptures. He loves the God who first loved him, and the faith and love is made known to others by the sacrifices and obedience of his life. Christ said, "First make the tree good, and the fruit will be good: for a good tree cannot bring forth corrupt fruit, neither can a corrupt tree bring forth good fruit; wherefore by their fruits shall ye know them." The subject is clearly presented by the apostle James thus: "Without works faith is dead, being alone: show me thy faith without thy works, and I will show you my faith by my works." "Was not Abraham our father justified by works, when he offered Isaac his son upon the altar? Seest thou how faith wrought with his works, and by works faith was made perfect?" That faith in the promise and power of God to raise the dead was the ground of Abraham's faith, is shown thus: "By faith Abraham, when he was tried, offered up Isaac: and he that had received the promises offered up his only son, of whom it was said, In Isaac shall thy seed be called: accounting that God was able to raise him up, even from the dead." (Heb. 11: 17–19.) "What doth it profit, my beloved brethren, though a man may say he hath faith, and hath not works? Can faith save him? If a brother or sister be naked, and destitute of daily food, and one of you say unto them, Depart in peace, be ye warmed and filled;

notwithstanding ye give them not those things which
are needful to the body ; what doth it profit ?   Even so
faith, if it hath not works, is dead, being alone.

"Thou believest there is one God ; thou doest well ;
the devils also believe and tremble.   [Such devils are not
on Ingersoll's side, as he claims all devils to be : they
are not so low in the intellectual scale as not to know
there is a God, nor in the moral scale as to oppose his
purposes and anticipate the consequences.]   But wilt
thou know, O vain man, that faith without works is
dead ?   [Here the fundamental principle is that a man
must be in a condition of heart which will lead him to
please God ; and in the very nature of things he made
man for this purpose, as it was impossible he should have
been made either incapable of doing that which would
have pleased him, or that God was indifferent as to
whether his creature pleased or displeased him ; or more
impossible still that he made him on purpose to displease
him ; and if he made man capable of being and doing
that which pleased him, he must have been capable of
being and doing that which displeased him—the one
carries with it the other.   But to please God, a man
must believe that he *is*—he exists—as it would be impossible to make the least effort to please that which had
no existence.   In order to do this it is also essential, as
it requires sacrifice on the part of man, to expect recompense for the service : "That he [God] is the rewarder
of them that diligently seek him."   And this is founded
upon the belief of God's unimpeachable veracity. (Heb.
11 : 6.)

It is evident that the argument presents the condition
of mind and heart so acquainted with the nature, disposition, and promises of God as revealed in the Bible, that
it implicitly relies upon their personal fulfilment.   This
is what the Scriptures teach of the nature of revealed
faith, and the crowning importance of the requisition :
"Have faith in God.   Without faith it is impossible to
please Him."   The last sentence of the passage shows God
is both just and good, neither of which do or can atheists believe ; and modern atheism, in order more effect-

ually to deceive, takes on the new form of expression in its rejection of the existence of God, and says: "It believes there is a God; but he is not a *personal* God." And then, for fear these atheists should be asked to define what they mean by "an impersonal God," reply, "we have the idea, but cannot explain it," a virtual acknowledgment of having a conception, an image, of a thing in the mind of which they are too ignorant of words, the signs of ideas, to describe it, or that paradoxically they have an idea of which they have no idea. In this revelation we see that the devils have such faith in the existence of a personal God that they tremble with apprehension for being devils, for which reason it is more sensible that they should expect favors from the hand of God, than that these impersonal-God idealists without ideas should thus hope. If, therefore, they continue in such a frame of mind, they make their destruction a philosophic necessity, as a coming universal peace is declared between God and all living creatures; and as they cannot destroy him, they must suffer this themselves. This destiny includes the father-devil and all his children, "children of the wicked one." Hence it is written: "For this purpose was the Son of God manifested, that he might destroy the works of the devil." (1 John 3: 8.) "Forasmuch, then, as the children are partakers of flesh and blood, he also himself likewise took part of the same; that through death [himself passing through death; for had he remained dead, he could neither have saved his friends nor destroyed his enemies, as a dead being can do nothing] he might destroy him who had the power of death, that is, the devil, and deliver them who through fear of death were all their lifetime subject to bondage." (Heb. 2: 14, 15.) As, therefore, Christ himself was raised from the dead, he is able to deliver, redeem, all his children from the power of the grave, and introduce them simultaneously into his new-made world; all being immortal, death had lost its dominion: "and there was no death."

Human Transactions Illustrate Faith.

The nature and work of faith is shown by the prosecution of all human transactions. To illustrate: Here is a man who has forfeited his property, which has been sold under foreclosure; but he has a year of grace in which to redeem it. Just after the sale, another, knowing of the transaction and desiring to win the man's love, sends a messenger to offer him the money to meet the claim, but will not give it until the day before the year of redemption expires. Until the day comes, he to whom the promise was made receives the money *by faith*—he believed the word of the friend who had made the promise; but the moment it was fulfilled, the faith was superseded by the knowledge of the fact, and ended. Suppose the proposition was not to loan the money, but that it was to be an absolute gift, compensation being out of the question. To this he who had forfeited the property objects, and informs his friend that he does not wish to be considered a helpless beggar. Well, says the friend, are you not such? If not, and are able to help yourself, why do you apply to me or to anyone else? Or why do you appear to be what you are not? Why do you pretend to have ability which you have not? This is both pride and hypocrisy of heart, and is the very object for which I make the proposition in this manner, that you may frankly and honestly acknowledge your true and helpless condition, thereby to humble you and honor me. Thousands in the same condition have applied to me, and with each have I had the same controversy. Some have yielded to my will and have received my bounty. Others held on to their self-will, pride, and hypocrisy; but all suffered the consequence of losing their property. This presentation of the case had the effect of humbling the applicant, and he waited patiently in faith and hope for the day of redemption. He reflected upon those who had refused the gracious offer of this friend upon whom the day of redemption expired, and who had lived only to reflect upon themselves, that they had but one friend who was able and willing to have saved them from the loss; but him they rejected, and from which they could never recover. All these now see that it would have ennobled themselves by publishing the praise of so kind, good, just, and merciful a friend, that others similarly circumstanced might also apply to him and receive his gracious bounties. Let us suppose, still further, that it was his life the man had forfeited by the crime of treason against the state, for which he had been tried, found guilty, and sentenced to be executed on a certain day, and that it was the law in that country that one might sacrifice his life to save that of another, and that in this case, owing to the greatness of the crime, the court had decreed that none but the life of a prince could be accepted in his stead—that if the king's son did not love the man so as to die for him, the culprit must suffer the penalty himself.

The king heard of it, and reasoned thus: This man is proud, self-willed, and wickedly ambitious, heading a seditious conspiracy to overthrow my authority and usurp my place; but instead of letting him die, I will die for him, in order to win him to be a loyal subject of my universal government which I have undertaken to establish, in which to love and obey me forever; indeed, so passionate will be his devotion that, if called to it, he will even lay down his life in defence of my honor. I know that if I could show him, and all others who hear of it, the full measure of my love, but which can only be done by making the greatest sacrifice of which I am capable, which is the life of my only begotten son—indeed, myself, embodied in human form. This is the demand, and the royal sacrifice shall be made. "Peradventure, for a good man, some would even dare to die." "Greater love hath no man than this, that a man lay down his life for his friend." (John 15: 13.) "But God commendeth his love toward us in that, while we were yet sinners, Christ died for us." (Rom. 5: 7, 8.) "Hereby perceive we the love of God, because he laid down his life for us; and we ought to lay down our lives for the brethren." (1 John 3: 16.) Before the day arrived for the execution of the condemned criminal, the king-father gave the life of his only son to ransom the life of his rebellious enemy.   The son, the prince, died, but the culprit lived, and, overwhelmed by the boundless love of the king and father, his pride gave way, and his self-will gave place to the deepest contrition and humiliation for ever having done an act displeasing to so good, loving, and gracious a friend ; and from thenceforth he would have laid down his life rather than offend his great saviour.   "He loved much, for he had much forgiven."   The father and son were glorified by such an act, and, becoming widely known, it drew around the king a class of such loyal, loving subjects as could have been gained in no other conceivable way.   Here is the philosophy of the grand and glorious gospel of God, as taught in the Scriptures of truth.   This is the system of revealed religion which Ingersoll utterly misconceives, and against which he wages an unnatural and, for himself, a ruinous warfare.   "Let the potsherds strive with the potsherds of the earth ; but woe unto him that striveth with his Maker !"   (Isa. 45 : 9.)

Two Resurrections to Fit Men for the Kingdom.

The great change through which a man must pass, in order to enjoy the association of his Maker, requires two resurrections.   The first comes by so believing the gospel that it produces penitence, humiliation, and godly obedience ; and the second, that to immortality at the last day ; he is then a fit subject for the kingdom of God to be established in the new-made world.   The fulfilment of all the promises relating to this reward is *salvation*.   It is salvation, because it places its recipients forever beyond the liability of possible want or harm.   They have obtained that world in which they cannot die ; and with whom God himself, in personal Immanuelization, forever dwells, just as they do with each other.   That he is the destined re-creator is the doctrine of Moses and the Prophets, and from whom it was revealed to John thus: "And I heard a great voice out of heaven, saying, Be-

hold ! the tabernacle of God is with men, and he will
dwell with them, and they shall be his people, and God
himself shall be with them, and be their God. And
God shall wipe away all tears from their eyes ; and there
shall be no more death, neither sorrow, nor crying,
neither shall there be any more pain ; for the former
things are passed away. And he that sat upon the
throne said, Behold ! *I make all things new.* And he
said unto me, It is done. Write ; for these words are
true and faithful. I am Alpha and Omega ; the beginning and the end ; which was dead and am alive again
forever more. I will give unto him that is athirst of
the fountain of the water of life freely. He that overcometh shall inherit all things ; and I will be his God,
and he shall be my son, but the fearful, and unbelieving,
and the abominable, and murderers, and whoremongers,
and sorcerers, and idolaters, and all liars, shall have their
part in the lake which burneth with fire and brimstone ;
this is the second death.'' (Rev. 21 : 3–8.) Here are
the inhabitants of the new heaven and new earth, constituting a world—"the world to come, world without
end "—all dwelling in perfect and endless safety ; they
are now saved. This is salvation, and until it is thus
possessed its inheritors and heirs are saved by faith, believing they will then be saved.

Salvation Completed at the End of this World.

It is obvious that until the saints are actually thus
saved, they are only saved by faith, and it is a contradiction in terms to say a man is actually saved—actually
safe—while he is liable to suffer the first or second death,
of the first of which it is written : " Who shall deliver
them who through fear of death were all their life subject
to bondage,'' and from which the resurrection to immortality alone exempts. It is also declared, " We are
saved by hope,'' that is, we hope to be saved when the
salvation comes, and, when bestowed, necessarily supersedes the possibility of faith, faith and possession being
incompatible with each other : " Receiving the end of

your faith, even the salvation of your souls" [yourselves].
(1 Pet. 1 : 9.) It is also called being saved by grace
through faith : the grace, the salvation, being the gift of
God.   The man who had forfeited his estate, and life,
had nothing wherewith to pay, and as both were restored
to him, it must have been by grace, gift, favor, which
terms mean the same in Scripture. The spirit of the grace
—the reflex power of the anticipation of such reward,
such triumph—commences in this life, by the resurrection
of the heart, the religious nature, from a state of indifference or hatred to one of absorbing interest and love for
its Maker ; but the salvation is the substance of all the
gracious promises God has given to his people, and to be
awarded "at the resurrection of the just."   Peter sums
up the argument thus : " Blessed be the God and father
of our Lord Jesus Christ, which, according to his abundant mercy, hath begotten us again unto a lively hope [a
hope of eternal life] by the resurrection of Jesus Christ
from the dead, to an inheritance incorruptible, undefiled, and that fadeth not away, reserved in heaven for
you [the new heaven] who are kept by the power of God
through faith unto salvation, ready to be revealed in the
last time [the salvation thus to be revealed is wholly inconsistent with the idea of its possession prior to that
time] : whom having not seen, ye love ; in whom, though
now ye see him not, yet believing, ye rejoice with joy
unspeakable and full of glory [if the anticipation of the
inheritance, the salvation, gives such joy, what will be that
of its possession ! but here, when faith ends salvation
begins].   Wherefore gird up the loins of your mind, be
sober, and hope to the end for the grace [gift of salva-
tion] that is to be brought unto us at the revelation of
Jesus Christ."   (1 Pet. 1.)

In this revelation of Jesus Christ's coming, he said to
John: " Behold ! I come quickly ; and my reward is with
me, to give every man according as his work shall be."
And to which the apostle responded : "Even so, come
Lord Jesus, come quickly ! " (Rev. 22.)   Here is the
salvation promised the saints of all ages, for having honored the word of the Lord of life and glory.   But when

he comes thus, it is to judge the world in righteousness, in view of which Isaiah says: "Behold! the Lord God will come with strong hand, and his arm shall rule for him. Behold! his reward is with him and his work before him." (Isa. 40 : 10.)   Here also the doom of those will be executed whose filthy lies and unholy rant ends in destruction.   How will the scoffer appear then in "standing up like a man," as Ingersoll says he is going to do? It is doubtful whether an angel-devil among the arraigned could be induced to stand by his side.   Hear him: "Faith is the infamy of infamies, and too absurd for refutation.   What man who ever thinks can believe that blood can appease God? and yet our entire system of religion is based upon that belief."   No, Mr. Scoffer! this is another of the low, blasphemous misrepresentations of which any man who has a respectable thought would be ashamed.   The religion taught in the Bible has its procuring cause in the love of God for man, and his incarnate death, involving the shedding of his blood, the sacrificial means to make it manifest to sinners, solely for the purpose of winning their love for himself in turn: "Thou shalt love the Lord thy God with all thy heart, and thy neighbor as thyself: on these two commandments hang all the law and the prophets."   In view of these revealed facts, what but a mixture of ignorance, hate, and madness, could make such a charge?

Again the scoffer says: "It is hard to conceive how the human mind can give assent to such terrible ideas, or how any sane man can read the Bible and still believe in the doctrine of inspiration."   In reply we may say, it is hard to conceive how any sane man could ever have read the Bible and remained so profoundly ignorant of the doctrines therein taught, or still to suppose them terrible, except to such sinners as he.   Thus far we have not found any of his ideas taught in the Bible; and it is impossible to conceive how a man who has the least respect for himself or for public opinion, who can put such lies and absurdities in the Bible as the teaching of inspiration or revelation.   Hear the lawyer and statesman again: "Whether the Bible is true or false, is of no consequence in comparison with the mental freedom of the race.'' The doctrine upon the question is that of obedience to law, whether civil or moral, as the basis of mental freedom, and everyone but Ingersoll knows that a man cannot lose his liberty but by violating the obligations law imposes. He says, '' Salvation through slavery is worthless.'' This is also a shallow untruth, for a man may submit to the most degrading form of slavery for a time in order to obtain a greater liberty ; and in order to obtain endless liberty he may submit not only to suffer the loss of liberty, but incur the severest imprisonment during his whole human life, even the loss of life itself, in order to obtain eternal liberty, '' the glorious liberty of the children of God in the world to come,'' and millions have suffered the loss of all things in the temporary world to make sure their salvation in the eternal.

He says, '' Salvation from slavery is inestimable.'' A man is a slave to the laws of his country when he violates their provisions, and he is the slave of sin when he has violated the laws of his Maker. The only freedom from either is by being pardoned by those against whom the crime was committed, or of suffering the penalty. But as Ingersoll don't believe in pardon, reconciliation, or atonement, which mean the same in Scripture, his slavery must remain ; and however inestimable eternal liberty may be, it is unavailable for him, except upon the condition that he gives up his fight against his Maker ; and we have no hope that he will do this. He is in the state of mind of a man who has told a lie so often that he believes it himself; he has repeated these studied lies so often and long about God and the Bible, that he believes them to be facts. The effect of receding from sunlight is to be involved in darkness, and to recede from the light of God's inspiration and revelation is to grope in mental and moral darkness. Christ says, '' If the light in you becomes darkness, how great is that darkness ! '' '' For this cause God shall send them strong delusions, that they may believe a lie ; that they all might be damned, because they believe not the truth, but had pleasure in unrighteousness.'' In the same line he also says, '' As long as a man believes the

Bible to be infallible, that book is his master. If a man believes the Bible to be infallible, he must believe an infallible being is its author, as a fallible being cannot write or dictate to be written an infallible book.'' Whether the Bible is a fallible or infallible book in nowise depends upon whether any man or all men believe or disbelieve it such, but wholly and absolutely upon its merits, or the evidence it contains of such an authenticity. If the Bible is infallible, having the Creator as its author, it is Ingersoll's master whether he believes it or not; and whether he believes in the existence of an infallible being or not, still God is his Maker and Master just the same. But it is not his master, nor is he its slave until he violates its commands and refuses to repent and obtain pardon; these acts master and enslave him, just as though he had violated the laws of his country, and there was power enough in the state to execute the penalty; they are his master and he is their slave. What a foolish idea that if he don't believe in the state or its laws, he is then a free man; and if he can succeed in inducing everybody to disbelieve the laws or the book containing them, then all will enjoy sweet mental and moral freedom !

Here is one of God's wayward creatures who objects to having even God his master; he cannot endure such slavery, but he would be master of God himself. His wrath cannot be appeased until he infuses his animus into the hearts of all others, and induces them to follow his example in not believing in God or the Bible; and that will be just the same as though there was no God, and the Bible was a fable.

What a conception of liberty, that cannot be contented so long as there is a being in the universe of superior power to his own, or as long as others believe in the existence of such a being ! This is the kind of freemen atheism with its freethinkerism makes, but who are, in fact, the slaves of perpetual anarchy.

We Cede One Claim to Ingersoll.

He says, " The civilization of this century is not the child of faith, but of unbelief—the result of free-thought." In replying to this claim we feel a little re-lief, as he does not charge it upon the Bible ; for it is a civilization when fraud and corruption are so general that men have lost faith in their fellow-men for the want of in-tegrity; and when oppression of moneyed monopolists upon even the bread and clothing of the people, are pro-verbially designated in their corporate capacity as having no souls ; and when robberies by bank-officers have be-come so general that men often prefer depositing their money in secret places and losing the interest, rather than in ordinary banks; and when the party spending the most money and giving away the greatest quantity of the drunkard's drink are the most likely to have their candi-dates elected to the offices of the United States and Eng-land ; when a large number of the bills passing Congress and the State Legislatures are known by the title of "put-up jobs ; " when the country is filled with crime, many of which are of the most unnatural character ; an almost universal disrespect for the aged and superiors, and of par-ents by their children ; and, to cap the climax, when In-gersoll can deliver this lecture "On the Gods," at Booth's Theatre, in New York City, and thousands pay extrava-gant prices for tickets and loudly applaud his blasphe-mous scoffs and low slanders of God and the Bible, and this, too, in full view of the historic fact that there never was any modern civilization where Christianity did not prevail. Yes ! Mr. Ingersoll, you are right for once— the civilization of this century is the child of unbelief, and if left to go on without intelligent and satisfactory ex-posure, its march must culminate in the re-enactment of the French atheistic reign of terror. The highest con-ception of freethought (so called) is that which rejects all restraint upon passion and reduces liberty to license, known better by the names—Socialism, Anarchism, and Nihilism. A freethinker said to the writer, at their convention in Rochester, New York, a few years ago: "We have reduced the number of capital crimes from thirteen in the laws of Moses, to only two." In reply we answered, "Yes, and you have increased the number and greatness of crime in the same ratio."

How the Prophecies may be Known to have been Inspired by God.

"All that it is necessary," says Ingersoll, "as it seems to me, to convince any reasonable person that the Bible is simply and purely a human invention, of barbarian origin, is to read it ; read it as you would any other book ; think of it as you would of any other ; get the bandage of reverence from your eyes ; drive from your heart the phantom of fear ; push from the throne of your brain the cobweb of superstition ; then read the Bible, and you will be amazed that for a moment you believed a Being of infinite wisdom, goodness, and purity, to be the author or such ignorance and atrocity." What he means to say here is, that if you wish to understand what the Bible teaches, you must read it just as I have done. Up to this point we have introduced and examined all the passages of Scripture which led Ingersoll to say those things just quoted about the Bible, and we feel certain that everyone who reads our book, just as he recommends to read the Bible, or in such a frame of mind and moral perception as to understand the ideas, they will be satisfied that Ingersoll does not deal honestly with a single passage, and that he does not understand one doctrine of the Bible ; and this conviction will be increasingly confirmed as we advance in exposing his ignorance of that book. It is amazing that a man thus ignorant of the Bible, should have the audacity to lay down rules before a New York audience, by which they should be governed in studying the Bible !—but

"Fools rush in where angels fear to tread."

To understand the Scriptures, is not simply to believe that the Being who made the world is their author, but to know that to be true, by logical demonstration, and to believe because of the evidence thus obtained. To know : First, that their teachings are in perfect harmony with themselves.   Second, that they are in perfect harmony with all the facts and phenomena of nature.   Third, that they contain the prehistoric record, or prophetic history of all the prominent events of the great nations of the world —more of which have been fulfilled in our day, or since the year 1848, than during any previous century—from which it follows that none but a Being able to see and calculate the development of events which he did not wish to come, but which would occur in the march of human society could thus write their history in advance ; and this is the character of the prophetic Scriptures, contained in Moses, the prophets, and the Book of Psalms.

As Ingersoll is profoundly ignorant of all this, of course he cannot conceive that anyone else knows what he does not know.   Hence the worthlessness of his opinions of the Bible.

God Challenges Man's Reason—Upon the Truth of Prophesy !

The great fact by which men may believe and know that the Scriptures originated in the mind of the Creator, is, that the events they predict come to pass.   Their author lays down this as a rule and test-principle by which every man may judge of the question for himself.   And if he will search the Scripture-predictions, and their historic fulfilment, as recorded by the civil historians of the world, some of whom are skeptics themselves, he will not only find evidence for belief, but a profound conviction amounting to experimental knowledge which leaves no room for doubt as to the truth of their inspiration.   The investigation is challenged by the use of such unequivocal language as the following, sent out to the priests of idolatry and reasoners—thinkers of the ages.   " Produce your cause, bring forth your strong reasons, saith the king of Jacob.   Let them show us what shall happen : Let them declare us things to come and show the former things what they be, that we may consider, and know the latter end of them; that we may know ye are gods; yea! do good, or do evil, that we may be dismayed." "Come and let us reason together saith the Lord." "I have declared the end from the beginning; and they went forth out of my mouth, and I did them suddenly, and they came to pass." (Isa. 49: 21–23, and 48: 3.) "And it shall come to pass, that whosoever will not hearken unto my words which the prophet shall speak in my name, I will require it of him. But the prophet, which shall presume to speak a word in my name, which I have not commanded him to speak, or shall speak in the name of other gods, even that prophet shall die. And if thou say in thy heart, how shall we know the word which the Lord hath not spoken?" [The answer is] "When a prophet speaketh in the name of the Lord, and the thing follow not nor come to pass, that is the thing the Lord hath not spoken, but the prophet hath spoken it presumptuously; thou shalt not be afraid of him." (Deut. 18: 19–22.) Here does the author of religious, prophetic Scripture subject it to the severest test of thought and reason. "I have not spoken in secret, in a dark place of the earth." (Isa. 49: 19.) That the predictions are general, covering the events connected with his Church in all ages and nations, running from the beginning of the world to its end, is thus also shown: "Surely the Lord God will do *nothing*; but he revealeth his secret unto his servants the prophets." (Amos 3: 7.)

All that had come to pass in former times he had revealed before they were done, and all that will come to pass, even to the end of the world, and beyond covering that of its recreation and the establishment of universal peace and righteousness. All this did he inspire his prophets to predict, and their scribes to write; therefore are the writings Scripture. Of course the prehistoric record is so complete, that nothing of importance connected with national and religious interests will ever come to pass which is not a subject of inspired revelation. The appeal is addressed to the intelligent of every age or period, to show by the history of their events or of the past, whether they have not been written in advance in this great book of God's inspiration. Hence, to read the Scriptures according to their own rules, therefore, understandingly, by comparing the predictions and their chronology of events with the records of profane history, is not only to believe, but to have certain knowledge of God being their author.

More of Ingersoll's Slander of Scripture.

The scoffer says: "One of these gods is reported to have given the following instructions concerning human slavery : 'If thou buy an Hebrew servant six years he shall serve ; but in the seventh he shall go out free. If he came in by himself, he shall go out by himself : if he were married, his wife shall go out with him. If his master have given him a wife, and she have born him sons and daughters : the wife and her children shall be her master's and he shall go out by himself. And if the servant shall plainly say, I love my master, my wife and my children ; I will not go out free : then his master shall bring him unto the judges ; he shall also bring him unto the door-post ; and bore his ear through with an awl ; and he shall serve him forever.' " (Ex. 21 : 26.) "According to this," says Ingersoll, "a man was given liberty upon condition that he would desert forever his wife and children. Did any devil ever force upon a husband, and father, so cruel and heartless an alternative ? Who can bend the knee to such a monster ? Who can pray to such a fiend ?" Here again we find the blasphemous scoffer belching forth his wilful ignorance and presumption. In proof of this charge, let us examine the terms and provisions of this law of the Mosaic code, with its modifications, and as limited by other laws and statutes.

In the first place, this was a Hebrew servant. Secondly, he went in to the employment of the master, knowing the terms of the service. Third, the wife his master gave him, was his own daughter, as he had no power to give any other woman in marriage, and the servant was his son-in-law, and the children his grandchildren. Fourth, he loved his master and did not want any larger liberty or better home than he already enjoyed. By this law the servant had a right to demand of his master that he should keep him, and this claim he put in before the judges. Instead, therefore, of its having been slavery for the servant to remain in the employment of this master, the law protected him against the power of the landlord to send him away, as he might not have been as profitable with his many children, to keep him, and there never were such laws as in this code for the protection of the poor against the rich. In the last place the term "forever," was not without end, as Ingersoll understands it, but was limited to the coming of the seven years' release, when this Hebrew servant, his wife and children, were as free as he who had been the master, and at which time his master was not to let him go away poor, but was compelled by the same law to give him liberally of everything he himself possessed, so that he should have another fair start in the battle of life.

Justice and Humanity of the Laws of Moses.

Some of the provisions of this law are as follows: " And if thy brother that dwelleth by thee be waxen poor, and be sold unto thee, thou shalt not compel him to serve as a bond-servant, but as an hired servant, and as a sojourner he shall be with thee, and shall serve thee until the [release] Jubilee: and then he shall depart, both he and his children with him, and shall return unto his own family, and unto the possession of his fathers, for they are my servants, which I brought forth out of the land of Egypt; they shall not be sold as bond-men. Thou shalt not rule over them with rigor, but shall fear thy God." (Lev. 25 : 39-45.) "And if thy brother, an Hebrew man, or woman, be sold unto thee, and serve thee six years; then in the seventh year thou shalt let him go out from thee free. And when thou sendest him out, thou shalt not let him go away empty, but thou shalt furnish him liberally out of thy flock, and out of thy floor, and out of thy wine press: of that wherewith the Lord thy God hath blessed thee thou shalt give unto him. For the poor shall never cease out of the land : therefore I command thee saying, Thou shalt open thy hand wide unto thy brother, to thy poor, and to thy needy, in thy land." (Deut. 15 : 11–14.) Here was so humane a law, that it enabled the poor to pay their debts without oppression. The creditor was obliged to give the debtor employment and support, including his family, while he was working out the debt. But if he was unable within a certain period to discharge it, there was a universal bankrupt law every fiftieth year, and which discharged every debt in the nation : not like the laws of our civilization, which Ingersoll claims to be the work of unbelief, which permits one creditor to seize on the property of a debtor and sacrifice the whole of it to get his pay, leaving the debtor still in debt, and all others unpaid, who, with his family, are thus reduced to a state of pauperism or starvation.

Here is the law which this master scoffer and blasphemer says is too bad for a devil to make, and he who made it is a monster—a fiend. Behold ! what a specimen of ignorance and madness ! But, lest Ingersoll or any of his freethinking clan of transformers, instead of reformers, should further object that the laws of the release and of the Jubilee only applied to Hebrews, and that all other nations might be bond-men and bond-women during life, we proceed to show that there are provisions in the Mosaic code by which all strangers and sojourners might become Hebrew citizens, thereby equal with them before the law, and share all its benefits. These were the keeping of the " Passover," and the offering of the " burnt sacrifice," which were in our language " the naturalization laws " of the Hebrew nation. " And the Lord said unto Moses and Aaron, This is the ordinance of the passover, there shall no stranger eat thereof ; but every man's servant that is bought for money, when thou hast circumcised him, then shall he eat thereof. A foreigner and a hired servant shall not eat thereof. And when a stranger shall sojourn with thee, and will keep the pass-

over to the Lord, let all his males be circumcised, and
then let him come near and keep it, and he shall be as
one born in the land. One law shall be for him that is
home-born, and unto the stranger and sojourner among
you." (Ex. 12 : 43, 49.) If it shall be said it was a
hard condition, the abandonment of their religion, we answer that every religion but that imposed by the Creator
is a corruption of it, and this made the demand of the
sacrifice of the false and ruinous corruption for the true
and holy religion of the one living and true God. The
passover taught the Hebrew nation to keep in remembrance their deliverance from a long and cruel bondage,
and continually reminded them not to subject others to
unjust servitude.

"And it shall come to pass, when your children shall
say unto you, What mean ye by this service? that ye shall
say, It is the Lord's passover, who passed over your
houses of the children of Israel in Egypt, when he smote
the Egyptians, and delivered our houses. And the
people bowed the head and worshipped." (Ex. 12 : 25–
27.) The passover also symbolically taught the death
of Christ : " For even Christ our passover is sacrificed
for us ; therefore let us keep the feast." (1 Cor. 5 : 7.)
The blood of the passover lamb was sprinkled upon the
lintel of the door of each Hebrew dwelling in Egypt,
seeing which the angel of death passed over all such,
while in all others the oldest son or daughter was smitten
with death that night. The passover therefore taught
the two fundamental principles of the Christian religion :
the sacrificial death of Christ to reveal his love for men,
and his resurrection from the dead as the pledge of that
of his saints. This is the religion, then, which the other
nations were to gain by offering the passover ; and if done
unto the Lord, done in the spirit of its intent, having
faith in Christ's death and resurrection, they became
joint heirs with him to the immortal resurrection and
endless inheritance of the new and redeemed world.
Thus would they answer the end and only end for which
they were made ; consequently, if they do not meet this
condition, every man is a failure. Instead, therefore, of

requiring the bond-servant to become a Hebrew convert being an objection, it was the greatest blessing which could have been conferred upon him.

Wisdom of the Laws of Moses to Secure Justice.

The wisdom of the laws of Moses to secure justice and equality may be further seen, and the wanton ignorance of Ingersoll exposed. We introduce its following provisions: " Judges and officers shalt thou make thee in all thy gates, which the Lord thy God giveth thee, throughout all thy tribes ; and they shall judge the people with just judgment. Thou shalt not wrest judgment ; thou shalt not respect persons, neither take a gift; for a gift doth blind the eyes of the wise, and pervert the words of the righteous. That which is altogether just shalt thou follow, that thou mayest live, and inherit the land the Lord thy God giveth thee. Thou shalt not plant a grove of trees near the altar of the Lord thy God [to add beautiful attractions of human invention to the place where God alone should be thought of and worshipped]; neither shalt thou set thee up any image; which the Lord thy God hateth. And if there be found among you a man or woman, that hath wrought wickedness in the sight of the Lord thy God, in transgressing his covenant, and hath gone and served other gods and worshipped them, either the sun or moon, or any of the host of heaven, which I have not commanded him ; and it be told thee, and when thou hast inquired diligently, and it is true and certain, then shalt thou bring forth the man or woman, unto the gates, and shalt stone them till they die. At the mouth of two witnesses, shall he that is worthy of death, be put to death ; but at the mouth of one witness he shall not be put to death. The hands of the witnesses shall be first upon him to put him to death, and afterward the hands of all the people. So shalt thou put away the evil from among you.'' (Deut. 16 : 17, 18.) Here is the very highest philosophy for·the prevention of crime, and there is no code of common law, in any civil state, whose substance and best features to secure this end are not borrowed from the laws of Moses. But here is Ingersoll, a lawyer, and yet sees nothing in them but a tissue of ignorance and oppression, too bad for a devil to enact and execute. "But wisdom is justified of her children;" and a man must be wise himself to discover and appreciate wisdom in others.

CHAPTER VIII.

FUTURE PUNISHMENT CONFOUNDED WITH MYTHOLOGI-
CAL TORMENTS.

In describing God's punishment of the wicked, Inger-soll uses the plural as though there were a number of gods thus engaged, while all the connections show he aims all his darts at the living God ; but even this is hypocritical, as he does not believe there is any such God, and is only used as a decoy, to drag the weak, who, for the time being may not have sufficient evidence to demonstrate God's existence in order to draw them to his own despicable level. He says : "All these gods threaten to torment the souls of their enemies forever ; did any devil ever make so infamous a threat ?" He evidently uses the word forever in the sense of the mythological tantalus tartareus, or in their tartarean dens, wherein endless miseries were inflicted ; but Christ said, " Fear him which is able to destroy both soul and body in hell." (Matt. 10 : 28.) Destroy does not mean to preserve and perpetuate. He said again : " These shall go away into everlasting punishment," and Paul explains the punishment to be everlasting destruction. " And to you who are troubled rest with us, when the Lord Jesus shall be revealed from heaven with his mighty angels, in flaming fire taking vengeance on them that know not God, and that obey not the gospel of our Lord Jesus Christ : who shall be punished with everlasting *destruc-tion* from the presence of the Lord and from the glory of his power, when he shall come to be glorified in his saints and to be admired in all them that believe in that day." (2 Thess. 1 : 7–10.) In regard to the punish-ment of the wicked, the Scriptures also speak thus : " Thou hast destroyed the wicked, thou hast put out

their name forever and ever, their memorial is perished
with them." (Ps. 9.)

The word forever, or forever and ever, does not always mean without end; but is limited to the duration of
the thing to which it is applied, and in this case to mortal man, and the wicked will always be mortal, in contrast to the righteous, who, from the resurrection, will be
immortal.   It was consistent for Pagan philosophy, or
Egyptian mythology, to inflict endless misery, as they
taught that the soul was the man proper, and that it was
immortal.   It was also consistent for them to change the
name of their gods to demons, who could be so cruel as
to keep man alive on purpose to torment him.   It was
also consistent for these Pagans, who believed all punishment should be reformatory, to invent the doctrine of
purgatory which was taught by Socrates, and his pupil
Plato.   It is also consistent for the Roman Catholic
Church, having adopted these heathen doctrines, to teach
endless misery.   But whatever is meant by the threat to
which Ingersoll alludes, as taught in the Scriptures, it is
the word of the Maker of those against whom it is pronounced, and it makes no difference.   Though it be esteemed infamous by those who incur its infliction, the
result will be the same; and as Ingersoll is one of God's
bitterest enemies, he is among the last who has any right
to remonstrate, and all that is necessary, in order to have
the experience, is to continue the fight against God, his
maker.   As to his praise of the devil for never having
made such a threat, it is illy founded, from the fact that
the devil has no power to do such an act, and the devil's
modesty, in comparison with that of Ingersoll, has kept
him from coming out in a public speech, loudly proclaiming he despised and defied God; and we have no doubt
but that the devil himself despises his would-be heroic son,
for having made such a fool of himself.

The scoffer says again: "The first account we have
of the devil, is found in that purely scientific book, called
Genesis."   This sarcastic fling is an attempt to make his
hearers believe him to be a scientist, and of such a high
type that he knows the statements of Genesis, touching

nature, and the creation of the world, to be erroneous. But we have already shown those statements, as to the origin of things, are philosophic necessities; and as a consequence the erroneous claims of modern geology, and evolution, whose conclusions Ingersoll adopts, not because of any evidence they furnish in defence of the hypothesis, but because he loves to have it so. " If the account given in Genesis is really true, ought we not, after all, to thank the serpent?   He was the first schoolmaster —the first advocate of learning, and friend of inquiry—of doubt—of investigation.   Give me the storm and tempest of thought and action, rather than the dead calm of ignorance and faith! Banish me from Eden when you will; but first let me eat of the fruit of the tree of knowledge!"   If Adam had not disobeyed the inhibition of his Maker until our day, Ingersoll would have done it, and if for no other reason, than to win the infamous popularity it would have given him.   The knowledge which his schoolmaster wished his pupils to learn, was the experience resulting from disobedience to the commands of their Creator, of course, becoming loyal subjects of their new schoolmaster—the Devil.

The Subtle Schoolmaster's Opening Address.

His Satanic majesty, in his opening address, said: " Kind friends, you are desirous of having knowledge—you wish to be wise, your Maker has endowed you with this passion, and you are ignorant of a good many things you should know: some of these I have experienced, others I anticipate and apprehend by faith, as I have every reason for believing I shall have fulness of such knowledge.   This you can only obtain by becoming my dutiful students.   God hath said, ' Ye shall surely die,' if you eat of the tree of the knowledge of evil.   You now have no conception of the nature of this death, and ye shall not surely die, as you have free access to the fruit of the tree of life.   By partaking of this, your physical system will be kept always youthful; you will therefore live forever, and as you are ignorant of what it is to die, you will then have this knowledge. To die, implies sickness and pain—its precursors and accompaniments. Take my advice, and you will no longer be ignorant—you will then be introduced into the storm and tempest ; but you will have the enjoyment of these my blessings of knowledge. In your present condition and environment, you have everything you wish—the very earth brings forth spontaneously, and you have the dead calm of ignorance, of want and labor : this knowledge I propose to teach ; and why should you continue longer in the dead calm ?

Then there is to be a second edition of death, preparatory to which you are to have a resurrection to shame and everlasting contempt, of which you will also remain forever ignorant, if you obey God ; but if you will investigate, think, and reason like a man, you will certainly be wise and know all about these things. I myself am laboring under the chains of the darkness of despair, against the judgment of the great day—last day, when the wicked of all nations shall be gathered together to be punished, because they knew their Lord's will, but did it not. The place of punishment is to be a lake of fire and brimstone, kindled on the earth at that time for the purpose, and into which a Being called the Son of man is to cast me and all liars, all my children, " all of whom are to be burned up, that shall leave of them neither root nor branch ; " " they shall consume away into smoke," " they shall become nothing," " shall be as though they had not been." This work is to be executed by his faithful angels. Of course you know nothing about this now, nor from my words can you have the least conception of them, and if you refuse to take me as your schoolmaster and give heed to my instruction you will always be ignorant ; but if you will listen to my voice, disbelieve the word and commands of God, doubt his existence and cherish your doubts, think, be a freethinker, reason and investigate, then you will be wise and have the experimental knowledge of evil, for you must take nothing by faith, and this will enable you to contrast what you have gained and what you have lost, what it is to be cast out of Eden and enter on the storm and tempest of freethink-erism, mental independence.   Then take my advice :

> Hear and obey my lies,
> Eat the fruit and be wise !

It is for this knowledge, Ingersoll says, " We should thank the serpent : he was the first to inspire in human ears the sacred word *liberty*—the creator of ambition." These satanic words were the lies : " Thou shalt not surely die ; ye shall become as gods."   This was a lie of the devil about his own experience.   He was an angel, and instead of being exalted by his ambitious war against his Creator, he became a devil, whose destruction the Son of man is to execute at the judgment in the last day.   This is not only the fate awaiting him, but all his men-servants who obey his lies and assume the ambitious liberty of setting up their will against that of their Maker. It is the spirit of Ingersollism to make war upon every-thing above itself.   It is that of the conspirator, anar-chist, the nihilist :

> " In pride, presumptuous pride, man's error lies ;
> All quit their sphere and rush into the skies.
> Men would be angels—angels would be Gods ;
> Aspiring to be Gods, angels fell ;
> Aspiring to be angels, men rebel :
> He who reverses nature's laws
> Sins against the eternal cause."   —POPE.

The Scoffer's Admiration of the Devil's Modesty.

He says : " The serpent was the author of modesty, of progress, and of civilization."   " The woman said, The serpent beguiled me, and I did eat."   This sneaking, deceptive manner of approach, Ingersoll calls modesty. He should have been bold, ambitious, like the Colonel, not lowly creeping into the garden, but walking up-rightly, confront his Maker face to face, and not wait to do it behind his back, just as this faithful servant of his is doing, but who has not the courage to meet a human antagonist face to face in public debate, as he refused to do when challenged by the author of this book ; and it should have been at the opportune moment, when the Lord had delivered his charge to Adam and Eve. Had the devil not been a coward, he would have walked up boldly and said, God, you want to keep these people in ignorance, which I despise, and I also despise you and defy your power ! and I call on these human progenitors to trample your restraining laws under their feet, and have a drink of knowledge, assert their liberty, and become gods themselves, and know all about evil, be wise. And I tell you, Adam and Eve, you had better obey me and become progressive, even though you are turned out of Eden ; have the noble consolation to know you are under no will but your own ; everything else is superstition :

"Better reign in hell than serve in heaven."

Behold how Ingersoll has cast off the modesty of his prototypic serpent !

Ingersoll's Foolish Criticism of Job's Trial.

To obtain a glimpse of the civilization and progress of our century, of which the serpent is the author, we must look into the cities, the centres of the civilization, in order to ascertain the standard of the devildom progress. We invite the candid attention of our readers to the incomparable number of infamous dens wherein is taught the knowledge the devil teaches, and seen the horrid combination of drunkenness, prostitution, and murder, and where every other crime is concocted. If the tree is known by its fruits, so certain is it, even in the closing period of our century, that men are led captive by Satan at his will to a degree of God-defiance, a depth and universality of crime, unknown in the annals of the world since the flood ; an era when almost universal distrust among men prevails, which is the legitimate outgrowth of as extensive dishonesty. As a house divided against itself cannot stand, or that Satan will cast out Satan, the development must go on, and the appalling harvest be

reached.   According to Ingersoll, this unbelief of the
devil and his children is the honorable source from
whence has flowed our modern civilization and progress,
but which the facts show to be the progress of all the low
sentiments and vile crimes ever known to human devilhood.   What has been the principle cause of this state of
things is the atheistic teaching of evolution, under the
false pretension of its being science.   As it leaves no
work for a God to do in bringing the world and man
into existence, he is not their owner, and has no right to
command their service.   In view of which these atheists
exhort men to give up the superstition and fear of a God
who has no existence.   Of course, the only remedy for
the evil is to expose the false science by showing the
true, as we have done in this and other works.

Ingersoll says: "The worst thing the devil ever did
was his abuse of Job," and in his narration of the circumstances he foolishly flatters himself that he sets the
whole book aside by a lie, a scoff, and a joke.   Here are
his words : "The basest thing recorded of the devil is
what he did concerning Job and his family ; and that was
done by the express permission of one of the gods, and to
decide a little difference of opinion between their serene
highnesses as to the character of ' my servant Job.' "   A
little mind belittles everything it looks at, especially if it
hates the thing ; and Ingersoll's intense hatred of all the
Bible records reduces his comprehension of them to the
utmost insignificance.   A striking example is what he
here sees and says about the book of Job.   In replying to
his funny words we may say, that in the east where Job
lived, and in his day, the people were not polytheists nor
atheists, and held to the existence of one, and but one,
living God.   Christ, Job's Redeemer, and the only Redeemer, promised Job deliverance from the power of
death and ransom from the grave, which would be his
salvation ; believing which, Job was saved by faith while
alive in the world.   The hope of such a salvation encouraged him to maintain his integrity amid all his sufferings and losses, so that when informed of the death of
all his children, he exclaimed, "The Lord giveth, and

the Lord taketh away; and blessed be the name of the Lord." Job's wife was one of the devil's modest children, free and ambitious, like her brother Ingersoll, and, using his phraseology, said to Job, "Curse God and die." She understood that kind of devilish progress would bring death, but being on the devil's side, he did not wish to afflict or kill her. In reply to the freethought of the woman, Job said: "You talk like the foolish women; shall we receive good at the hand of the Lord and not evil?" He did not think, with Ingersoll, that the Lord was his servant, and had no right to do anything that crossed the will of his serene highness.

The philosophy of Job's friends did not comprehend the doctrine of the resurrection of the dead, the fundamental truth of Christianity, and that they might be thus informed, God gave Job an inspired revelation, or transfiguration of it, just as he saw it would appear when accomplished; as an architect sees and knows a mansion will appear, when built according to his plan. When Job received the vision, and for fear it might be lost to the world, or corrupted by tradition, he exclaimed: "Oh! that my words were now written! Oh! that they were printed in a book! that they were graven with an iron pen and lead in the rock forever! for I know that my Redeemer liveth, and that he shall stand at the latter day upon the earth: and though, after my skin, worms destroy this body, yet in my flesh shall I see God: whom I shall see for myself, and mine eyes shall behold, and not another; though my reins be consumed within me."

Job here saw the God whom his friends entitled "the Almighty," but not being in the Abrahamic line, who alone had the written Scriptures, these had by corrupting tradition mostly lost sight of the knowledge of the resurrection of the dead, as introductory to future life. In order to give Job and the other branches of the human family, outside of the chronological line of Adam's generations, a clearer revelation of the resurrection and of the Redeemer, being God himself in human form, who was the resurrection and the life, the devil was permitted to afflict him to the utmost of his ability, without taking his life ; God foreseeing that these miseries would call together the other wise men of the country to mourn with their friend, and that hearing this truth from Job would correct their errors.   Job was now confronted with death and desired to die, but was kept back from suicide by his vague hope of living again, implied in the question : " If a man die, shall he live again ? "   After the Lord had given Job the new revelation and healed him of his sufferings, he said to Eliphaz the Temanite, My wrath is kindled against thee, and thy two friends : for ye have not spoken of me the thing that is right, as my servant Job hath.   Therefore take unto you now seven bullocks and seven rams, and go to my servant Job, and offer up for yourselves a burnt offering ; and my servant Job shall pray for you ; for him will I accept : lest I shall deal with you after your folly, in that ye have not spoken of me the thing which is right, like my servant Job.   So they did as the Lord commanded them ; the Lord also accepted Job, and the Lord turned the captivity of Job when he prayed for his friends ; also the Lord gave Job twice as much as he had before." (Job 42 : 7–10.) Another object for permitting this occurrence was to give an example of patience under the most extreme losses and sufferings which, by the ordinary concurrence of events, would never be exceeded, and if Job bore it without turning against his God, who he believed inflicted it, there would be no excuse in the future for those who suffered less to do so.   That it is used for this purpose in Scripture shows it to have been one of these objects.   James says: " Take my brethren the prophets [and Job was one of God's prophets], who have spoken in the name of the Lord, for an example of suffering, affliction, and patience. Behold, we count them happy which endure.   Ye have heard of the patience of Job, and we have seen the end of the Lord ; that the Lord is very pitiful, and of tender mercy." (James 5 : 10, 11.)

The event also shows that the devil cannot inflict physical evil upon the servants of the Lord, if he can upon others, and the latter are his friends—" our friends," says Ingersoll ; and if he does afflict these thus, he is meaner than his servant Ingersoll gives him credit for. The only use the devil makes of his faithful servants is to seduce the saints of God to become his servants. Another fact taught in this Scripture is that the devil is not yet in hell, but walking up and down in the earth, and that he is often unable to accomplish what he undertakes, and which may do his cause vastly more harm than good. As the devil is a liar, he may here falsify his location ; but it is confirmed by the apostle Peter, thus : " Be sober, be vigilant, because your adversary the devil, as a roaring lion, walketh about, seeking whom he may devour : whom resist, steadfast in the faith, knowing that the same afflictions are accomplished in your brethren that are in the world." Thus are we obliged to follow this man's cavils, not merely by opposing assertion by assertion, opinion by opinion, sarcasm with sarcasm, or ridicule with ridicule, but by reason and argument to have investigated those passages of Scripture against which the scoffer aims his illogical, unphilosophic, and unscientific thrusts, as to show them to be such, and to present the ideas which the same passages teach ; and by this means qualify those who have read or heard Ingersoll to refute him, as well as all other sceptics of the past, present, or future.

Did we not know that this lecture on the gods of Ingersoll's has been published in various forms and spread over the country, it would be a serious question whether we should give it this publicity. Neither can what he pulls down in a single lecture be built up in the same brief space. A city of a thousand years' growth may be laid in ashes in a single night. What Ingersoll says about the record of Job's affliction and what we were obliged to say in answer illustrates the idea. We may also add, that to defend the Scriptures to the satisfaction of careful readers, against which the arch sceptic says of them, forever disarms him and all classes of infidels who question the fact that they teach the existence of a personal devil and a personal God, the one a creature and the other his Creator. Ingersoll is armed with all of that which all the sceptics of the past have said, and with the conclusions or assertions of modern sceptical science—astronomy, geology, and evolution, as to the origin of the world, which are held to be irreconcilable with the statements of the work as recorded in the book of Genesis—and of course to refute him is to refute all the rest. Not to do this thoroughly, producing a sufficient amount of evidence to expose the fallacy of all such attacks, might better not have been attempted.

Hard Driven for Matter to Ridicule.

Says Ingersoll, " Man, having always been the physical superior of woman, accounts for the fact that most of the high gods have been males. Had woman been the physical superior, the powers supposed to be the rulers of nature would have been women, and instead of being represented in the apparel of man, they would have been caricatured in trains, low-necked dresses, and back-hair." If he had legitimately carried out the idea by saying the men would have been beardless, and their voice tuned an octave higher—in a word, that the sex had changed places, it would have shown the absurdity of the allusion, heightened by the supposition that women could have been the leaders in war and government simply by exchanging habiliments, and not letting their hair grow long. All we were going to say in answer to this was, Foolishness ! but we will add that it shows to what an extremity its author is driven to drag in such silly things in attempting to degrade the gods, as he expresses it, but means the only living and true God ; for who would have paid to hear him lecture on the gods if none believed there was a living God in existence ? The sentimental sympathy so often expressed by Ingersoll for the suffering women, sinners against the laws of God, forbids his making any other comparison of superiority of man than the mere physical brute force, not being able to attain to the conception that all power is of the mind. " Nothing," says he, " can be plainer than that each nation gives to its god its peculiar characteristics, and that each individual gives to his god his personal peculiarities.'' In the history of idolatrous worship, no image or likeness of man or woman has been so universally adored as those of the sun, moon, and planets. Even the names of the days of the week had their origin in the division of the worship paid to the divinities, commencing with that of the sun. Sun-day, so named because dedicated to the worship of the sun. Moon-day (Sax.), the particular day for the worship of the moon. Tues-day (among the ancients, Tug), the Teutonic deity of war and combat which it deified. Wednes-day derives its name from Oden, the Scandinavian deity, the father of Thor and the Woden of the Saxons. Thor, in Scandinavian mythology, was the son of Odin and Frega, the god of thunder, and from which we have Thursday. Fri-day is from Frigga (Sax., Frician); the sixth day of the week was consecrated to the worship of these gods. And Satur-day to the worship of the planet Saturn.

These, and not men and women images, were the most ancient gods of idol-worship, and the most elevating, because of their shining splendor and importance to the vitality and fruitfulness of plants and animals ; and yet the nations thus worshipping gave no national peculiarities to these gods, much less were they conceived to possess any peculiarities of the worshipper, but rather that they gathered from them their own most prominent peculiarities ; and instead of the people making these national gods what they were, the gods made the people what they themselves were, exactly reversing Ingersoll's statements and conceptions of ancient mythology. It would have been amazing had any other than he to have so construed the lessons taught by the existence of the mythological gods ; but any absurdity may be expected from this man's reasonless rant. From Ingersoll's flippant talk about ancient mythology it might be inferred that he was a classical scholar, at least well acquainted with the mythic sciences, while the effort shows his ignorance both of its historic facts and their philosophic teaching, which almost universally goes to show that the gods the people made were conceived only to represent or symbolize the one living and supreme God and Creator of

the world, and its lowest form of worship was that which
made the lights and flames they themselves had kindled
sacred; but this sacredness was conceived to symbolize
the great lights of heaven—the sun, moon, and stars.

Plato's Discourse on the Formation of the World.

We learn from the discourse of Plato on the formation
of the world, that he attributed the existence of all gods
and things to the fiat of the one Supreme Deity.   On
one occasion Plato's friends implored him to guide them
to the true origin of the world ; complying, he seated
himself in the temple of Minerva, and said : " Feeble
mortals that we are ! is it for us to penetrate the secrets
of the divinity ? for us, the wisest of whom is to the Supreme Being what an ape is to us ! [Behold, how our
generation has degenerated; taking Ingersoll as its representative, who, being an evolutionist, traces his pedigree
to an ape, and which seems to be confirmed by contrasting the sublimity of this discourse of a Grecian philosopher who lived more than two thousand years ago, with
the low, foolish harangue delivered by Ingersoll at
Booth's Theatre on the gods.]   I entreat him to inspire
me with such ideas and such language as will be pleasing
to him and conformable to reason.   The God which I
declare unto you is a God, single, immutable, and infinite ; the centre of all perfection, and the inexhaustible
source of intelligence and being.   Before he had created
the universe, before he had externally displayed his
power, he *was ;* for he had no beginning, he was in
himself, he existed in the profundity of eternity.   No !
my expressions do not correspond to the elevation of my
ideas, nor my ideas to the sublimity of my subject.
Thus, from all eternity existed God, the author of all
good ; and that model according to which he had determined to reduce matter to order."   That it was not the
opinion of heathenism that men created even the subordinate gods, as Ingersoll says, we have the following
from the same discourse : " And now the Author of all
things thus addressed the genii whom he had made and

to whom he had committed the government of the stars : Ye gods, who owe to me your birth, listen to my sovereign commands. You have not a title to immortality, but you may participate in it by the power of my will, more potent than the bonds which unite the parts of which you are composed. It remains for you to give perfection to this grand whole, to fill with inhabitants the seas, the earth, and the air. Were these creatures to receive life from me, they would be exempt from the empire of death, and become equal to the gods themselves ; I therefore commit to you the care of producing them : delegates of my power, unite to perishing bodies the germs of immortality, which you shall receive from me ; and form those beings who may command over animals to remain subject to you. Let them receive birth at your command, live to increase by your benefactions, and after death, let them be united to you and share in your happiness." How does this philosophic reasoner reverse Ingersollism—that the people made the gods, and that in his narrow conception no god or being exists higher or greater than himself? This is the testimony of Plato, the pupil of Socrates, and having had his education in Egypt, understood the mythological doctrines of all the past ages.

Testimony of Xenophon : God in Nature.

Xenophon was one of the pupils of Plato and the historian of Socrates, whose testimony upon the nature and history of gods whom Ingersoll says the people made, may appear in contrast. Xenophon has transmitted to us a conversation of Socrates with Euthydemus upon providence, which is one of the finest passages found in the writings of the ancients, and which is as follows : " Did you ever reflect within yourself, how much care the gods have taken to bestow upon man all that is necessary for his nature ? Never, I assure you, replied Euthydemus. You see, continued Socrates, how necessary light is, and how precious that gift of the gods ought to appear to us. Without it, added Euthydemus, we should be like the blind, and all nature as if it were dead, or were not; but because we have occasion for suspense and relaxation, they have also given us the night for our repose. You are right, and for this we ought to render them continual praises and thanksgiving.

They have ordained that the sun, that bright, luminous star, should preside over the day, to distinguish its different parts, and that its light should not only serve to discover the wonders of nature, but to dispense light and heat; and at the same time they commanded the moon and stars to illuminate the night of its darkness and obscurity. Is there anything more admirable than this variety, or vicissitude of day and night, of light and darkness, of labor and rest; and all this for the good and convenience of man?" Socrates enumerates in like manner, the infinite advantages we receive from fire and water, in the occasions of life, and continues to discourse upon the wonderful attention of providence in all that regards us.

"What say you, pursued he, upon the sun's return after winter, to revisit us, and that as the fruits of one season wither and decay, he ripens new ones to succeed them? That, having rendered man this service, he retires, lest he should incommode him by excess of heat; and then after having removed to a certain point, which he could not pass without putting us in danger of perishing with cold, that he returns in the same track to resume his place in those parts of the heavens where his presence is most beneficial to us? And because we could endure neither the cold nor the heat, if we were to pass in an instant from the one extreme to another, do you not admire, that whilst this star approaches, and removes so slowly, the two extremities arrive by almost insensible degrees? Is it possible not to discover, in this disposition of the seasons of the year, a providence and goodness, not only attentive to our necessities, but even our delights and enjoyments? All these things, said Euthydemus, make me doubt, whether the gods have any other employment than to shower down their gifts and grace upon mankind. There is one point, however, that puts me at a stand, which is, that the brute animals partake in all these bless-

ings as well as ourselves.   Yes, replied Socrates; but do
you not observe, that all these animals subserve only
man's service?   The strongest and most vigorous of
them, he subjects to his will, and makes them tame and
gentle, and uses them successfully in his wars, his labors,
and the occupations of life.   What if we consider man in
himself?"   Here, Socrates examines the diversity of the
seasons, by the ministry of which man enjoys all that is
best and excellent in nature, the vivacity of his wit, and
the force of his reason, which exalt him infinitely above
all other animals; the wonderful gift of speech, by means
of which we communicate our thoughts reciprocally,
publish our laws, and govern states.   "The Great God
himself [this shows that Socrates acknowledged but one
supreme God, the sole author of all beings, and as superior to all others as the Creator is to the creature, all of
which, whether animate or inanimate, are ministers of
his will], who has formed the universe, and supports the
stupendous work, whose every part is finished with the
utmost goodness and harmony; and who preserves them
perpetually, in immortal vigor, and causes them to obey
him with a never-failing punctuality, and a rapidity not
to be followed by our imagination: this God makes
himself sufficiently visible by the endless wonders of
which he is the author."   But to all this and of all this
Ingersoll is totally blind and ignorant !

Socrates continues: "Let us not then refuse to believe
even what we do not see, and let us supply the defect of
our corporeal eyes, by using those of reason ; but especially
let us learn to render the just homage of respect and veneration to the divinity, whose will it seems to be, that we
have no other perception of him than by his effects in our
favor.   [The progressive Ingersoll says: "I despise him
—I trample him under my feet—I defy him !"   What
a degraded piece of humanity, when compared with the
heathen Socrates !]   "Now this adoration, this homage,
consists in pleasing him, and we can only please him by
obeying his will.   In this way," says Xenophon, "Socrates instructed the youth ; these are the principles he
inspired in them ; on the one side a perfect submission to

the laws and magistrates, in which he made justice consist; on the other hand a profound regard for the divinity, which constitutes worship.   In things surpassing our understanding, he advises us to consult the gods, and as they only impart to those that please them, he recommends, above all things, the making them propitious by a wise regularity of conduct.   The gods are wise, says he, and it depends upon them either to grant what we ask, or to give us directly the reverse of it.   He cites an excellent prayer from an anonymous poet: ' Great God, give us, we beseech thee, those good things of which we stand in need, whether we crave them or not; and remove from us all those things which may be hurtful to us, though we implore them of thee.'   The vulgar imagine that there are things which the gods observe, and others of which they take no notice; but Socrates taught that the gods observe all our actions and words; that they penetrate into our most secret thoughts, are present in all our deliberations, and inspire us in all our actions.''

Although Socrates talked of the gods as a polytheist, yet when men came to pray, praise, and worship, it must always be to the great Supreme Creator, the single divinity.   Here he was a theist.   He recognized but one God, the Creator of all things and beings.   He knew of the actions, words, thoughts, and motives of his creature, man—hence of his abilities and susceptibilities—just as men know the possibilities of those things they design and make, and that, too, before they are made.   These are the creatures of man's creation, and no matter who made them, he has a perfect knowledge of all, and whether they will answer the purpose for which the mechanic designed them; and in the comparative scale of being, has not the Creator of man the same knowledge of him, and when there will be a sufficient number of them, in a given time, who will be induced by his goodness and love to please and obey him, thereby answering the purpose for which he made all?

What makes a Man a Philosopher?

It was by the observation of nature and relation of things that made the thinking, reasoning Socrates a philosopher ; he thus discovered the existence of God, his attributes, moral and mental qualities, from those of his own—the reflex from the image, the like from the likeness. It was not merely a matter of faith, but of logical knowledge. To him it were as fanatical to talk about believing there is a God, the Creator of man and the world, as for the man to talk about believing he made the machines, or that he himself exists ; that it is his belief he is pleased with some of his own works and displeased with others ; that he believes he will destroy everything he has made which fails to answer the purpose for which he designed it. We may believe, upon evidence, in things which are things of promise ; but things of existence must be known by observation or historic fact, and hence it becomes logical knowledge. But Ingersoll, not knowing enough about these themes of natural, moral, and religious science and the philosophy of things, supposes everybody equally deficient, talks about this knowledge as that of mere faith.

The Scripture doctrine of faith, as we have seen, relates to the fulfilment of the reward promised to his people at the end of the world ; which can only become knowledge by such fulfilment. Neither of these principles of the knowledge of God by his works and word come within the present conception of Ingersoll, though adapted to the mental calibre of mere youth ; which fact is only to be explained by his wilful ignorance—the love of moral and religious darkness. How does the reasoning or freethinking of such a man look by the side of those of Socrates, whose mental and religious faculties exalted him to such a knowledge of the Creator by the revelation of his works, without that revealed in Scripture, which rendered it impossible for him to be an atheist on the one hand or a polytheist on the other. In this exalted state of mind, he was as true a worshipper, as loving and obedient ser-

vant of God, as the Scripture revelations could have made
him. The highest standard set up in the word of God
is the supreme motive of a man to please and obey his
Creator ; from such a heart everything else of Christian
requisition, in relation to God or man, follows. This is
the man whose estimate of the progress of our age is to
be attributed to freethinkerism, but which to describe
truthfully in all these relations, the word retrogression
should be substituted for that of progress ! For once we
agree with Ingersoll, that the boasted progress of our
age must be accredited to the freethinkers, of whom and
among whom Ingersoll is held to be chief.

Heathen Philosophers in Advance of Freethinkers.

These advanced views of God and nature were also
those of Democrates, Euclid, and Aristotle. In fact, not
one of the philosophers contemporary with any of those
differed upon these great truths, or confounded God with
nature. Not one was either a pantheist or an agnostic,
the latter of whom theoretically accepts everything, but
merges all into a heterogeneous mass of impenetrable
and indefinable confusion, a death and burial of all certain knowledge and all faith, though founded upon the
most conclusive evidence. We have the telescope and
microscope, with superior chemical apparatus, furnishing
greater facilities for the study of nature, with this same
open book which lay before those wise men of antiquity ;
and what a reflection upon our modern scientists (so
called) that, instead of elevating their minds to sublimer
thoughts and conceptions, the most prominent of them
are busily engaged in searching among the lowest animals
and insects for the lost links of the chain which unites
them to such an evolutionary ancestry, instead of being
the most noble work of God. This so-called freethought
sees no being in the universe higher or better than themselves. Alas ! what progress is this ? Those ancient philosophers knew nothing of the Scriptures, except as coming through the necessarily corrupt channel of tradition,

which shows that their knowledge of God as the Creator, and that of his moral and natural goodness, was not derived from that source ; and yet their statements clearly show they obtained the same knowledge by the study of nature, the works of God, as that revealed in the Bible, thereby answering the highest end of his being, the spiritual service of God his Maker. Take the following as an example of such instruction : " For the invisible things of God, from the creation of the world, are clearly seen ; being understood by the things that are made, even his eternal power and Godhead ; so that they are without excuse." (Rom. 1 : 20.) We have seen that these heathen philosophers learned the goodness and grace of God by the study of nature, and that it drew from them perpetual homage and praise, and the acknowledgment that the interest for the happiness of man occupied the whole time and attention of God ; and this goodness led them to love, please, and obey him.

The following passage also conveys the same instruction, which is brought as a reproof for its ignorance : " Or despisest thou the riches of his goodness and forbearance and long-suffering ; not knowing that the goodness of God leadeth thee to repentance." (Rom. 2 : 20.) Here is God's goodness, eternal power, and Godhead revealed by the nature of his works, and which can only be predicated of an eternal being, and which comprehends him in all forms of his manifestation, especially that of his Immanuelization and personality, all of which are revealed by the things that are made known to his (God's) thinking, reasoning students. By the Immanuelization, God became visible and palpable to the senses, as he was invisible from the creation of the world down to this event, and in which form he is the destined re-creator of man and the world. These successive manifestations and creations are contrasted in scores of passages of Scripture. Here is one : " For our light afflictions, which are but for a moment, worketh for us a far more exceeding and eternal weight of glory ; while we look not at the things which are seen, but on those things which are not seen [the coming glory, not seen as yet] : for the things which

are seen are temporal; but the things which are not
seen are eternal." (2 Cor. 4: 17, 18.)

A heathen poet gives us the following beautiful lines
upon the subject of future being, the same common reasoning of the philosophers upon the nature of man, and
which like that of the Scriptures, as inducement, points to
purity and perfect self-sacrifice as fitness for association
with the pure and holy God :

> " If there's a power above us—and that there is,
>   Nature cries aloud, through all her works—
>   He must delight in virtue, and that which
>   He delights in must be happy.
>   'Tis the divinity that stirs within us—
>   'Tis heaven itself, that points out an
>   Hereafter, and intimates eternity to man ! "
>   —CATO'S SOLILOQUY.

Ingersoll's Ignorance of Scripture.

Nothing is clearer in the lecture of Ingersoll on the
gods, than that its author does not claim to know anything about any of them, and he does not disappoint his
readers by betraying any knowledge upon the subject.
It is also clear that, whatever is intended, his warfare is
not waged against those who know about God, but those
who believe about him.   Upon these he has exhausted
his vocabulary, spent his noisy thunders, and issued all his
painted lightnings, so that he has nothing left for those
who have knowledge of God.   By this attitude he confesses profound ignorance of two things: to wit, that as
he does not know there is a God, of course he can know
nothing about him ; secondly, that he has no evidence
for believing there is one.   If he is an honest man and
has no such evidence, he would not oppose others for
entertaining similar sentiments, much less abuse them
for so doing.   If he had such knowledge or belief, how
could he enter into an irrepressible conflict with those
who claimed to have the same.   It will be seen that this
reasoning exposes the notion of some who say that Ingersoll does not believe what he says, and thus charge him

with hypocrisy; while our idea is that he is one of those
who tells a lie so often that he believes it himself. He
not only professes perfect ignorance upon the general subject, but upon all its particulars, as he sees no God in
nature but nature herself; and this shift is only an am-
biguous shift, to appear to modify the rancor of the venom turned against those who know that the living God
of nature and Scripture exists, and whom both books
equally reveal.

In the same manner he acknowledges his igorance of
Scripture. Says he, " To read the Bible, is to reject it."
He need not have informed us of this fact, so far as his
reading is concerned, for, thus far, we have seen that in
all his attempts to criticise it, he was profoundly ignorant of every passage and subject. In opposition to this
we may say that to read and study the Bible according
to its own prescribed rules, is to understand it as a whole
and in every particular part, and this knowledge demonstrates it to have had the living God, who made the
world, as its author; and we may submit whether up to
this point, the exposure of Ingersollism does not vindicate such an assumption? As, therefore, the scoffer has
no such evidence, he can have no rational belief, as
such belief is founded upon evidence; and thus having
no understanding of its scope and design, he can have no
knowledge of the Bible. Then how can it be expected
that such a mind in such a frame should see anything else
in any passage of Scripture but senseless absurdity? In
view of which, we would ask our readers and Mr. Ingersoll's readers, What is his opinion of any passage worth?
Before answering, remember that he confesses there is no
evidence to prove the Scripture to be what it claims—
the inspired Word of God. The book of Revelation,
which makes known the coming important events of the
world, before declared to the prophets, all of which is
known to be that of prehistoric and historic record of the
four universal kingdoms, in their successions, divisions,
and subdivisions, including that of their religions, even
down to the present day, describing and identifying them
as accurately as profane history records them: these, in

his ignorance and blasphemy, the scoffer characterizes as "the insane ravings of the lunatic of Patmos." This is a specimen of the modesty he learned from Satan, his honored schoolmaster.

Why Men Love God, Incomprehensible to Ingersoll.

Ingersoll does not see how a sane man can love the God who could have done or proposes to do such things as the Bible relates. Not understanding the narration of any of those things, nor the objects he accomplished or intends to accomplish by them, he sees nothing but inconsistency in loving a being who is so unlovely. This ignorance is not to be mitigated on his part by the plea of necessity ; for nothing is clearer than that it is not for the want of mental capacity or opportunity, but that it is wholly wilful. The following charge illustrates this. He says : " The God of the Bible drowned a whole world." That is, he drowned a whole generation of people living at a particular time. But had he been an honest investigator and seeker for truth, he would have observed that the God of nature, even if it is nature herself, did introduce, or permitted the introduction, at some period of the existence of mankind, some physical derangement into her works which would cause the death of the two hundred generations of mankind, one-third of whom have been little children. This god *Nature* thus kills and gives no reason for the killing ; while the God of the Bible reveals both the object and necessity for the introduction of universal death, especially for shortening the life of the generation by the flood.

Now, Mr. Ingersoll, let us expostulate a little with you and ask, why you should fight the God of the Bible for thus killing a single generation, and adore your god Nature who has killed the other one hundred and ninety-nine generations. If you reject the inspiration of the Scriptures for the small killing, must you not reject the records of nature for the great killing, and then tell us that you don't believe in *Nature* because he kills people, even little children, or deny the record that nature kills anybody—in fact, that there is no such thing as nature in existence—that it is only a god the priests have made? Come, now—"honor bright!" Behold the marvellous wisdom and consistency of the king of freethinkers! The most advanced atheistic scientist of the nineteenth century declares he has no knowledge of the existence of God—no evidence for such a belief! See what a great bluster of a fight against the God whom he holds to be a mere phantom of the imagination, and wishes people to believe him a very courageous man for the undertaking!

How can a man who is professedly ignorant upon a subject, be anything, if he talks about it at all, but its burlesquer? He despises a God whom he does not believe exists; he defies a phantom which he knows cannot harm him—brave man! But as Ingersoll is the representative freethinker of our time, and whom the sceptical world holds as a kind of demi-god, it leaves us no other alternative than that of stripping every vestige of reason for the veneration from the shrine of their idolatrous matter-god.

The Scoffer's Defective Metaphysics.

He says, "Man has no ideas, and can have none, except those suggested by his surroundings. He cannot conceive of anything utterly unlike what he has seen or felt. He can exaggerate, diminish, combine separate, deform, beautify, improve, multiply, and compare what he sees, what he feels, what he hears, and all of which he takes cognizance through the medium of his senses; but he cannot create. Having seen exhibitions of power, he can say omnipotent. Having lived, he can say immortality." No, sir! man cannot say immortality because he lives, for all the life he has seen comes to an end; therefore, between the two ideas, mortality and immortality, there is no comparison possible; and immortality does not come within the range of human observation, which is limited to death on every hand, and he can only say, from the light of the revelations of the laws of nature, *mortality!* But a man may have an idea of immortality, even a knowledge of it, as the result of logical reasoning, thus : Man lives ; a living being must have caused him to live, as the laws of his own being gives the only true definition of life, making it consist in the existence of every physiological part in the structure of the body essential to life as a part of the life itself.   From this wonderful mechanical involvement man may infer that the Being who made it liable to death is able to remake it exempt from such liability—hence he can say immortality ; and his Maker has given this revelation in another book, with that also for which he made the world itself—an endless world for an immortal man.   In order, therefore, that a man may say immortality, as designed for him or any one else, he must have satisfied himself that the Author of the revealed design and promises is the Creator of nature, and his own nature, as none other would be able to accomplish the work ; and that he has the evidence in his own mind, which enables him to depend upon his ability and veracity to fulfil them.   If a man masters and complies with these conditions, he has as positive knowledge upon the subject as upon that of his own existence.

Ingersoll says, "Man cannot create, or have any idea of anything utterly unlike what has come within the scope of his senses."   In order to make the assertion answer his purpose, it is necessary to show that as man has never seen, felt, heard, tasted, or smelt God, with his bodily senses, therefore there is no God.   It is a fact that there was a time when there were no fire-arms, steam-engines, electric telegraphs, and ten thousand inventions, all of which are the creations of man, and the first of each was utterly unlike anything which had ever come within the scope of human sense.   According to Ingersoll, no man can make a new discovery or have an original idea ; he can only imitate what he has seen. This may be true of him, and is so upon the subjects of his infidel lectures ; and we must allow every man to know what he does not know, or that he knows of what he is ignorant ; and charity should concede that what a man announces as a fact of his own experience, is honest ; hence Ingersoll knows nothing utterly unlike that of which his own senses have been cognizant; the sequence of which is, that he never had an original thought or idea, and this is the limitation of his intelligence; or he must logically know things which have never been tested by his own senses—such as the existence of a living God, and that he is the Creator of the world. If he was a man of thought and reason, the result of a logical mind, he would reason from the known to the unknown—the universal law of mental philosophy—and the conclusions would not be the rant of agnosticism, but the positive knowledge of a man, seen by the eye of the mind, just the same as though started by images struck upon the retina of the eye. In confirmation of this limitation of ideas in the mind of Ingersoll, we have the fact that a hundred years before he was born, everything he says about God and the Bible was substantially said and written; so that his supposed progress, at the head of the boasting freethinkers, runs backward.

He says, "Knowing something of time, man can say eternity." No, sir! he cannot say eternity so as to have a sensible idea of it, for an idea or even an inference can only be obtained by comparison, and the two things so utterly unlike as time and eternity, bearing no proportion to each other, cannot be compared. He says, "Conceiving something of intelligence, man can say God." But Ingersoll cannot thus say God, because, by his own confession, he has not intelligence enough to know that there is one. He says, "Having seen exhibitions of malice, man can say devil." But he cannot say or infer the existence of a devil from that of malice; for he himself manifests more malice, and that, too, toward his God and Creator, than the devil ever did or dared to do; besides he is too ignorant of the Scriptures to know their statements to be true as to the existence of the devil, and therefore the exhibition of no amount of malice can give him the idea of a devil. He says, "A few gleams of happiness having fallen athwart the gloom of his life, man can say heaven." Well, whatever any other man can say about heaven or happiness hereafter, he has no such prospect, for he is too ignorant of the Scriptures to know there is or ever will be a heaven of happiness, and he cannot infer it from the present life of man, as the sources of misery vastly exceed those of happiness, which indicate future misery, if anything; and if, as he says, all the gods are worse than devils, they certainly can have no motive for making men happy hereafter. What a dreadful plight does Mr. Ingersoll's philosophy involve! These are the lessons of wisdom his schoolmaster the devil has taught him. Who would pay for such learning?

The Scoffer's Bad Logic.

He says: "The superstructure has been reared, combining, separating, diminishing, beautifying, improving, and multiplying realities, so that the edifice or fabric is but the incongruous grouping of what man has conceived through the medium of his senses. It is as though we should give a lion the wings of an eagle, the hoofs of a bison, the tail of the horse, the pouch of the kangaroo, and the trunk of the elephant. We have in imagination created an impossible monster, and yet the various parts of this monster really exist. So it is with all the gods that man has made." Here we have Mr. Ingersoll's conception of God, and all the gods, in the form of an illustrated conclusion. It must be remembered that among all the gods, with whom Ingersoll blasphemously includes the living God of the Scriptures—in fact, this seems to be the only God that calls forth his bitter animosity—it must also be remembered that in this man's estimation there are no gods except those which men have made, and the making is nothing but an imaginative manufacture. As, therefore, there is no God within this man's conception, or he has no idea of a god, and as it is impossible to illustrate no idea, he gives us this incongruous attempt to do an impossibility, producing the monster representative of his conceptionless talk; and supposes that if all the named features of these animals belonged to a single one, that would fitly represent all the ideas mankind have ever entertained of God. A man may attempt to illustrate his own ignorant notions of

7

God ; but if he has no idea of the existence of a living God, then how can he with any sense make even this incongruous attempt ? and how much more ridiculous that he should assume it to illustrate all the ideas mankind have entertained respecting God ? Is it not also absurd to suppose that the Being who made all these animals, with their peculiar features, could not have combined them in a single one ? and had it been a domestic animal .of common observation, would it have been a monster ? Besides, the illustration concentrates all the gods in one, and this shows the scoffer aims his weapons, such as they are, at the single God of holy Scripture ; and to crown the silly effort he acknowledges all through his sayings that he does not know or believe there is any living God in the universe ; and because he is thus ignorant, concludes all men are in the same category. Here is the king of the self-styled freethinkers, who makes war upon God, on the alleged ground that he calls on him to sacrifice *his reason.* But if he should do even this, would it be much of an oblation ?

The scoffer says : "Pain, in its numberless forms, having been experienced, man can say hell." Not knowing the Bible, which teaches there is a hell or is to be one, of course he does not know or believe anything about it ; and being thus ignorant, he considers all opinions about hell as imaginary as his own, as it requires knowledge in one mind to appreciate it in another ; and though it puts him and the freethinkers in contradiction to all the intelligence of the world in their estimate of the science and philosophy of God, heaven, and hell, entertained by the scholars of the ages, as equally ignorant with themselves ; and everybody understands by the senseless manner in which their chief talks about these subjects that he has no evidence for the belief of the existence of any being in the universe higher or greater than himself, who must therefore be as devoid of any reason for his own existence or object proposed by it.

CHAPTER IX.

WHY INGERSOLL IS POPULAR.

In order to appear to be original, Ingersoll puts the old, stale witticisms and atheistic phrases in something of a new dress; but there never was a public sceptic who reasoned so little and used less argument against God and the Bible; but even on this account his lectures are popular in our age, in which it is painfully true that not only the young people, but their parents are not distinguished for thought. It is a fact that they are great readers, though the reading is mostly that of newspapers and light literature, while the historic and philosophic literature of the ages lies like buried rubbish upon the shelves, if it is there at all. He says: "Some nations have borrowed their gods [we have just heard him declare as a fact that each nation made its own gods; but now this is not a fact]. Of this number, we are compelled to say, is our own. The Jews having ceased to exist as a nation, and having no further use for a god, our ancestors appropriated him, and adopted their devil at the same time. [A funny blasphemy.] This borrowed god is still an object of some adoration, and the adopted devil still exists and excites the apprehensions of our people." [His people must be those like him; but the devil does not excite their apprehensions, as they are ignorant of his existence, and to excite their apprehensions might lead them to flee his company and escape his doom.] He is still supposed to be setting traps and snares for the purpose of catching our unwary souls, and is still, with reasonable success, waging the old war against our God." The very latest trap set by the devil is to make men believe he has no existence, and into this trap Ingersoll has fallen headlong. So pleased is his satanic majesty with the capture, that he has made him chief agent, proclaiming through the country the paradox, " My master has no existence —the great liar of Eden is dead, so that you, *my people*, need have no fears of my traps and snares." It would not only be ungrateful, but foolishness, for the devil to wage war upon his own faithful children, ignorant of the famous truism, " A house divided against itself cannot stand ; " and there is but one God against whom the devil makes war—all others are on his side, as Ingersoll claims for his confederates. The book that knows about this parent and his children, says : " Who are led captive by Satan at his will."

This *Wiseacre* says : " To me it seems easy to account for these ideas concerning gods and devils. They are a perfectly natural production : man has created them all." We have shown that God made the devil an angel, and he made himself a devil ; and having lived six thousand years, he knows well enough how to lay snares to catch such simpletons as those who know nothing about him. In contrast to such, those who do know about him are addressed in such language as the following : " Lest Satan should get an advantage of us : for we are not ignorant of his devices." (2 Cor. 2 : 11.) So, Mr. Ingersoll, keep it ringing in the ears of your people : " Man has created all the gods and all the devils," though you have just said, " Man cannot create anything." What a foolish thing a man is to create devils to lay snares and traps to catch his soul and fill him continually with apprehension, and also to make gods to punish himself for serving another one of his creatures ! Of course Ingersoll knows nothing about living gods or devils, so has his master blinded his mind, and so does he keep the tongue of a thoughtless brain in locomotion.

The Scoffer Claims Originality for One Thought.

He says, " Man has not only created these gods and devils ; but he has created them out of the materials by which he has been surrounded." This unknown God to him, says, " To whom, then, will ye liken God ? or what likeness will ye compare unto him? The workman melteth a graven image, and the goldsmith spreadeth it over with gold, and casteth silver chains. He that is impoverished that he hath no oblation, chooseth a tree that will not rot; he seeketh a cunning workman to prepare a graven image, that shall not be moved. They that make a graven image are vanity, and their delectable things shall not profit, and they are their own witnesses; they see not, nor know; that they may be ashamed. Who hath formed a god that is profitable for anything? Behold, all the fellows shall be ashamed together. The smith with his tongs, worketh in the coals, and fashioneth it with hammers, and worketh it with the strength of his arms; the carpenter stretcheth out his rule; he marketh it out with a line and with a compass, and maketh it after the figure of a man, according to the beauty of a man; that it may remain in the house. He burneth part thereof in the fire [part of the material, the chips whereof he is surrounded]. With part thereof he roasteth a roast, and is satisfied; yea, he warmeth himself; and saith, Aha, I am warm, I have seen the fire; and with the residue thereof he maketh a god; and falleth down and worshippeth it, and prayeth unto it, and saith, Deliver me; for thou art my god.

"They have not known me [the living God], nor understood; for he hath shut their eyes [because they love darkness rather than light, and because their deeds are evil] and their hearts, that they cannot understand." (Isa. 40 and 44.) "But is there a God beside me? yea, there is no God; I know not any." Thus did the people create gods, and out of the material with which they were surrounded; and Ingersoll should have given the Scriptures credit for the quotation, and not have said, "It seems perfectly natural to me that the people made all the gods and devils," as though he had arrived at this conclusion by his own reasoning.

But Ingersoll, either ignorantly or designedly, overlooks a most prominent fact in this mythological history, namely, that these god-makers believed in the existence of but one living and supreme God, and that the gods they made were but symbols to put them in remembrance of him; and we defy this iconoclastic upstart of a god-slayer and degrader, to produce a single testimony from the idolatrous priests or those who practised its rites, who claimed that there were no gods or God superior to those they themselves made, or that any of these were alive, or that they did not claim there was one supreme living God! Again he says, "Each nation made its own gods and devils, who not only speak its language, but put in their mouths the same mistakes in history, geography, astronomy, and in all matters of fact, generally made by the people. No god was ever in advance of the people or nation that created him." What a foolish thing is this to say, when we have just seen how the mechanics, as he says, made the gods out of the material that surrounded them, and that the gods so made never made a mistake. How can a piece of carved wood or metal make a mistake. He means this fling for the God of Scripture; but we have seen that all Ingersoll's supposed mistakes of Moses or Genesis are to be credited to the false and foolish so-called science of the atheistic evolution and chronological geology, and that the statements of the Scriptures, touching the origin of the world and its inhabitants, are philosophic and astronomic necessities; that is, that if no account had ever been written of that work, what we know now of science demands that it should be written in exact accordance with Scripture statements!

He says: "The negroes represented their gods with black skins and curly hair. The Mongolian gave to his a yellow complexion and dark, almond-shaped eyes. The Jews were not allowed to paint theirs or we should have seen Jehovah gods with a full beard and oval nose." See how the arch-scoffer goes out of his way to give vent to the infamous venom of his heart against God! No, here is your lying blasphemy; for you have seen the record of their idolatrous gods in the shape of a golden calf, or a pile of stones, which the Jews made and worshipped. See how he attempts to degrade the living God, by such association as this: "Zeus was a perfect

Greek, and Jove looked as though he was a member of the Roman Senate. The gods of Egypt had the painted face and placid look of the living people who made them. The gods of northern countries were represented warmly clad in robes of fur; those of the tropics were naked. [It is not true that they thus represented the people, for there is not an uncivilized race on the earth, or ever was one of which there is authentic history, who went, or go, naked.] The gods of India were often mounted on elephants; those of some islands were great swimmers. [How could an image-god represent a great swimmer? The fact is Ingersoll is fixing up the god-picture to suit his purpose in names, color, and shape of the gods manufactured by his own imagination and that of his freethinking confederates.] The deities of the Arctic zone were passionately fond of blubber. [How could a god in the shape of man represent an appetite? He wanted to say something funny, and calls that about the blubber a fact.] Nearly all people have carved or painted representatives of their gods, and these representatives were, by the lower classes, treated as the real gods, and to these images and idols they addressed prayers and offered sacrifices." The scoffer is here unwittingly led into a correct statement, that the people generally came to worship these idols as the real gods, with the exception that he should have said " the real God," and this before they became mentally degraded to the level of the freethinkers who reject his existence, and morally desire to have it so, and worship the symbol-god as the real. The existence of an idol-god cannot be reasonably accounted for, but as implying the prior existence of a living God.

Idolatry Proves the Existence of a Living God.

It is evident that Ingersoll uses these universally existing gods to prove there is no real God. A more absurd effort could scarcely have entered an uninfatuated mind. All these gods were representative. Representatives necessitate something to be represented, and the god-representative could not have been the god represented ; consequently representative gods prove the existence of a real god represented.   If all the gods of nations and in- dividuals were in character representative, which fact is historically notorious, not even questioned by Ingersoll himself, then there is one God all these represented and represent, and the testimony of all the gods at once demonstrates the truth of our position.   The conception of God, entertained by the image god-makers, as shown by the names, structure, and adornment of the idols, was that they possessed unlimited wisdom and knowledge, omnipotent power, justice, goodness, love, hate, and mercy to the penitent ; but who would in nowise spare the stubborn guilty.   These intellectual and moral attributes it is impossible to have conceived as belong- ing to any but a living, personal God, and this is the God of nature, as the idolators saw him revealed in their own, the workman in the work, as well as in the bounties of inanimate nature for man's support and pleasure.   That such is the God of Scripture revelation, exhibits the sublime harmony of truth for the contempla- tion of all sentient beings.   If it should be asked, Why, then, is the practice of image-making and worship for- bidden in the Scriptures? we answer, Because of their tendency to divide the worship between the image and the living God.   But instead of idolatry making atheists, no god at all, it made polytheists—"lords many and gods many "—while freethinkerism makes the gods repre- sentatives, but no god represented.

We have a Congress of the United States, one branch of which is composed of representatives chosen by the people ; but Ingersoll's logic says there is no people they represent.   What, however, he fails to do logically he attempts by sophistry : " The gods," says he, " repre- sented the conception, the ideal of the people."   To dis- lodge him from this attempt at further deception, we may say that a man can have no conception or idea of a thing of which he has no reasonable knowledge, or of which he is totally ignorant, and he must be totally ignorant of that which does not exist.   If, therefore, there is no God, he cannot have a representative or symbol. Ideas or conceptions originate by observing and comparing things which come within the range of our senses, or from their description given by others, from which it follows that if there were *no things* there would be no ideas, or conceptions, as we can have no idea or conception of *nothing*, other than that of non-existence. Hence, ideas or conceptions of God depend upon and prove the existence of a living, personal, intelligent God, the Creator of nature. Here again we see Ingersoll's specious sophistry and spurious logic.

Origin of Image-worship Natural.

How natural were the existence of these traditions and universal conceptions and idol-god representations ! God made the first pair of mankind in his own image, and after his own likeness, and these precise words are defined in describing the form of the third man born into the world, thus: "And Adam lived an hundred and thirty years, and begat a son in his own likeness, after his own image: and called his name Seth." (Gen. 5 : 3.) As Seth was in the form, likeness, and image of his father Adam, so was Adam in the form, likeness, and image of his father God. That this was a personal image or form, is corroborated thus : "Who [the son of God] being the brightness of his [God's] glory, and the *express image of his person.*" (Heb. 1 : 3.) And this Son in the form of God "was found in fashion as a man." (Phil. 2 : 6, 8.) In the beginning the first pair of the human species must have had a personal acquaintance with their father God, as their children had with themselves. From this centre the human family spread over the earth, but having no books, and wishing to retain and transmit their knowledge of God's person, and object of the worship he imposed, they made images like themselves, and therefore like their Maker. As corrupt as were the antediluvians, they are not charged with the sin of idolatry ; but after the flood, the practice being forbidden in the Scriptures shows its existence. Thus is In-

gersoll without the least defence for wickedly confounding
the living God with the men-made gods of idol-worship ;
but of this Being, by his own confession, he knows nothing, and has consequently no idea or conception of him.
For his enlightenment and that of this class we copy their
picture, drawn by the dictation of the God who knows
them, if they do not know him : " For there are certain
men crept in unawares, who were before of old ordained
to this condemnation [they were not ordained to do the
diabolical work, but were condemned for doing it], ungodly men, turning the grace of God into lasciviousness,
and denying the only Lord God, and our Lord Jesus
Christ. Likewise also these filthy dreamers defile the
flesh, despise dominion, and speak evil of dignities [even
of the great God and his dominion]. But these speak
evil of those things which they *know not ;* but what they
know naturally as brute beasts, in those things they corrupt themselves. Woe unto them ! for they have gone in
the way of Cain, and ran greedily after the error of Balaam for reward, and perished in the gainsaying of Core.
Clouds they are without water, carried about of winds ;
trees whose fruit withereth, without fruit, twice dead,
plucked up by the roots ; raging waves of the sea, foaming out their own shame ; wandering stars to whom is
reserved the blackness of darkness forever." (Jude.) The
error of Balaam was that he wanted to curse the children
of God for money, so that they might become an easy
prey to their enemies ; while Ingersoll and his class not
only curse the children of God, but God himself, and
for the greedy reward of the mammon of unrighteousness
—the god they worship, and which is the most sordid and
degraded god before whose shrine human beings ever
prostrated themselves. The scoffer says : " The Christians now claim that Jesus is God. [Yes ! and they always
did claim that Jesus was God ; but because the sceptics
of our day deny this, it necessitates its prominent defence ;
and his ignorance even of this history leads him as here
to suppose it to be a new doctrine.] If he was God,
[he also says] of course the devil knew that fact, and
yet, according to the account, the devil took the omnip-

otent God and placed him upon the pinacle of the temple, and endeavored to induce him to dash himself against the earth.   Failing in that, he took the creator, owner, and governor of the universe up into an exceeding high mountain, and offered him this world, this grain of sand, if the god of all the worlds would fall down and worship him, a poor devil, without even a tax-title to one foot of dirt.   [We have seen that in this lecture Ingersoll thanks the devil for teaching him all he knows and for all the liberty he enjoys, but see how disparagingly he here talks about his devil friend and benefactor !]   Is it possible the devil was an idiot ?   Should any great credit be given to this deity for not being caught with chaff ? Think of it !   The devil, the prince of sharpers, the king of cunning, the master of fitness, trying to bribe God with a grain of sand that belonged to God !   [Was the devil so much of an idiot and fool as this scoffer, who makes public war upon God himself ?]   Is there in all the literature of the world anything more grossly absurd than this ? "

There is nothing ever said, either by God or man, which may not be made to appear inconsistent by ridicule ; in consequence of which it is generally conceded that nothing sacred should be made a subject of ridicule, and it is generally apparent that when a man has recourse to ridicule he has no reason or argument for what he is attempting to teach.   Knowing nothing of the teaching of Scripture, about God, Christ, or the devil, but still talking roughly upon the subjects, of course he says senseless things, and then draws his famous conclusion by asking if anything was ever more absurd ?   If he knew enough about these things, which he might learn from the Scriptures and the philosophy of intelligent being, he would know that the devil, being a creature, only knows what he learns, and foreknows nothing ; hence that he is disappointed and defeated every time he tempts another to do a thing and fails, thereby exposing his ignorant calculation. And in this case, to make the account of Christ's temptation in the wilderness appear ridiculous, Ingersoll ignorantly assumes that the devil knew all about Christ, that he was God, etc. : "If Jesus was God, of course the devil knew that fact." But this effort of the devil was to ascertain who Christ was, and this effort, Mr. Ingersoll, relieves these acts of the devil of all absurdity in the transaction, and credits them to your account, exposing the foolishness and arrogance of your effort in setting up this straw-devil, to have the honor of his demolition.

Christ's Temptation Free from all Incongruity.

Some of the facts and the philosophy of the temptation of Christ by the devil in the wilderness are as follows :

1. Jesus Christ was made of a woman, as truly as Eve was made of Adam, and by God the Creator. There was some difference in the manner ; but so far both were creatures.

2. The life of that which was born of Mary, or, as Paul expresses it, "made of a woman," was a natural, mortal life, the demonstration of which was the fact that Jesus Christ died ; but God was not born or made, nor did he die, and this was not even the body of God while it hung dead on the cross, except in the predestination that he was to take it again.

3. This life being mortal, was never taken again, but was made a sacrificial offering to show his love for men, that he might thus win them to become his friends. Had God taken the mortal life again, it would still have been subject to death, and that which is subject to death must at some time die.

4. That God had been preparing a human body for himself for the space of thirty-three and a half years, and had lived in it during that time, but forsook it while it hung on the cross.

5. While it lay dead in the grave, God, as he was before making it for himself of the woman, invested, incarnated, or Immanuelized himself with it the second time, which act raised it from the dead, and whose life from thenceforth became the life of the Immanuel-man-God, before which in decree, type, and prophesy he had been all these, but now in fact in history. Now it could be

declared and interpreted by the angel Gabriel: "This Jesus that is born this day in Bethlehem, the city of David, is Immanuel, God with us" [God with our nature]; and by Paul: "In him dwelleth all the fulness of the Godhead bodily." (Col. 2 : 9.)

Here were two distinct living forms of being. A man in every respect human—"in all points tempted like as we are, and being so tempted, he knows how to succor them that are tempted." (Heb. 4 : 15 and 2 : 18.) It was not God as he was before this birth of the Son of Man who was thus tempted; hence it is written: "Let no man say when he is tempted, I am tempted of God: for God cannot be tempted with evil [and this temptation was with the evil of idol-devil worship], neither tempteth he [thus] any man." (James 1 : 13.) The prophet anticipating this transaction, and personating God thus in human form, exclaims: "A body hast thou prepared for me." And again: "When he bringeth in his first-begotten into the world [not from another world, but into existence, born of a woman, born into life], he saith, Let all the angels of God worship him. And unto the Son he saith, Thy throne, O God, is forever and ever: a sceptre of righteousness is the sceptre of thy kingdom." Here was the same lying devil who had cunningly deceived the first Adam, telling him that if he would obey him he would become a god, be wise, and not die. And now the second Adam comes into the world, and the devil makes the same kind of effort to induce him to disobey the Creator, and obey him. This Adam, however, is his master, and gives the devil every opportunity, going with him wherever he proposes, and wherein he had every advantage; but after all his presumption and lying insinuations is completely foiled and vanquished, and leaves his Lord and God, whom alone it was his duty to worship, a wiser devil than he was before; and immediately angels—his angels—came and ministered unto him. Christ quoted Scripture prediction of the temptation to the devil, thus: "Get thee behind me, Satan: for it is written, Thou shalt not tempt the Lord thy God." "Thou shalt worship the Lord thy God, and him

only shalt thou serve." And we learn from this Scripture that no matter how much any of God's creatures
have degraded themselves, or how long he has been a
sinner, though it is the devil himself, still it has been his
duty, and ever will be, to love the Lord his God and
Creator every moment of his being, and to obey him
because he loves him. God was the Creator of man-
angels and of the world, before he assumed human form ;
and was he any the less such after its assumption ? To
say that the God who made all the living forms of the
universe could not have made any one he pleased for himself, will do well enough for freethinkers, or no-thinkers,
like Ingersoll, but it is too absurd for common sense. He
also exposes his bad science and worse philosophy by calling our world "a grain of sand." Of course he borrowed the idea from the groundless speculations of the
nebular theory of Laplace, adopted by Darwin, Lyell,
Proctor, etc., who also did the same thing, just as he does
his opinions of God, Christ, the devil, heaven, hell, etc.,
from the sceptics of the past, and without the least thought
or reason on his part. And such is the mind which attempts to grapple with these great questions !

Providence of God in Nature.

Ingersoll says : "Since the invention of steamships
and railways, so that the products of all countries can
be easily exchanged, the gods have quit the business of
producing famine." That it is impossible to respect what
the scoffer says is shown by the fact that since these
inventions were in full blast, we have had the famines of
India, China, and Ireland, and a score of others of less
note, in which more people died of starvation than in
any other three famines recorded in ancient history.
Besides, every famine is as truly the work of God as an
eclipse of the sun is his work ; both equally result from
the operation of the principles which run the machinery
he made and put in motion at the creation of the world,
and to say he did not know what his machine would
accomplish, at any particular time or place, is forbidden

by the detailed adjustment of the works of nature themselves. According to this principle, the Creator involved
in his machinery of nature whatever irregularities or derangements which would result from its operation during
all periods of time, thus providing for every famine and
every other natural evil. These constitute the providence
of God, all of which have resulted from man's disobedience to the rightful laws of the only proprietor of the
universe, the revealed purpose of which is to make the
present world an uncomfortable abode for man, that he
might be induced easier to seek one of endless duration,
one in the re-created world of his righteous and eternal
government. It is this end that justifies the means for
its accomplishment, and without a knowledge of which
involves all in incomprehensible mystery.

The Creator cursed the earth and its productive powers when man became a sinner, and for his sake. The
second curse took place at the deluge, when he broke up
the entire crust of the earth, the greatest source of physical derangement. Whatever of these calamities would be
modified by a prayer or life of a saint, important in
facilitating the more rapid populization of this coming
New World, having foreseen it, he could also have involved, interwoven it in the machinery itself, at the
foundation of the world. Any other view makes God
careless and uncertain what will take place in these great
departments of his work. This providence, with the
above exceptions, if indeed they are such, can have
nothing to do in producing the moral or Christian character of men, but befall all equally. Men have will and
mind which must be consulted, and they are as free to
act within their sphere as the Creator himself is within
his sphere. Of course, if he cannot be induced to do and
be that which is pleasing in the sight of his Maker, he
must take the consequences, and such may infer, from
the severity with which his laws of nature are made to
execute themselves, what will be done in the infliction
of the revealed penalties against the finally impenitent
when the time comes appointed for that work. Being
ignorant of all this, Ingersoll continues to talk thus:

" Now and then God kills a child because " it is idolized
by its parents. As a rule he has given up accidents on
railroads, exploding boilers, and bursting kerosene lamps.
Cholera, yellow-fever, and small-pox are still considered
heavenly weapons; but measles, itch, and ague are now
attributed to natural causes. [He should have known that
everything in nature are effects, and she is the cause of
nothing.] As a general thing God has stopped drowning
children, except as punishment for violating the Sabbath
[a cunning little scoff].

" In wars between great nations God still interferes;
but in prize-fights the best man, with an honest referee,
is almost sure to win. [See the scoffer's low design to
degrade the God of nations by associating him with
prize-fighting; but it shows that the prize-fighter is held
in high esteem by this God-hating Col.] The church
must insist that prayer is answered; that some power
superior to nature [nature has no power, all power is in
mind] hears and grants the requests of the sincere and
humble Christian, and that this same power in some
mysterious way provides for all." As Ingersoll is not one
of these sincere, humble Christians, having nothing of
their experience, he knows nothing of the subject, and
which is of course mysterious and incomprehensible to
him. If he wishes to know whether God answers prayer,
let him ask these sincere, humble Christians, and he will
receive the testimony of intelligent witnesses, who have
experience in the matter.

Another Young Ingersoll Discovered.

The conceited scoffer discovered another such prodigy,
about whom he says: " A devout clergyman sought every
opportunity to impress upon the mind of his son the fact
that God takes care of all his creatures; that the falling
sparrow attracts his attention, and that his loving-kind-
ness is over all his works. Happening one day to see a
crane wading in quest of food, the good man pointed out
to his son the perfect adaptation to get his living in this
manner. ' See,' said he, ' how his legs are formed for

wading ! What a long slender bill he has. Observe how
nicely he folds his feet when putting them in or drawing
them out of the water; he does not cause the slightest
ripple. He is thus enabled to approach the fish, without
giving them any notice of his arrival. My son,' said
he, ' it is not possible to look at that bird without recog-
nizing the design as well as the goodness of God, in
thus providing the means of subsistence.' ' Yes,' replied
the boy, I think I do see, so far as the crane is concerned ; but, after all, don't you think the arrangement is
a little tough on the fish ? ' '' Of course Ingersoll is the
bright boy, and the father is the dull clergyman. This
fact of the bird and fish confounds the one, and satisfies
the other that God is not good ; and the story illustrates
the food question, relative to organic beings, of supply
and demand, as well as the adaptation of each to prey upon
the other for food. Nature does nothing of this work, has
no economy, and is simply the means in the hand of God
for the purposes they subserve, just as the tools are in the
hand of the mechanic with which he builds the locomotive. God asks no such superficial and sentimental
defence to screen him from the production of the earthquakes, or hardships of living beings, by ascribing them to
nature. It is God himself who assumes the responsibility
for all things called '' natural evil,'' concerning which he
speaks thus : '' I am the Lord, and there is none else.
I form the light, and create darkness; I make peace,
and create evil ; I the Lord do all these things.'' (Isa.
45 : 6, 7.) '' Shall there be evil in a city, and the Lord
hath not done it ? '' (Amos 3 : 6.)

The direct source of all these evils results from the curse
of the inanimate world, inflicted by the Creator in consequence of the disobedience of man. To Adam he said :
'' Cursed is the ground for thy sake.'' (Gen. 3 : 17.)
The next curse was by the deluge, which left the earth in
as bad a condition as the Creator ever intended to reduce
it. '' And the Lord said unto Noah, and in his heart, I
will not again curse the ground for man's sake.'' (Gen.
8 : 21.) '' The earth is also defiled under the inhabitants thereof, because they have transgressed the laws,

changed the ordinances, and broken the everlasting covenant; therefore hath the curse devoured the earth."
(Isa. 24 : 5.)   It is a fact that a very large proportion of
animals cannot live but by devouring others, and man is
the greatest devourer of all.   He is provided with vegetable teeth to grind and animal teeth to tear.   Indeed, he
kills and appropriates almost everything—fish, flesh, and
fowl—for his food, clothing, comfort, and decoration; even
the women adorn their bonnets with the plumage of birds
killed for the purpose.   The pain and suffering incident
to the killing of an ox is as great to it as the killing of a
man to the man, and the pain of death is a universal evil
from which the saints of God do not escape.   Pain resulting from the sensitive nervous system, revealing organic
derangement to the individual, is essential to the preservation of health; while that of dying comes as a necessity.
These provisions of nature make known the disposition of
the God who made them, and from which men may learn
that he that offends against the written and religious laws
of God will equally suffer their pains and penalties.

It were well for Mr. Ingersoll to think and investigate
beyond the clergyman and his boy to learn the lesson
thus written : "Behold the goodness and the severity of
God" (Rom. 11 : 22); and "It is a fearful thing to
fall into the hands of the living God" (Heb. 10 : 31).

Beauties of a Cancer, the Sceptic's Argument.

"Even the advanced religionists," says Ingersoll,
"although disbelieving in any great amount of interference by God in this age of the world, still think that in
the beginning God made the laws governing the universe.
He believes that in consequence of these laws a man can
lift a greater weight with than without a lever; that this
God so made matter, and established the order of things,
that two bodies cannot occupy the same space at the same
time; that it is a greater distance around than across a
circle; that a perfect square has four equal sides; that a
whole is greater than a part; and that had it not been for
this power, superior to nature, twice one might have

been more than twice two, and sticks and strings might have had only one end." [See what silly and false things he charges to be held by the most advanced religionists. Did any man ever know of one who held that, under any possible circumstances, "twice one might have been more than twice two, that a stick or string might have but one end," if God had not made the world. What a fellow-fool a man must be who supposes Ingersoll either wise or honest!] Again he says : " These religious people see nothing but design everywhere, and personal intelligent interference in everything. They insist that the universe has been created, and that the adaptation of means to ends is perfectly apparent. They point to the sunshine, and to all there is of beauty and use in the world." [We may now expect that this biblical scholar and philosophic scientist is going to give us argument to prove all these advanced views of Christians absurd—that God did not create the world, that means are not adapted to ends, that like causes do not produce like effects ; and, doing this, he will easily expose the error and credulity of the most intelligent religious people. Let us hear him, and be disappointed.]

" Did it ever occur to them that a cancer is as beautiful in its development as the reddest rose ? [What an æsthetic.] That what religious people are pleased to call the adaptation of means to ends, is as apparent in the cancer as in the April rains? [Who ever said it was not ? The law is universal.] How beautiful the process of digestion ! By what ingenious methods the blood is poisoned so that the cancer shall have food ! By what wonderful contrivances the entire system of man is made to pay tribute to this divine and charming cancer ! See by what admirable instrumentalities it feeds itself from the surrounding quivering flesh ! See how it grows, with what marvellous mechanism it is supplied with long and slender roots that stretch out to the most secret nerves of pain for sustenance and life ! What beautiful colors it presents ! Seen through a microscope it is a miracle of order and beauty. All the ingenuity of man cannot stop its growth. Think of the amount of thought it must have required to invent a way by which the life of one man might be given to produce a cancer. Is it possible to look upon it and doubt that there is a design in the universe—[has he not just been describing the design in the mechanism of the cancer? and do they not always produce the same effect, death? "Of dust thou art, and unto dust shalt thou return." "It is appointed unto men once to die"—that the inventor of this wonderful cancer partook of the infinite?" [Yes, we answer; for it baffled all finite skill either to make or cure it, as you have just said.]

The introduction of pains and diseases into the world, growing out of the universal curse, was one of the elements of God's plan, through which he is able in less time to accomplish his purposes with man and the world, which is indicated in the acknowledgment: "Before I was afflicted I went astray." If Ingersoll, at the head of human skill, with all mankind as his assistants, cannot make or cure such a cancer, then there is a Being above him and all others, of superior power and intelligence, who did make it. If all the ingenuity of man cannot make such a piece of mechanism, then ignorant nature, not possessing a particle of skill or ingenuity, could not have made the wonderful cancer; and as its organization partakes of the infinite, an infinite Being made it; therefore was it a supernatural and superhuman work, a most wonderful miracle, because one of which nature, with man as one of her parts, was incapable. So you see, Mr. Ingersoll, whether you select one of God's healthy organic formations or a cancer of transformation to show there is no Creator, it equally necessitates and demonstrates his existence, and the works of all nature, the adaptation of means to ends, for the accomplishment of his purposes. Ingersoll's brain is so mixed up and confused upon these subjects, that he utterly fails to distinguish between knowledge—matter of fact—and belief. He has here introduced a dozen self-evident truths, mathematical demonstrations, which, he says, are "believed." Does a man believe or does he know that twice two are more than twice one? Is it a matter of belief or knowledge that a man can lift a greater weight with a lever than without one? Now how can a man talk intelligibly upon the subject of faith who entertains such ideas? The substance of Ingersoll's lectures are repetitions from Paine's "Age of Reason," especially about Christ and the Bible, which are old and stale, written a hundred years ago; and yet he puts himself at the head of this age of progress. But to show Paine's superior knowledge of nature and philosophical science, in contrast to the silly talk of Ingersoll, scoffing at the existence of God, the Creator of the world, we introduce the following passage from Paine's "Age of Reason."

CHAPTER X.

PAINE SHOWS NATURE DEMONSTRATES THE EXISTENCE OF GOD.

SPEAKING about God, Paine says: "Do we want to contemplate his power? We see it in the unchangeable order by which the incomprehensible universe is governed? Do you want to contemplate his munificence? We see it in the abundance with which he fills the universe? Do we want to contemplate his mercy? We see it in his not withholding that abundance from the unthankful. In fine, do we want to know what God is? Search creation. The only idea man can affix to the name of God is that of a first cause—the cause of all things; and incomprehensible and difficult as it is for a man to conceive what a first cause is, he arrives at the belief of it from the tenfold greater difficulty of disbelieving it. It is difficult beyond description to conceive that space can have no end; but it is more difficult to conceive an end. It is difficult, beyond the power of man, to conceive an eternal duration of what we call time; but it is more impossible to conceive a time when there shall be no time. In like manner of reasoning, everything we behold carries in itself the internal evidence that it did not make itself, that he did not make himself; neither could his father have made himself, nor his grandfather, nor any of his race; neither could any tree, plant, or animal have made itself; and it is the conviction arising from this evidence that carries us on, as it were by necessity, to the belief of a first cause eternally existing, and this cause man calls God. It is only by the exercise of reason that man can discern God; take away that reason, and man would be incapable of understanding anything. So also must it be believed that he organized the structure of the universe for the benefit of man, and that the Creation we behold is the real and ever-existing Word of God, in which we cannot be deceived. It proclaims his power, it demonstrates his wisdom, and manifests his goodness and beneficence.

"That the whole duty of man consists in imitating the moral goodness and beneficence of God, manifested in the creation toward all his creatures, that seeing as we do daily the goodness of God to all men, it is an example calling upon all men to practise the same toward each other; and, consequently, that everything of persecution and revenge between man and man, and everything of cruelty to animals, is a violation of moral duty. When impressed as fully and strongly as we ought to be with the belief of God, man's moral life would be regulated by the force of that belief; and he would stand in awe of God, and of himself, and would not do anything that could be concealed from others. We can know God only through his works. We cannot have a conception of any one attribute, but by following some principle that leads to it. We have only a confused idea of his power, if we have not the means of comprehending something of its immensity. We have no idea of his wisdom, but by knowing the order and manner in which it acts. The principles of science lead to this knowledge; for the Creator of man is the Creator of science, and it is through this medium that man can see God, as it were, face to face. Could a man be placed in a situation, and endowed with the power of vision, to behold at one view, and to contemplate deliberately, the structure of the universe; to mark the movements of the several parts, the cause of their varying appearances, the unerring motion in which they revolve and depend on each other; and to know the system of laws, established by the Creator, that governs and regulates the whole—he would then conceive, far beyond what any church theology can teach him, the power, the vastness, the munificence of the Creator; he would then see that all the knowledge man has of science, and all the mechanical arts by which he renders his situation comfortable, are derived from that source. His mind, exalted by the scene and convinced by the fact, would increase his gratitude as it increased his knowledge; his religion or his worship would become united with his improvement as a man; any employment he followed that had connection with the principles of Creation, as everything of agriculture, of science, and of the mechanical arts, would teach him more of God, and of the gratitude he owes to him. Great objects inspire great thoughts; great munificence excites great gratitude."— PAINE'S "Age of Reason," pages 151, 152.

What makes a Deist, a Christian, or an Atheist?

It is easy to see from these passages that Paine had studied nature, as he tells us, and from his boyhood. The proof is in the ideas themselves; not that the ideas were original, for they were taught by Socrates substantially the same. This study made Paine a deist. Had he studied from his youth Christianity alone from the Scripture, and not confounded it with that of the Papal Church with which he was surrounded, it would have made him a Christian. It was in the latter part of his life that Paine wrote "The Age of Reason." He finished Part First without having read the Bible, and could not procure one; and what he said about it was from his early recollections, received from his father, who was a Quaker. The criticisms its publication provoked induced him to get a Bible, in order to attempt to vindicate himself, which he thinks he did in publishing the second part. He gave the Bible a cursory reading while he was writing the second part. But to learn its principles in so short a time was as impossible as to learn the science of the universe in the same period, and which was rendered more difficult by the pride of opinion he sought to sustain of his former views. Indeed, had he told us that he had studied the Bible from his boyhood, it would have been refuted by the ignorant things he says about it. He thinks he demolished the Bible by showing that some of the New Testament writers, whose names the books bear, were not their authors.

Of course, he failed ; but had he succeeded, it would have been an error, as all the writers claim God to be the author of the words they wrote. He might with the same propriety have said that there is no law of gravitation, because Kepler's and Newton's writings about that law were not written by them. While Paine's philosophical knowledge of nature compelled him to know there was a God that made him, Ingersoll's ignorance of the science of nature compels him to reject these conclusions. While Paine's knowledge of nature forced him to believe in God and made him a deist, his ignorance of the Bible produced no conviction of its truth ; while Ingersoll's ignorance of both makes him an atheist. To know nature may make a man a deist ; to know the Scriptures may make a man a Christian ; but to know neither is to make a man an atheist or a freethinker !

Ingersoll's Prayer for an Idea—Pitiable Object.

He says : " If the church wishes us to believe, let one of the intellectual saints perform a miracle, and we will believe. [This puts us in mind of the equally wilful and blind Pharisees who had within their observation scores of miracles performed by Jesus, and when they had nailed the Intellectual Saint to the crucifix, said : " Let him now come down from the cross, and we will worship him."] We are told that nature has a superior. Let him for a single moment control nature, and we will admit the truth of your assertions. [After such a confession of ignorance of nature, not seeing that this superior is controlling nature in all her phenomena, no reflection can attach to us by giving him credit for it. So profoundly ignorant is he of nature that he thinks she made herself, and, while moving, set herself in motion, and that therefore the motion was before the motion.] In the olden time [says he] the church, by violating the order of nature, proved the existence of her God. At that time miracles were performed with the most astonishing ease; they became so common that she ordered the priests to desist; and now the same church and people, having found some little sense, admit not only that she cannot perform a miracle, but insist that the absence of miracles, the steady unbroken march of cause and effect, proves the existence of a power superior to nature. [It is only such atheists in the church who raise this question, by the adoption of the modern science of evolution and the geological antiquity of the world, and who contend that like causes do not produce like effects. But after stating these things he calls facts, and in a defiant manner, he becomes exalted to an awful altitude of self-esteem, and comes down on our poor church with the hollow noise of puffed-up thunder and painted lightning, thus:] We have heard talk enough. We have listened to all the drowsy, idealess, vapid sermons that we wish to hear. We have read your Bible; we have read the works of your best minds [and read both to pervert them]. We have heard your prayers, solemn groans, and reverential Amens. All these amount to less than nothing. [If he wanted experience, so as to make his opinions of any value, why did he not pray himself, according to the Bible directions?] We want one fact. We beg at the doors of your churches for just one fact. We pass our hats along your pews, and under your pulpits, and implore you for just one fact. [Having not one fact in all your foolish, atheistic lectures and sceptical books, you would not be able to identify it as a fact. If one of the saints should condescend to give you one, even at the risk of violating the instruction, "Cast not your pearls before swine, lest they turn round and rend you," you would not know it.]

"We know all about your mouldy wonders and your stale miracles. We want a this year's fact. We ask only one; give us one fact for charity. Your miracles are too ancient; the witnesses have been dead for nearly two thousand years. Their reputation for truth and veracity in the neighborhood where they resided is wholly unknown to us. Give us a new miracle, sustained by witnesses who still have the cheerful habit of living in this

world. Do not send us to Jericho to hear the winding
horns, nor put us in the fire with Shadrach, Meshach,
and Abed-nego. Do not compel us to navigate the sea
with captain Jonah, nor dine with Ezekiel. There is no
sort of use in sending us hunting with Samson. We have
positively lost all interest in that little speech so elo-
quently delivered by Balaam's inspired donkey. It is
worse than useless to show us fishes with money in their
mouths, and call our attention to vast multitudes stuffing
themselves with five crackers and two sardines. We want
a new miracle, and we demand it now. Let the church
furnish at least one, or forever after hold their peace.''
The scoffing blasphemy and funny merriment has its explanation in Ingersoll's greed to make the fools laugh and
get their money. But such importunity, such an object
of intellectual starvation, should excite the sympathy of
even the passer-by, especially when the beggar only asks
one idea, one fact—with a little doubt attached to it ; for
this purpose he advises everyone to cherish his doubts, as
they lead to the knowledge taught by Satan. It is clear
from this ardent plea that Ingersoll is the most abject
case of intellectual penury the world ever saw, lower even
than that of Balaam's ass, for he had one fact, that of seeing the angel, which the false prophet could not do, and
with which experience the animal could talk more to
the purpose than the man who tries to slander him, unless he is the veriest hypocrite of a tramp that ever lived,
and we are rather disposed to give him credit for the ignorant poverty he professes. Think of it, ye who have
facts, and spare just '' one little one '' in relation to the
great subjects of the origin of the world and the Bible, and
the harmonious revelation of both books, and bestow it in
charity upon this New York lecturer on the gods, so that
he may not die without '' one idea ! ''

There are but two sources from which all facts and
their scientific and philosophic teaching are derived—two
books in which every atom of human knowledge is contained upon these subjects—God's book of nature, and
his book of inspired revelation ; but from neither of these
exhaustless fountains has the scoffer Ingersoll ever been

able to extract a single fact, or one idea as even a rudiment of knowledge. The inspired book has not taught him a single idea, as he himself confesses ; and though pretending otherwise, it is just as certain to those who understand the book of nature that he has not learned a single one of her facts or ideas, the knowledge of which depends upon that of their origin, and this upon that of the prior existence of God the Creator as the only scientific and philosophic power adequate to their production, or to the origin of any power whatever. Every fact has its philosophy and science, and as such involves its origin and moving phenomena.

To be Taught of God too Humiliating for Sceptical Pride.

It may be thought that we should have omitted quoting some of the most scurrilous and blasphemous things Ingersoll here says ; but had we done so, he or some of his friends, in reviewing our book, might have attempted to make capital out of it, as things we were unable to answer ; and it should also be remembered that the whole of this lecture has been published by the New York *Tribune* and the general press of the country ; and where is the man who has not read it or heard it ? The scoffer says, " The Deity has demanded the most abject and degrading obedience. [It is a universally conceded sentiment that to serve the greatest king or emperor is to be the most honored, and this reaches its infinitude when the service is accepted and the obedience paid by man to his Creator ; but in his insolent pride and cowardly pretence, this is intolerable to the will and heart of Ingersoll, and were he equal to his desire, rather than submit he would reduce his Maker to the most abject servitude.] In order to please him, man must lay his face in the dust.''

It was said by one of the ancients, " That evil partook of the infinite, and good of the finite ; as the evil is that which a man in heart desires to do, and would do if opportunity was afforded, and not that alone which he performs.''

The scoffer-in-chief says again : " Gods have always been partial to the people who created them, and have generally shown their partiality by assisting those people to rob and destroy others." [We need only remark upon this that gods whom people make to worship should be obeyed by them, and equally should the God that made us receive our worship and obedience ; but one of the most prominent characteristics of the God of the Bible is his impartiality, having no respect for persons, but wholly respecting character—looking at the heart, the thought, the motive.] He says, " Nothing is so pleasing to these gods the people make—[the foolishness, to talk about such gods being pleased !]—as the butchery of unbelievers. Nothing so enrages them, even now, as to have someone deny their existence. [What a senseless mass is this ; that men should make gods, and then the ungrateful, wrathful things turn round and deny the existence of their makers, even subject them to butchery ! It seems as though the unfortunate people would never make but one set of such gods.] Few nations have been so poor as to have but one god ; gods were made so easily, and the raw material so plenty and cheap, that generally the god market was glutted, and heaven crammed with these phantoms. The gods not only attended to the skies, but were supposed to interfere with all the affairs of men. They presided over everybody and everything ; all was under their immediate control ; nothing was small, and nothing was large ; the falling of sparrows and motion of planets were alike attended to by these industrious and observing deities. From their starry thrones they frequently came to the earth for the purpose of imparting information to men."

The magician seems never to tire in repeating the legends about these many gods, their deep interests in the affairs of the people ; but why should they not minister thus, when the people made them for the purpose, and also to aggregations of families, called nations? It is therefore no wonder that the gods should become excited, and even indignant, at these wicked and foolish people who had made them, and then denied their existence.

What could they expect for such atheistic treatment and infidelity than condign punishment. If Ingersoll should make one of these gods, he would be the last man to bow the knee before him, but would want to become the god himself, and command the deity-servant to worship at his shrine, proclaiming *man* to be the head of nature, and that no being exists superior to him! Nor do we see why the god should make a fuss about the abject demand: did he not make the god to please him, and could not the maker appropriate him as he saw fit? could he not do as he liked with his own? So if God made Ingersoll, and demands his most servile obedience, abject humiliation, and had promised him nothing for the service, what right has he to object? God made him, and every being owns what he makes; and this settles the question, rendering remonstrance impossible, except as impudent arrogance.

But instead of this, God graciously offers to reward him for the service with immortal being, and everything he needs to make him eternally wealthy and happy, and still he disobeys. Can such conduct do otherwise than call down destructive wrath upon such a vessel for which he has fitted himself? Hence it is written by the dictation of the living God, which harmonizes with natural necessity: "Because I have called, and ye have refused; all day long I have stretched out my hand, and no man regarded it [no such man]; but ye have set at naught all my counsel, and would none of my reproof, I also will laugh at your calamity; I will mock when your fear cometh like desolation, and your destruction as a whirlwind; when distress and anguish cometh upon you. Then shall ye call upon me, but I will not answer; ye shall seek me, and shall not find me: for they hated knowledge, and did not choose the fear of the Lord. They despised all my reproof. Therefore they shall eat of the fruit of their own way, and be filled with their own devices: for the turning away of the simple shall slay them, and the prosperity of fools shall destroy them. But whoso hearkeneth unto me shall dwell safely, and shall be quiet from the fear of evil." (Prov. 24 : 33.) The sin of Ingersoll in turning away the simple from the fear of the Lord, and the prosperity of the fool (who hath said in his heart, There is no god) in his success, both fits him for destruction. " Behold, ye despisers ! wonder, and perish; for I will work a work in your days, which ye shall in nowise believe, though a man declare it unto you." (Acts 13 : 41.) This work of final destruction is that at which Ingersoll scoffs and makes ridicule for the entertainment of the simple, turning them away from God, and into his destructive pathway.

He says again : " It is related of one of the gods, that he came amid thunderings and lightnings, in order to tell the people that they should not cook a kid in its mother's milk. [That is a lie.] He left his shining abode to tell a woman she should have a child [This is another lie, for it was an angel who thus came, and the birth of the child, whose name was Isaac, was a miracle, to typify the birth of Christ] ; to inform a priest how to cut and wear his apron, and to give directions as to the proper manner of cleaning the intestines of a bird." That God came upon mount Sinai for this purpose, is a most wanton and slanderous falsehood. He came there to give the world a system of laws which contains the righteous principles of the common law of all civilized nations ; and these little details were typic of great events and duties connected with Christ and the destiny of mankind : a slain lamb signified the slaying of Christ, and a sheaf of the first ripe fruits of the harvest that of his resurrection from the dead—" Christ the first-fruits of them that slept." To cleanse these internal organs typified the necessity of cleansing the internal evil heart and its thoughts, the purity of which will be measured by that law in the judgment at the last day, and by whose principles Ingersoll will then be tried, whether he likes it or not, and by Christ in person, " the judge of quick and dead," whom he now delights to abuse. He did not make this God, nor can he control or bribe him, even though it degrades him and his like to " shame and everlasting contempt." He and God are at great enmity, and he declares, " I hate them that hate me ; " therefore one or the other must go down ; and Ingersoll wants no mercy—

and if he did, it will be too late then to apply ; in his pride he must therefore perish.   He would destroy his Maker, but cannot ; and according to the law of God, sin is measured by the disposition, the malignity of the intent, and not by the circumstance or the power to gratify it— not what the sinner commits, but what he would commit if he had the power and opportunity.

He says : " When the people failed to worship God, or to clothe and feed his priests, he generally visited them with pestilence and famine."   A portion of the sacrifices which the law imposed upon the people were to feed and clothe the priests, whose time was wholly occupied in offering them and teaching its principles to the people ; and in the worship of God he esteems " obedience better than sacrifice, or than whole burnt offerings."   But the spirit, the intent of the sacrificial law typically pointed to Christ, and this education introduced him to the faithful and devout of every age, since God instructed and commanded Abel to offer the lamb, the firstling of his flock, and a sheaf of the first ripe fruits of his harvest, and to repeat the offering once every year : " For Christ is the end [intent] of the law for righteousness to everyone that believeth."   (Rom. 10 : 4.)   " Wherefore the law was our schoolmaster to bring us to Christ, that we might be justified by faith."   (Gal. 3 : 24.)   In a word, the law comprehended the gospel of Christ, which God himself preached to Abel and Abraham, the glad tidings of the work he was to perform at his first and second personal visits to the world.   The lesson taught by the law of animal sacrifice was that when the lamb was offered, it shadowed forth the fact that Christ, the Lamb of God, was going to make an oblation of himself, in order to manifest his love, the love of God for man.   Christ says : " Greater love hath no man than this, that a man lay down his life for his friends."   Hence, seeing and believing that God would make this immense sacrificial offering, and which in purpose, revelation, and practicability was already made, and that Christ was to be the Saviour to justify and the Judge to condemn, presents the revealed doctrine and philosophy of salvation, at which Ingersoll scoffs and makes funny allusions. Besides, there is not an instance on record where God visited the people with pestilence and famine for refusing or neglecting to offer the sacrifices required by the law, the penalty for which was simply that such were not numbered among his people, but classed with infidels and unbelievers in Christ and his proposed work. Had God thus visited sinners, it would have made the present world one of retribution, while that work is reserved for the judgment at the last day, according to the whole tenure of Scripture.

"Sometimes," he says, " the god of the nation allowed some other nation to drag them into slavery, to sell their wives and children [this was done but once, and then God abandoned the whole nation, who had first abandoned him and his service, his worship, and paid it to gods made by men. If the sceptics were able to point to a single instance in Scripture where God abandoned a nation or a man before it or he first abandoned him, it would put another face on the whole subject] ; but generally he glutted his vengeance by murdering their firstborn. [Here are a number of lies: that this was general, when it occurred but once ; and that it was his people for refusing to support the priests, the fact being that it was visited upon the Egyptians for refusing to release his people from the four hundred years of the most cruel bondage, killing all their male children as soon as they were born, to prevent their becoming the dominant party in the nation.] The priests always did their whole duty, not only in predicting these calamities, but in proving, when they did happen, that they were brought upon the people because they had not given quite enough to them." There is no such record in the Scriptures, which adds another wanton lie to his account.

An Ignorant Attempt to Account for the Difference of Gods.

The scoffer says : " These gods differed just as the nations differed ; the greatest and most powerful had the most powerful gods, while the weaker ones were obliged

8

to content themselves with the very off-scourings of the heavens!'' This is a misstatement of the facts of history, to the effect that the god of each nation existed before the nation; that no nation ever changed its gods except for the worship of the living and true God; that every nation had its childhood and was weak, but in all its periods had the same gods. This man makes history to suit his iconoclastic warfare. Why should any nation at any period be obliged to content itself with one god, or a weak god, as the off-scouring of heaven, if the material out of which the people made them was so cheap and plentiful? According to another of his sayings, '' the heavens made gods and imposed them on the people and nations,'' and this contradicts the other saying, that '' the people made their own gods.'' This, however, is as well as Ingersoll's jargon usually holds together.

As an example of a weak people having a strong god, and showing also that the people only made shrines for the gods, we introduce the following history: Ephesus was once a city of Greece; but at the time we are about to speak, her dominion had passed away and Rome was her mistress; but still she worshipped Diana as her goddess, and which, their tradition said, fell down from Jupiter. Paul visited the city of Ephesus and preached unto them the gospel of the living and true God, and it made a great stir, as the following account shows: '' A certain man named Demetrius, a silversmith, which made silver shrines for Diana, which brought no small gain unto the craftsmen; whom he called together, and said, Sirs, ye know that by this craft we have our wealth. Moreover, ye see and know that not alone in Ephesus, but almost throughout all Asia, this Paul hath preached and turned away much people, saying that they be no gods which are made with hands; so that not only this our craft is in danger to be set at naught, but the temple of the great goddess Diana should be despised and her magnificence destroyed, whom all Asia and the world worshippeth. And when they heard this, they were full of wrath, and cried out, saying, Great is Diana of the Ephesians! and the whole city was filled with confusion; and having caught Gaius and Aristarchus, men of Macedonia, Paul's companions in travel, they rushed with one accord into the theatre. And when Paul would have entered, the disciples suffered him not to enter.

"And certain of the chief of Asia, which were his friends, sent and desired him not to adventure into the theatre. Some, therefore, cried one thing, and some another, for the assembly was confused [just as they were in Booth's Theatre when they laughed and shouted at the foolish things this other silver lover said about Diana and the rest of the gods, from which he also derived no small gain, and who himself was so confused that he thought the laughing was intended for applause]. And they drew Alexander out of the multitude, the Jews putting him forth. And Alexander beckoned with the hand, and would have made his defence. But when they knew that he was a Jew, all with one voice cried out, Great is Diana of the Ephesians? And when the town clerk had appeased the people, he said, Ye men of Ephesus, what man is he that knoweth not how that the city of the Ephesians is a worshipper of the great goddess Diana, and of the image which fell down from Jupiter? Seeing then that these things cannot be spoken against, ye ought to be quiet, and do nothing rashly. For ye have brought hither these men, which are neither robbers of churches nor yet blasphemers of your goddess. Wherefore, if Demetrius and the craftsmen which are with him, have a matter against any man, the law is open and there are deputies; let them implead one another. But if ye inquire anything concerning other matters, it shall be determined in a lawful assembly: for we are in danger to be called in question for this day's uproar, there being no cause whereby we may give account of this concourse. And when he had spoken thus, he dismissed the assembly." (Acts 19.) Instead of each nation having its own god and having made it, here is Diana, the god of all the nations of Asia, whether in their independent strength or subjects of the Roman Empire, all of whom worshipped this image that fell down from Jupiter; and we may add that there is not in all ancient mythology as intelligent

and consistent an account of idol gods and worship as this
of Ephesus, every feature of which is in contrast to Ingersoll's talk about the gods.

The Gods and Future Punishment.

The magician says, " Each of these gods promised happiness here and hereafter to all his slaves [yes, but all the
world were slaves in this sense—all worshipped some god,
and there was not an atheist living], and threatened to
eternally punish all who either disbelieved in his existence,
or suspected some other god might be his superior.   But
to deny the existence of all gods was and is the crime of
all crimes.   Redden your hands with human blood ; blast
by slander the fair fame of the innocent ; strangle the
smiling child upon its mother's knee ; deceive, ruin, and
desert the beautiful girl who loves and trusts you, and
your case is not hopeless.   For all this, and for all these,
you may be forgiven.   For all this and for all these, that
bankrupt court established by the gospel will give you
discharge ; but deny the existence of these divine ghosts
of the gods, and the sweet, tearful face of mercy becomes
livid with eternal hate.   Heaven's golden gates are shut,
and you, with an infinite curse ringing in your ears, and
the brand of infamy upon your brow, commence your
endless wanderings in the lurid gloom of hell, an immortal vagrant, an eternal outcast, a deathless convict."
    This is what Ingersoll calls dealing with subjects in
reason.   Intellectually, we do not call attention particularly to this passage as lacking in reason and intellect, especially as seeming to imply that other parts of the lecture
are not thus defective ; but we venture nothing by the
assertion that there never was a lecture on record of its
length so utterly devoid of reason : the reason is sophistry,
the argument witticism, and the grade of intellect buf-
foonery.   He says, " The court established by the gospel
is bankrupt."   No institution of trust, or of a state which
has incurred liabilities, is or can be bankrupt until the
legal day for payment has arrived, and which has then
repudiated its obligations.   Neither has the court of a

state become bankrupt until it has become too feeble to execute the penalties of its laws ; and this implies that the session of the court has been held and its decisions passed, but no existing power is able to execute them.

Is the Court of the Gospel Bankrupt ?

One of the principal events of which the gospel is tidings is the coming of a court of rendition—who is to be the judge ; what characters will be acquitted ; what condemned and executed ; the rules of decision ; and the time appointed for its session. The following are a few of the passages of Scripture which give this information : " Forasmuch then as we are the offspring of God, we ought not to think that the Godhead is like unto gold, or silver, or stone, graven by art and man's device. And the times of this ignorance God winked at [he was and is, and will continue the delay, the execution of his law upon the wicked until the coming of this day], but now commandeth all men everywhere to repent : because he hath appointed a day, in the which he will judge the world in righteousness by that man whom he hath ordained ; whereof he hath given assurance unto all men, in that he hath raised him from the dead." (Acts 17 : 29–31.) " For the Father judgeth no man ; but hath committed all judgment unto the Son." (John 5 : 22.) " If any man hear my words and believeth not, I judge him not [now ; I wink at it, pass it by now] ; for I came not [now] to judge the world [he comes again for this purpose]. He that rejecteth me, and receive not my words, hath one that judgeth him : the word that I have spoken, the same shall judge him in the last day." (John 12 : 47, 48.)

" For we shall all stand before the judgment seat of Christ ; for it is written, As I live, saith the Lord, every knee shall bow to me, and every tongue confess to God." (Rom. 14 : 10, 11.) " I charge thee therefore, before God and the Lord Jesus Christ, who shall judge the quick and the dead at his appearing and his kingdom." (2 Tim. 4 : 1.) " For the Son of Man shall come in the glory of his Father, with his angels; and then shall he reward every man according to his works." (Matt. 16 : 27.) " Behold, I come quickly ; and my reward is with me, and my work before me, to give every man according as his work shall be." (Rev. 22 : 12.)

" And I saw a great white throne, and him that sat on it, from whose face the earth and the heaven fled away ; and there was no place found for them. [They had been dissolved into their original elements, as Isaiah and Peter declare, out of which it is then to be again created.] And I saw the dead, small and great, stand before God ; and the books were opened, and another book was opened, which is the book of life : and the dead were judged out of those things which were written in the books, according to their works. And the sea gave up the dead which were in it ; and death and hell [the hell of the grave] delivered up the dead which were in them : and they were judged every man according to their works. And death and hell [contents of the grave, who had just been raised to life] were cast into the lake of fire. This is the second death. And whosoever was not found written in the book of life was cast into the lake of fire." (Rev. 20 : 11–15.)

Court of the Gospel Condemns for Works of Omission.

That it may be seen upon what principles and for what actions the coming judgment is to proceed, we quote the following scene, at which the Son of Man, Judge and King, has come to the earth to do his appointed work of trying, judging, rewarding his servants, and punishing his enemies. " When the Son of Man shall come in his glory, before him shall be gathered all nations ; and he shall separate them one from another, as a shepherd divideth his sheep from the goats : and he shall set the sheep on his right hand, but the goats on the left. Then shall the king say unto those on his right hand, Come, ye blessed of my father, inherit the kingdom prepared for you from the foundation of the world : for I was an hungered, and ye gave me meat ; I was thirsty, and ye gave me drink : I was a stranger, and ye took me in : naked, and ye clothed me : I was sick, and ye visited me : I was in prison, and ye came unto me. Then shall the righteous answer him, saying, Lord, when saw we thee an hungered, and fed thee ? or thirsty, and gave thee drink ? When saw we thee a stranger, and took thee in ? or naked, and clothed thee ? Or when saw we thee sick, or in prison, and came unto thee ? And the king shall answer, and say unto them, Verily, I say unto you, inasmuch as ye have done it to one of the least of these my brethren, ye have done it unto me. Then shall he say unto them on the left hand, Depart from me, ye cursed, into everlasting fire, prepared for the devil and his angels : for I was hungered, and ye gave me no meat : I was thirsty, and ye gave me no drink : I was a stranger, and ye took me not in : naked, and ye clothed me not : sick, and in prison, and ye visited me not. Then shall they also answer him, saying, Lord, when saw we thee an hungered, or thirsty, or a stranger, or naked, or sick, or in prison, and did not minister unto thee ? Then shall he answer them, saying, Verily, I say unto you, inasmuch as ye did it not unto one of the least of these, ye did it not unto me. And these shall go away into everlasting punishment ; but the righteous into life eternal.'' (Matt. 25 : 31–46.)

This is the court of the gospel, which, as we see, is not to sit until the end of this world ; and it is another of Ingersoll's blunders to declare it bankrupt before it attempts to do its work. Of course, that the court is bankrupt is the man's only hope, hence his desire to have it so ; and the foolish thought, upon which he seems to act, that if he can only make all men believe with him that the court is bankrupt, why, so it will be ; while the only effect will be their identification with the goats on the left hand of the Judge in the last day. At this court is promised blessed reward for the kind and merciful acts of men, and punishment to those who have selfishly refused to perform them upon Christ's brethren ; and this is the scoffers' plea for the selfish conduct of his life toward Christ and his people, and everyone can see that the wish for the bankruptcy of his court is father to the thought and desire.

God is too Merciful and too Unmerciful, says the Wiseacre.

This man seems to hate God so intensely, that if he cannot make it appear from the Bible that he is merciless and cruel, he slanders him for being too merciful and forgiving.   He has given above a list of the dreadful crimes God will forgive; indeed, every crime but atheism.   He seems to be acting upon the supposition that if he can induce men to disbelieve in the existence of God it will accomplish every other purpose, and thus succeed in ruining himself and fellow-men.   That we may see the hatefulness of atheism in the sight of God, and the reason for it, let us suppose that a thousand criminals had been tried in our state for crimes and doomed to die.   Suppose now, as their last resort of hope, they should appeal to the governor for pardon, and he should grant it to nine hundred and ninety-nine, could the one, because he was the ring-leader, call the judge a cruel tryant?   Yet for doing this very thing Ingersoll slanders the court as bankrupt, and calls such talk reason.   Suppose the prisoners, thus doomed to die and waiting the day of execution, were yet ignorant of the merciful provision of law, investing in the governor the pardoning power, and no one but Ingersoll to give them the information, and instead of doing it, which would be preaching the gospel of their salvation, he should go and tell them there was no danger, that the court was bankrupt and unable to execute the death-penalty, and in their ignorance they should believe his lies until the day of execution arrived. Suppose, further, that the qualification to induce them to become law-abiding citizens thereafter was the goodness and mercy of the governor shown in granting the pardon, such love winning them to love him in turn, and that the criminals, laboring under unbelief because of the ignorance in which the scoffer's lies had involved them, had failed to comply with the only condition in which the governor could interfere in their behalf.   They must make personal application to him for pardon, and to condone and pardon criminals without this would not only show the court bankrupt, but offer license for continual criminality. Had Ingersoll thus preached to these culprits the gospel of the governor's clemency, assigning the object of the pardon to be to induce them to become loyal citizens thereafter, connected with this was the necessary duty that the criminals were to believe the promise of the governor that he would pardon them on the morning of the day on which the execution was to take place. This promise of life they received by faith during the period after they had complied with the conditions, and up to the day of the promised pardon.

Here is the philosophy of the gospel of Jesus Christ, and who cannot see that the only effect of Ingersoll's lies is the ruin of himself and his fellow-men, and in no other way can interfere with the accomplishment of God's plan, except to delay it a little longer so as to give others the offer to take their place and crowns? and this delay was taken into the calculation in appointing the day for that of the judgment.

It is not true, as Ingersoll says, that the crime of all crimes which is not to be forgiven is that of atheism; for nowhere does the Scriptures deny pardon to the atheist, if he will accept it upon the same conditions offered to all sinners. The effect, however, of the crime of saying in his heart, There is no God, and acting as though there was none, upon himself, renders his case about hopeless. It is not God, but the sin of hating and abusing him, makes it almost impossible for the man to repent and apply for mercy and pardon in the spirit of such humility as will alone beget love and loyalty to the righteous government of God. It is no more certain that a man cannot respect another whom he has abused, slandered, and defied without cause, than that such men can be brought to love, reverence, and worship the God whom they have thus abused. One may forgive another who has wronged him, but he cannot forgive himself for wronging his best friend. If repentance would do it, it might be answered: "What can repentance do, when one cannot repent?" The punishment is not only vindictive, but consists in loss, loss of character, loss of companionship with Christ, angels, and holy men, the only qualification for the incorruptible inheritance in the new and eternal world, and that of immortal life. This is the fatal bankruptcy in which both the neglecters and defamers of God and his gospel are involved, and from that day it is without remedy. It is at the judgment of the last day, where and when the victims of Ingersoll's lectures and writings will be forced to answer the question which they themselves will ask, "What is a man advantaged, if he shall gain the whole world and lose himself, or be cast away?" (Luke 9 : 25.)

The only arbitrary feature in the whole revealed plan of God, is in limiting the opportunity to the present life, in which men may obtain the necessary fitness of character for the incorruptible inheritance and its associations, and the whole period to the duration of the present world. But of this they are forewarned, thus: "Behold! I come quickly; and my reward is with me, and my work before me, to give to every man according as his work shall be. He that is unjust, let him be unjust still; and he which is filthy, let him be filthy still; and he that is righteous, let him be righteous still; and he that is holy, let him be holy still." (Rev. 22 : 11, 12.) Now apply to Ingersoll, who has been the cause of this calamity upon thousands, the charge whether atheism is not the crime of crimes. The loss of salvation is damnation, whatever that word may mean, just as the loss of life is death, whether temporal or eternal: "The soul that sinneth it shall die." (Ezek. 18 : 20.) "The wages of sin is death." (Rom. 6 : 23.) "He that believeth not the Son [his promises and threatenings, his words] shall not see life; but the wrath of God abideth on him." (John 3 : 36.) The sin of Ingersoll is *atheism ;* and we can account for his terrible characterization of its turpitude only upon the hypothesis of his approximating a just apprehension of its nature and the punishment in justice it merits.

CHAPTER XI.

"If we abandon the doctrine that some infinite being created matter and force, and enacted a code of laws for their government, the idea of interference will be lost." So says the Oracle. If he or any other man ever had the evidence—and to have been such, it must have been founded upon known facts—it would have been impossible to have abandoned it; and if he or they never had such evidence, they could not have abandoned it, as they could not have abandoned that which they never possessed! This is absurdity No. 1.

Force is matter in motion, and originates in mind. Ingersoll supposes we can abandon this fact; but if we abandon it, we abandon the existence of force and that of matter in motion. This is absurdity No. 2. Says this wonderful scientist: "The real priest will then not be the mouthpiece of some pretended deity, but the interference of nature." Laws for the government of nature exist in nature, every one of which is an incorporation with the substance governed. Nature is her own interpreter, and the testimony she gives is that there is a cause superior to me, and to which I owe my existence and all my phenomena; everything from the falling of a leaf to the ruling of a world within my vast dominion are effects—I am all effect. And Ingersollism supposes effects came without cause. This is absurdity No. 3.

He says: "From that moment the church ceases to exist." The existence of the church depends upon her knowledge of God, based upon that derived from the two revelations of nature and Scripture. Can knowledge become no knowledge? which is the supposition here entertained. This is absurdity No. 4. "The tapers will die out upon the dusty altar ; the moths will eat the fading velvet of pulpit and pew.   The Bible will take its place with the Shastras, Puranas, Vedas, Eddas, Sagas, and Koran, and the fetters of degrading faith will fall from the minds of men.''   Here he virtually says all this will happen if we abandon the scientific and philosophic necessity for the creation of the world, and, therefore, for the prior existence of the Creator.   It is as though he had said, '' If we abandon the fact of gravity, there will then be no gravity.''   This prince of sagacity does not know that there is a God, or that he interfered to construct the principles, laws of nature.   If, therefore, he abandons his ignorance upon these subjects by becoming enlightened, which he must do if he abandons anything, why, that will be the last of the church.   This is absurdity No. 5.

His classification of the Bible with these heathen fables, which at best are its traditional corruptions, is absurdity No. 6.   '' If we admit that some infinite being has controlled the destinies of persons and peoples, history becomes a cruel and bloody farce.''   If we deny the control of the Emperor Nero, then the history of blood of that period did not exist ; a theoretic denial or admission can change the bloody history of the world.   The fact is that the history of the world has been one of cruelty and blood, and if we deny that an infinite being controlled it, why, that would make it a beautiful farce, or one of serene peace.   This is absurdity No. 7.   '' Age after age the strong have trampled upon the weak, the crafty and the heartless have ensnared and enslaved the simple and innocent ; and nowhere, in all the annals of mankind, has any God succored the oppressed.   Man should cease to expect aid from on high.   By this time he should know that heaven has no ear to hear, and no hand to help.''   Ingersoll has told us that he has read the Bible.   If he had, did he not see it recorded in its annals that its God delivered the oppressed Hebrew nation from the Egyptian powerful oppressor and from that of every other nation, as long as they obeyed his laws.   So proud and averse to the ways of God are mankind, that not one of them ever applied to

God for aid until every other source of help and happiness had been tried and failed, and even in such extremities multitudes have applied and received present aid;
while all who have applied upon the conditions the proprietor proposed, received information which encouraged
them to bear the cruelties, even of personal torture and
death; which was to the effect of promising them an inheritance in his coming endless world, wherein they were
to be brought by a resurrection to life immortal.

This hope gave the intelligent contentment and joy a
family would experience while living in a mere hut of a
house, about ready to tumble down, but who had a
beautiful marble mansion almost finished for its occupa-
tion.   To deprive them of this aid from on high is the
diabolical work of Ingersoll and his fellow-atheists.   This
is absurdity No. 8.   "The present is the necessary
child of the past.   There is no chance, and there can be
no interference."   By no interference he means there
has been no creation of the world, the antithesis of which
is that all things came by chance, or they did not come
at all, and nothing exists.   Here Ingersoll puts himself in
contradiction to all other atheists of the world, and
equally to all modern scientists, who claim that all things
did come into existence either by evolution or creation;
and yet he professes to adopt the doctrines of these very
scientists.   According to Ingersollism, therefore, the
world was not created, did not come by chance, nor by
evolution, and it was not eternal.   This is presumptuous absurdity No. 9.

That Ingersoll fails to comprehend the argument of
interference or chance [perfect opposites], that they came
into existence, and did not come into existence, presents
an insight into the most muddled brain of all the public
characters of the world; and gives the crowning absurdity
No. 10.

The Archsceptic Quarrels with Nature.

"What would we think of a father who should give a
farm to his children, who should first plant upon it thousands of deadly shrubs and vines, stock it with fero-

cious beasts and poisonous reptiles, put a few swamps in the neighborhood to breed malaria; should so arrange matters that the ground would occasionally open and swallow up a few of his darlings; establish a few volcanoes in the immediate vicinity that might at any moment overwhelm his children with fire? Suppose the father should have neglected to tell his children which of the plants were deadly, that the reptiles were poisonous; failed to say anything about the earthquakes, and kept the volcano business a profound secret—would we pronounce him angel or fiend? And yet this is exactly what the orthodox God has done.'' We may remark that we have no God to defend, and if such a duty depended upon us, the defence would be like that an infant might make in behalf of his grandsire. No! if God cannot defend his acts, then man nor angel can do it. The highest qualification of man is his ability to study and understand God's two great books of nature and Scripture, which together give the facts and reasons for all his works, and answer the prayer of John Milton, offered while contemplating these great subjects:

> "What in me is dark, illumine;
> What is low, raise and support;
> That to the height of this great argument,
> I may assert eternal Providence,
> And justify the ways of God to man."

To give the facts without the reasons for all the works of God, as Ingersoll has done in this passage, is to vilify and belie the Father and Maker of man. We accept the picture, and do not think it too highly drawn. We also acknowledge that the God who created the world is the Author of all these evils, no matter whether he is called the God of Scripture, the God of nature, or the orthodox God. Another important lesson taught by these calamities which befall man is that this God is not such a sentimental, pusillanimous being that he will not hurt his creatures or let them suffer for a purpose. It should also be remembered that there is not a pang of pain on this planet but which results from the violation of some law, either natural, moral, or religious, all of which God is the Author, and knew these consequences when he made the laws; in fact, were necessary accompaniments of his work with man and the world, of all of which the Great Father gave his children timely information.   If we admit the charge that this God is a tyrant, a fiend, even then he should be obeyed, though he could not be loved.   What madness and folly to make war upon our Maker because he does not do everything to suit our notions, as though we could overcome, overpower him.

God's Vindication for Introducing Natural Evil.

Let us suppose a father had two children—man and wife—Adam and Eve; and before they lived he made a beautiful farm for them.   It was an island in the midst of the sea, and without a barren rock, or bluff shore; of an undulating surface, all covered with deep luxurious soil. It was harvest time when they were given possession, and every tree was loaded with ripe, luscious fruit: there was not a poisonous plant on the island.   The father had made every kind of cattle and animals for the use and pleasure of his children—not one had a disposition to hurt another; and to those children were given the dominion over all.   There were beautiful streams, rivers, and placid lakes filled with tame and splendid fishes.   All the variety of plumaged birds played and sang among the trees, and the fowl sported amid the beauteous verdure, rich foliage, and spicy groves of the island garden.   The air was so harmoniously blended in chemical composition and temperature that rendered its motion, except as a fanning, mild zephyr, impossible.   So symmetrically were the strata laid beneath the soil, that no pent-up gases could form, and therefore no earthquakes as results existed.

In addition to this lovely environment there was a certain tree whose fruit was of such a chemical composition as to counteract the ossifying tendency of the human system, that which we call the effect of age, by partaking of which the inhabitants of the island might perpetuate their

life indefinitely, indeed live forever.   In view of this relation, and giving these children possession of the whole
island, he naturally and reasonably wished them to please
and obey him.   They were created with power to obey,
and this carried with it the power to disobey.   But
either of these rendered a law and its revelation a necessity—something must be permitted, and something must
be forbidden ; and the latter must be that which they
did not need to do, or the temptation would have been
an element of weakness, and with such a defect the
Creator could not have pronounced their nature "very
good."   That they might learn obedience, the father
said, Children ! I have given you this beautiful island
home, and you may freely use all it contains for your
gratification with the exception of the fruit of a single
tree, which stands in the centre of the garden ; of that
you must neither touch nor eat.   This was the law, and
a law without a penalty or execution, if violated, is a
farce, and especially impossible for this father to enact
and pronounce.   Hence he said : "In the day thou eatest thereof thou shalt surely die."   When the father had
thus spoken, he retired, leaving the happy couple to
themselves.   But notwithstanding all this munificence
and manifestation of love, with the blessed gift of life,
and everything adapted to make it one of perpetual happiness, these children most wantonly disobeyed their loving father, dishonoring him in the most aggravating
manner, by obeying his enemy, another of his creatures
like themselves, though they were under no obligation to
do him service.

The design the father had in view, in the creation of
the island, was to populate it with children who would
be eternally loyal to his commands, loving him and his
government.   Although these children, the parents of all
future generations of the island, had thus offended and
died, yet it in nowise baffled the great purpose or induced him to change his plan ; but only rendered a
greater number of generations to be born a necessity,
from among whom the requisite number of such subjects
would be induced to become such by the offer of an in-

heritance in the same island, re-created and beautified for the purpose, but which would never have an end, and from which the whole family of the unlovely and disobedient would be forever excluded. But so few comparatively in each successive generation would accept the inheritance upon the conditions it was or would be offered, that it became necessary to subject both the good and bad of each generation to removal by death, the one after they had rejected the offer of the island home, in order to give place to others of human born, who, the father foresaw, would accept the offer by complying with the conditions.

The Philosophy of Future Existence.

The introduction of death rendered a resurrection, which is equivalent to a re-creation of these destined subjects, a necessity, and to take place when the complement was full. Christ was the resurrection and the life for the dead saints, all of whom died in the faith and hope of its accomplishment. Hence the record in which their names were registered was called "the Lamb's book of life," at the head of whose first page stood the name of Abel. Nothing is more reasonable than that the father of this family should desire the completion of the great work in the shortest time its nature would admit. The father informs the first two men born into the world of this purpose; preaches the gospel to Cain and Abel. One believes and dies a martyr to his faith; the other refuses to offer the lamb, and thus rejects Christ, becomes an infidel, hates, persecutes, and kills his brother. That men may become dissatisfied with the island garden, and easier induced to sacrifice its small pleasures for an inheritance in its re-creation, the father curses the very ground that henceforth it should bring forth briers, thistles, thorns, and poisonous plants, and to be overrun with troublesome weeds, in consequence of which it will be said : "By the sweat of thy face thou shalt eat bread all the days of thy life." Thus, for sixteen hundred years was the new island gospel preached, and converts

made. Now a generation had come into existence who,
notwithstanding these physical evils, loved the present
world so much that although the father sent them a
preacher of righteousness, by the name of Noah, who proclaimed the gospel of the re-created island for a hundred
and twenty years, yet failed to make a single convert.
The father had not obtained the number of loving inhabitants for his permanent government. This forced
the alternative of abandoning his purpose, or of destroying the whole generation of his rebellious children, and
of commencing anew ; and he had resolved on the latter,
and gave the warning for this long period.

The original curse produced so little physical derangement that the members of the family lived an average age of five hundred years, and every generation
before this had died a natural death, while the life of this
one was cut short one hundred and twenty years by the
flood. By this catastrophe the whole crust of the earth was
broken up, and three-fourths of its surface left covered
with briny oceans; a large portion of the rest with
swamps, sending up malaria ; huge rocky mountains,
thrown up by the convulsion ; deep chasms, left by sunken
continents, filled with seas, which till then·had been
buried in the heart of the circling earth. This vast derangement laid the foundation for volcanoes and earthquakes, and all the fearful meteorological phenomena of
the heavens since witnessed. The effect of this was to
render the climates of the earth so unhealthy that the
period of human life was cut down to three score and ten
years, and by the progress of the derangement growing
still shorter, until the present generation is but about
thirty years.

The Earth Doomed to a Universal Conflagration.

The history of the island, given in advance and written
in a book dictated by the father of this family, shows it is
destined to pass through a universal conflagration. This
history also shows that the wickedness of each generation
will increase until the last, which will become as godless

and defiant at the commands of God, and as unbelieving
in relation to the coming end, as that which was destroyed by the flood, to which Christ testifies as follows:
" But as the days of Noah were, so shall also the coming
of the Son of Man be: for as in the days that were before the flood, they were eating and drinking, marrying
and giving in marriage, until the day that Noah entered
into the ark, and knew not until the flood came and took
them all away; so shall also the coming of the Son of
Man be." (Matt. 24: 36–39.)   As then, this state of
sin and general unbelief is assigned as the reason for the
second destruction of the world.   But when this condition of things arrives the number of loving, loyal inhabitants for his new island farm will be complete.   The
father comes again to the island, resurrects his saints,
takes them above the heavens, that they may be uninjured
by the conflagration and re-creation.   After this work is
accomplished, he then comes with his angels and immortal
saints, takes and holds eternal possession.   There is not a
child in all the family who will be excluded from the
island, when made new, who had not deliberately rejected
the merciful and gracious offer of its possession; not one
can rise up in court and make a righteous defence, and all
will have an opportunity.   The father himself will put in
a defence against the accusations of his disloyal children
in order to justify himself before his faithful sons and
daughters, and show both classes that he had done what
was consistent for him to do, to induce all to love and
obey him.   Hence it is written: " That every tongue
may be stopped, and all the world become guilty before
God."

The little children of every generation will be there,
whether of Christian or heathen parentage.   Instead of
the lost ones being the dear children of their heavenly
Father, as those of the farmer of Ingersoll's illustration,
they evinced no love, no sympathy for their God and
Father.   On the contrary, every one of them did his best,
both by precept and example, to expel God from his
world; every one of them joined in heart in the cry of
the rejection of Christ, their rightful Lord, King and

Saviour: "Away with him, he is not fit to live." Even Ingersoll, with the malignity of a devil, after drawing his picture of human suffering, asks: "Did a god or fiend do this?" To what purpose can the Father appropriate such children? How could they answer any end that by any possibility could be pleasing to him? What kind of salvation even would it be to such were they admitted into his palace and presence, with every feeling of their heart revolting against his will and government? What kind of heaven would it be where such men as Ingersoll and Paine lived? How would it rouse the ire of such proud hearts to behold Jesus Christ adored by angels and the whole multitude of glorified immortals? No! If they were alive they would rush from such presence and such employment, even into outer darkness, seeking natural companionship with kindred devils. No! The exclusion of the wicked from God and his presence lies not so much in arbitrary enactments as in the very nature and fitness of things. "How can two dwell together except they be agreed?" It is the philosophy of the mind in thinking and willing, the heart in feeling, and the cherished habits of life, that raises the barrier, that digs the impassable gulf between God and sinners. Every student of Scripture will see that the picture we have drawn is but a transcription of the revealed purpose and plan of God with man and the world, while that of Ingersoll's, giving the facts without the reasons, is a monstrous effusion of ignorance and blasphemy. "A prudent man foreseeth the evil, and hideth himself; but the simple pass on, and are punished." (Prov. 22 : 3.)

The Sceptic's Arrogance : he would have made a Better World.

Says he: "A very pious friend of mine, having heard that I had said the world was full of imperfections, asked me if the report was true. Upon being informed that it was, he expressed great surprise that anyone could be guilty of such presumption. He said that in his judgment it was impossible to point out an imperfection. Be kind enough, said he, to name an improvement that you could make, if you had the power.   Well, I said, I would make health catching, instead of disease." Yes ! his pious friend, in short, might have rejoined ; but if the proprietor had appointed unto men once to die, as necessary to the acco..plishment of his purpose of making an eternal world of li.. and perfect exemption from disease, and were you the proprietor, you could not have carried out the appointment had you made perpetual health in this world the order of things, the order of nature.   But if any one expects Ingersoll to see more than one side of any question involved in these subjects, he will be disappointed.   He continues thus : "The truth is, it is impossible to harmonize all the ills, pains, and agonies of the world with the idea that we are created, watched over, and protected by an infinitely wise, powerful, and beneficent God, who is superior to and independent of nature."   The reason these things cannot be harmonized in Ingersoll's estimation is his erroneous idea that the present world is a Theocracy, or that God in Scripture claims it to be such, which would make all men loyal subjects of his government ; the fact being that every adult is at heart and spirit opposed to it, and the vast majority remain thus during their natural life, and God understands all about their rebellious nature.   Upon the question we have such information as the following : "Lo, this only have I found, that God made man upright ; but they have sought out many inventions."   (Ecc. 7 : 29.)   The world is represented as being under the reign of sin and death, and that the world itself is the object of man's love and worship, instead of God his Creator : "They love the creature more than the Creator."   Thus have they made a god of the world itself : "The god of this world hath blinded the minds of them that believe not, lest the light of the glorious gospel of Christ, who is the image of God, should shine unto them.   But if our gospel be hid, it is hid to them that are lost."   (2 Cor. 4 : 3, 4.)   The inhabitants of the present "evil world," as it is called, are in open revolt against the laws and government of God as he would and will have it in his coming new world, and there is not a pang of human suffering but which results from the ignorant or wilful violation of moral, religious, and physical law, and all the ignorance and sin has been transmitted by the precepts and example of sinners. In fact, God does not even propose to protect and provide the necessaries of life for his own loving children in the present world, millions of whom have starved for the want of food. In fact the loving, loyal children of God have suffered in the present world more than the " lovers of the world," and they were forewarned of this before they became his disciples. Said their Master : " The time will come when he that killeth you will think that he doeth God service. And ye shall be hated of all nations for my name's sake ; but not a hair of your head shall perish, for I will raise it up at the last day."

This cruelty was inflicted upon them from the foundation of the world. Abel lost his life for obeying his Lord. "They were tortured, not accepting deliverance ; that they might obtain a better resurrection. Others had trial of cruel mockings and scourgings ; yea, moreover, of bonds and imprisonments. They were stoned, sawn asunder, tempted, slain with the edge of the sword ; they wandered about in sheep-skins and goat-skins ; being destitute, afflicted, tormented ; of whom the world was not worthy ; they wandered in deserts, and in mountains, and in dens and caves of the earth. These all having obtained a good report through faith, received not the promise [things promised], but died in the faith and hope of the resurrection at the last day." (Heb. 11 : 35–39.) God has subjected the whole world, including his righteous children, to the sufferings and physical derangements to which Ingersoll refers ; so that by the mouth of the prophet he declares : " The curse hath devoured the earth," and under which it is doomed to groan until God redeems it for his children. With this prospect lying before them we have such language as the following : " And if children, then heirs ; heirs of God, and joint-heirs with Christ ; if so be we suffer with him, that we may be also glorified together. For I reckon that the suffer-

ings of the present time are not worthy to be compared
with the glory which shall be revealed in us ; for the
earnest expectation of the creature waiteth for the manifestation of the sons of God.   For the creature was made
subject to vanity [liable to have been made in vain, not
answering the purpose for which they were made], not
willingly, but by reason of him, who hath subjected the
same in hope ; because the creature itself shall be delivered from the bondage of corruption, into the glorious
liberty of the children of God.   For we know that the
whole creation groaneth and travaileth in pain together
until now.   And not only they, but ourselves also,
which have the first-fruits of the spirit, even we ourselves
groan within ourselves, waiting for the adoption, *to wit*,
the redemption of our body." (Rom. 8 : 17, 18.)

God did not willingly subject the world to this derangement; but by the losses thus sustained men would
more easily be induced to seek an inheritance in his new
creation.   He thus subjected it in hope.   Its language is,
" Cursed is the ground *for thy sake*."   Christ gave John
a prefiguration of it as he saw it would be and appear
when made new, and his redeemed children had taken
possession, and for whose encouragement he was directed
to write thus : " And I saw a new heaven and a new
earth ; for the first heaven and the first earth were passed
away ; and there was no more *sea* [this shows that the
sea, now covering more than two-thirds of the earth's
surface, was a part of the curse—the second curse, that of
the flood].   And I John saw the holy city, New Jerusalem
[capital city of the new world, " the city of the great
King "], coming down from God out of heaven, prepared
as a bride adorned for her husband.   And I heard a
great voice out of heaven saying, Behold ! the tabernacle
of God is with men, and he will dwell with them, and
they shall be his people, and *God himself* shall be with
them, and be their God.   And God shall wipe away all
tears from their eyes ; and there shall be no more death :
neither sorrow, nor crying, neither shall there be any
more pain ; for the former things are passed away.   And
there shall be no more curse.   And he that sat upon the

throne said, Behold, I make all things new. And he said unto me, Write; for these words are true and faithful. And he said unto me, It is done! I am Alpha and Omega, the beginning and the end. He that overcometh shall inherit all things; and I will be his God, and he shall be my son." (Rev. 21 and 22.) Here, Jesus that was dead is the God of all the immortal saints.

"Jesus answered and said unto them, If a man love me, he will keep my words; and my Father will love him, and we will come unto him, and make our abode with him." (John 14: 23.) "In my Father's house are many mansions; if it were not so, I would have told you. I go to prepare a place for you. And if I go and prepare a place for you, I will come again, and receive you unto myself; that where I am, there ye may be also." (John 14: 2, 3.) Here, Christ and his Father, who are "one," has come, according to his promise, and brought the mansions with him—the New Jerusalem—and has taken his abode, made his dwelling place, on the earth and among men, safe, because beyond the susceptibility of death or evil. This is therefore salvation—"They that shall be counted worthy to obtain that world, and the resurrection from the dead, are the children of God, being the children of the resurrection; neither can they die any more." (Luke 20: 35.) Here is the solution of God's grand design with man and the world. It is this innumerable multitude of re-created men and women, no more liable to suffer, that vindicates the wisdom, protection, goodness, and mercy of God, in subjecting the present short life of man, and that of the death-period of the world itself; for its six thousand years bears no proportion to its redeemed and re-created eternity. Ingersoll, knowing nothing about this end, clearly taught throughout the Scriptures, leaves him floundering in ignorance, and complaining of the irreconcilable condition of things; to prove to the pious friend of his, that the present world is not under the government of God, while there is not an intimation in all the Scriptures that it is under his government. He might have given an illustration of his own experience to prove that God did not govern the present world, thus: "Here am I engaged in openly defying God, and using the most scornful language toward him, which he would not permit if he governs mankind; he does not even defend his own character against my charges. If he did govern and control men, why, when I was about to utter one of my common blasphemies, he would instantly smite my tongue with speechless paralysis; but as I do this with impunity, therefore there is no God, or he does not govern the world."

The modest ex-Colonel says: "I hold that the man who roots up the tares from out the path of life confers some benefit, even if he never sows a seed of good." Christ's servants, in the parable, said: "Wilt thou then that we go and gather out the tares? And he said, Nay; lest while ye gather up the tares, ye root up also the wheat with them. Let both grow together until the harvest; and in the time of harvest I will say to the reapers [his angels], Gather ye together first the tares, and bind them in bundles to burn them; but gather the wheat into my barn. The tares are the children of the wicked one. The enemy that sowed them is the devil. The wheat-seed are the children of the kingdom." (Matt. 13.)

Ingersoll, being a rank tare himself and seeing the present suffering of mankind, which he cannot destroy, he is endeavoring to dissipate all future hope from it by preaching eternal annihilation.

The hope of exemption from suffering and death in the future world encourages men to endure the sufferings of the present, even gives joy under them; but he calls those who indulge this hope tares, and would root them out of the world. Infinite arrogance! Behold, the devil's supreme tare sower!

CHAPTER XII.

THE scoffer says: "For three hundred years the Christian world endeavored to rescue from the infidel the empty sepulchre of Christ. For three hundred years the armies of the cross were baffled and beaten by the victorious hosts of an impudent impostor. The immense fact sowed the seeds of discontent throughout Christendom; and millions began to lose confidence in a God who had been vanquished by Mohammed. The people also found that commerce made friends where religion made enemies, and that religious zeal was utterly incompatible with peace between nations or individuals. They discovered that those that loved God most loved men least; that the arrogance of universal forgiveness was amazing; that the most malicious had the effrontery to pray for their enemies; and that humility and tyranny were the fruit of the same tree."

Here we have another list of this man's slanders of God, Christ, and his religion. Not one of the things to which he refers is authorized by the Scriptures. First, there is no "Christian world;" there are Christians in it, and the reason why they are such is because they follow Christ in being harmless, and separate from sinners, keeping his instructions and commands, one of which is, "Put up thy sword, for he that taketh the sword shall perish by the sword." These crusaders, therefore, disobeyed Christ and obeyed the popes. Christ's converts were only made by believing the gospel and obeying its precepts; theirs, by the sword of aggressive warfare. Second, Christ never told his disciples that the sepulchre in which he once lay had the least sacredness about it, or ever intimated that his servants were to rescue and hold it by any means, much less by the sword of blood; hence, he nor his religion were in nowise responsible for the crusades; and Christians, his followers, never marched to Jerusalem to prosecute a bloody fight for an empty cave; consequently they were not beaten back by an impudent impostor. The immense fact, therefore, that God had been beaten by Mohammed, is no fact at all; but is one of this other impostor's lies, though, like a parrot, he only repeats the stale story.

Third, the Bible condemns all religious zeal which is not according to knowledge, and it is always such when it leads its possessor to execute acts unauthorized or condemned by the Scriptures; and if it makes aggressive war upon other nations, it is of this character. The discovery that those who loved God most loved men least was never made at all, and it is as contrary to common philosophy as to Scripture, thus: "If a man say, I love God, and hateth his brother, he is a liar. For he that loveth not his brother, whom he hath seen, how can he love God, whom he hath not seen? And this commandment have we from him, That he who loveth God loveth his brother also." (1 John 4: 20, 21.) Those, therefore, to whom Ingersoll alludes were anti-Christians like himself, hating both their brother and their God. He stigmatizes universal forgiveness "arrogance." If in the last great judgment God should forgive him, would he consider that arrogance? Besides, such is not the doctrine of the Bible. Its Author proposes to forgive none who do not heartily repent of their wickedness and work righteousness thereafter. He says: "The most malicious prayed for their enemies, and this showed them to be hypocritical at heart." Well, then they were not Christians. A man who can say, "Humility and tyranny are the fruit of the same tree," has audacity and ignorance equal to any statement, having no regard for truth, propriety, reason, or self-respect. As well say light and darkness have the same root, grow on the same tree.

The scoffer says: "The clergy balance all the ills of life with the expected joys of the next life." Having no

hope of future happiness himself, he seems to be maddened at the idea of joy in any future world for others,
and consoles himself by imitating his father-devil in trying to destroy the future hope of everyone else.   His pen
and tongue turns God into a tyrant, angels into fiends,
and heaven into hell, if there are such places.   He has
discovered that the most effectual weapons to accomplish
this object are ridicule,. abuse, sarcasm, sophistry, and
presumptuous lies, which he adopts and wields with the
vengeance of cowardly audacity.   That we do him no injustice, listen to the following : " We are assured that all
is perfection in heaven ; there the skies are cloudless,
there all is serenity and peace.   Here empires may be
overthrown, dynasties extinguished in blood, millions of
slaves may toil beneath the fierce rays of the sun and
the cruel strokes of the lash ; yet all is happiness in heaven.
[But none of these things would happen if men would
obey their God, loving him with all the heart, and their
neighbor as themselves.] Pestilences may strew the earth
with corpses of loved ones ; the survivors may bend
above them in agony ; yet the placid bosom of heaven is
unruffled.   [That is not the heaven where God and his
angels reside.   So intensely are they interested in that
which takes place among men on earth, to hasten the purpose of God in obtaining subjects for his coming endless
empire, that when a single convert accepts the conditions
the master of the place says, " I say unto you, there is joy
in the presence of the angels of God over one sinner that
repenteth." (Luke 15 : 10.)]
   " Children may expire, vainly asking for bread ; babes
may be devoured by serpents ; while God sits smiling in
the clouds.   [Never in the Bible is God represented as
sitting in the clouds smiling ; and, wherever he sits, he is
long-suffering with men, not willing they should perish,
but come to repentance and live.]   The innocent may
languish in the obscurity of dungeons ; brave men and
women may be changed into ashes at the bigot's stake ;
while heaven is filled with song and joy.   [God's remedy
for the martyrs is provided for thus : " He that loseth
his life for my sake shall find it again ; " and that life will

be without end : "And this is the will of him that sent me, that every one which seeth the Son, and believeth on him, may have everlasting life ; and I will raise him up at the last day." (John 6 : 40.) Ingersoll fabricates a heartless God and a fictitious heaven, in order to prejudice men and women, whom he supposes as ignorant upon these subjects as himself, against the God and heaven of the Scriptures.] Out on the sea, in darkness and storm, the shipwrecked struggle with the cruel waves ; while the angels play upon their golden harps. [There is not a passage in the Bible that says or intimates that angels play on golden or any other kind of harps in heaven. Those who thus rejoice are the redeemed and resurrected saints of God, and it is at their eternal victory in the new heavens and new earth, and all the innocent children of all ages and the repentant sinners are to be the harpers ; nor is it until all the impenitent have suffered the second death, and all saints are saved beyond the liability of harm. This is as near as Ingersoll ever gets anything right which is taught in the Scriptures.] The streets of the world are filled with the diseased, deformed, and helpless ; the chambers of pain are crowded with pale forms of suffering ; while the angels float and play in their happy realms of glory. In heaven they are too happy to have sympathy ; too busy singing to aid the imploring and distressed. Their eyes are blinded, their ears are stopped, and their hearts turned to stone by the infinite selfishness of joy." [This is another picture of his fictitious heaven, not an item of which is taught in the Bible. Its place of rejoicing is to be the new heaven and new earth, in which, as we have seen, there will not be a pang of suffering, all of which belonged to the past and had passed away, and also in which there is not an existing will of man or devil hostile to the will of God, therefore nothing to mar the joys of God, angels, or men. Who would have thought Ingersoll had ever read the Bible, had he not said he had ?] He says, "Heaven barely glances at the miseries of earth." [God, angels, and his saints did all they could to induce such as he to seek this life of future happiness ;

but they scoffed at all the gracious offers, and abused them for sacrificing the mere animal joys of the present short life for that of this immortal world.]

He says: "The terrible religious wars that inundated the world, tended at last to bring all religions into disgrace and hatred." The contrary of this is the historic fact, whether of false or true religion. There never were as many Mohammedans, Roman Catholics, Jews, and Protestants on earth as at the present day. Besides, all the rest of the world are Pagans. Among the Pagans there are no atheists; among the Mohammedans none; among the Jews none; among the Roman Catholics none; and only here and there a professing atheist among nominal Christians. How, then, is all religion held in contempt? Such assertions show that whatever Ingersoll desires he states as a fact. He says: "Thoughtful people begin to question the divine origin of a religion that made its believers hold the rights of others in contempt." One of the cardinal principles of the Christian religion, everyone but Ingersoll knows, is absolute respect for the rights of others, and if he means the right of the crusaders to take Jerusalem from the Mohammedans, it was Papacy and not Christianity that did it; and that religion claims the right to use the sword of war in its establishment, but which the laws of God forbid. Christianity recognizes her subjects as aliens in this world and heritable citizens of the world to come.

Says the Lying Oracle: "A few began to compare Christianity with the religions of heathen people, and were forced to admit that the difference was hardly worth dying for." Yes, very few; for during the first three centuries of the Christian era, the Christian religion almost superseded the Pagan religion of the Roman empire, though supported by the civil power, and that too by its natural means, the preaching of the gospel. And if he refers to the days of the crusades, then Romanism had so far corrupted nominal Christianity, that scarcely an example either of its faith or practice could be found. It was the "*Dark Ages.*" He says: "They also found that other nations were even happier and more prosperous than their own, and they began to suspect that their religion, after all, was not of much real value." These are not true statements, for history shows that during the Christian era there has not been a heathen nation as happy and prosperous as those which were merely nominal Christian; and how would this have been increased had everyone of them been a real Christian nation, whose practice is the golden rule! It is another fact that no mere nominal Christian country ever went back to heathenism, which it would have done had the people found it would have made them more prosperous and happy.

Progress of the Gospel in the First Three Centuries.

In order to rightly estimate the value and purity of the gospel, its history must be taken when it stood alone upon its merits, and against all the religions of the world, though sustained by the military and legal power of their states; and this period was from the days of Christ until it became the legal religion of the Roman Empire, which began in the days of Constantine the Great, who came to the throne A.D. 319. To show what it was during this period we introduce the following testimony of its enemies: " Most of the Roman Emperors who reigned in the second century were of a mild and lenient character, and under their administration the churches enjoyed many seasons of tranquillity, though they were occasionally called to pass through the fire. Before the close of the first century, Nerva had granted toleration to the Church, and restored the Christian exiles; but his successor, Trajan, renowned for his philosophic virtues, managed the question so as to put the Christians without the protection of law. If he did not issue edicts against them, he suffered the populace to wreak their vengeance on them and destroy them at pleasure. A violent persecution raged in Bethynia. Not knowing what course to pursue, Pliny, the governor of the province, addressed a letter to the emperor, which gives such an account of the Christians as a candid and intelligent heathen would form, and being an official document of the age, as well as its answer, is entitled to the fullest credibility. It was written about A.D. 107.

Pliny's Letter to the Emperor Trajan.

" Health : It is my usual custom, Sir, to refer all things of which I harbor any doubt, to you ; for who can better direct my judgment in its hesitation, or instruct my understanding in its ignorance ? I never had the fortune to be present at any examination of Christians before I came into this province ; I am therefore at a loss to determine what is the usual object of inquiry or of punishment, and to what length either of them is to be carried. It has been with me a question very problematical, whether any distinction should be made between the young and old, the tender and the robust ; whether any room should be given for repentance : for the guilt of Christianity, once incurred, is not to be expiated by the most unequivocal retraction : whether the name itself, abstracted from any flagitiousness of conduct, or the crimes connected with the name, be the object of punishment. In the mean time, this has been my method, with respect to those who were brought before me as Christians. I asked them whether they were Christians. If they plead guilty, I interrogated them twice afresh, with a menace of capital punishment. In case of obstinate perseverance, I ordered them to be executed. For of this I had no doubt, whatever was the name of their religion, that a sullen inflexibility called for the vengeance of the magistrate. Some were infected with the same madness, whom on account of citizenship I reserved to be sent to Rome, to your tribunal. In the course of this business, information poured in, and as usual, when it is encouraged, more cases occur. An anonymous libel was exhibited, with a catalogue of names of persons, who yet declared they were not Christians, and never had been ; and they repeated after me an invocation to the gods and to your image, which, for this purpose, I had ordered to be brought, with the images of the deities. [They did not think the images were the deities themselves, as Ingersoll charges.] They performed sacred rites with wine and frankincense, and execrated Christ, which, I am told, no Christian can be compelled to do.

" On this account I dismissed them. Others, named by an informer, first affirmed and then denied the charge of Christianity, declaring that they had been Christians, but had ceased to be such some three years before. All of them worshipped your image and the statues of the gods, and also execrated Christ. This was the account they gave of the nature of their religion, whether it deserves the name of crime or error, namely, that they were accustomed on a stated day to meet before daylight, and to repeat among themselves a hymn to Christ as a God [thus did the Christians at this early day worship Christ as God], and to bind themselves with an oath not to commit any wickedness, but to abstain from thefts and not to break their pledge, after which they separated and met again at a promiscuous, harmless meal, from which last practice they desisted after the publication of your edict, in which, agreeably to your orders, I forbade any societies of that sort. On which account I judged it more necessary to inquire by torture, from two females, who were said to be deaconesses, what is the real truth. But nothing could I collect, except a depraved and excessive superstition. Deferring any further investigation, I determined to consult you, for the number of culprits is so great as to call for serious consideration. [That the Christians should increase so as to justify this admission, and under such circumstances, can only be attributed to the power of the gospel.] Many persons are informed against, of every age and of both sexes ; and still more will be in the same situation. The contagion of the superstition hath spread, not only through cities, but even to villages in the country. Not that I think it impossible to check and correct it. The success of my endeavors hitherto forbid such desponding thoughts ; for the temples, once almost desolate, begin to be frequented,

9

and the sacred solemnities, which had long been inter-
mitted, are now attended afresh, and the sacred victims
are now sold everywhere, which once could scarcely find
a purchaser. Whence I conclude that many might be
reclaimed, were the hope of impunity on repentance absolutely confirmed."—PLINY.

Here is indisputable testimony, showing that in about
eighty years after the crucifixion, Christianity had almost
destroyed the worship of the gods, and in the most popular part of the Roman Empire ; and that, too, when its
converts were outlawed and martyred for its profession.
Surely it could not have been this period that the heathen
discovered no value or difference between the Christian
religion and that of heathenism. And shortly after
this Christianity became corrupted to the level of pagan-
ism by its espousal by the Roman Empire, bringing the
world into the church, and from which she has never recovered ; and Ingersoll's blunder is in confounding the
fallen with the true Church, Christ with antichrist,
light with darkness, truth with error, and condemning
both alike !

Trajan's Answer to Pliny.

" You have done right in the inquiry you have made
concerning Christians ; for, truly, no one general rule
can be laid down which will apply to all cases. These
people must not be sought after. If they are brought
before you and are convicted, let them be capitally punished ; yet with this restriction, that if any one renounces
Christianity, and evidences his sincerity by supplicating
our gods, however suspected he may be for the past, he
shall obtain pardon for the future, on his repentance.
But anonymous libels ought in no case to be attended to,
for the precedent would be of the worst sort, and perfectly incongruous to the maxims of my government."—
MARCH'S " Ecc. History," pages 171–173.

Here is the admission that in the highest court of the
Roman world, the profession of the Christian religion
was a crime punishable by death ; and yet, in little more
than half a century, the idol temples were forsaken, and

the sacred victims could not be sold in the shambles ; and, as we have seen, the dreadful effort of the Emperor and his successors not only failed to exterminate it, but it continued so to prosper that, in the beginning of the fourth century, it was a popular and easy task for the Emperor Constantine the Great to change the religion of the state to that of Christianity.

Testimony of a Distinguished Martyr.

The most distinguished martyr of the age—the latter part of the second century—was Polycarp. This venerable man was a disciple of John, and intimate with the other disciples. He belonged to the church of Smyrna ; and in that age there was but one church in a locality, and from it always took its name. Ireneus informs us that he had often heard from his lips an account of his conversations with John and others who had seen the Lord, whose sayings he rehearsed. Polycarp was brought before the tribunal in the hundredth year of his age. The proconsul commanded him to reproach Christ, and he would release him ; but he replied : " Eighty and six years have I served him, and he hath never wronged me. How can I now blaspheme my King ? " " I have wild beasts," said the proconsul. " Call them," said the Christian. " I will tame your spirit by fire." " Do what you please," said the martyr, " and why do you delay ? " The fire was brought and he was bound to the stake, his hands tied behind him, which he clasped, and said : " O Father of thy beloved and blessed Son Jesus Christ ; O God of angels, principalities, and of all creation ; I bless thee that thou hast counted me worthy of this day and hour, to receive my portion in the number of martyrs—the cup of Christ, for the resurrection to eternal life, both of soul and body." The fire consumed the martyr, but Rome was unable to subdue the humble trophy of the grace of God, and he triumphed even in death !

Tertullian's Apology for the Church of the First Three Centuries.

The benevolence of the Christians up to the last part of the third century was such as has never been witnessed since. They not only gave their treasures to their own poor, but they exerted themselves to relieve distress-and suffering everywhere they found it, and at this time the Church in Rome supported a thousand widows. Christians felt that they did not deserve the name unless they spent their lives in imitation of that of Christ their Master. Immense estates were consecrated to public charity. Having renounced the luxuries of the world, they did not need great wealth, and they viewed their poor brethren on a level with themselves, as sinners to be ransomed by the Son of God. The number of the Christian converts, their crucifixion to the interests of the world, and the extent of their good works, is best shown by one of their own number. In his apology for the Christians, Tertullian says : " We pray for the safety of the emperors to the eternal God ; that they may have a long life, a secure empire, a safe palace, a faithful senate, a well moralized people, and a quiet state of the world. Were we disposed to act the part, I will not say of secret assassins, but open enemies, should we want forces and numbers ? Are there not multitudes of us in every part of the world? It is true, we are but of yesterday, and yet we have filled all your towns, cities, islands, boroughs, councils, camps, courts, palaces, senate, and forum. We leave you only your temples.

" For what war should we not be ready and well prepared, even though unequal in numbers ; were it not that our religion requires us rather to suffer death than to inflict it ? If we were to make a general secession from your dominions, you would be astonished at your solitude. We are dead to all ideas of worldly honor and dignity ; nothing is more foreign to us than political concerns. The whole world is our republic. We are a body united in one bond of religion, discipline, and hope. We meet

in our assemblies for prayer.   Every one pays something
into the public chest once a month, or when he please
and according to his ability and inclination, for there is
no compulsion.   These gifts are, as it were, the deposits
of piety.   Hence we relieve the needy and bury the dead,
support orphans and decrepid persons, assist those who
have suffered shipwreck, and comfort those who, for
teaching the word of God, are condemned to the mines
for imprisonment.   This charity of ours has caused us to
be noticed : See, say they, how these Christians love
one another.''

It is as certain that this church, this religion, was that
of the holy Scriptures, as that it is in palpable contrast to
that which was established by the sword of Constantine
at the beginning of the fourth century.   Can it be said of
this church, that '' It is dead to all ideas of worldly honor
and dignity ; that nothing is more foreign to it than political concerns ; that we are united in one body, one discipline, one bond of religion, and one name ; winning the
poor and needy from the Pagan selfish religion, by first
feeding and clothing them, to that whose test and standard
is thus written ? ''—'' Whoso hath this world's goods, and
seeth his brother have need, and shutteth up his bowels of
compassion from him, how dwelleth the love of God in
him ? ''   Their religion was the embodiment of humanity
in its highest form—the implantation of the spirit, disposition of God, personally manifested in Jesus Christ.
Their future hope rested alone in the resurrection of both
soul and body from the dead.   For having a religion so
humane, a worship so rational, and a hope so palpable
and philosophical, they were called atheists by the mythological priests of heathendom.   They had no creed but
the Bible.   Christ's disposition, precepts, and words
were the guide of their life and the groundwork of future
life and hope.   Of course, any system of religion, whether
called Catholic or Prostestant or by any other name,
lacking any of these features, is a fallen system, and it is
an abusive degradation to Christ and his religion to judge
it by these worldly, men-made standards.   As well hold
Michelangelo responsible for his most masterly painting,

after being defaced by the brush of ignorance or design. It is as though the great principles of human freedom are responsible for its destruction by the hand of ambitious tyranny. Nothing, therefore, is more wicked and absurd than for Ingersoll and his confederates to first confound Christianity with its corrupt counterfeits, and then scoff at the incongruity of their own work. It is the duty of Ingersoll, and his God and Creator holds him responsible for its discharge, to preach a reformation, taking as the standard the church of the first three centuries, when there were no creeds, and which popery destroyed by making one, and that one was the first creed! If he would do this, he would enlist not only the sympathy, but the co-operation of every Christian, whether Jew or Gentile, in the civilized world. But here, with the power of truth, we put a hook in the jaw of this dastardly cowardice of the self-styled freethinkers, who are engaged in this crusade against their Maker, because they see they may do so at present with impunity, but without regard to the wrath they thus treasure to themselves against the day of wrath: " Because sentence against an evil work is not executed speedily, therefore the heart of the sons of men is fully set in them to do evil." (Ecc. 8 : 11.)

Ingersoll says : " For years a deadly conflict has been waged between a few brave men and women of thought and genius upon one side, and the great ignorant mass on the other. This is the war between science and faith. The few have appealed to reason, to honor, to law, to freedom, and to the known, and happiness here in this world. The many have appealed to prejudice, to fear, to miracle, to slavery, to the unknown, and to misery hereafter. The few have said, Think. The many have said, Believe." Against this flight of egotistic boasting we place the facts of history, facts of physical, moral, and political science, facts of philosophy, facts of Scripture, facts of common observation and of experience, facts of the power of the gospel to ameliorate human suffering in the highest possible degree in the present world, as well as to inspire human happiness by the promise of eternal wealth and life. Of course, it is only a deadly conflict to the few who wage the war against their Maker. Who would suppose that such men and women think? He says: " It is a war of religion against science." No, sir, there is no war between the science of nature and the religion of Christ, as the religion is the highest philosophic science itself, and that of nature, being the work of God himself, must be as perfect as its author. There may be war between your ignorant conceptions of both of these departments of the works of God. Belief, to Ingersoll, is incomprehensible; having no knowledge of the God of nature or of his written revelation, he has no grounds upon which to base belief, and evidence is the inseparable condition of belief—this being an unquestionable principle of mental, philosophical science. Hence the fictitious warfare is in the vain imagination of the " Brave Thinker."

Mythological Nomenclature.

In the passage from Ingersoll we are about to quote, and in which he has collected the names of many of the prominent heathen deities, among whom he blasphemously ranks Christ, the God of the Scriptures, with the hope of degrading him to the level of his animosity. It might be supposed from this effort that he was well acquainted with the ancient classics and modern history, as well as with the religious facts of the present day; but we shall see that such an inference is without justification. The god of any man is that object which he loves most, honors, and serves, and for which he will make the greatest sacrifices to please; and every man has such a god. While many of these gods in name and form have passed away, their places have been filled by others; and the principal religions, of which they were the outward symbols twenty-five hundred years ago, remain until the present day, and have more worshippers than in any period of the past; and so God's prophets predict it will be to the very last age of the world. We may also remark that these gods of the ancients represented every passion of human nature, every depraved appetite, and every ambitious scheme of revenge; and it was the indulgence of these that constituted the worship, while that of the true God is unique and requires the crucifixion of all these passions. For example, to get intoxicated in the days of Alexander the Great was called the worship of Bacchus, the god of drunkenness; and to perform the same devotion, to become the servant of the same base appetite, is the same worship—the service of the passions being the service of the gods—and is in direct hostility to that of the living God. Hence he must forbid all such worship and reject all such service. Paul gives us the philosophy of the question, thus: "Know ye not that to whom ye yield yourselves servants to obey, his servants ye are, whether of sin unto death, or of obedience unto righteousness." (Rom. 6 : 6.)

Another of these gods of antiquity was called Mammon, the god of riches. Of course, the service of this god is the love of money, and is hostile to the Christian religion. Christ says: "Ye cannot serve God and Mammon." (Matt. 6 : 24.) The gospel gives this species of idol-worship the name of "covetousness:" "Covetousness, which is idolatry." (Col. 3 : 5.) That the devotees to this god have not passed away, but are very numerous at the present day, is shown by the popular name given to our times—"the age of the almighty dollar." Even for money Ingersoll curses God and looks upward. He says: "In that vast cemetery, called the past, are most of the religions of men, and there, too, are nearly all of the gods. [The love of the world is called the god of this world, "who blinds the minds of them that believe not," and has so blinded the mind of Ingersoll that he thinks all the gods and their worship is interred in the cemetery of the past.] The sacred temples of India were ruins long ago. Over column and cornice, over painted and pictured walls, cling and creep the trailing vines." [But the idolatrous religion of India lies not thus buried, and her devotees are more numerous than ever before, though her symbolic gods may have become crystallized in the lower form of atheism, even more degrading than the pronounced worship of Brahma or Mohammed.]

He says : " Brahma, the golden, with four heads and four arms; Vishnu, the sombre, the punisher of the wicked, with his three eyes, his crescent, and his necklace of skulls ; Siva, the destroyer, red with blood ; Kali, the goddess ; Draupadi, the white-armed ; and Chrishna, the Christ—all have passed away and left the thrones of heaven desolate."

There is more beauty in this paragraph than sense or truth, as Chrishna—interpreted Christ—is no heathen god, though millions of heathen have learned to worship him ; and the only fact relative to his having passed away is that he is to return and reign forever, King of kings and Lord of lords, in his own re-created world.   He says : " Along the banks of the sacred Nile Isis no longer wanders and weeps, searching for the dead Osiris.   The shadow of Typhon's scowl falls no more upon the waves. The sun rises as of yore, and his golden beams still smite the lips of Memnon, but Memnon is as voiceless as the Sphinx.   The sacred fanes are lost in the desert sands ; and the dusty mummies are still waiting for the resurrection promised by their priests.   [This is a fabrication of Ingersoll, or one which he quotes, made to degrade the doctrine of the resurrection, as though it was taught elsewhere than in the Bible, while there is not an intimation, even in Egyptian mythology, that the priests entertained the least conception of a resurrection of the dead, and it was unknown to Orpheus, Socrates, Plato, or Aristotle, which completely exposes the fraud of any attempt to so interpret Egyptian hieroglyphic, or the cuneiform slabs dug from Babylon and Nineveh.   All of these men studied at the schools of Alexandria, in Egypt.

While it may be true that the notion of Egyptian metempsychosis was a corruption of the doctrine of future existence by the resurrection, understood by Joseph, Jacob, and Moses, the latter of whom was taught in all the learning of the Egyptians, it is inconceivable that such a man, the virtual king of Egypt, should not have in turn taught in their schools the Scripture doctrine of the resurrection, more elaborately revealed in the Old Testament than in the New.]   And the old beliefs wrought in curiously sculptured stones, sleep in a language lost and dead. [If the language is lost and dead, what right has he to say it teaches a resurrection?] Oden, the author of life and soul—[this Scandinavian deity is the same as the Woden of the Saxons, who never was claimed to be the author of life or the creator of man, and the highest honor paid him was dedicating to him the Wednesday, the fourth day of the week, " Woden's day "] ; Vili and Ve, and the mighty giant Ymir, strode long ago from the icy hills of the north ; and Thor, with his glove-glittering hammer, dashes mountains to the earth no more.   Broken are the circles and cromlecks of the ancient Druids ; fallen upon the summits of the hills, covered with the centuries' moss, are the sacred cairns.

The divine fires of Persia and the Aztes have died out in the ashes of the past, and there is none to rekindle and none to feed the flames.   The harp of Orpheus is still ; the drained cup of Bacchus has been thrown aside [never was there such devotion paid to the god of wine, as at the present day ; Bacchus was the god of wine, and son of Jupiter] ; Venus lies dead in stone, and her white bosom heaves no more with love.   [Christ says : " Every one that loveth father, mother, sister, brother, wife or husband, houses or lands, more than me, is not worthy of me," and all such are the devotees of " Venus ; " and O how her symbolic bosom heaves with the " love of the creature more than the creator " in our day !]   The streams still murmur, but no naiads bathe ; the trees still wave, but in the forest aisles no dryads dance.   [A dryad is a nymph of the woods.]   The gods have flown from high Olympus.   Not even the beautiful women can lure them back.   Danaë lies unnoticed, naked to the stars. Hushed forever are the thunders of Sinai.   [And they were never heard but a part of forty days ; but the laws that were given amid their voices have not, and never will, cease their thunderings against all ungodliness and the perpetrators of crime, and especially against the blasphemers who associate them with the imaginary voices of dumb idols ; and never will those flaming laws cease their thunders until they are opened in the judgment at the last day, and then, according to their writings, every scoffer and slanderer's voice will be forever hushed: " And they were judged out of those things written in the books, according to their works."] Lost are the voices of the prophets. [No, sir ! never did their voices speak with such clearness, or were understood so well, as at the present day, being vindicated by the fulfilment of the events of our own times, both national and religious.] And the land once flowing with milk and honey is but a desert waste. [And this fact is a perfect fulfilment of the predictions of the prophets thus voiced.] One by one the myths have faded from the clouds. [There never were any myths located in the clouds, by the voice of the prophet.] One by one the phantoms have disappeared, and one by one, facts, truths, and realities have taken their places. The supernatural has almost gone, but the natural remains : the gods have fled, but man is here."

It is not a fact that the gods have fled, but quite otherwise, and they are more numerous than ever before ; and the devotees, instead of being formal worshippers of the gods, as the ancients were, have set up their idols in their hearts : its phantoms have passed away, but its realities have become crystallized in the huge idol, " The love of the world." The God of the prophets, foreseeing this, inspired them to write : " Love not the world, nor the things of the world. He that loveth the world, the love of the Father is not in him." The universal *love of the world*, as in our day, is universal idolatry. Here is the god of this world, who hath " blinded the minds of them that believe not," who, laboring under the deception, leads them to think, with Ingersoll, that the gods have passed away.

Of course, the more follow the gods, the less follow the living God. Of course, there is but an insignificant number who are willing to be called atheists ; but who masquerade under the specious title of *scientists*. That, in the estimation of Ingersoll, the supernatural is almost gone, has its explanation in the fact that he does not know enough about the natural to see the philosophic ne-

cessity for the existence of the supernatural ; that everything in nature, in its inherent perpetuity and commencement, bears the stamp of the supernatural.

A Supposition—a Counter Supposition.

The speculator says : " Suppose, upon some island we
should find a man a million years of age [this is a geological period, or one of evolution, and indicates that Robert
is going to give us something to show he has dabbled
into modern science], and suppose we should find him
in possession of a most beautiful carriage, constructed
upon the most perfect model. And suppose, further,
that he should tell us it was the result of several hundred
years of labor and thought ; that for fifty thousand years
he used as flat a log as he could find [This is foolish,
for there never was a flat log, without the hand of man to
make it such.] before it occurred to him that by split-
ting the log he could have the same surface with half the
weight ; that the wheels he first used were solid, and that
fifty thousand years of thought suggested the use of spokes
and tires ; that for many centuries he used the wheels
without linch-pins ; that it took a hundred thousand
years more to think of using four wheels instead of two.
That for ages he walked behind the carriage when going
down hill, in order to hold it back, before the tongue
was thought of ; would we conclude that man, from
the very first, had been an infinitely ingenious and perfect mechanic ? " We may say that there is no relic of
a cart or a wagon, ever having been found, which never
had a tongue, or linch-pin ; and those of solid wheels
were only used in new countries, while the most beautiful carriages were used at the same time in other countries,
or other parts of the same country. And the foolishness
of the supposition is seen in the fact that a wooden relic
could not be kept from decay even fifty years, without
the hand of art. " Suppose we found a man living in an
elegant mansion, and he should inform us that he had
lived in that house for five hundred thousand years before he thought of putting on a roof." [Why, we should

suppose the man told us a lie, and thus confessed that he was a greater fool of a mechanic than a beaver, who always makes the roof of his house first, to shelter him while he makes the sides. In fact, we should conclude that this genius of a thinker in mechanics was a striking type of such freethinkers as Ingersoll. All of these allusions are too absurd to admit of being respectable suppositions. In exposure of such fabrications, we refer their authors to the fact that there is a long list of artistic productions, the work of ancient men, which are catalogued among the *lost arts.*]

He further supposes that this dunce of an old mechanic, who concentrated all the wisdom of the past for one hundred and fifty thousand years, had not been able to invent windows and doors for his dwelling. At the second beginning of the world, sixteen hundred and sixty-six years after its creation, we have the account of the construction of a human habitation, which was at once a house and a vessel, and which had both doors and windows. In order to expel an infinitely wise God from being the inventor and constructor of nature, this prodigy of a logician argues that because things exist answering a supposed purpose which always existed, thereby showing improvement, and that improvement in things created shows a corresponding improvement in the Creator. But to show an improvement in a created thing, it is necessary to show that the thing existed before, but in a different form, and that the purpose was always the same. God made the man, and if he was a perfect artist and a mechanic at first, though the man perfectly answered the temporary purpose for which he was made, yet he was defective if he did not answer an eternal purpose, or that his temporal environment was not eternal. That because the man himself made improvement shows a corresponding improvement in the Creator. What folly !

God could invent and construct the wonderful machinery involved in the physiological structure of the man himself—a mouth to open and shut at will—transparent windows in his head through which his mind could see and distinguish objects ; but he could not make a door for a man's house, or tell a man how to make them, unless he improved in mechanic skill. Behold! what an example—what a man of thought, reason, and intelligence is this Ingersoll? Created things were at least as perfect at the beginning, as the Creator designed them to be; and many of them more so than they manifest at the present day; in fact some species of the most noble animals have degenerated to extinction. The comparison presents the same ratio of difference as that between a new and an old garment, and that this is according to the original plan of the Creator, is shown in his written book, thus: "And thou, Lord, in the beginning hast laid the foundation of the earth; and the heavens are the works of thine hands. They shall perish, but thou remainest: and they all shall wax old as doth a garment; and as a vesture shalt thou fold them up and they shall be changed; but thou art the same, and thy years shall not fail." (Heb. 1 : 10-12.) This change of the heavens and the earth is written in the twenty-first and twenty-second chapters of Revelation, all of which is copied and condensed from the Scriptures of Moses, the prophets, and the Book of Psalms. These suppositions of Ingersoll bear the general stamp of his pretended arguments against the existence of the infinite intelligence and almighty power of the Creator: false statement, false premise, and consequently false conclusion, all prompted by a desire to have it so, and pushed forward by boundless conceit and arrogance.

The Wisdom of God Questioned by the Scoffer.

Says he: "Would an infinitely wise God, intending to produce man, commence with the lowest possible forms of life; with the smallest organism that can be imagined; and during immeasurable periods of time, slowly and almost imperceptibly, improve upon the rude beginning, until man was evolved? Would countless years thus be wasted in the production of awkward forms, afterward abandoned?" Ingersoll has adopted Evolution as true science, every item of which is demonstrated to be false in published works, of which he must be ignorant ! No, Mr. Ingersoll ! nature gives the facts, whose philosophic necessities of coming into existence, show that the most perfect living and mature forms were created first, and in so short a time that the parts first formed would not decompose before the last were finished ; that life is inconsistent with a single rudiment in an animal or plant form. Your blunder is in adopting evolution as to the origin of things, and holding the Creator responsible for its foolish theory.

He asks, " Can the intelligence of man discover the least wisdom in covering the earth with crawling, creeping horrors that live only upon the pangs of others ? " I wonder if Mr. Ingersoll can see the wisdom and humanity of every day devouring parts of cattle, sheep, and innocent lambs, whose pangs would not exist if he and others did not thus devour. Or if he does not sustain his valuable life by causing the death pangs of the turkey and harmless dove. Is his wisdom indeed so superficial that he has not yet learned the fact that there is not a living thing but which furnishes food for some other living thing ; and that man himself devours more living creatures than any other animal ; and that finally worms devour him ? Now, who can see the wisdom in the Creator thus providing for man—composed of those things which reproduce themselves—keeping pace with the march of the living generations.

Besides, were there no animals to live, die, and decompose, in order to restore to the atmosphere the carbonic acid from which vegetation manufactures their own food, in a very little while it would poison animals to breathe, and they would all become extinct. Of course, his mind never comprehended the teaching of natural science, of the interdependence of the plant and animal life of the world. Had he done this, he would never have asked such silly questions, which imply the possession of superior wisdom to that of his Maker. This is the man who says science is on the side of atheism, and such are the things he dispenses with the self-confidence of ignorance, as science. He asks, " Can we see the propriety of so

constructing the earth, that only an insignificant portion
of its surface is capable of producing intelligent man?"
Here we have more sagacious thought, from the boasting
thinker who dares think for himself—there is too small a
portion of earth congenial enough to produce—grow
man.   If he did not believe in evolution, we might suppose he meant to say, " to sustain the life of man."   But
as men grow like trees, it seems to us that there is abundance of soil capable of producing men of such ideas,
and it would not be much detriment, were there no such
soil—none which would not produce a higher type of intelligent and good men than this scoffer !   It is clear
that, whether this man attempts to grapple with questions
of philosophy, science, or Scripture, he makes equally
bungling work.   Here he assumes an intelligence so
much higher than that possessed by his Maker, that it
enables him to see innumerable mistakes, blunders, and
incongruities in his works, failing to perceive as the conditions of living existence the relation one thing bears to
another.   He would have made everything independent,
all capable of resisting each other.   It is the repetition of
the almost idiotic sentiment, of the machine finding fault
with its maker—the creature with the Creator—which
was long since philosophically answered thus, " Nay
but, O vain man, who art thou that repliest against God?
Shall the thing formed say to him that formed it, Why
hast thou made me thus ? "   (Rom. 9 : 20.)   Think of
it, a thing that cannot explain how he moves a finger,
undertaking to instruct the Maker of the world !

Killing Animals for Food no Part of the Original Creation. ·

It will have been seen that it has not been merely
our object, in this work, to expose the shallowness of this
man's talk as the mouth-piece of freethinkerism ; but to
present reasons for the works of the Creator as they are.
In regard to the question of food for man and the lower
animals, we may remark that killing was no part of
the creation, but grew out of the curse of the earth and

man for his disobedience; hence it is written, "By sin, death entered into the world, and so death passed upon all men, for all have sinned." The original food for animals was provided and described thus: "And God said, Behold, I have given you every herb bearing seed, which is upon the face of all the earth, and every tree, in the which is the fruit of a tree yielding seed; to you it shall be for meat. And to every beast of the earth, and to every fowl of the air, and to everything that creepeth upon the earth, wherein there is life, I have given every green herb for meat: and it was so." (Gen. 1 : 29–31.) An herb is a plant or vegetable with a soft succulent stalk or stem, and which dies to the root every year, and is thus distinguished from a tree or shrub, which have ligneous, or hard woody stems. Even after sin entered into the world with all its concomitant evils, the order of meat was not changed. "And God said unto Adam, Because thou hast hearkened unto the voice of thy wife, and hast eaten of the tree of which I commanded thee saying, Thou shalt not eat of it; cursed is the ground for thy sake; in sorrow shalt thou eat of it all the days of thy life: Thorns and thistles shall it bring forth to thee; and thou shalt eat the herb of the field. In the sweat of thy face shalt thou eat bread [This shows that the expression herb comprehended bread-stuffs.] till thou return unto the ground; for out of it wast thou taken: for of dust thou art, and unto dust shalt thou return. And the Lord God said, Behold, the man is become as one of us, to know good and evil: and now, lest he put forth his hand, and take also of the tree of life, and eat, and live for ever: therefore the Lord God sent him forth from the garden of Eden, to till the ground from whence he was taken. So he drove out the man; and he placed at the east of the garden of Eden cherubims, and a flaming sword which turned every way, to keep the way of the tree of life." (Gen. 3.)

By this deprivation of access to the fruit of the tree of life, which had the properties of its indefinite perpetuation, man necessarily lost everlasting life, or died, and as the deprivation reached all subsequent generations, death thus passed upon all men. Because of these calamities upon man and the ground, hard labor became a necessity, and a corresponding necessity for more substantial food. As this necessity increased, man began to kill the lower animals for food, whose existence was provisionary in the wisdom of God to meet the necessity which had now come. He foreknew because he foresaw it would come, and he also arranged the single, double, and mixed teeth to meet it. Nothing in the scientific world is better known than that vegetables and animals furnish food for each other. The organism of the lamb and ox converts vegetation into their own individual and peculiar structure, so that when men devour these animals they indirectly devour vegetables, and Ingersoll's objection against animal food is of equal force against vegetable food, with the exception of the pain experienced in the act of killing, but which would be the same in natural death ; but this being a philosophical necessity of organic life, and only lessening the days of the life of those animals used for food, was a necessity in their creation. The objection is founded on the foolish notion that it was possible for God to do an impossibility. Hence to have made animals with sensations and yet without them. Was it not an act of goodness, love, and mercy to have made man, and all other animals, with an organic system of sensitive nerves, from which every pleasure flows, every flower, every strain of music, every variegated color, and every luxury from cold or heat, and every motive resulting in protection from their extremes. Indeed, were it not for the pleasure of eating and drinking, or the feeling of relief they afford, men would forget to eat and drink, and die in consequence.

The question therefore is, whether it would have been a wise provision to have had no pleasure or phase of animal happiness for a lifetime, if it would free us from a few pangs of pain while consciously dying? According to Ingersoll's reflection upon the Creator for its existence, it would be an act of love and mercy for one man to deprive another of all sensation during natural life, in

order to relieve him from a few moments' pain just before
it ended, and thus convert murder into goodness.   Here
again do we behold the absurdity of Ingersoll's criticism
on infinite wisdom and love.   But the extent of the folly
is only seen by taking into the account the fact, that in
this short and suffering life, we may avail ourselves of the
proposition made by the Creator, to introduce us into a
re-created world, where death will never come, and as a
consequence physical derangement in no degree can exist.
Ingersoll being ignorant of this promised destiny, which
every man holds in his own hands, he talks about the
present moment's living and dying as though it was without end ; while it is only the industrial school to prepare
the scholar for an endless life of health and happiness.

What Kind of Reformers are Atheists?

The sceptic says : " If abuses are destroyed, man must
destroy them."   [And, we may add, that Christians are
the only men who do such work.]   " If new truths are
discovered, man must discover them."   [And the history
of discovery reveals the fact that its most splendid periods
have been those wherein Christianity was unrestrained by
. civil enactments ; and the vast majority of discoveries
have been those inspired by Christian principle and hope,
while atheism quenches its fires and blunts every noble
sentiment.]   He says, " If justice is done, labor rewarded,
the hungry fed, and the naked clothed, man must do it."
Yes ! but this is not and never has been the work of
atheism—an inseparable mixture of pride, jealousy, and
selfishness—while this work is ranked among the most
prominent enjoinments of the Christian religion.   Listen
to its voice upon the subject : " Go to now, ye rich men,
weep and howl for your miseries that shall come upon you.
Your riches are corrupted, and your garments are moth-
eaten.   Your gold and silver is cankered ; and the rust
of them shall be a witness against you, and shall eat your
flesh as it were fire.   Ye have heaped treasure together for
the last days.   Behold, the hire of the laborers who have
reaped down your fields, which is of you kept back by fraud,

crieth : and the cries of them are entered into the ears of the Lord of Sabaoth. Ye have condemned and killed the just ; and he doth not resist you. Be patient therefore, brethren, unto the coming of the Lord.'' (James 5.) Here is the work of the Christian Church—its suffering from the oppression by the rich, its promised reward, and the coming of the Lord to confer it.

He says : '' If superstition is to be driven from the mind, man is to do it.'' This enunciates a good work ; but whatever is done toward it, must be the work of Christians, and not atheists : Satan makes bad work in casting out Satan. Superstition means a belief of that which is absurd—that for which there is no evidence, and which is connected with religion. Atheists believe either that the world was never made, or that it made itself, or that it came by the laws of nature, which they interpret to be active myths, abstract from nature and existing before it. In the days of Paul, there were men in Athens of this class, who had no evidence for the belief of a God, and this because they knew nothing about him, and yet like Ingersoll wrote and talked about him : '' Then Paul stood in the midst of Mars' hill, and said. Ye men of Athens, I perceive that in all things ye are too superstitious : for as I passed by, I beheld an altar with this inscription, TO THE UNKNOWN GOD.'' Ignorance and superstition are Siamese twins ; and Ingersoll professes to know nothing about God—has no evidence for his existence—totally ignorant of the science of nature, whose principles demonstrate his existence, and as totally ignorant of the fulfilment of the prophetic Scriptures, which also demonstrate them to have originated in the Mind of God. This ignorance he calls unbelief, being too proud to call it by its proper name : ignorant superstition. The pretender continues : '' If the defenceless are protected and the right finally triumphs, all must be the work of man. The grand victories of the future must be won by man, and by man alone.'' Yes ! but the voice of history declares that no victories for the good of mankind were ever won by atheists, and if we heed its warning voice, no good is to be looked for from that source. This is an attempt to hypocritically steal the principles of Christianity with which to oppose it.

He says: " During that frightful period known as the ' dark ages,' faith reigned, with scarcely a rebellious subject. [No, sir, faith in its very nature is founded upon evidence, and what then reigned was the sentiment, " Ignorance is the mother of superstition." It won't do, Robert, to confound the knowledge and fear of offending God with ignorance and no fear of him !] Her temples were carpeted with knees, and the wealth of nations adorned her costly and numerous shrines. The great painters prostituted their genius to immortalize her vagaries, while the poets enshrined them in song. At her bidding man covered the earth with blood. The scales of justice turned with her gold, and for her use were invented all the cunning instruments of pain. She built cathedrals for God, and dungeons for men. She peopled the clouds with angels and the earth with slaves." No ! Mr. Ingersoll, this is the picture of the false Church—the very antithesis of Christianity. It was the martyrer of the true Church, whose sacrificial blood you have just described ; the prehistoric record of which occupies a very large part of the prophesies, to predict, and two-thirds of the book called Revelation, to reveal ; besides being the burden of profane history for a thousand years, which simply records the fulfilment of the prophetic events. But Ingersoll being destitute of this knowledge, fits him to commit this blunder also.

That Jesus Christ and his system are not responsible for this work of slavery and blood, is shown by the prehistoric record, announcing him as the grandest emancipator of which it is possible to form a just conception. " And he came into Nazareth, where he had been brought up, and as his custom was, he went into the synagogue on the sabbath day, and stood up to read. And there was delivered unto him the book of the prophet Isaiah, and he found the place where it was written. And the spirit of the Lord God is upon me, because he hath anointed me to preach deliverance to the captives, and recovering of sight to the blind, to set at liberty them that are bruised,

to preach good tidings unto the meek, to proclaim liberty
to the captives, and the opening of the prisons to them
that are bound." "Is not this the fast that I have
chosen? to loose the bands of wickedness, to undo the
heavy burdens, and to let the oppressed go free, and that
ye break every yoke? That thou deal thy bread to the
hungry, and that thou bring the poor that are cast out to
thy house? When thou seest the naked, that thou cover
him, and that thou hide not thyself from thine own flesh."
(Isa. 61 : 1, and 58 : 6, 7.) (Luke 4 : 16–18.) " Remember them that are in bonds as bound with them, and them
which suffer adversity as being yourselves also in the
flesh." (Heb. 13 : 3.) "If the Son shall make you
free, ye shall be free indeed." (John 8 : 36.)

That Christianity was not responsible for the persecution to which Ingersoll alludes, or was authorized by its
founder, is further shown by such language as the following : "Remember the word that I said unto you, the servant is not greater than his Lord. If they have persecuted me, they will also persecute you ; if they have
kept my sayings, they will keep yours also. But all these
things will they do unto you for my name's sake, because
they know not him that sent me." (John 15 : 20, 21.)
"These things have I spoken unto you, that ye should
not be offended. They shall put you out of the synagogues ; yea, the time will come, that whosoever killeth
you will think that he doeth God service." (John 16 :
1, 2.) "Offences must come, but woe unto that man by
whom the offence cometh : it were better that a millstone
were hanged about his neck and that he were cast into
the depth of the sea, than that he should offend one of
these little ones which believe in me." Ingersoll thinks
that if we induce men to reject Christ and his religion,
all superstition and persecution will be gone. There is,
however, no surer test of Christianity and contrast between saints and sinners, than that of persecution : those
who suffer it for Christ's sake are saints ; while those who
inflict it are sinners, even though they think that thus
they do God service. This was the work of the false
Church for a thousand years, and which is symbolized by

the Great Babylon of the Revelation and the prophets, and when the punishment predicted by Christ comes upon her : that a great millstone, as it were, sinks her into the depth of the sea, and which he inspired John to write was in these words : " Rejoice over her, thou heaven, and ye holy apostles and prophets ; for God hath avenged you on her. And a mighty angel took up a stone like· a great millstone, and cast it into the sea, saying, Thus with violence shall great Babylon be thrown down, and shall be found no more at all." (Rev. 18 : 20, 21.) What horrid darkness of mind and wilful ignorance must Ingersoll labor under, to confound these two classes and characters, denouncing the killed with the killers—the offended with the offenders—the flowing blood of the persecuted with the bloody work of the persecutors ! If he does this knowingly, he manifests the character of the most public defamer of Christ and his Church ; and if he does it ignorantly, he is twice guilty—for not enlightening himself, as well as for the persecution.

Atheism has had but one Period of Power and Success.

In the history of the world, atheists have never had but one period of civil power, and if you want to know how they used it, ask the crammed prisons and guillotine of the Parisian reign of terror. Ingersoll animadverts against the dark ages, but had the atheist held its power for a thousand years, the people of every nation to which it extended would have been robbed and murdered, just as the Parisians were. It therefore comes with an ill grace from this representative of freethinkerism to reflect upon any period or nation, as covering the earth with blood, or building dungeons for men. These are the men that promise the people liberty if they will only turn against God, and adopt their boundless pride and conceit —that no being exists superior to themselves, and the foolish superstition that man and the world came into existence without the aid even of a living myth.

The Scoffer Harangues the People to Rebel Against God.

He says: "Of what use has God been to man? [We might change the form of the question and ask, of what use are men to God, especially such as those who are only happy in Satanic glee, when they are abusing him and trying to induce others to do likewise?] It is no answer to say that some God created the world, established certain laws, and then turned his attention to other matters, leaving his children too weak and ignorant to fight the battle of life alone. [In answer we may say, that none but Ingersoll and those of whom he is the mouth-piece, and a few devil-worshippers in the interior of Africa, ever said that God abandoned the world after having made it, leaving his children alone.] It is no solution to declare, that in some other world God will render a few, or even all, his subjects happy. What right have we to expect that a perfectly wise, good, and powerful being will ever do better than he has done, and is doing? The world is filled with imperfections. If it was made by an infinite being, have we any ground for saying that he will render it nearer perfect than it is now. If the infinite Father allows a majority of his children to live in ignorance and wretchedness now, what evidence have we that he will ever improve their condition? Will God have more power? Will he become more merciful? Will his love for his poor creatures increase? Can the conduct of infinite wisdom, power, and love change? Is the infinite capable of improvement?"

As Ingersoll is ignorant of the will and power of God, revealed in his Word and in the nature of man, even of this man himself, who hates what little he does know, it is natural that he should ask such questions. As an example, let us ask, how can God improve him? He is so ignorant of the Bible that he cannot expound a doctrine it contains. God has said to him, "Search the Scriptures, that they are they which testify of me," and that such knowledge is able to make him wise unto salvation; but he has despised the command and disobeyed the instruction. Now, suppose infinite power took possession of, and controlled his mind, compelling him, for the time being, to love the teachings of the Bible, to love to search it for the truth; love to teach it to others, to do which would make him an entirely different man; but what credit would that be to him—what virtue would it be to Ingersoll? He fought against the change and never yielded, what he now did and became was because his volition had been destroyed by the compelling power of the being that made him. Let that being remove the mental and physical force from the organism of the sceptic, and he would be the same hater of God and his word he was before. Whatever good was said or done by him after being reduced to a mere machine, must be put down to the credit of the compelling power of his God: How can God improve a persistent rebel?

In his fight with his Maker, he has the infernal audacity of abusing his Creator because he will not change to suit him—and such a change wrought as we have supposed, would show an improvement on the part of God. No man could say such things who had the faintest conception of the physical, mental, and moral philosophy involved in his own nature, that renders him with all the species so high in the scale of being, that it is impossible to compel him to do the least act, not even to lift a foot or finger. A stronger than he may lift the foot or raise the finger, just as he might if the man was dead; but it would be the act of the physically stronger, and he alone would be responsible for it. If infinite power forced the will to move the foot or finger, or compelled the mental and moral organism to pray, it would not be the act of the man, but that of him who exerted the force. It was God and not the man that prayed. To force a man to do a voluntary act, is a contradiction in terms. It virtually says, the act is at once both voluntary and involuntary. It is the same indomitable power with which even all the lower animals are endowed; and to which the adage gives expression: "You may lead a horse to the water, but you cannot make him drink."

CHAPTER XIII.

METAPHYSICAL PHILOSOPHY OF POWER.

WHEN we ascribe wisdom and power to God, and then interpret it to mean that he can do things inconsistent with the nature and power of other minds he has made—repugnant and antagonistic to his own wishes and purposes—we do that for which we have no authority. According to the dynamical philosophy in the nature of beings of mind, each grade and individual is omnipotent within his sphere of action. When God made a man a man, it carried with it the alternative that he could do as he pleased, and that the power to please and obey his Maker conferred also the power to displease and disobey; leaving the alternative to make him thus, or not to make him with a will, and therefore like a plant. Reasoning from the known to the unknown, the analogy forces the conclusion, that the Maker of man had a purpose to accomplish in the act of his creation, as it is impossible for man to do the least act without first forming a purpose; and as it is the accomplishment of that purpose which constitutes the motive actuating it, the analogy teaches that the purpose of God in the act of man's creation must have been that he should please and obey his Maker, and the power to please and obey carried with it the power to displease and disobey. These acts must not only be voluntary, but in accordance with the inducement held out to the creature by the Creator; and as the mental processes involve the impulses or feelings of the heart, it also follows that the man, won by the inducement, becomes a loving, loyal subject of the will of his Maker, and has a rational hope of an immortal resurrection and an incorruptible inheritance in the coming re-created world. It cannot be denied that

if one man may accept this offer, every other man may
do the same, and if either may accept it they may also
reject it.   It is another universally acknowledged fact
that every man and woman have experienced feelings of
aversion to that which they conceived to be the will and
wishes of God concerning them at the time ; and have
therefore done acts which they knew were displeasing to
him and rebellious against his will.   It is another fact
attested by millions of living, rational beings, and from
among the same class of people, that subsequently they
passed through another experience by which the same
God, without change on his part, looked upon them with
complacency, as of a loving Father.

It is another fact, that all those who had ceased to
hold the unnatural and hopeless conflict with their Maker,
have been induced to do so upon the condition that his
service, as described in the Bible, was to be performed
during natural life, and the pay, or reward not to be
given until the re-creation of the world, and faith in the
anticipation of this made them happier in the mortal life
than though they possessed all the wealth, pleasure, and
honor the present world affords.   The trouble with Ingersoll and his like is, that being still on the rebellious
side of the question, he is involved in the total darkness
inseparable from ignorance upon the subject, and has
none of the loving, loyal experience of which we speak ;
being still without God and without hope in the world,"
as the Scripture expresses it.   Of course, he can have no
other conception than that all men are in the same condition of mind as himself.   Hence the folly of the reflection upon God for not making him a saint.   It seems as
though the man has mental calibre sufficient to comprehend the theory of our argument—the experimental part
we doubt whether he will ever know : not that the
mercy of God is too limited to reach such a sinner ; but
the difficulty lies in the fact that he has abused God,
Christ, and the Bible so inveterately, and so publicly
committed himself against the gospel, that his pride of
heart and opinion will forever prevent him from repent-
ing, so as to look upon God as his Creator, and Christ

as his Saviour, or from receiving the Scriptures as containing the revealed will of God to man.

> " Try what repentance can ; what can it not ?
> Yet what can it, when one cannot repent ? "—SHAK.

Nature and Philosophy of Worship.

The infidel says : " Nations, like individuals, have their periods of growth, of manhood, and of decay." Religions are the same, and the same inexorable destiny awaits all. The gods created by the nations must perish with their creators. They were made by men, and like men they must pass away. The deities of one age are the by-words of the next. Ingersoll said this about the gods before, in answer to which we showed every statement of it to be in contradiction to the history of the national gods. But in answer to what he says about religion we may reply, that it is not a fact that man created it, of whatever form ; but that its existence, like that of man himself, is a truth of nature, a truth of the highest philosophical science, of which man is the natural exponent, the illustration, the manifestation. It is as natural to him as that he is a mental and moral being, of which religion is the appetite and the Word of God the food, equally universal as that his physical appetite exists and finds its food in the provisions of God, in nature.

The first development of childish abstract reasoning, asks " Who made me ?" conscious of the existence of a being above the inquirer of sufficient knowledge and power to have performed the work, and by the implied concession beginning to pay the honor, the worship which is his due. [No child ever asked the atheistic questions, implying doubt, " Did anyone make me ?" or " Was I made ? "] This is religion, and these universal and almost infantile expressions demonstrate it to be inborn. Thus every human being finds himself endowed with intellectual faculties, which compel him to search after a being superior to himself, as well as with a set of moral faculties, such as veneration and love, inciting him to adore this higher something, and to love him for the goodness implanted in his capacities for pleasure and happiness, and the surrounding resources in nature for their gratification.

This is religion, and whether written in a book, or expressed in outward symbols, as the existence of the gods, or their images, still it is religious worship and originated by creative implantation; and we may add, that if the errors in religious faith and practice of the individual do not prevent him from honoring and loving this living God, to which these noble faculties of the gospel of nature, his nature, points his faith, then he is one of his children and with them awaits the glorious destiny of all. It is clear from this that religion is a *unité* unchanged by the variety of the modes in which it manifests itself, either among nations, governments, or generations. If this be so, it may be said that all worship God but the freethinkers, who have so blunted their natural sensibilities that they see no God in the universe; each of whom considers himself the highest living being, which reduces his worship to self-worship, and his hope, if he has any, to self-reward. This is the culmination of his poverty-stricken independence; the champion of whom is Robert G. Ingersoll. National religion is the honor and loyalty paid to a sovereign, or chief-ruler, and for a citizen of one nation to pay to the ruler of another, is treason to his own lawful chief; of course, for any religionist to so confound an idol with his God and Creator, as to honor and love it, is idol treason to his only lawful God. Nothing is more universally conceded, and justly so, than that a father should receive the honor and obedience of his children, and for them to repudiate this by rendering it to another, without repentance and reformation, is an unpardonable affront; it is the sin of idolatry to the father; and yet he is but the agent of their existence, while God is the Creator, and therefore the proprietor of all men, hence the deeper turpitude of the offence, and merited punishment.

It is self-evident that these intelligent creatures of God's handiwork cannot please and obey him without being first instructed in the nature and character of those things pleasing to and approved by him, as that a child cannot perform the will and pleasure of his human father, unless that father should instruct him in relation to those things he approves and disapproves. A bright child may infer the will of the father by his goodness toward him, without further revelation, and be thus induced to honor and love him; and so a philosopher may see God revealed in nature, and be thus induced to honor and love him, which is natural and true religion; but to facilitate this knowledge and to enable the Creator to accomplish his object with man and the world, in the shortest time the nature of the elements will admit, it becomes necessary that a written revelation of his will should be made to man, clearly describing those things he approves and disapproves. The investigation of such a revelation becomes an individual necessity, if he would meet the demands of his great Father, which are imposed by such language as the following; "Search the Scriptures; for in them ye think ye have eternal life; and they are they which testify of me." (John 5 : 39.) They reveal the fact and nature of endless being, and the conditions upon which it is offered. To encourage the investigation, they give such assurance as this, "If any man will do his will he shall know of the doctrine whether it be of God." (John 7 : 17.)

The Gods the People Make.

In this relation to image-worship, its tendency to lead to the veneration of the images themselves, we would expect to find the will of God clearly and emphatically expressed, and the practice forbidden. A few of these passages read as follows: "Every man is brutish in his knowledge: every founder is confounded by the graven image, for his molten image is falsehood, and there is no breath in them. They are vanity, and the work of errors; in the time of their visitation they shall perish." (Jer. 10 : 14, 15.) "Thus saith the Lord, learn not the way of the heathen, nor be dismayed at the signs of heaven ; for the customs of the people are vain : for one cutteth a tree of the forest, the work of the hands of the workman, with an axe.   They deck it with silver and gold ; they fasten it with nails and with hammers, that it move not.   They are upright as the palm-tree, but speak not ; they must needs be borne, because they cannot go. Be not afraid of them, for they cannot do evil, neither is it in them to do good." (Jer. 10 : 2–5.)   " They tempted and provoked the most high God, and kept not his testimonies ; they moved him to jealousy with their graven images ; when God heard this he was wroth, and greatly abhorred Israel." (Ps. 78 : 56–59.)   " I am the Lord : that is my name : and my glory will I not give to another, neither my praise to graven images." (Ps. 42 : 8.)   " Thou shalt have no other gods before me.   Thou shalt not make unto thee any graven image, or any likeness of anything that is in heaven above, or in the earth beneath, or that is in the water under the earth ; thou shalt not bow down thyself to them, for I, the Lord thy God am a jealous God, visiting the iniquity of the fathers upon the children unto the third and fourth generation of them that hate me ; and showing mercy unto thousands of them that love me and keep my commandments." (Ex. 20.)

Here we see the folly and wickedness of the infidels in confounding image worship with that of the living and true God, and because some of these nations abandon the religion of idol worship, and if the religion dies, that the same destined extinction awaits the religion and worship of the living God—that because the corruption of a thing dies, becomes extinct, the same destiny awaits the pure ; because counterfeit dollars become extinct, the same destiny awaits all pure dollars.   This is the shallow reasoning of the infidels.   They rob God of the honor due him, by rendering it to other things, and commit the same offence by withholding it from him ; and in their ignorant pride the freethinkers suppose they worship no god, while they have only changed it to other objects of love and sacrifice ; even the very love and pride that they worship nothing, is the idol of their heart's devotion.   Of such it is said, " Ye have set up your idols in your hearts."

The love of vain glory, empty boasting pride, is the god of the atheist, and ranks him below any heathen religionist, all of whom held and hold their gods to be greater than themselves, while the conceit of the atheist puffs him up higher than anything or being in the universe, and who thus performs self-devotion.

Let us listen to our oracle's floundering fulminations among the gods, things of which he is totally unacquainted. "The religion of our day is no more exempt from the sneer of the future than the others have been," just as though all the religions but Christianity had become extinct. Of course, the religion of Christ never did and never will escape the sneer of the scoffer, especially as the world approximates the ignorance and irreligion of the antediluvians, which Christ says it will reach, at the time he comes to put an end to it. Hence we read, "Knowing this first, that there shall come in the last days scoffers, walking after their own lusts, and saying, Where is the promise of his coming? for since the fathers fell asleep all things continue as they were from the beginning of the creation, for of this they are willingly ignorant." (2 Pet. 3: 3-5.) "These are murmurers, complainers [Even complaining against God for his imperfections.], walking after their own lusts; and with their mouth speaking great swelling words, having men's persons in admiration because of advantage, clouds are they without water, carried about of winds; trees whose fruit withereth, without fruit, twice dead, plucked up by the roots; raging waves of the sea foaming out their own shame; wandering stars to whom is reserved the blackness of darkness forever." (Jude.) How near Ingersoll and the rest of the puffed up atheists and scientific freethinkers who were to come in the last days, answer to this predicted picture our readers must judge, but to our mind and in our day, these have gone beyond its highest coloring. "But as the days of Noah were, so also shall the coming of the Son of Man be: For as in the days that were before the flood, they were eating and drinking, marrying and giving in marriage, until the day that Noah entered into the ark, and knew not until the flood came and took them all away ; so shall also the coming of the Son of Man be." (Matt. 24 : 37–39.) Who cannot see, that the scoffing success of Ingersollism is bringing about precisely such a state of the world, through whose ignorant sneers and ridicule, bringing Bible study and teaching less than ever before since the reformation. Even those who pretend to teach it, substitute the opinions of men, and thus drag it down to the level of the sceptical science of chronological geology and evolution ; for whose conclusions science is no more responsible than is the Bible for the corrupt compromise.

Ingersoll asks, Who Will Supersede Christ ?

The scoffer says : " When India was supreme, Brahma sat upon the world's throne. When the sceptre passed to Egypt, Isis and Osiris received the homage of mankind." [This is contrary to history, for ancient Egypt, and it is about those times he speaks, was always superior to India, and never borrowed her gods. Nor is it true that any one of the idol gods ruled the world, nor that they succeeded each other in receiving the homage of mankind ; for no god or religion was ever universal.] " When Greece, with her fierce valor, swept to empire, Zeus put on the purple authority." This is also an historic blunder, as it skips the Chaldean and Medo-Persian monarchies, both of whom held Egypt as a dependency before Greece swept to power. Neither did Greece put on the purple, which was the badge of the Roman empire. Nor did Zeus become the national god of Greece, for this god of her's was always " Diana." This, however, has nothing to do with the argument ; but it serves to show the superficiality of the scoffer's learning, and detracts from the reliability of what he quotes as matter of fact, including what he quotes from the Bible and history. He continues : " The earth trembled with the tread of Rome's intrepid sons, and Jove grasped with mailed hand the thunderbolts of heaven. Rome fell, and Christians, from her territory, with the red sword of war, carved out the ruling nations of the world, and now

Christ sits upon the old throne. Who will be his successor?" Here is a conglomeration of the most unjustifiable ignorance and misrepresentation. Nothing is more positively forbidden, both by the example and laws of Christ, than the use of the sword, even for the defence of himself and his cause; and as no one can be a Christian and disobey either source of the instruction, therefore, the Christians in the Roman empire never did this work, whoever else did, nor does Christ sit upon the world's throne, the erection of which is yet future, and to be built upon the destruction of all other thrones, at his personal return in the end of the world. No! Christ has no contemporary sitting upon a throne, nor is his throne ever superseded.

This determination is one of the principal subjects of prophecy, and Christ grouped the events to transpire at the erection of the throne and commencement of his reign, and revealed them to John, thus: " The second woe is past; and, behold, the third woe cometh quickly. And the seventh angel sounded; and there were great voices in heaven, saying, The kingdoms of this world are become the kingdoms of our Lord and of his Christ; and he shall reign for ever and ever. And the four and twenty elders, which sat before God on their seats, fell upon their faces, and worshipped God, saying, We give thee thanks, O Lord God Almighty, which art, and wast, and art to come; because thou hast taken to thee thy great power, and hast reigned. And the nations were angry, and thy wrath is come, and the time of the dead, that they should be judged, and that thou shouldst give reward unto thy servants the prophets, and to the saints, and them that fear thy name, small and great; and shouldst destroy them that destroy the earth." (Rev. 11 : 14–18.)

" Then Pilate entered into the judgment hall again, and called Jesus, and said unto him, Art thou the King of the Jews? Jesus answered him, Sayest thou this of thyself, or did others tell it of me? Pilate answered, Am I a Jew? thine own nation and the chief priests have delivered thee unto me; what hast thou done? Jesus

answered, My kingdom is not of this world ; if my kingdom were of this world, then would my servants fight,
that I should not be delivered to the Jews ; but now is
my kingdom not from hence. [It does not now begin.]
Pilate therefore said unto him, Art thou a king, then?
Jesus answered, Thou sayest that I am a king; to this
end was I born, and for this purpose came I into the
world."   (John 18 : 33–37.)   Here are the facts taught
that Christ was born to be a king, though his kingdom
did not then begin ; but he is coming again to take possession of the whole world, which becomes his kingdom
without successor or end.   The universal government
shall be upon the shoulder of the child that was born,
the Son that was given : " His name shall be called the
Wonderful, Counsellor, the Mighty God, the Everlasting
Father, the Prince of Peace.   Of his government there
shall be no end.   His Kingdom will be established with
judgment and justice from henceforth [thenceforth] even
forever.   The zeal of the Lord of hosts will perform
this."   (Isa. 9 : 6, 7.)

When Christ was on earth he said, " Now is my kingdom *not from hence;* " but when this prediction shall
have its fulfilment, Christ having returned and having
assumed the government and kingdom of his new-made
world, he will say, " My kingdom *is from henceforth even
forever.*"

History and Philosophy of Suffering.

The scoffer says : " We are informed by the clergy
that this world is a kind of school ; that the evils by
which we are surrounded are for the purpose of develop-
ing our souls ; and that only by suffering can men become pure, strong, virtuous, and grand."   There is a
broad and well-defined distinction in the Scriptures between the suffering consequent upon physical derangement, disease, and death, and that which men suffer at
the hand of persecution for allying themselves with the
cause of Christ.   Such persecution has by no means been
confined to what is called " the Christian era," but has

been the common lot of the saints beginning with Abel.
As proof of this we quote the following : " Take my
brethren the prophets, who have spoken in the name of
the Lord, for an example of suffering, affliction, and patience." (James 5 : 10.) " Moses refused to be called
the son of Pharaoh's daughter, choosing rather to suffer affliction with the people of God than to enjoy the
pleasure of sin for a season ; esteeming the reproach of
Christ greater riches than the treasures in Egypt ; for he
had respect unto the recompense of the reward." (Heb.
11 : 24–26.) " If ye suffer for righteousness' sake, happy
are ye ; and be not afraid of their terror, neither be
troubled ; but rejoice, inasmuch as ye are partakers of
Christ's sufferings ; that when his glory shall be revealed,
ye may be glad with exceeding joy ; if ye be reproached
for the name of Christ, happy are ye ; for the spirit of
glory and of God resteth upon you ; on their part he is
evil spoken of, but on your part he is glorified. But let
none of you suffer as a murderer, or a thief, or an evil
doer ; yet, if any man suffer as a Christian, let him not
be ashamed, but let him glorify God on this behalf."
(1 Pet. 2 : 20 ; 3 : 14 ; 4 : 13.)
Christ forewarned his followers that for his sake they
would continue to suffer throughout all ages of the world.
Hear him : " Blessed are they which are persecuted for
righteousness' sake, for theirs is the kingdom of heaven.
Blessed are ye, when men shall revile you, and persecute
you, and shall say all manner of evil against you, falsely,
for my sake, rejoice, and be exceeding glad ; for great is
your reward in heaven, for so persecuted they the prophets
which were before you." (Matt. 5 : 11–12.) " Behold,
I send you forth as sheep in the midst of wolves, be ye
therefore wise as serpents and harmless as doves. But be-
ware of men, for they will deliver you up to the councils,
and they shall scourge you in their synagogues, and ye
shall be brought before governors and kings for my name's
sake, for a testimony against them and the Gentiles. And
the brother shall deliver up the brother to death, and the
father the child, and the children shall rise up against
their parents, and cause them to be put to death. And

ye shall be hated of all men for my name's sake, but he that endureth to the end the same shall be saved.   The disciple is not above his Lord.   If they have called the master of the house Beelzebub, how much more shall they call them of his household ?   Whosoever therefore shall confess me before men, him will I confess before my Father which is in heaven ; but whosoever shall deny me before men, him will I also deny before my Father which is in heaven.''

''Think not that I am come to send peace on earth : I came not to send peace but a sword, for I am come to set a man at variance against his father, and the daughter against her mother, and a man's foes shall be they of his own household.   He that loveth father or mother more than me is not worthy of me, and he that loveth son or daughter more than me is not worthy of me, and he that taketh not his cross, and followeth not after me, is not worthy of me.   He that findeth his life [By abandoning Christ to save his temporal life.] shall lose it, and he that loseth his life [Falls a martyr for his sake.] shall find it.   And that shall be the immortal resurrection life.'' (Matthew 10.)   From such instruction, it seems that even Ingersoll cannot fail to see that the kind of suffering here taught, and which develops the soul, the whole man into an immortal inhabitant of Christ's new world and endless kingdom, is to be reproached for being so much like him as to be known to be his disciple, which those cannot have or be who reproach him, and choose rather to reproach him and enjoy the pleasures of sin for a season, and lose those of immortality ; of course, they reap the harvest of the seed they sowed.

Salvation of the Little Children.

Ingersoll asks : '' Supposing this to be true, what is to become of those who die in infancy ?   The little children, according to this philosophy, can never be developed. They were so unfortunate as to escape the ennobling influence of pain and misery, and as a consequence are doomed to eternal mental inferiority.''   We have seen that the advantage of suffering for Christ's sake is, that it shows the sufferer loves him and is identified with his cause, and this the little children cannot have, nor do they need, as Christ pronounces such already fit for the kingdom ; and this shows Ingersoll to be ignorant even of the theory of salvation, and when adult sinners are converted to his discipleship they are then exalted to the standard of the little child. Said he, "Suffer the little children to come unto me, for of such is the kingdom of heaven, and except ye be converted and become as a little child, ye can in no case enter into the kingdom of heaven." This objection of the scoffer shows how hard pressed he is for exceptional matter against the Bible and its religion, and secondly, his profound ignorance of plain scripture teaching. That he is, however, satisfied in establishing the necessity for evil to do the work of righteousness, he asks: "If evil is necessary to the development of man in this life, how is it possible for the soul to improve in the perfect joy of paradise?"

The absurdity of the question consists in supposing that evil, which shows what good is by contrast, begets the good. As though darkness begets light—cold, heat—death, life. In a word, that opposites are the product of the same conditions, the same causes. Not understanding the revealed fact, that the suffering of the present world, of whatever name, nature, or degree, is the result of sin, and that this ends with the present sinful world and with all its evil consequences. Absence of these in the world to come—paradise restored, proposes infinite and endless facilities for intellectual and moral development. There are angelic teachers with six thousand years' experience, to begin with, and the close, personal association with the Immanuelized God, "In whom dwells all the fulness of the Godhead bodily." Think of the grandeur of such a future, and of the limitless attainments even of the little children. Little, only when first entering the place, and soon growing to mature physical size, and then with the redeemed millions running the race of immortality together with their Lord, glorified to an exaltation of eternal honor. A nature so attuned to that of their

Maker, that whatever they wish to do will be lawful to be done—"The glorious liberty of the children of God."

This is the proposition and promise of our glorious gospel, while atheism leaves its votaries buried in the oblivion of dark annihilation: such a man dies as the fool dieth.

The Scoffer's Closing Harangue.

This brings us to consider the last passage of the lecture. The oracle says: "Day by day, religious convictions grow less and less intense. Day by day, the old spirit dies out of the book and creed. The burning enthusiasm, the quenchless zeal in the early Church have gone, never to return. The ceremonies remain, but the ancient faith is fading out of the human heart. The worn-out arguments fail to convince; and denunciations that once blanched the faces of a race, excite in us only derision and disgust. As time rolls on, the miracles grow mean and small, and the evidences our fathers thought conclusive utterly fail to satisfy us. There is an irrepressible conflict between religion and science, and they cannot peaceably occupy the same brain and the same world." It is unnecessary here to say that there is no conflict between the revealed religion of the Bible and the true science of nature, as the arguments in these pages demonstrate, and this disposes of the strongest weapon in the hand of atheism. It is a fact that the conflict exists, and that it is irrepressible, but the idea Ingersoll borrowed from Christ, who declared: "I came not to send peace on earth but a sword." But the conflict is between truth and error, light and darkness, sin and righteousness, Christ and Belial; and the picture drawn by the pen of inspiration, and sang by the angels of Bethlehem, is that of universal and endless peace on earth, but it is the peace which results from the existence and reign of universal righteousness, and in the very nature of the two principles could not be otherwise. The elements of sin are war, and those of righteousness peace; but it was the new earth about which the prophets discoursed and the angels sang; it was the earth "brought back from the sword," the earth with the curse taken off: "Behold, I create new heavens and a new earth; and the former shall not be remembered, nor come into mind. But be ye glad and rejoice forever in that which I create; for, behold, I create Jerusalem a rejoicing, and her people a joy. And I will rejoice in Jerusalem, and joy in my people; and the voice of weeping shall no more be heard in her, nor the voice of crying. The wolf and the lamb shall feed together, they shall not hurt nor destroy in all my holy mountain." (Isa. 65th.)

Mountain in prophecy symbolizes kingdom. Here is paradise restored to what it was when God first made it. "For as the new heavens and new earth, which I will make, shall remain before me, saith the Lord, so shall your seed and your name remain. And they shall go forth and look upon the carcasses of the men that have transgressed against me; for their worm shall not die, neither shall their fire be quenched; and they [the carcasses] shall be an abhorring unto all flesh."

They have had their resurrection to weakness, dishonor, corruption, shame, and everlasting contempt." The fires of God's execution have put out their life, and could not be arrested in their work: they were unquenchable fires, and no power could arrest the work of decomposition upon the wicked. The carcasses are beheld by the immortal righteous: as described thus: "When the wicked are cut off, thou shalt see it." (37th Psalm.) "A thousand shall fall at thy right side, and ten thousand at thy right hand; but it shall not come nigh thee: only with thine eyes shalt thou behold and see the end of the wicked." (Ps. 91: 8.) "For behold, the day cometh that shall burn as an oven; and all the proud, yea, and all that do wickedly, shall be stubble: and the day that cometh shall burn them up, saith the Lord of hosts, that it shall leave them neither root nor branch. But unto you that fear my name shall the Son of righteousness arise with healing in his wings; and ye shall go forth, and grow up as calves of the stall. And ye shall tread down the wicked; and they [their carcasses] shall be ashes under the soles of your feet in the day that I shall do this, saith the Lord of hosts.'' (Mal. 4 : 1–3.) '' The wicked shall perish, and the enemies of the Lord shall be as the fat of lambs : they shall consume away into smoke. Yet a little while, and the wicked shall not be, and the earth shall not be [Both are consumed into their elements by the fires of the last day.], but the meek shall inherit the earth.'' [The new earth.] '' Wait on the Lord and he shall exalt thee to inherit the land.'' '' Blessed are the meek, for they shall inherit the earth.'' (Matt. 5 : 5.) '' Fear him which is able to destroy both soul and body in hell.'' (Matt. 10 : 28.)

If in his search Ingersoll cannot find hell, let him be a little patient until its fires are kindled at the last day, as we here see is the time appointed for the work, and he will surely find it unless he repents : '' For behold, the Lord will come with fire, and his chariots like a whirl-wind [And his chariots are thousands of angels.], to ren-der his anger with fury, and his rebuke with flames of fire : for by fire and by his sword [His executing angels.] will the Lord plead with all flesh, and the slain of the Lord shall be many.'' (Isa. 66th.)

The Final Doom : The Galilean has Conquered.

Christ has now accomplished his revealed purpose upon his enemies, '' Who would not that he should reign over them.'' The devil and his servants, whether of angelic or human origin, are gathered out of his kingdom—the field—the present world, and are cast into the furnace of fire and burned to destruction: '' For this purpose the Son of God was manifest that he might destroy the works of the devil.'' (1 John 5 : 3.) The works of the devil are his obedient children, the children of the wicked one, the tares of the field. '' Forasmuch as the children are partakers of flesh and blood, he [Christ] himself likewise took part of the same ; that through death [His resurrection from the dead.] he might destroy him that had the power of death, that is the devil [The devil used this power by introducing sin into the world, and death came in consequence.], and deliver them who through fear of death were all their life-time subject to bondage." (Heb. 2: 14, 15.) When the time comes, according to these Scriptures, appointed for the destruction, and a devil or one of his children is left alive, then the Son of God has failed of his purpose; none, however, but men like Ingersoll suppose such a thing possible. This is the manner, Mr. Sceptic, in which the irrepressible conflict between you and Christ will be repressed. Here the Prince of Peace begins his reign of righteousness, never to be interrupted by a note of discord, or a seed of corruption. Every hostile will to the reign of righteousness are no more: "Behold! a king shall reign in righteousness." (Isa. 32: 1.) This has now commenced, and embraces all living, re-created animals, the lower as well as man. "The wolf also shall dwell with the lamb, and the leopard shall lie down with the kid; and the calf and the young lion and the fatling together; and a little child shall lead them. The cow and the bear shall feed; their young ones shall lie down together: and the lion shall eat straw like the ox. And the suckling child shall play on the hole of the asp, and the weaned child shall put his hand on the cockatrice den. They shall not hurt nor destroy in all my holy mountain [kingdom]; for the earth shall be full of the knowledge of the Lord, as the waters cover the sea." (Isa. 11: 6–9.)

"And the work of righteousness shall be peace; and the effect of righteousness, quietness and assurance for-ever. And my people shall dwell in a peaceable habita-tion, and a sure dwelling, and in quiet resting places." (Isa. 32: 17, 18.) Here the prophetic song of the angels, "Peace on earth, good will toward men," is ful-filled. Christ came at first, not to send peace on earth, but a sword. But he has now come the second time, and established a universal government of righteousness upon earth, the effect of which is eternal Peace. It is the kingdom under the whole heaven, covering the now paradisiacal earth, "The kingdoms of this world have become the kingdoms of our Lord and of his Christ, and he shall reign forever and ever."

General Unbelief Reigns when the World Ends.

In our opinion, no living man has done so much as Ingersoll toward bringing about the unbelief which the Scriptures declare will exist at Christ's return to the world, consequently preparing it for destruction.   But this he took into the account when drawing and revealing the picture as he foresaw it would be, but not as he would have it, "Who would have every man to be saved." The scoffer predicts that the old zeal is dying out of the church, while he is doing all in his power to fulfil the prediction by the use of the arts of a most wily magician, and with infinite effrontery calls the success "progress," "improvement."   Instead, however, of this delaying the end, they are so many voices of alarming apprehension to these willing victims of the deceptive arts, that the world is fast filling up the cup of its iniquity, "ripening the vine of the earth," for the work of the reaping angels of destruction, the conflagration of the last day.   This general unbelief is implied in the question Christ asked thus, "Nevertheless, when the Son of Man cometh, shall he find faith on earth."   (Luke 18 : 8.)   Here we may remind our readers, that the first two chapters of the Bible record reveal the history of the creation of the temporary world.   The rest of the Bible, the object of that creation to be a re-creation, delineating the character of its contemplated inhabitants, the requisite qualifications and conditions upon which it may be obtained. The last two chapters record the prehistoric revelation of that object when accomplished ; the winding up scene of which is as follows : "He that sat upon the throne said, I am the first, and I am the last, I am he that liveth and was dead.   I will give unto him that is athirst of the fountain of living water freely and he shall inherit all things, and I will be his God and he shall be my son." The achievement of this end vindicates and justifies the Creator in making and keeping the first world and its inhabitants in existence for its six thousand years.   The indefensible blunder of the freethinkers, including in our day every grade of infidels, is, in attempting to account for the condition of things in the preliminary temporal world, without taking into the account the end proposed, the perfect, re-created, and endless world.

CHAPTER XIV.

HISTORY OF THE DEBATE, CHRISTIANITY DEFENDED BEFORE THE FREETHINKERS' CONVENTION.

INTRODUCTION.

[From the New York "Herald."]

"Freethinkers' Convention—Orthodoxy to be Vindicated at Rochester—Elaborate Preparations for a Notable Gathering.

"ROCHESTER, N. Y., August 3, 1883.

"There is every prospect and promise that the Freethinkers' Convention, to be held at the Corinthian Academy of Music in this city, on August 29, 30, 31, and September 1 and 2, will be one of the most notable gatherings they have ever held in this country. A large number of conspicuous men and speakers have been engaged, among whom are Thaddeus B. Wakeman, of New York; Courtlandt Palmer, Z. C. Deland, and Samuel P. Putnam, of New York City; the ex-Rev. George C. Miln, C. B. Waite, Professor John Stolz, and E. A. Stevens, of Chicago; Elizur Wright, George Chainey, William S. Bell, and George N. Hill, of Boston, Mass.; Charles Watts, editor of the *Secular Review*, of London, England; Mrs. Amelia Colby, of Buffalo, N. Y.; Samuel H. Wixon, of Fall River, Mass.; Mrs. H. S. Lake, of Milwaukee, Wis.; J. H. Burnham, of Saginaw City, Mich.; M. Babcock, of St. Johns, Mich.; W. F. Jamieson, of Lake City, Minn.; Allen Pringle, of Selby, Can.; C. Frederick Farlin, M.D., of Binghamton, N. Y.; J. A. Seitz, of North Conway; N. H. J. Chapel, of Brighton, N. Y.; Z. L. Brown, M.D., of Binghamton, N. Y.

" It is confidently expected that the following named will also be present: Colonel Robert G. Ingersoll, Horace Seaver, Professor Felix Adler, B. F. Underwood, and Professor Van Buren Denslow.

"*Orthodox Clergyman to Speak!*

" The leading spirits in this modern movement propose to make the coming convention one that will greatly surpass in interest and importance all their other conventions. For a number of years the secretary has publicly invited the orthodox people of the country to send a representative to speak in behalf of Christianity on their platform, but no one has ever responded to the invitation until this year. The acceptance of the challenge by the Rev. Thomas Mitchell, of Brooklyn, heretofore announced in the *Herald*, has stirred up a deep interest in all sections. It has caused much comment in religious circles in this city. At first the Christian people were in doubt as to Mr. Mitchell's ability to defend orthodoxy, but the well-informed ones in the church have quieted these doubts by asserting that he is one of the best theologians in the Methodist denomination, They add that no better man could be chosen in the United States to meet and put to flight the infidel horde. Thaddeus B. Wakeman, of New York, well known as a lawyer and one of the ablest men in the ranks of the freethinkers, has been chosen to reply to Mr. Mitchell, and it seems likely that the conflict between two such men will be watched with considerable interest, both by the Christian and infidel parties all over the country. The prospects are, too, that during the discussion many of the ablest men of the country, of all shades of opinion, will be present.

" The announcement made in the *Herald*, in June, that the convention will be happy to meet with them as their guest a representative of the orthodox churches, attracted wide attention, formed the subject of numberless editorials throughout the country, and succeeded in arousing one champion for the cause of Christianity. This is the Rev. Thomas Mitchell, a distinguished Methodist clergyman and author, of Brooklyn, N. Y. His letter to the secretary of the Freethinkers' Association of the State of New York, was in the following quaint style:

"I accept the invitation of the Freethinkers' Association of the State of New York, to make an address before their convention, to assemble at Rochester, N. Y., on August 29, 1883, in defence of the Christian religion, as published in the New York *Herald* of June 10th. Please find enclosed papers, which, as we suppose, meet the conditions of your invitation in recommending me to appear and make the proposed address. That you may not be confused, permit me to say that I am not now a pastor of a church, though an ordained minister in the Methodist Episcopal Church, having devoted my time for a number of years, almost exclusively, to the work of authorship. My church relation is in Hanson Place Methodist Episcopal Church, having a membership of 1,400, and of which the Rev. J. O. Peck, D.D., one of the most prominent ministers in the denomination, is now pastor.

"Dr. Peck gave me the letter of recommendation enclosed the day before he went on his summer vacation. Wishing to be unobjectionable, we have availed ourselves of the clause of the invitation which says: 'Or either branch of the orthodox Church of the United States may send such representative.' Hence we applied to the Presbyterian branch, and send you the enclosed papers, signed by Samuel D. Burchard, D.D., late chancellor of Ingraham College, New York, now president of Rutgers College, and pastor of Murray Hill Church, being also moderator of the Session.

"'DEAR SIR: I need not say to you that I wish to have it decided as soon as possible whether I am to be the representative to your Convention, as the task of preparation imposed is so great, and which suspense increases. I shall be relieved of the latter by hearing from you that I am accepted, and of the former by being rejected.

"'Yours respectfully,
"'THOMAS MITCHELL,
"'No. 248 Lafayette Ave., Brooklyn.'"

The Champion's Indorsers.

This letter was accompanied by the following indorsements:

"Brooklyn, N. Y., July 9, 1883.

"This will certify that Rev. Thomas Mitchell, of this city, is personally known to me, and that, in defence of Christianity as against materialism and free religion and modern scepticism, I consider him candid, able, and fearless. I approve of his meeting the challenge of the Freethinkers' Association to meet in Rochester, N. Y.

"J. O. PECK, D.D.,
"Pastor Hanson Place Methodist Episcopal Church."

"New York City, July 16, 1883.

"*To the President of the Freethinkers' Association of the, State of New York.*

"DEAR SIR: Being acquainted with the character and ability of the Rev. Thomas Mitchell, we feel prepared to recommend him to represent our individual church and the cause of evangelical Christianity in your Association, which is to meet in the city of Rochester, August 29, 1883.

"S. D BURCHARD,
"Pastor of Murray Hill Presbyterian Church, New York City, and Moderator of the Session."

To these communications the secretary of the Association immediately forwarded the following reply to the Rev. Thomas Mitchell:

"Salamanca, N. Y., July 18, 1883.

"MY DEAR SIR: Yours of yesterday received. I think you have substantially complied with the invitation of the New York State Freethinkers' Association as made through the *New York Herald,* and we shall be very much pleased to welcome you as a representative of evangelical Christianity at Rochester. And if it meets your

mind, you may deliver your address at the Academy of
Music, at which our convention is to be held, on Thursday evening, August 30th. The headquarters of our
convention will be at the Clinton House, where my wife
and I shall put up, and we should be pleased to have you
stop where we do. Personally, I shall do all in my
power to make your visit with us pleasant.

" Truly yours,
" H. L. GREEN,
"Secretary Freethinkers' Association."

It has been arranged that Mr. Mitchell's address shall
be delivered before the convention on Thursday evening,
August 30th. The Hon. T. B. Wakeman, of New York
City, will reply to him on the following evening.

The Address.

GENTLEMEN OF THE FREETHINKERS' ASSOCIATION OF
THE STATE OF NEW YORK: On accepting your invitation
to make an address " defending or sustaining the claims of
the Christian religion against infidelity, or both, as the
speaker might choose," I cannot but avail myself of the
whole extent of the option, not only because it is liberal,
but because the defence implies the attack thus broadly.

It cannot be intelligently questioned that the Bible
sets up the claim that the words clothing the ideas describing the Christian religion are of divine inspiration,
and which are not to be changed or modified to the end
of the world. Its language is : " All scripture is given
by inspiration of God." (2 Tim. 2 : 16.) " The prophecy came not in old time by the will of man ; but
holy men of God spake as they were moved by the Holy
Ghost." (2 Pet. 1 : 21.) " For I testify unto every man
that heareth the words of the prophecy of this book, if
any man shall add unto these things, God shall add unto
him the plagues that are written in this book ; and if any
man shall take away from the words of the book of this
prophecy, God shall take away his part out of the book
of life, and out of the holy city." (Rev. 22 : 18, 19.)

If, therefore, this book admits of no change of phraseology, then it admits of no change of meaning; and any attempted change for improvement is positive corruption. It is equally unquestionable that the Bible claims God created the word according to the account given in Genesis, which is quoted throughout the Scriptures as the plain statement of the facts as they occurred, the two most prominent of which are that the whole work was done in six days of twenty-four hours each, and that the work in all its parts was as perfect as it has ever been. The hypothesis of evolution is the exact opposite of this; hence there is an irreconcilable conflict between the two. We are also free to admit that science cannot prove that the world came into existence according to both of these claims; therefore all true science must be on one side or the other, and the question is on which side? Here is the clearly defined issue, and we take the Bible side of the question—King James's version, without note, comment, or marginal reading—asking no accommodating rule of interpretation not equally necessary to the language of any other book.

We acknowledge the fact of the spread of infidel sentiments in our day, as never before in the history of the world; but, as we conceive, it has not been by the discovery of new defects in Christianity, nor by really new truths in science, much less in philosophy; but what is called "modern science," which we shall show is not science has been the chief cause of the evil. Of course, we refer to its ideas about the geological antiquity of the world, and its evolution, with that of man, from a supposed inherent potency in organic or in inorganic matter, to which the work is to be ascribed, leaving nothing for a supernatural workman to do. If this be true science, then whether there is a living God or not, is of but speculative consequence to us. If God did not make the world and man, he is not their proprietor, and he has no right to impose duties and restraints upon mankind; and the freethinkers are right and philosophic in rejecting the Bible containing them, together with the impositions of the Christian religion. But if we show by the resources

of nature, her facts of science, and its highest type, philosophical science, that she has no such potency, and is
utterly inadequate to the performance of the work, then
their thinking has been erroneous, and their opposition
to the creation of the world should forever cease.

We shall not only show this, but that they cannot fall
back upon atheism, which asserts that there has been an
endless succession of living generations; for even their
superficial investigation has demonstrated to the intelligent evolutionists that there was a beginning of the world
and of its inhabitants. At the outset it becomes necessary to know the formidability or feebleness of our antagonist, whether he is a giant or a pigmy. Taking into
the account the nature of the proof which the originators
of modern science have adduced, let us hear their own
testimony as to whether they themselves claim it to be
science, which means " certain knowledge or understanding of truth by the mind." It is admitted by the four
principal authorities on evolution—Darwin, Huxley,
Tyndall, and Haeckel—that if it does not account for the
origin of organic beings and things, the only alternative
is the Biblical account of creation. Another admission
granted by all these leaders in modern science is, that the
claim, the primordial, originated by inherent forces in
nature without supernatural interference, is a pure hypothesis; and an hypothesis means, " something not
proved, but imagined, or assumed for the sake of argument." Darwin begins his argument on evolution
with the assumed existence of a single living form—the
primordial of all living forms, and which was the simplest
of all living things. In contrast to this, the primordial
of Scripture is the grandest and most perfect living Being.
That the Biblical account of the world's primordial is the
most consistent with philosophy and the facts of science,
is demonstrated by the necessities of that which preceded
the evolution, the unfolding—namely, the work of infold-
ing, putting the things in which afterward came out, or
were evolved. It is simply absurd to put evolution before involution; it supposes that living things can come
out from whence even their embryons or seeds had not

been put in ; especially when the embryon of an animal or plant is as grand a piece of workmanship as the animal or plant itself.   It is self-evident, that the primordial, if it was a single one, from which every species of animals and plants have come into existence, whether it was that of Darwin or of Scripture, had the knowledge and ability to make the first pair of each, and involve in them the embryons or first rudiments, including every shade of difference or susceptibility of variation which have or ever will manifest themselves in the evolution of all subsequent generations.   This demonstrates the fact that the primordial involving such mechanical and physiological skill was the very paragon of a complete living organism himself, the living all-knowing—all-powerful creator, to whose existence every living thing, points and ascribes its own origin.   If it was Darwin's primordial from which all these things have evolved, then, instead of its having been the simplest, it must have been the grandest embodiment of living being, as it involved the embryons within embryons of each link in the chain of being, losing one of these at each generation ; therefore becoming simpler and simpler until man was evolved, who, having lost all his embryons of different species, was the very simplest of all living things !   This argument completely reverses evolution, and shows that its primordial, instead of being the simplest, had the same involved ability as the Bible gives the living God of creation.   Hence philosophical science and the well-known facts of physiological relation between parentage and organic transmission, prove the living God of Genesis to have been the primordial of the life of the world.

What science demanded of Darwin before he proceeded another step in his hypothesis of evolution, was to show how lifeless nature was capable of performing the prior involution at least of embryonic rudimental life within the structure of the primordial ; and this implies the absurdity of a thing communicating life, or the seed of life, before it lived itself—of organic nature acting before she was born ; and certainly this would have been a miracle. Had he done this, we should have been obliged to bow with reverence before the demonstration—having ceased to be an hypothesis—because it would have presented us with the work which science shows must have been performed in the origination of nature. The conditions upon which the first living things were brought into existence demanded work of which nature was incapable, hence superior, supernatural work ; for a miracle is simply a work of which nature is incapable. Though Darwin had not descended far enough from his quadruman ancestors to comprehend the philosophic and scientific necessity in nature for the work of a creator, he did descend far enough to see that evolution was only an hypothesis. In his Belfast speech, Professor Tyndall asked : "Whence came the primordial of Mr. Darwin?" and declared that he "saw the potency of life in those material atoms which we cover with opprobrium." But if he did see the primordial thus coming into life, his vision was so distorted that he has failed to give us the facts or to describe the process, so that others might behold the marvellous phenomenon. In his later published "Fragments of Science" he says : "Having adopted the nebula theory, I am bound to show that living things originated without the existence of antecedent life ; but all observation in proof of this has failed, and all experiment in its defence has utterly broken down." According to this testimony, there is no proof that evolution ever had a beginning, and that which never began cannot continue ; therefore this modern sceptical science has no existence, not even an hypothetical one. Professor Huxley corroborates these testimonies. In his "American Lectures," delivered in New York and reported in the New York *Tribune* Extra, he said : "Man came into existence originally either according to the account in Genesis, or upon the hypothesis of evolution," and left it where he found it, a mere hypothesis. Since then Professor Huxley has publicly abandoned the godless myth of evolution, as being unable to account for the origin of the world's inhabitants. Professor Haeckel, in his "History of Creation," says : "Though spontaneous generation is a pure hypothesis, never having been observed or proved

by experiment, yet it is essential to the non-miraculous
origin of living things ; and the evolutionists [Of whom
he is one ·of the most intelligent and devoted.] must accept spontaneous generation, or the creation of living
things.'' Thus evolution, according to its own showing,
is unsustained by evidence.   It is therefore a pigmy, and
not a giant !

It is evident that that which gives vivacity to this controversy is the existence of a personal God.   The sceptics say, '' We will agree with you, if you will give up
the claim to the existence of a personal God, of a personal Christ, and call it the Godly, the Christly principle.
This is beautifully modest, when all the evidence is on
our side ; while they have nothing but hypothesis to begin with, inferences as continuity and irrationality to
end with, not one of their propositions being established
by philosophical science ; while all the real facts and
well-known principles of natural science prove that evolution, according to natural selection, never had a starting-point ; and surely that which never started could not
continue nor exist.   The sceptics know full well that
nothing but a personal being can issue laws to restrain
their conduct and execute their penalty.   They equally
know that these penalties are not executed in the present
life ; as they violate the laws with impunity, their course
evinces a conviction and apprehension of *future punishment*, and act as though they supposed that if they did
not believe in the existence of a personal God, why then
there would be none.   All the facts of observation show
that persons only can deviate from one source, and pursue another ; that persons only originate things, form
purposes, and carry them into execution, that persons
only have the conviction of moral responsibility, and the
conception of the existence of persons or a person higher
in the scale of being than themselves ; the exceptions
being those who in their pride have so distorted their
moral sensibilities, and perverted their reasoning faculties,
that they can honestly believe or accept the foolish notion that there is no personal God, and nothing in the
universe higher or greater than themselves !   It is no

wonder that such minds are capable of accepting any absurdity, as the supposition that the Christian religion is an abstract principle—"the God, the Christ principle."

What folly to suppose the Christian religion, which imposes laws, and enforces duties, offers rewards, threatens punishment, and demands worship which can only be paid by the recognition of a superior Being, having the right to make the laws and to demand obedience to them, could exist without having originated in the mind of a personal God—a personal Christ! As well suppose a moral law without a moral lawgiver, a religious principle imposed without a Being to impose it! In a word, Godliness [Godlikeness] Christliness, without a God—without a Christ, the characteristics without the character! As well talk about the laws of Lycurgus without the existence of the Grecian lawgiver; the code of Justinian if the Roman emperor had never existed; or of the Newtonian system of astronomical science, had Sir Isaac never been born. The evolutionists having proved nothing, we might here claim a verdict against modern science, and in favor of the Scripture account of the origin of the world ; but we propose to vindicate the statements of Genesis by the well-known facts of natural science, both as to the manner of its construction and the time consumed in the origin of the world and its living inhabitants. The nebula theory of Laplace (and its name admits it to be a mere hypothesis) may be considered the foundation of animal and plant evolution, as well as that of the inorganic world, even of the solar system ; for if from this supposed form of matter, as the theory goes, the stars, as centres of revolving systems, formed themselves from this matter, it would be reasonable to conclude that their living inhabitants followed the same course of coming into existence ; and had he demonstrated the hypothesis, it would have settled the question ; but if he failed, and did not even make the attempt, then what right has any man to dignify it by the name of science, and how much less to adopt and build specious theories such as evolution upon it ?

Humboldt talks about creation, but nothing is more

apparent from his writings than that he attaches no other idea to the word than nature. He says : " Among the many wonderful things discovered by science and art, by the aid of powerful instruments scanning the regions of space, we see the remote nebulous mass resolving itself into worlds of stars." It is held by this scientist that the stars thus formed are suns, each having a planetary system like that of our own. Of course, if the nebulous mass resolves itself into stars, it leaves no work for the creator to do in forming suns, and therefore in bringing our sun and solar system into existence ; consequently, man is under no responsibility to him, even if there be such a being, and he may pay his devotions to his god " Nebula " with impunity. The nebula theory is the strongest expression of sceptical materialism, and for which Humboldt virtually acknowledges its author has given no evidence. He says : " Laplace has combined the results of the highest astronomical and mathematical bodies, and has presented them to his readers *free from all processes of demonstration.* The structure of the heavens is here reduced to the simple solution of a great problem in mechanics ; and yet his work has never been accused of incompleteness and want of profundity." Yes, indeed, a very simple process ; for is it not childish simplicity to suppose that nebula—white cloudy vapor—should commence to work and resolve itself into suns and systems of worlds replete with vegetable and animal life ? If it is a tax upon human intellect to admit this work to have been that of a living person, how infinitely greater is the tax upon human credulity to believe that a quantity of diffuse, lifeless vapor did the mighty work. If it is credulous bigotry to believe that this work was achieved by a person possessed of the wisdom and power it demanded, how infinitely greater the faith which believes that the white vapor of space commenced of itself and made all the suns and their planetary systems ! How such a faith should put the unbelief of church members to the blush ! If it is a reflection upon men for believing the origin of things to have been miraculous, how much more severe do those merit it, who believe the greater miracle, that lifeless cloudy vapor, or any other form of inorganic matter, achieved the mighty work !

Sceptics also say, We do not know where this God is, nor whence his origin. Well, do they know where or from whence is the power that brought them into existence, whatever it was ? What we know is the fact that we exist, and that nature had no power to cause our existence. Hence, correlatively, and of philosophic and scientific necessity, we know that there exists a being of wisdom and power equal to the task of our creation. This is what we know. Now, if we do not know where this Being resides at present, or whence his origin, and have never seen him, does such ignorance destroy what we do know ? We know that the sun produces light and heat upon our planet. If we do not know how the sun came into existence, nor the origin of its light, nor the mechanical and chemical principles involved in its production, does such ignorance destroy our knowledge that the sun exists, and that the light is its effect ? We know that we had a father and a mother, because we have seen them, and for other reasons. But suppose you had not seen your grandparents, would you not know you had them also, and be equally positive that every generation before them had parents ? and, by analogous reasoning, do you not know that your ancestors run back to a single man and woman ? and that these, being the first, could have had no parents ; for if they did have them, they could not have been the first, who, therefore, must have been the work of creation. You know, also, that dead parents produce no children, and therefore that the first pair—and there must have been a pair, male and female—were alive before the second generation was born.

You know by the physiological science of life that the possession of vital organs is essential to life — lungs, heart, stomach, spinal column, anterior brain, etc. In a word, the involvement in a single body of all the parts, the removal of any one of which would prevent the continuance of life, and as certainly its commencement. This establishes the fact that all your ancestors, including the first, possessed all these parts, the combination of which is life ; and the first pair must have had them all, as any succeeding generation, and each performing its function as an integral part of the life. Again, as nature always acts uniformly [and nōt to act thus she would work miracles], and does not now produce living things and beings from lifeless matter, nor children without parents, while she is in her maturity and not in a nascent state—as she is claimed to have been in when these things began—therefore nature had no power to bring the first pair into existence without parents ; and that, just as certainly as the second generation of men, or of any living thing, required parents in order to their existence, so certainly did the first pair require a living being to bring them into existence ; and the process must have been so short that the parts made first would not have decomposed until the last were finished ; and this would not have admitted more than a single day to have commenced its ravages. The work was therefore done in exact accordance with the account given in Genesis, and physiological science shows it could not have been done by the false science of evolution. This, then, is what we know by logical reasoning upon the facts and processes of nature ; from which it follows that that account is demonstrated to be the exact truth, both as to the manner and time it consumed.

What kind of reasoning or thinking is that which denies we know anything concerning a fact of existence, because we do not know everything about it ? Or, what is equally absurd, for a man to reject all phenomena the origin of which he cannot comprehend, when, as a matter of fact, he cannot explain the mechanical principles involved in the motions of his finger ? And yet we hear one great scientist [Humboldt] complimenting another [Laplace], because he has not deigned to prove his scientific opinions ! Praising him because he has not demonstrated them, and falling in love with the scientific world for not calling in question their completeness and profundity ! Think of it, undemonstrated profundity ! These are the men who stand at the head of the school of

modern scientists, the one the author of the nebula
theory, and the other, one of its ablest defenders, acknowledging that Laplace, its author, gave no evidence in
its defence. Let it, then, be remembered that all the
inferences and conclusions of the evolutions drawn from
the nebula theory are without force, philosophy, science,
or fact ; therefore .the structure of evolution built upon
such a foundation is nothing but a fanciful myth, without
the least claim to truth, or to be honored by the name of
science. Then comes Professor Proctor, with his fiery
astronomy, wholly founded upon the nebula theory,
which of course has no more scientific existence than its
imaginary foundation. The Professor says : " It has
been found that the sun and the whole solar system—the
earth, moon, and planets—are moving in one direction ;
and this uniformity of movement would seem to indicate
a community of origin ; that at the same time the same
influence was at work to set it in motion in the same direction. It is at this point, when we look into the
heavens for the solution of the mystery, that we come
upon the nebula hypothesis. This supposes [mark it,
supposes—not proves] that the bodies composing the
solar system once existed in the form of nebula ; that this
had a revolution on its own axis from west to east : that
by the effect of gravity, the matter composing the nebula
gradually became condensed toward the centre ; that the
exterior thus had the velocity of their revolutions increased until, by centrifugal force, they were separated
from the mass, and left behind in the form of a ring ;
that thus the material of each of the planets was separated,
while the main body was condensed, forming the sun ;
and finally that each of the planetary rings, by a similar
process, deposited other rings, _ ' of which, by condensa-
tion, its secondaries, or satellites, were formed."

In one of his American lectures, delivered in New
York, in giving some of his incomprehensible periods for
the cooling of the earth's crust, so as to make it a suitable
habitation for living beings, the professor said : " But
back of all this lay the time occupied in the gradual cooling of the earth's crust, when the earth was a fiery mol-

ten mass, whirling through space, a mass many times larger than it is now. As to the duration of this period, when the crust was slowly forming, it was very much longer than the subsequent one. According to Bischoff's calculation, the time occupied in the formation of the earth's crust could not have been less than 350,000,000 years; and this, the professor thought, erred rather on the side of deficiency than excess. But this did not fully measure the time since the earth began; for back of the molten condition there lay another period, the vaporous stage, when the whole solar system was a mass of nebula vapor. This could only be obtained by approximation, and perhaps a period of 500,000,000,000 years may be assigned as the duration of the time. Adding these figures together, it gave the age of the world. How can such baseless speculation lay claim even to a respectable supposition? It must be remembered that these calculations are all based on the supposition of the existence of the nebula supposition of Laplace, and for which there is absolutely no evidence; hence the whole scheme is an atheistic fabrication of greater marvellous credulity, than to believe all the miracles recorded in the Bible, the refutation of which admits of no argument, since nothing is proved. We have however shown, in our published "Cosmogony," that the nebula in none of its stated forms could burn; that a fiery mass has no gravity, electrical or chemical attraction; without which formation is impossible; and that destruction, not formation, is the result of conflagration. We shall, however, in the sequel of the scientific part of our address, expose its absurdities by a number of syllogisms; and if the nebulous fiery mass never existed, then it never cooled, and the periods of the cooling are the children of their parent myth. If the house never burned down, it consumed no time in the process. In the same work we have also examined what purport to be facts in Sir Charles Lyell's "Principles of Geology," giving the world a greater age than the Bible record admits, as well as the same pretentious things found in other geological works; and we have no hesitation in saying that not a fact of fossilization or of formation has been discovered which demonstrates the world to be even six thousand years old, or as old as Biblical chronology makes it.

We return to Professor Huxley's American lecture for the purpose of showing still further that the origin of animal life necessitated a creation just such as Genesis reveals. He says: "The hypothesis of evolution [here it is admitted that evolution is mere hypothesis, supposition] that in any given time in the past we should meet with a state of things more or less similar to the present, but less in proportion as we go back in time. That the physical form of the earth could be traced back in this way to a condition of things in which its parts were separated as little more than a nebulous cloud, making part of a whole in which we find the sun and other planetary bodies resolved [He finds this nebulous condition of things just as Laplace found it—that is, he found no such thing, neither by observation nor calculation.]. And at no point of the continuity could we say, this is a natural process, and this is not a natural process; but that the whole might be strictly compared to that wonderful series of changes which may be seen going on under our eye, in virtue of which there arises, out of that semi-fluid homogeneous substance we call an egg, the complicated organization of one of the higher animals. That, in a few words, is what is meant by the hypothesis of evolution." [Hypothesis and nebula express the two corner-stones of evolution.] "The universe has come into existence somehow, and the question is whether it came into existence in one fashion or another," says the professor. In the hen and egg illustration, is the conclusion true that "at no point in relation to the manner in which the universe and its inhabitants came into existence, from the nebula to the hen, can we say, this is a natural process, and this is not." We answer, it is not true. It makes no difference as to the nature of the work, whether it was a hen, egg, plant, or man, which was the first living thing. In the example of the egg, what are the facts and their correlation?

1. An egg exists.

2. By subjection to a certain temperature, a chicken is hatched from it.

3. The hen is possessed of a voluntary and an involuntary department of machinery. The first enables her to go in quest of food, and to eat it when found. The second takes the food and from it manufactures the egg.

4. If the egg had a father and mother, it might evolve a chicken. If it had no father and mother it could not evolve a chicken ; therefore all eggs in the process of evolution had a father and mother. And also, if the egg had an air-space containing air for the chicken to breathe after it began to live, and until it gathered strength enough to break the shell of its confinement, then it could hatch a chicken ; but if it was full of meàt, leaving no such space, then it could not hatch a chicken.

5. The egg had in it the rudiments of every vital organ and every feature of the hen that laid it, and its products would be identical with its parents'.

6. If nature, in violation of this uniformity, should make an egg without an egg or hen, which would produce and reproduce chickens, hens, and eggs persistently, *that would be a miracle ;* and according to evolution she did this very thing in making the first egg before a hen existed. And if the hen was first, then she made the living hen and evolved in her a chemical laboratory and mechanical apparatus capable of making the egg. Hence nature wrought a most stupendous miracle in bringing the first living thing into existence. But she has never repeated that act ; she only evolves subsequent generations, which is simply the unrollment of the one original miracle of involving all in the first ; and which makes the whole, from first to last, the one grand miracle of God, manifested in the phenomena of nature, and of which nature is utterly incapable. Surely, in view of this the honest sceptic will not object to our ascribing the miraculous work to a living being, when he sees that if his god " Nature " did it, it was the same miraculous work, the unrollment of which comes under observation in every thing that is born. Each species of animals and plants, with all their generations, being these miraculous ma-

chines, which for six thousand years have worked so perfectly that a second interference on the part of the great Engineer of nature has been entirely unnecessary. Here we see Huxley's narrow conception of the subject which he attempts to handle, concluding that the process of bringing the first egg or hen into existence, was so like that which brings every succeeding egg or hen into existence that we cannot say, " this is a natural process, and this is not a natural process."

7. The process of bringing one egg into existence requires about one day, and that of hatching a chicken from it less than one month. Expose an egg to the necessary temperature, and it will either hatch or decompose in less than one month. Therefore, the process of bringing the first chicken from the first egg could not have been longer than a single month ; and if the egg was formed first, no matter what power did it, the process must have been limited to this short period, and was so rapid that the parts formed first would not have decomposed before the last were finished. Of course, this argument admits of none of the indefinite periods which modern science appropriates for the work of bringing living things into existence, and shuts us up to the twenty-four hour-day statements of Genesis as the scientific and ultimate truth.

In the history of the first hen, we have the fact that there was a moment before it lived, before it breathed, and the next moment it drew its first breath and lived ; and this implied that it had every vital organ as perfectly developed as any living thing has at the present day ; and so also has it been with every succeeding generation ; for at no time does nature admit of a different or longer process ; therefore, the long periods and incipient stages of evolution for the performance of the work were always unscientific and impossible. These facts and principles of natural science demonstrate that the first progenitors of every species of animals were as perfect, and came into living form as suddenly, as the book of Genesis records them ; which equally demonstrates the so-called modern science to be no science, mere nonsense.

Hence we have the classic account of the work dictated by the great Naturalist himself, thus : " And God created every living creature that moveth and creepeth upon the earth, after his kind ; the birds of the air and the fishes of the sea after their kind ; male and female created he them." The perpetual miracle manifested in the work is seen in the fact that each species was to be " after its kind," never to be lost in another ; and its confirmation is the fact that nature, assisted by the cultivating and rearing skill of the great naturalists of the world, has never produced a generation different from its kind, and not a new species of animal or plant has ever come into existence. The test of species is that by crossing they will not reproduce and persist ; while races are the modification of species, and will always reproduce and persist !

Latest Discoveries Confirm our Position.

To show that no later discoveries have been made to relieve evolution from these embarrassments, we quote the following from the July number of *Nature*, one of the most popular scientific periodicals of the day. It is a review by Henry De Varigny, an evolutionist, of a book by Albert Gaudry, another evolutionist, and Professor of Paleontology in the Museum of Natural History, Paris. De Varigny says, " A great deal has been written on the transformism-theory of Lamarck and Darwin, and it must be expected that much more will be written. One of the principal objections made to it is that, if a man is really the descendant of the ape, and the ape that of other mammalia ; if, generally, there exist links between all animals, living and extinct, so that all animals trace their origin to a common ancestor, how is it that no link really exists between man and ape, or between fish and frog, or between vertebrate and invertebrate ? Embryological considerations, it is said, show a real connection between very different animals ; a frog, for instance, is a fish for some time during its youth, and amphioxus looks very much like an ascidian. But, notwithstanding numerous arguments to support Lamarck's theory, no transformist can show any species gradually losing its peculiar characters to acquire new ones belonging to another species, and thus transforming itself. However similar the dog may be to the wolf, no one has found any dead skeleton which might be as well ascribed to wolf as to dog, and therefore be considered as being the link between the two. One may say exactly as much concerning the extinct species; there is no gradual and imperceptible passage from one to another. Moreover, the first animals that lived on this earth are not, by any means, those that one may consider as inferior and degraded. M. Gaudry, in the first pages of his work, states very clearly that he prefers the theory according to which links do exist between the extinct animals of different groups, but he does not show any facts to support it.''

Here we have two facts developed by the researches of evolutionists down to the present time. First, that the first animals which inhabited our earth were by no means inferior to those which now inhabit it. Second, that each species has preserved its identity; both of which confirm the statements of Genesis as to the origin of animals, and as perfectly refute the theory of evolution. For more than half a century the evolutionists have been searching for the links which gradually connect different species. They have ransacked all nature; visited and searched every continent and island on the earth's surface, explored every sea, lake, and river; climbed every mountain; hunted every cave; sunk shafts in the soil, and bored the rocks. They have paid particular attention to snakes, snails and tortoises; hunted burial-places for skulls, and calculated their age; and for their pains have not found a living creeping thing or fossilized specimen upon which to hang the hypothesis of evolution; but, on the contrary, have found all nature protesting against their folly; and here are the latest witnesses, two eminent French authors and evolutionists, who would love to have the sceptical science true, but find no evidence by which to prove it.

23

Scientific Origin of Plant-life.

Let us now examine the origin of plant-life, in order to see whether it was the work of evolution or creation. The position we take in regard to the question is, that nature did not have the materials of which all plants are known to be composed, therefore the first plants were the work of supernatural power. In discussing the question we quote what is known upon the subject of scientific botany from the best text-books. What then is the nourishing media, or food of plants? We can only satisfactorily and precisely answer the question by stating what the simple and chemical component parts of vegetables are, because it is an established fact that everything they contain must be formed of that which is received from without. The bulk of every plant is composed of cellular and vascular tissue and woody fibre, and their cellular membranes contain starch, resin, salts, chlorophyl, and a watery sap holding in solution sugar, gum, and acids in union with metallic oxides, albumin, volatile and fixed oils, with other fatty matters. The chief part of every plant passes, by combustion, into gaseous combination and disappears, and only the non-volatile metallic oxides and salts remain as ash, which forms an inconsiderable proportion of the weight of the plant. These substances are not in nature, for we never meet with woody fibre, starch, sugar, albumin, etc., except in the plant itself. It must therefore be the manufacturer of those articles out of the constituents of nature which it inhales from without—which is principally carbonic acid gas, composed of carbon and oxygen. Plants cannot receive carbon in its solid form into their circulation. Carbon is insoluble in water, but mixing with the oxygen of the air and water, for which it has a strong affinity, it is reduced to carbonic acid gas. This substance is received into the plant by its roots and leaves, and is decomposed by the plant itself, which expels the oxygen not needed in its formation; retaining the carbon, and from it alone forms all the starch, sugar, albumin, woody fibre, etc., existing in nature, and which constitutes not only the food for all plants, but that also for all the animals of the world.

All plants are formed of cells of about the same size and shape, of which there are 22,800 in a square inch. They are formed of layers from the outer to the inner layer, and down to the centre. Each of these cells form other cells exactly like themselves, adding cell to cell, and thus the plant enlarges or grows. As the cells thus succeed each other in coming into existence, if we begin at the last and count back, we come to the first—the primordial. If it was a plant-cell, it had the faculty of inhaling carbonic acid gas from the surrounding air and earth, and then of separating the oxygen from it and of expelling it. It also had the faculty of manufacturing from this substance starch, sugar, albumin, etc., the elements of which itself was composed, and of forming other cells of these materials, and of transmitting to these all its own faculties. This argues the prior existence of the first cell, and of which nature was always incapable of producing, because she did not possess any of the score of different compound substances of which the first was composed; and, as the cell existed, demonstrates it to have been a work of which nature was incapable, and therefore a superior, supernatural, or a miraculous work—the work of a living Creator, who made the first plant of each species before there was any growing or any second generation. Hence we read the only scientific and satisfactory solution of the problem in the scriptural account of the manner in which the first plants came and must have come into existence: "And God made every plant of the field *before it was in the ground*, and every herb of the field *before it grew*, yielding fruit after his kind whose seed is in itself upon the earth." (Gen. 1: 11; 2: 5.) Here were the first plants of each species made, involving the mechanical department of producing "seed after their kind," all of which have followed this identical order of reproduction—after their kind. "Never have men gathered grapes of thorns, or figs of thistles." Never, therefore, has there come into existence since the sixth day of creation a new species of plant kind; and by no art of man has it been possible to produce one. With these proclamations of fact and science, all corroborating the Genesis of Scripture, how does the myth of evolution appear, which declares that all species came from one, and all kinds from a single kind ! Here again does science and the Bible as perfectly agree as that both disagree with this so-called modern science of evolution, and the geological fiction of the age of the world.

Let us briefly consider the conditions and law of vegetable growth, and which will also show, by the interdependence of natural phenomena, how great a portion of the solar system is necessary to sustain the life of man. A seed must first exist ; yet not one atom it possesses would ever move toward life of itself. A seed, therefore, is not a law of nature, of plant production. Neither is soil such a law, nor yet solar light ; nor is the heat received from the sun such a law. These may exist, yet if the seed is kept out of the soil, no vegetable effect would follow. If the seed were planted in good soil yet amid perpetual darkness, still no vegetation would result, as no plant can be brought to maturity without sunlight. The law of vegetation, therefore, necessitates the astronomical motions of the earth and correlatively those of the solar system. Suppose the earth did not revolve on its axis : in that case the half turned from the sun would be always dark and cold ; hence, if the seed were planted on that side of the earth, not one of its particles would ever move toward germination, and not at all, except to decompose, as they certainly would, unless the temperature was so low as to keep them frozen. We will also suppose the seed planted in a dry soil ; but as moisture is an essential element of vegetable growth, dew or rain must fall upon the soil to prepare it to do its work. But this can only come from the atmosphere ; and as water is not a constituent of the air, it must be drawn into it by an inherent principle designed for the purpose. This is its evaporating power.

The water is principally taken up from the oceans, lakes, and rivers, and it would fall again directly into those bodies, were it not for the motion of the clouds,

themselves formed by the evaporation. This motion is
produced by the unequal expansion of the air, principally
resulting from the ecliptic motion of the earth, and that
upon its axes, perpetually changing its temperature.
These correlative principles necessitate not only the existence of the whole solar system, but its motions as perfect
as at the present day ; all of which present us with the following fundamental facts of the science of vegetable life :
First, no plant or seed would grow unless it was first organized according to the law of plant-life.   Secondly,
not the simplest plant could live in any nascent or half-
formed condition of the globe, or in one less perfect than
that which now exists, and without vegetable food animals, with man at their head, could not have existed.
Third, that the laws of nature are not abstractions, susceptible of existence prior to nature, and as the evolutionists claim brought her into existence, but that they inhere
chemically and electrically as integral parts of the bodies,
giving them their peculiarities, with which they were incorporated by the Creator at the formation of the world.
Thus does nature, or the solar system, the great law of
vegetation, exhaust herself in sustaining the temporary
life of man, demonstrating him to be the great object for
which it was made.   Thus does the well-known voice of
botanical chemistry negative the airy thing called evolution.   If man is thus dependent upon the universe, let us
briefly inquire how much of it depends upon him for its
perpetuation.   One of the commonest objections scepticism makes to the Bible is that it regards man as the
great object for which the world was made, delegating to
him supreme dominion, and of course making all animals
and living things subservient and dependent upon him.
Man's desire to survive death, to live again, and his hope
of eternal being, are attributed to his pride ; ''for,'' say
they, ''he has really no more grounds for indulging such
a hope than have the lower animals. As with these, so
with him, death ends all.''   Indeed, modern science
completely reverses this order, and makes man dependent
upon a long line of ancestral weeds, shell-fish, and
monkeys for his existence, through which he has crawled

into being, so that in his devotions to his numerous progenitors he can sing,

> All hail thou mighty monkey! all hail thou ancient clam !
> Through you, by evolution, I came to be a man !

Our answer is, that the sustenance and continued existence of the lower animals, fish and fowl, depend upon
the simultaneous existence and labor of man.   Man is the
only animal who clears the land of trees, and cultivates
the soil, sows seeds, plants trees, and reaps harvests.
There is no account of any race of men so low in the
scale of being, that they did not do these things, nor of
one that did not rear and use domestic animals.   Wild
wood will grow wherever there is soil enough to sustain
any kind of plant, and they will be numerous in proportion to the richness of the soil.   No cereals or fruit will
grow in dense woods, not even grass for hay, while it
does not require fifty years to grow a forest of oaks, and
not half that time for one of various other kinds of trees.
A large portion of the vegetable matter produced upon
the earth is washed into the rivers, lakes, and seas by the
falling rain, which supplies the food for the smaller fishes,
while the larger ones prey upon and devour the smaller.
Birds and fowls feed on fruits, vegetables, fish, and car-
rion, while birds of prey devour the smaller ones, and the
domestic birds and fowls.   Let us now suppose the sudden extinguishment of mankind, and that the catastrophe
took place in the spring, too early to sow or plant.   As a
result, there would be no harvests reaped that autumn.
By the next spring all the domestic animals would have
died of starvation and exposure, while the carnivorous
animals and birds of prey fattened and increasingly mul-
tiplied.   But the domestic animals being dead, they could
only live thereafter by devouring each other, and before
the end of ten years the last two of these would have
met in deadly conflict, after which the survivor would
have died of starvation.   The flowers, vegetables, fruits,
and dead animals—the food for insects—being gone, they
too would have ceased to be, and the smaller birds, which
fed upon these insects, would soon join the number of the

dead. Those birds of prey which depended upon insect-feeding kind for food, would soon devour the few that remained, and finally also have died of starvation. Those birds which preyed upon the small fishes living close to the shore in shallow waters, would soon also perish for lack of food. These fishes had fed upon the living and dead insects, and vegetable matter washed from the cultivated farms, but the supply became exhausted, and they extinct. Upon these smaller fishes the larger ones of the deep depended for their food; but the supply being cut off, they too preyed upon each other, and the last contest soon comes between the two surviving monsters of the deepest sea. The two strongest and most savage, uncivilized and therefore the most unfit to survive, kills and devours his antagonist, and then himself dies by starvation, after which universal death reigns over the animal creation. Look ahead to the end of a century, and see in what a condition are all the once cleared lands—the rich cultivated farms! Not a spot which would produce grass for cattle can be found uncovered by wild brush-wood and trees. The fruit-trees, overtopped and choked by wild-wood, long since became extinct. These facts not only confirm but demonstrate the Bible statements of the creation, that all organic beings and things, plants and animals, with man at their head, came into existence simultaneously, and that the world was made for man, and man for the world.

CHAPTER XV.

HAVING now discussed the principal questions of science
and philosophy in defence of the Bible statements as to
the origin of the world, we proceed more directly to consider those which relate to the nature of the Christian religion—that of man to it, and that of Christ to both ; and
the first inquiry is, Who is Christ ? An article in the
" Encyclopædia Britannica," headed " Confucius," men-
tions it as a distinguishing mark of the greatness of the
Chinese philosopher, that he deduced " the Golden Rule "
from the needs of human society. As this fact is used by
sceptics to degrade Christ to the level of a mere philosopher, we call attention to the subject to show that he borrowed nothing from the Chinaman, and that Confucius
had no conception of " the Golden Rule." Confucius
lived three hundred years before Christ, and Moses lived
one thousand five hundred before Christ, and Christ declares that the " Golden Rule " he taught was deduced
from the laws of Moses and the prophets, so that if either
borrowed it, it was the Chinaman. The rule of Confucius was only negative. Its language is, " What you
would not like to be done to you, do not do to others."
It is obvious that a perfectly selfish miser may keep the
rule of Confucius, which simply requires that we do no
evil to others ; while the rule of Jesus requires this, and,
in addition, to do every good to others which lies within
our power—everything we would have others do to us,
were we in their circumstances. The practical part of
the Christian religion therefore consists in doing those
unselfish works which were exemplified in the life and
taught by the injunctions of its author ; and its best de-

fence are the laws its founder enjoined. The Golden
Rule of Christ, is in these words: "Therefore all things
whatsoever ye would that men should do to you, do ye
even so to them: for this is the law and the prophets."
(Matt. 7 : 12.) As proof of our position, we present a
brief summary of those principles from Moses and the
prophets, and from which Christ deduced the Golden
Rule, and we may add they were the constitution of revealed religion from the foundation of the world.

"The stranger that dwelleth with you shall be as one
born among you ; thou shalt not vex him, and thou shalt
love him as thyself." "Thou shalt rise up before the
hoary head, and thou shalt honor the face of an old man."
"Ye shall do no unrighteousness in judgment, in mete-
yard, in weight, in measure ; just balances, just weights, a
just hin, shall ye have." "Regard not them that have
familiar spirits, neither seek after wizards, to be defiled
by them : I am the Lord your God." [The supposed
gods of space, after which the familiar spiritualists seek
for the living among the dead, are no gods—refrain from
consulting those who have this animal magnetic power to
glide familiarly into your mind, reading the brain-pict-
ures of your history and returning them to you as revelations from the ghosts of the dead—do not thus defile
yourselves.] "If there be among you a poor man thou
shalt not harden thine heart, nor shut thine hand from
thy poor brother ; but thou shalt open thine hand wide
unto him ; thou shalt surely lend him sufficient for his
need, in that which he wanteth." "Thou shalt not de-
fraud thy neighbor, nor rob him." "The wages of him
that is hired shall not abide with thee until morning."
"Thou shalt not hate thy brother in thy heart." "Thou
shalt not avenge, nor bear any grudge against the children
of thy people ; but thou shalt love thy neighbor as thyself, and thou shalt love the Lord thy God with all thy
heart." "Thou shalt not deliver unto his master the
servant that is escaped ; but he shall dwell among you
within thy gates, in the place where it liketh him best :
thou shalt not oppress him." "And when thou sendest
away thine hired servant, thou shalt not let him go away

empty : thou shalt furnish him liberally out of thy flock, and out of thy floor, and out of thy wine-press, of that wherewith the Lord thy God hath blessed thee." (See Leviticus 19th, Exodus 6th, and Deuteronomy 15th, 18th, and 24th chapters.)

These scriptures are quoted by Christ and his apostles as the Code of the Christian religion. Says Paul. " Remember them that are in bonds, as bound with them," " Bear ye one another's burdens, and so fulfil the law of Christ." " Love worketh no ill to its neighbor." " Love is the fulfilling of the law." Jesus said, " Thou shalt love the Lord thy God with all thy heart ; and thou shalt love thy neighbor as thyself, and on these two commandments hang all the law and the prophets." In his sermon on the mount, Christ reaffirms the provisions of these laws as the principles of his religion, and, in closing, resolves them all into the Golden Rule, which covers all the reciprocities of human relationship and obligations : " Whatsoever ye would that men should do to you, do ye even so to them ; for this is the law and the prophets." Is it not marvellous that in this late age anyone should be called on to defend such a system ? and should not its boasting pride feel the rebuke of its utter inability to add the least shade of improvement to the perfection and grandeur of its standard ? Every system of mechanics or art, and of natural and social science, have their fundamental principles. These not only relate to each other, but are dependent upon the physical laws of the universe, limiting the term to signify the solar system and its Creator. If we understood the entire correlation of natural existences, we would be able to deduce the purpose of an existence from the fact of its existence ; the whole phenomena from a knowledge of a part, and its parts from the whole. For example, the globe from an atom, and the atom from the globe ; the ocean from a drop, and the drop from the ocean ; the atmosphere from a breath, and the breath from the atmosphere ; the vegetable from the animal, and the animal from the vegetable ; man from the universe, and the universe from man ; the existence of the Creator from that of man, and man's existence from that of his Maker. In a word, if nature is a system, any part correlates the whole, and especially does it include the end it proposes, namely, the development of man, the head of nature, to the highest mental, moral, social, physical, and religious exaltation of which his nature is susceptible, both in the temporary and endless world.

If these postulates are true, it follows that any partial view of the supposed teaching of nature which does not blend with the whole, or which antagonizes some known part, demonstrates its error, and thereby excludes it from being any part of the universal science; and this carries with it every assumption, hypothesis, inference, or supposed phase of natural teaching which is in opposition to any of its known parts. These principles of nature which for brevity we call truth, must be in harmony with each other, and all the truth and evidence must be on one side of every question, and on that side on which some truth is known to be arranged. There may be that which, for the time being, seems to involve truth and error on both sides of a question; but this is because of superficial knowledge of the subject at the time, or science falsely so called. This involves the conclusion, that the principles adapted to such development may be deduced from the physical, moral, and religious necessities of mankind, and would be true if taught in no book; so that if the principles of the Christian religion are adapted to such development, then the universal science and all its parts demonstrate their fundamentality and truth. If, then, all nature is interdependent, and each department is essential to the highest development of man, including what is called humanity as a part [for, as it cannot exempt man from death, the greatest deranging element in human society], it follows that such a state cannot be attained in the present world, and as conclusively, that there must come another world, wherein exemption from death will make it possible. The effect upon those in this world who have complied with the conditions of obtaining an entrance into the world of purity and universal righteousness, and have therefore been actuated in their human career by the purest motives and highest aims, which has made them the brightest examples of human society; because they have refrained from every evil and practised every good within their power, which the real followers of Christ must and will do.

As this temporary development is reached by belief in the promises of God of an inheritance in that world, exemplified by submission to the necessary sacrifices demanded in this life of all degrading indulgences, a society composed of unbelievers in that purpose and those promises, cannot but be low in its aspirations, selfish in its spirit, and inconsistent in its acts; all of which tend to degrade and disintegrate human society. If unbelievers are too self-willed and proud to obey their Maker, how can they act otherwise toward their fellow-men? This development is simply according to the philosophy which, while it aims at the higher, recedes from the lower; and, while aiming at the supremely high—the possession of the eternal world of righteousness to come—it reaches the highest virtue and knowledge in the present world, namely, the knowledge of God's will and purposes with man and the world. The fundamental principles and bonds of social union are not statutory enactments, secret compacts, communistic engagements, or conventional arrangements of whatever name or nature, but that which inheres in the character of the individuals composing it. What each member is in himself is his standard of the social state. He acts out what he is within, evolves what he involves, and cannot for any considerable time do otherwise, because no man can be a permanent hypocrite and it not be known to others. These principles of deduction indicate both those of the highest human and immortal society; the former being unattainable without proper conceptions and hopes of the latter. The anticipation of an endless life induces men to shun every evil and practise every virtue in this life; and when this is done for Christ's sake, it makes them Christians. This is the Christian religion, thus deduced from the wants, hopes, and susceptibilities of mankind, and its corroboration by the gospel statements demonstrates it to be the universal science of God, man, and nature for time and eternity.

Let us hear the great Philosopher discourse upon the subject : " Every tree is known by its fruit.   Every good tree bringeth forth good fruit ; but a corrupt tree evil fruit.   A good tree cannot bring forth evil fruit, neither can a corrupt tree bring forth good fruit.   A good man, out of the good treasure of his heart, bringeth forth good things ; and an evil man, out of the evil treasure, bringeth forth evil things.   First make the tree good, and the fruit will be good ; or make the tree corrupt, and the fruit will be corrupt.   O generation of vipers ! how can ye, being evil, speak good things ? for out of the abundance of the heart the mouth speaketh." (Matt. 7 : 17, 18 ; 12 : 33–35.)   We see by these sayings, which our daily observation confirms, that it is the heart of man— his moral, feeling, sensitive nature—which is the standard of human rectitude, purity, and virtue, and its action the development of the standard ; and that these principles divide mankind into but two classes.   All are good or bad, as their hearts are such.   We may also learn from these facts the utter impossibility of forming a permanent community composed of both these classes and characters, for " how can two walk together, except they be agreed ? "   The attempt may be made, as it has often been, but the effort to counteract nature with nature always fails.   No conventionalities instituted by man change selfishness to kindness and benevolence, nor pride to humility ; therefore, all schemes for the development of a permanent and prosperous social community, whose aims and hopes are limited to selfish human nature and the present world—call it what you will, even the religion of humanity, or moral cultured humanity without religion—must always prove a failure, from the fact that all such efforts reverse the great philosophy of God and man, by attempting to cure the social evil tree by doctoring its evil fruit.   Its devotees seek to " gather grapes of thorns and figs of thistles."   They make efforts to sweeten the bitter fountain by medicating its streams.

It is the attempt to practise the highest conditions of development without obeying the essential mandate, "Thou shalt love the Lord thy God with all thy heart." This is first, and gives the qualification to fulfil the second requisition, "Thou shalt love thy neighbor as thyself."

As though the Creator had said, "Thy mental powers shall first be devoted to the investigation and practice of those things which please me; and secondly to those which will be best adapted to develop the highest interests of thy fellow-men. The love which proceeds from the heart is always characterized by purity of intention, will both please me and work the greatest good to thy fellow-men." Therefore the second requisition is, "Thou shalt love thy neighbor as thyself." Hence the absurdity of supposing a man can act toward his God whom he does not love as though he did love him, and of thinking that a man can act toward his brother-man whom he does not love as himself as though he did thus love him, or for a selfish man to be unselfish at the same time. This truth is read and confirmed in the decline and fall of all the great states of the world, and the ruins of cities. Human nature being the same, must always repeat itself in history. In our day it clamors for freedom from all religious restraint. Abolish the Sabbath, give us easy divorce. It ridicules God and the Bible, blasphemes Christ, and many make him the principal wizard in the spiritualistic religion, and give us the ghostly revelation of free love, and with whom progress is the obliteration of all restraints upon passion. They repeat the cries of their prototypes, and say unto God, "Depart from us! we desire not the knowledge of thy ways." They proudly exclaim, "Who is the Lord, that we should serve him?" and indignantly cry, "Cause the Holy One of Israel to cease from before us!" The two fundamental principles of the Christian religion are love and sacrifice; the latter being the means of its manifestation. One person may love another, but the only manner in which it can be made known is by sacrifice. The one has wants, and the other possesses the means and disposition to supply them; and the degree of love is measured by the degree of sacrifice made to please the object loved. Our Maker, desiring to be pleased and obeyed by the first pair, while they did not know what would please or displease him, was obliged to make a revelation, and tell them what they might and what they might not do, and of the consequences. But if the man obeyed, his loyalty might be precarious, because it was not prompted by love, and to make it supreme and constant he must be brought to love him who imposed the duties. This the man could not yet do, because he had no wants which might be graciously supplied, he must therefore feel independent of his Maker. The possession and dominion of the earth had been committed to him ; all nature was subservient to his happiness ; he knows of nothing he does not possess. But now he violates the obligation imposed, and deprives himself of the means of everlasting life.

The loss carries with it the consciousness of shame and want, and teaches him what evil is. He can now love him who is able and willing to supply these wants, and relieve him of the apprehensions, even though it be by promises to be fulfilled in the future, and for which he may in faith and hope confidently look. These gracious promises the Creator made to the first generation of mankind, and they have constituted the hope of the saints of all ages. To win the love and obedience of this pair, and of their offspring, God must make the greatest sacrifice in his power so as to afford them the very strongest inducement to love and sacrifice for him in turn—and that must be the sacrifice of a life ; anything less would not show the greatest love for man and the world. Hence the revelation—" For God so loved the world that he gave his only begotten son, that whosoever believeth in him might not perish, but have everlasting life." " For greater love hath no man than this, that a man lay down his life for his friend." But as the immortal God could not die, he must take on him a living nature in which he could die, which he did when he became " Immanuel, God with us—God manifest [seen] in the flesh." In this form God was both Father and Son. Before this he was only such in purpose, made known in decree, prophecy, and typical revelation. This Immanuelized being is the Christian's God, as taught in the Bible, the one living and true God, the Creator of all things. "Hereby perceive we the love of God, because he died for us." (1 John 3: 16.) To show that this Redeemer, Saviour, and destined King of the coming new world is the only living God, as taught in the Scriptures, we quote but one of its predictions and its revelation in the New Testament. " Thus saith the Lord, the king of Israel, and his Redeemer, the Lord of hosts: I am the first and I am the last ; and beside me there is no God. Is there a God beside me? Yea, there is no God ; I know not any." (Isa. 44: 6, 8.) This passage is revealed by Christ himself to John thus : " I am Alpha and Omega, the beginning and the ending, saith the Lord, the Almighty. I am the first and I am the last ; I am he that liveth, and was dead ; and behold, I am alive for evermore, Amen, and have the keys of hell and death." (Rev. 1: 8, 17, 18.) It was not the human form which was Jesus Christ, nor was God Jesus Christ before he took this form ; but God in it was both God and Christ, the Father and Son—the Lord of Glory, and the man Christ Jesus.

That this human form was the whole Godhead is also proved by the following apostolic declaration : " For in him dwelleth all the fulness of the Godhead bodily." (Col. 2: 9.) He was the Creator before he took human form, and was he any less the Creator afterward ? If God could make bodies for men, could he not make one for himself, involving himself in it ? If he could live in it as a man, could he not die in it as a God ? and while he was thus dead would not God be the same being as he was before the Immanuelization ? Or could he not on the third day become Immanuel the second time, thus investing himself with the same dead body, the human-mortal life of which he had sacrificed for men to win them to become his loyal, loving servants and thus, by his own living, immortal self, rendering it no more susceptible of death ? And if this resurrected Lord thus became Christ again, can he not by [with] Christ, the whole embodiment of God, resurrect his saints from the dead, when the time appointed for that work arrives? Whatever was the substantial nature of God before he became Immanuel, he now becomes the palpable God-man revealed in human form ; a form in which he might sacrifice himself for his creatures, in order to win loving friends for his kingdom and that he might be seen— " God manifest in the flesh," and in this his last form to reign with his subjects and be like them in his endless world. From henceforth he is no more the invisible God, whose face no man had seen or could see ; but in the very glorified nature of his glorified brethren, becomes forever visible. Upon this subject we have such testimony as the following : " I know that my Redeemer liveth, and that he shall stand at the latter day upon the earth, and in my flesh [the flesh of man] I shall see God." John testifies : " We shall be like him, for we shall see him as he is." " No man hath seen God at any time, but the only begotten Son, he hath declared him ; " and Christ's declaration is, " I and my Father are one, and he that hath seen me hath seen the Father also." No more the invisible, impalpable, but the Immanuelized God-man—" The Lord of lords, and King of kings : the first and the last, and beside whom there is no God."

It is evident that the second creation of the world and its inhabitants demands the same wisdom and power as did its original creation ; and as Jesus Christ is the revealed re-creator and Saviour, it follows that, if he is anything less in wisdom and power than the original Creator, he is inadequate to the work ; but after his second Immanuelization from the dead, we hear him declaring, " All power is given unto me in heaven and in earth." (Matt. 28 : 18) ; and Paul, in 1 Cor. 1 : 24, says that " Christ is the wisdom of God, and the power of God." He therefore embodies it all, and which the Immanuelization alone explains. Indeed, the power and wisdom he displayed in his mortal history over organic and inorganic matter—in stilling the tempest, raising the dead, and controlling the laws of vegetable and animal life—

24

were manifestations of all the wisdom and power which the creation of the world demanded ; and when this work is accomplished, it is the promised salvation of which the gospel is the glad tidings ; the re-created world being the kingdom of God and of Christ—one God with various titles. All the revealed instruction concerning its nature and coming is the gospel of the kingdom ; and when its immortal inhabitants take possession of it, then they are saved—safe beyond all future liability. This is expressed in such language as the following : '' Receiving the end of your faith, even the salvation of your souls ''—yourselves ; for the Christian religion does not propose, like heathenism, to save a disintegrated part—a mere ghost of a man, but the man himself—body, soul, and spirit—'' Man all immortal.''

In this world Christians are saved by faith. '' That is, they believe they will be saved when the salvation comes. Then faith is superseded by possession, and ends. In the present world they '' walk by faith and not by sight.'' Their eye is fixed on the salvation which they do not yet see. They are also declared to be '' saved by grace.'' This is the gift of God, comprehending the bestowment of eternal life in the endless world. This gracious promised reward has been a sufficient inducement to encourage the saints of all ages to sacrifice everything of the present world, even life itself, rather than forfeit their heirship to it ; and in their trials they hear the cheering words, '' My grace is sufficient for you.'' '' He that shall endure unto the end, the same shall be saved.'' '' He that overcometh shall inherit all things : and I will be his God, and he shall be my son.'' '' Wherefore gird up the loins of your mind ; be sober, and hope to the grace that is to be brought unto you at the revelation of Jesus Christ.'' Again it is said. '' We are saved by hope, and if we hope for that we see not, then do we with patience wait for it.'' (Rom. 8 : 24, 25.) '' Looking for that blessed hope, and the glorious appearing of the great God our Saviour, the Lord Jesus Christ : who shall change our vile body, that it may be fashioned like unto his glorious body, according to the working whereby he is able even to subdue all things unto himself." (Phil. 3 : 21.) Here Jesus Christ, the Saviour, is to come and give the great salvation for which the saints of all ages have hoped. Hence " we are saved by hope "—we hope then to be saved. Abraham looked for a heavenly country, and was heir of the world—the world to come—the new heaven and new earth. Hence says Christ, " But they which shall be counted worthy to obtain that world, and the resurrection from the dead, neither marry nor are given in marriage; neither can they die any more ; for they are equal unto the angels and are the children of God, being the children of the resurrection." (Luke 20 : 35, 36.) It is also said, " We live by faith." Jesus said, " I am the resurrection and the life. He that believeth in me, though he were dead, yet shall he live." Paul says, " For ye are dead, and your life is hid with Christ in God. When Christ, who is our life, shall appear, then shall ye also appear with him in glory."

Who can see an inconsistency in this instruction, or an impossibility of its execution ?

Let us for a moment return to our Protoplast. Here is a man and a woman physically mature, bearing the corresponding marks of age, as did all animals, plants, and rocky strata, though but one week old. " And God called their name Adam, in the day when they were created." (Gen. 5 : 2.) They possess faculties to think, will, and act. But a man can only act after he wills to act. He can only will after he thinks. He can only think after he has brains and organs of sense ; and only then after he is alive. As no man can think for him or will for him, so no man can act for him, not even his Maker ; for if the Maker should compel his will, and he should act under such compulsion, it would not be the act of the man, but that of the controlling will ; and for such an act the will which prompted it would be alone responsible. Here are two persons, each having a will. Each person must have a will, and no person can have two wills. One is the Creator, the other the creature. The creature desires to be pleased with what he makes, and expects it to subserve the purpose he designed—that it should in some way minister to his pleasure and satisfaction. From these characteristics of the creature, we reason that the Creator also desires to be pleased with what he makes, and that it should answer the purpose for which he designed it, and thereby minister to his pleasure and gratification. Indeed, it is no more possible for the Creator to make a thing on purpose to displease him, than for a creature to commit such folly. If, then, the man can will and act, and act independently of the Creator—which simply means that he can do a voluntary act at all—it follows that he has the ability to act in accordance with the will of his Creator, and to obey him. This implies the ability to act contrary to his will, and to disobey him.

Having thus made him a man, and endowed him with the gift of volition and the power to displease him, how to win such a being to love and obey his Creator, is the vital question; for, to secure his love and fidelity, and rescue him from infidelity, would afford him greater pleasure than to behold all the glories of the universe besides, which had no power to disobey him. And how is this enhanced when we consider man's intellectual faculties? By the use of these man alone is capable of investigating and of appreciating the wonderful wisdom and power displayed by the Creator in the mechanism of the world, and the adaptation of its parts to work out God's purposes and ends; thus pleasing his great Father as a precocious son pleases his natural father; for man alone has the power to discover the grandeur of the great Architect of the universe; and every such conception draws from the mind of him who entertains it an act of merited honor and worship, elevating to himself, and, as a consequence, brightening the halo of glory encircling the great Inhabitant of eternity.

Now, if some of his creatures thus " give the Lord the honor due unto his name," is it not arrogant for others who, in their selfish pride and jealousy, desire all honor to be paid to themselves, to question the right of the Maker to have made those who remain proud and conceited ? That because one refuses to perform the duties which another recognizes and discharges, and thereby gains his Maker's approval and promised reward, God had no right to cause both men to exist! That the Creator has no right to be honored and obeyed, because some persist in dishonoring and disobeying him ! As if the disobedient father of an obedient son should not have been born, thus depriving the obedient son of existence. Or, as all fathers are disobedient at some period of their lives, and have violated the laws of God, although multitudes of them would have repented of their folly, seeing that the loss would fall only upon themselves, and would have been "converted from the error of their way."

This complaint against God for having made man, is the argument of the disobedient, the self-willed and proud, but never of the lover and worshipper of God. If God was morally like themselves, would they not glory in having such a distinguished leader, just as they glory in such men as Robert G. Ingersoll and Charles Bradlaugh? The weakness of their defence obliges them, against their own reason, to make every effort to dissipate from their minds the conviction of the existence of God, and the truth of the Christian religion, which are the greatest sources of their trouble. If they would make half the effort to end the contest with their Maker that they do to prolong it, O ! what changed men would they become ! Has not God blessed these men with life ? If they did not esteem life a blessing, would they not commit suicide ? For its preservation they submit to three score and ten years of toil, hardship, and suffering. If temporal life is the gift of God, and for which he demands and they pay such an enormous price, can they expect him to give them eternal life without any price or sacrifice, and while they continue his enemies ? If nature is the god that brought them into being, does he deal so mercifully and mildly with them that they should praise and worship him ? They complain against God, because he threatens to punish them if they continue all their life to disobey his laws and refuse to be his loyal subjects;

but they praise their god nature, while he instantly and implacably punishes friend and foe alike for every trans-'gression of his laws, and mercilessly sends forth his conflagrations to burn, his gravity to crush and mangle, hurricanes to scourge, famines to starve, pestilences .to devour, floods to drown, lightnings to kill, earthquakes to engulf, and lets loose the whole host of deadly diseases to torture his devotees; and at death executes upon them hopeless annihilation! Why should they prefer such a god?

Another of these complaints against God is, that he knew when he made these opposers and detractors of his character and honor that their end would be punishment and destruction; and because such an end is inevitable, they say they will not serve a god that would inflict it. We admit that God foreknew this destiny. He foreknew it because he foresaw it just as a man foreknows that a steam-boiler which he has made will explode under certain circumstances; but did his knowledge explode the boiler? God foreknew, because he foresaw, that sin and death would reign six thousand years in the world which he was going to make. The disobedience of men would make this reign, and God saw it. Had mankind always been loyal to his laws, death had never entered the world. This history he would also have foreknown, because having foreseen it; but in neither case would his knowledge have produced any effect upon the result. Knowledge simply qualifies to act, but does nothing. God determined on having a certain number of inhabitants in his new world, and foreknew, because he foresaw, how long it would require him to induce this number to accept the conditions of the citizenship, and thus become candidates for the eternal empire; and he appointed the very day on which he foresaw the last man needed to complete the number would accept the terms of loyalty, as that upon which he would return and finish the work he had determined to accomplish. To deny this right of the Proprietor of the world, involves the absurdity that a universal government of virtue and righteousness has no right to exist, because it displeases the vicious and rebellious ; or that a government has no right to destroy those who would destroy it ; that a king has no right to exclude from his dominions those who had taken the lives of millions of his subjects and would exterminate them all, and the king himself, rather than be themselves exterminated.

Who can but desire the establishment of a government covering the whole earth, wherein all apprehensions of decay or death have been superseded by organic immortality ? wherein those who had been the righteous poor in the former world, have taken possession of incorruptible riches ; wherein pain and sorrow have been exchanged for strength, health, and endless pleasure : wherein ignominious persecution for Christ's sake is repaid by eternal honors ; wherein the weakness of mortality is superseded by the power of an endless life, and the badge of the despised and abused Nazarene is exchanged for the eternal companionship of God, angels, and immortal men ? Who is so in love with sin and the present world that he cannot be induced to make the necessary sacrifices to obtain such an exalted reward ?

Such are the provisions, such are the promises, and such the hope of the Christian religion ! Who would blot it from the records of the world ? If any—" Father, forgive them ! they know not what they do ! "

Forty Syllogistic Conclusions.

That the force and conclusiveness of the principal arguments we have now presented may be more readily perceived, we resolve them into the form of syllogisms and aphorisms.

1. Persons exist ; impersonality cannot create persons ; therefore the Creator is a person.

2. Persons are creatures ; creatures had a Creator ; therefore there is a creator.

3. A thing has locality ; space has no locality ; therefore space is not a thing.

4. A thing has locality ; God is something ; therefore God has locality.

5. The origin of nature demands volition ; nature is

incapable of volition; therefore nature did not originate nature.

6. The Creator could not have been created; that would have made him a creature; therefore he was uncreated.

7. All things in nature are effects; effects are less than their cause; therefore the cause was supernatural.

8. The cause could not have begun to be; that would have made it an effect; therefore the cause was uncaused.

9. All minds are causes; causes are limited to first and second orders. Man is a second cause, as his existence was caused.

10. Created minds cannot create the simplest thing of nature; therefore all had a Creator, as much greater than man as he is greater than the greatest work of art.

11. Whatever makes things of which nature is incapable [a locomotive engine, for example], is a creator. Man makes such things; therefore man is a creator.

12. The mechanical power of each mind is limited to that which it can comprehend. Man cannot comprehend the mechanical principles involved in his own nature; he therefore acknowledges the existence of that which he cannot comprehend.

13. Everything is a miracle of which nature is incapable; nature is incapable of making a living animal or plant; therefore the origin of living things was miraculous.

14. Every act of nature is involuntary; involuntary acts originate nothing; therefore the origin of all things was a living, supernatural Being of voluntary power.

15. All power is of mind; nature manifests power; therefore nature is the work of mind.

16. Whatever nature evolves must have been first involved in her; all nature is evolution; therefore involution was first, was creation, and brought nature to birth.

17. There was a time before nature existed; a thing cannot act before it existed; therefore nature did not cause her own existence.

18. All acts of nature are upon conditions; conditions exist before their resultant acts; therefore the conditions was nature's creation.

19. Inorganic things move by necessity; that which moves by necessity had no power to commence the motion; therefore the power was supernatural.

20. Organic things are greater than inorganic things, the lesser cannot make the greater; therefore the organic was miraculous work.

21. Living things cannot evolve from those which do not involve their embryons; living things do evolve from embryons; therefore the embryons and the living things which possess them were creations.

22. Rudiments cannot perform functions; the first living things performed all the functions of life; therefore it was a perfect living organism, without a rudiment.

23. The process of bringing the first living thing into existence must have consumed so short a time that the part made first could not have decomposed before the last part was finished; therefore the time and process must have been according to the statements made in the book of Genesis.

24. Whatever is essential to life is a part of the life; all the vital organs are essential to life; therefore the first living things were as perfect organizations as any of their successors have been.

25. Each species preserves its own identity; no new species has ever come into existence; therefore the first pair of each were created at the beginning of the world.

26. Each species has natural parents; the first pair of each had no natural parents; therefore the first pair of each species were creations.

27. The food of plants is not in nature; plants make their own food; therefore the first plants were creations.

28. Living things succeed each other in coming into existence. Beginning at the first and counting back, we come to the first; therefore there was a first.

29. Inorganic things cannot form purposes; such things manifest purposes; therefore a supernatural power involved these dynamics.

30. Nothing but a reasoning being possesses economy; unreasoning nature shows economy; therefore a reasoning Being involved this principle in her works.

31. The solar system [it is said] was once a fiery, molten mass. Fire destroys that upon which it preys; therefore the world did not come into existence upon the fiery hypothesis.

32. Nebula vapor cannot burn [it is said the nebula was before the fire]; therefore the fiery world never existed.

33. Evolutionists say the original matter was homogeneous: homogeneous matter has no chemical compounds to dissolve; therefore it could never have burned, as burning is dissolution.

34. Gases must have been formed into compounds before they could have dissolved by burning; therefore the world was never in a state of gaseous fusion.

35. The atmosphere contains only twenty-seven parts of inflammable gases; therefore it was never a fiery mass.

36. Fossils are found in rocks; liquid fire leaves no fossils; therefore the rocks were never liquid fire.

37. If left to cool, fire leaves nothing but ashes and cinder. The crust of the earth is not ashes and cinders; therefore it was never a fiery, nebulous mass.

38. Gravity was essential to the formation of the solar system; a world of liquid fire has no gravity; therefore the world never commenced its existence upon the nebula theory.

39. If the Creator ever caused the account of the origin of the world and its inhabitants to be written, that account must bear the stamp of the highest philosophical science. As we have found the Scripture statements of that work to be philosophic necessities, therefore the author of those statements was the Creator of nature.

40. To suppose there was no higher object in bringing the world and its inhabitants into existence than that which they manifest, argues the Creator acted without a reasonable purpose; but as everything in nature answers such a purpose, forbids such a reflection, and indicates the ultimate purpose to be of future development, and cannot be of less perfection than that consummation revealed in the Bible.

41. The Scriptures contain the prehistoric, or pro-

phetic, record of the civil, moral, and religious march of the family of man down through all the ages to the present day, therefore none but a Being who saw the end from the beginning, could have been their author.

42. Man is a being of mercy ; a merciless being could not have made one of mercy, because he would have been better and greater than himself ; therefore God is merciful.

43. God made man with power to obey him ; that carried with it the power to disobey ; therefore man can only become a subject of God's government by inducement offered to his understanding. If he persistently refuses to obey, his Maker may destroy him ; but destruction is not government, and the man still triumphs.

44. The proprietor of man's existence must desire his obedience, as the disobedience of his creatures mars his happiness ; therefore, if he would be supremely and endlessly happy, there must come a time when every created being, whether of human or angelic origin, will be reconciled to the will and government of the Creator, or have perished.

45. The interest manifested by the Creator in the details of organic and inorganic nature, forbids his indifference to the smallest acts of his intelligent creature ; yet in the present world his most loving and loyal subjects suffer the greatest hardships. This demonstrates the necessity, upon the ground of justice, that there shall be another world, in which all this will be reversed, and "Lazarus will have his good things, and the rich man his evil things."

Man Cannot Corrupt the Scriptures.

In conclusion, permit me briefly to allude to the charge that the Scriptures have been corrupted in passing through various translations. Our answer is a flat denial ; and we assert that there cannot be produced a translation which has omitted or inserted a single doctrine not taught in every other. We affirm, moreover, that the corruption has always been impossible. They were given in such diversity of manner and division, that an error by addition or omission in one part may be corrected by reference to another. What we mean to say is, that they are so divided that the distinctive parts are each complete in themselves, and each contains the whole system of revealed truth. The first division is the types and revelations of Genesis, from which God preached the gospel to Abraham. (Gal. 3 : 8.) Second, It is all taught in the commands, types, and precepts of the laws of Moses. Third, The whole gospel is taught in the Scriptures of the prophets. Fourth, It is also as comprehensively written in the book of Psalms. Fifth, The sermon on the mount and plain teachings of Jesus while on earth also contain the whole gospel; all of which was taught before in the Old Testament. Sixth, Christ's parables, most of which were copied from or built upon Old Testament records, leave no part of the gospel out. Seventh, It is equally full in the book of Acts. Eighth, The epistles of the apostles also give us a complete gospel. Ninth, The book of " The Revelation of Jesus Christ," all of which is the unfolding of inspired prophecy, contains an unbroken chain of gospel truth, and the whole of it.

Each of these grand divisions of the Word of God is such a perfect expression of his will and purposes with man and the world, that had we anyone of them, and were there but one instead of nine, we would be furnished with a perfect system of Gospel truth. Hence the wisdom of giving it thus, so that each age of the world had it all, and in such a manner as to render all the divisions impossible either of corruption or destruction. The following declarations show that Paul preached the whole gospel from the Old Testament, and before there was a New Testament : " Wherefore I take you to record this day, that I have not shunned to declare unto you all the counsel of God." (Acts 20, 26, 27.) " But this I confess unto thee, that after the way which they call heresy, so worship I the God of my fathers, believing all things which are written in the law and in the prophets ; and have hope toward God, that there shall be a resurrection of the dead, both of the just and of the unjust." (Acts

26: 22.) " Having therefore obtained help of God, I continue unto this day, witnessing both to small and great, saying none other things than Moses and the prophets did say should come."

Upon what, then, let me ask, is the gigantic superstructure of modern scepticism founded? We answer, ignorance· of the book of nature, and equal ignorance of the written revelation of the will of God to man. And to-day, by the blessing of God, we break the spell of its lying charms, and strip the gauzy drapery from the shrine of the goddess of modern science [so called] and ancient scepticism; and that, too, at the very moment of its greatest expected triumph; thus not only leaving Christianity untarnished and unscathed in the conflict, but more radiant by the accumulation of the testimonies of all known science, philosophy, and history, written alike in great nature's profundity and the hallowed harmonies of the book of nature's God—presenting its Author more sublimely enthroned for the contemplation of his creatures, as the centralized power, wisdom, goodness, and glory of his vast universe.

We now submit the question whether every honest sceptic is not bound to disprove all these arguments, or put himself in harmony with what they indicate?

We close by saying that we feel abundantly able to brush away the sophistry from all objections to these arguments, and to defend by philosophy, science, history, and scripture every position we have taken, for which our allotted time may not have afforded sufficient opportunity.

We heartily thank the Freethinkers' Association for the courtesy shown us, and for the patient and respectful attention with which the Convention has listened to our humble effort; and may the blessing of the great God, my Maker and your Maker, rest upon you.

CHAPTER XVI.

EFFECT OF THE ADDRESS ON THE CONVENTION AND FREETHINKERISM.

AT the close of the session we were congratulated, seemingly from all quarters, as having turned the tide against the Freethinkers. This is confirmed by the fact that, during the nine years which have elapsed since, they have not challenged another minister to meet them in public discussion. On this occasion, though an admission fee was charged, the Corinthian Academy of Music was filled, and it was the sixth annual convention of the Freethinkers. We did not commence our Address until eight o'clock, and knew it would take two hours and a half in delivery. For fear of not being able to finish, we began too rapidly to produce the effect it might otherwise have done. Feeling this, we stopped abruptly, and said we are spoiling our lecture fearing there will not be time to finish. At this point a gentleman rose and made a motion to give us all the time we needed, which was carried without a dissenting voice. This gave the needed relief, and we consumed the full two hours and a half, and we may add, that none left the hall until it was finished.

The Secretary of the United States League of Freethinkers said to us, "Our people have not studied these subjects as you have done, and cannot answer your arguments. He also said that Mr. Wakeman and Mr. Palmer had made about a dozen appointments to hold Freethinker conventions or deliver lectures in Western cities, the next at Buffalo, and that he was to accompany them and make the arrangements ahead. Thaddeus B. Wakeman's Address, purporting to be an answer to ours, was delivered the following evening, at the conclusion of which the convention voted us an half-hour to answer.

We commenced by congratulating the convention for having chosen Mr. Wakeman, of course in its estimation the best qualified to answer our arguments and demolish Christianity, leaving the inference that if he failed neither could be done. As we desire to know the truth, no matter what may be the effect in exposing our ignorance and error, we want the same test applied to this convention and in this discussion. We are compelled to say, that though we followed Mr. Wakeman's speech as closely as possible, we were unable to discover that it refuted or even weakened one of our arguments. Possibly he may have done this and we failed to perceive it; we therefore appealed to anyone in the audience who heard both addresses to rise in his place and refer us to any such exposure; and we paused to give an opportunity; but as there was no response, we continued: Surely, it cannot be that the whole convention considers our arguments conclusive in the defence of Christianity [and we considered them to be such]; that the Freethinking talent of the United States and of England here assembled, is unable to find a single objection. Come, gentlemen, come up to the confessional! Here we paused to give another opportunity; but still no reply was made, or a word heard from any of the dozen orators of Free Thought who were with us upon the platform. After a little longer time, a man rose in the audience and said Mr. Wakeman said things which were true, not needing argument, and sat down. We replied, That is beautiful! Then, we are to understand that the free thought of Free-thinkers requires no thought at all, only free talk; unfounded assertion to satisfy and confirm them in their scepticism. Who would suppose that such men think! In contrast to this, we receive no assertion, no opinion, coming from whatever source, even from that of the Bible itself, unsupported by evidence, the result of thought and reason. To this effect its author has issued this challenge to the world, "Come, let us reason together, saith the Lord." We still wait to give the convention every chance to extricate itself from the meshes into which the false theories of Freethinkerism have plunged it, and which our arguments have made manifest.

In a few moments another man rose and said, "I did not hear Mr. Mitchell's address," and intimated that had he done so, he could have made fatal objections to it, and sat down. We replied, That is wonderful! Here on the platform are assembled the most able representatives of the infidelity of the civilized world, and not one of them is able to rise in his place and point to a single one of our arguments as objectionable, or one which Mr. Wakeman showed to be inconclusive in the establishment of revealed Christianity ; but if this gentleman had heard them, he would have been abundantly able to have done it. It is a great pity for the now lost cause of Freethink-erism that he was absent! Here, however, is a man who is not afraid to say something in attempting to raise up the fallen Dagon, and this illustrates the fact that ignorance, as well as knowledge, gives confidence, while he who has part of both is afraid. [Immense applause.] We appeal to this audience whether the conclusion is not legitimate, that by their silence here manifest, the Freethinking talent of the country, here assembled, have no reason, no objection, no argument or evidence against Christianity, which to their own satisfaction gives them confidence enough to rise before this audience and state it, either philosophic, scientific, or biblical, and must we not press the consideration demanded by the most ordinary regard for truth and consistency, that not one of their voices shall ever again be heard protesting against its inspired and revealed system, which cannot be done but at the expense of honest courage, and in the absence of those, as here, able to expose the sophistry and ignorance which prompt them.

And now we have consumed more than the time kindly allotted us by the convention, and have not considered one of the sophistries which make up Mr. Wakeman's speech. As we turned to take our seat, amid cheers and cries from all parts of the house, except the platform—"Go on—go on," and a vote was unanimously carried, giving us all the time desired, and we continued by say ing, There was one thing Mr. Wakeman talked about at great length, and as it is one lying at the foundation of the sceptical science of evolution, though so late we may spend a few moments upon it. This was Protoplasm. This substance is said to be composed of very little creatures, and these were our ancestors. It cannot be questioned that if these little fellows exist, it has been determined by observation—they have been seen either by the naked eye or microscopic art. It is laid down by all logicians and mental philosophers, as a fundamental principle, that if a thing is a fact at all it is a universal fact; a single exception proves it to be no fact. There was a very learned lecture upon protoplasm delivered some time ago, at the Liberal Club Rooms, in Eighth Street, New York, to which Mr. Wakeman and myself listened. Before the lecturer concluded he undertook to answer the objection—why, if these little creatures exist they have not been seen, even by the aid of the microscope—and assigned as the reason that each one of them was smaller than a ray of light, which, therefore, completely envelops it. Now, if these little folks have never been seen by the human eye, aided by the microscope, how does anybody know they exist? Of course the ingenious sophism was to prevent its detection, which can only result from analogous reasoning between things known to exist, while the protoplastic myth was not known to exist.

It struck us at once that the fraudulent attempt to shut off investigation upon the starting-point of the evolution machine, was nevertheless fatal to its existence, except as false science; for the microscope offers no relief, because it magnifies the ray of light equally with the object it covers; and we thus knock the bottom out of the evolution tub, which buries all the mythic speculations of the protoplastic foundation stone of evolution. It was now eleven o'clock and we took our seat, but still amid cries of "Go on." Although we make no apology for being found at this meeting of the Liberal Club [for we would not hesitate to go into the very ante-chamber of any kind of devils, in order to obtain facts with which to cripple their influence for further evil], we may, however, say

25

that on this occasion we had been invited to lecture before the club on biblical criticism.   In order to form an estimate of the talent to whose criticisms we would be subjected, we attended two of the previous weekly meetings, and Mr. Wakeman will never forget the answer to his criticism upon our lecture, which set the audience in a roar of applause at his expense.   At the conclusion of our reply to Mr. Wakeman's speech, the convention also voted him time to reply, which he did simply by saying : "We supplied facts in our address, leaving the audience to supply the reasons ; it was an intelligent one and needed no further light."   A vote of thanks was given us, and the session adjourned near midnight.   We refer to this admission of Mr. Wakeman, as confirming our charge, that he offered no argument, reason, or evidence against anything in our address.

Reply to Courtland Palmer's Speech on Spiritual Life.

That Mr. Wakeman felt the weakness of his effort to destroy the force and influence of our arguments, is also shown by the fact of having called Mr. Palmer to his assistance, a part of whose speech he anticipated thus : "I am glad that before this Association adjourns, my friend, Courtland Palmer, who has thought this new world out with me, and whose poetic nature feels it clearer, will lay this wonderful story before you in his own words.   He will show you that, just in proportion as the integrations of mankind have advanced, the spiritual and altruistic life has become more and more, and that the higher integrations will surpass all others and extend the glory of spiritual conceptions of every form."   On Saturday evening Mr. Palmer delivered his address, which abounded in three high-sounding phrases—spiritual life, religion of humanity, and immortality ; but all of which had their realization in human life.   When Mr. Palmer finished he took his seat next us, and we said to him, "Mr. Palmer, that address must have cost you a great deal of labor ;" to which he replied, "Oh ! the Holy Ghost helped me."

And we responded, "Then the Holy Ghost was alive until he helped you out!" He looked chagrined, but
made no reply. We were sorry for not having an opportunity of answering it, as the convention was to close on
Sunday morning by a lecture from Hon. Elizur Wright,
of Boston, one of the oldest and most talented Freethinkers of the country; for which reasons his address was
given the honorable place of closing the convention, and
was looked forward to as a great feast.

On Sunday morning a very large audience assembled, and the president, Dr. Brown, was making some
remarks in relation to the business matters of the Association when we came in, and no sooner had become
seated, than applause began and cries from the audience
for a speech. The president turned toward us, and
said, "They want you to speak." We rose and said,
"Please excuse us; we came to hear Mr. Wright. Let
us hear him." But this only increased the cries for
a speech. The president said again, "You will be
obliged to speak." So, as we advanced toward the front
of the platform, it came to us like an inspiration to expose the atheism of Palmer's speech, and we were almost
overjoyed at having the opportunity; so, when the applause had subsided, we commenced by saying: "Most
of us listened to Mr. Palmer's lecture last evening, and
although it was a very labored and beautiful composition,
I noticed that it called forth but little applause. One
reason to our mind for this was that the audience thought
it too religious, by its frequent expressions of the religion
of humanity, the higher spiritual life, and that of immortality, which men should seek after. But there was one
objection we thought we discovered while it was being
delivered, and which we would be glad to make before
you if an opportunity presented itself, and which you
have now most unexpectedly given. The objection to
which we allude is that it was atheism from beginning to
end." This remark created a stir, but no voice of dis-
approval was heard. Mr. Palmer talked fluently about
immortality, but made it consist in great achievements of
individuals in the present life by which they would be

remembered in coming generations; but it began with human life and ended with it, so far as they were concerned. No matter how renowned or long the applause of the living, no sound could awaken the dull, cold ear of the dead to its appreciation. Had we time, we might present an unanswerable argument from the philosophy of human action to disprove such a theory, which supposes a man capable of acting without an adequate motive—one which would in some way and at some future time administer to his interest and happiness, which, in the nature of moral and physical philosophy, is impossible for the remembrance immortality to accomplish.

But let us endeavor to illustrate the fallacious theory. Some are remembered by the living for their good deeds, and others detested for their bad ones, and there are more of the great deeds of the wicked, who have oppressed the poor and trampled upon the rights of mankind, remembered and detested than of those of the righteous dead. What satisfaction would it be to a dead man, supposing him capable of appreciating what may be said of him when he was dead, which atheism denies and which Mr. Palmer's immortality denies? On the one hand he knows that the living are pouring contempt upon the great deeds of his life, and for the same acts others are awarding him honor and praise. In common life, can a man be happy as long as half of those who know him curse him for the deeds of his life which have, or are supposed to have, made them suffer?

For example : A Washington may be receiving the immortality for having acted the most conspicuous part in wresting the American Colonies from the government of England, while King George is receiving the immortality for having put a price upon his head, as a traitor to his country. You have heard of Julius Cæsar and Brutus, who, by their deeds have the remembrance immortality for which Mr. Palmer contends, and for which we should strive in the present life :

> "They waded through slaughter to a throne,
> And shut the gates of mercy on mankind."

According to evolution by natural selection, their immortality should have developed in steadily increasing honors through all succeeding ages ; instead of which their very names have degenerated to the use of canine symbols—Cæsar is a dog and Brutus keeps sheep.   Do you want such immortality as that ?   Audible responses were made, No, no.

You have also heard of Dr. Franklin, who had the remembrance immortality in a very high degree ; but would it be any honor to him to know that in every city his name has degenerated to be a sign for liquor saloons —The Franklin House ?   Would it be any compensation for you to labor and sacrifice in the present life to have your name used for such a purpose after you were dead ? Voices responded—No, no !   Well, this is all Mr. Palmer's address offered you after death !   Is such an immortality worthy of your life-long effort ?   Again responses came from the audience—No, no.   Better say with Paul, " If in this life only we have hope, then we are of all men most miserable."   At this point, Mr. Palmer rose and said, " Mr. Chairman, has not the time arrived for the regular lecture ? "   To this we replied before the president could speak, " Yes ! but the audience compel us to speak."   And " Yes," responded the president, " but what can I do, only to wait for Mr. Mitchell to get through."   To which we responded : " Do you think we shall become exhausted ? "   " No," he replied, " but that the audience will hear Mr. Wright."   During this interruption the audience were applauding and cheering, amid cries of Go on—go on, which we did as soon as the applause ceased and said : " These are the men who have made their mark in the history of the world ; but what hope, even of such immortality, is there for such little folks as you and I ?   Alas for us ! we shall always remain mortal and be forgotten in a brief space after we are dead !   According to our observation [we continued] based upon the developments before us, there are but a very few real atheists.   To become such requires a long stifling of reason and servile subjugation of the noble powers of mind and heart to the low passions and desires

to have it so ; and an obliteration of every vestige of future hope.   It is the philosophy of hope that encourages
us to bear the ills and disappointments of life, and endure
the heart-sickness of hope deferred for the long life of three
score and ten years ; but the sufferer will not despair so
long as he hopes for future life—the true immortality ;
but blot hope from his mind and fear goes with it, and
the crazed victim flies to suicide ! ¬Without hope a
man cannot be held long in the human furnace of affliction.

In philosophic necessity and scientific harmony with
this mental endowment, Christianity offers a man a resurrection from the dead, which is equivalent to a re-creation ; and can it be questioned that the Being who made
him live once, is able to make him live a second time?
The proposition is not to reduce, and leave a man a ghost,
a thousand of whom can stand upon the point of a needle
and all the room be left ; but to reproduce the man himself—his vital organism— his moral, phrenological brain,
upon whose tablets every event of his history stands photo-
graphed, by which it is possible for a man to remember
and become identified with himself.   But gravity renders
it impossible for such a man to live in an ethereal ghost-
house forever, and therefore the same Being who created
the world has revealed his purpose to re-create it into one
of perfection and endless duration, thus adapting it to a
suitable habitation for man—all immortal, soul, body,
and spirit.   Atheism is the antithesis of this glowing
prospect—the Christian's future hope.   Its victims die
like the beasts, and remain dead forever.   No ray of hope
illumines the grave of its loved ones.   The interest you
have manifested in calling us to speak in the place of
others—a stranger in the place of admired friends—and
the applause with which we have been greeted, for which
we return our personal acknowledgments, convince us
that it has been because of what we have said in brushing
away the cobwebs of atheism from your minds and hearts.
This truth has drawn out the numerous expressions of
grateful approval, and convinces us that no sceptical delusion will ever be able to draw many of you back into its

ruinous embrace! Here we took our seat; but still amid cries of Go on!

Hon. Elizur Wright was then introduced and gave his lecture on Miracles, which was received almost without applause. Feeling this, the lecturer hurried through, turning over a half-dozen pages at a time. It was evident that something had been done to quiet the enthusiam of the convention for atheism. After the audience was dismissed the reporter of the New York *Herald* came to us and said, "Your exposure of Mr. Palmer's speech was more than he could bear, as his attempt to prevent you from going on showed." Dr. Brown, president of the convention, said to us, "I will never attend another Freethinkers' convention, unless you are there," and expressed a strong desire to converse with us. Mr. Charles Watts of London, editor of the *Secular Press*, the organ of the Freethinkers, congratulated us, and in a manner indicating approval of our efforts at the convention. In reply we said, Mr. Watts, we have one more important act to perform in this direction, and one which we think you can bring about, and that is a public debate in London between Hon. Charles Bradlaugh and myself, where we will go at our own expense for the purpose: occupying the same platform an equal part of the time each evening, until one of the parties succumbs. If you will do this it will confer a great personal favor upon us, and aid in spreading light upon these all-important subjects. In reply he promised to try and bring it about; but we have heard nothing more about the challenge. At the hotel the Secretary of the National League of Freethinkers said to us, "I have just returned from Buffalo and in great haste to see you before starting for Brooklyn," assigning as a reason that he had been to Buffalo, and that their friends said the people of Buffalo, having read the reports of the debate at Rochester—which they considered unfavorable to the Freethinkers—it would be impossible to get an audience in the city to hear Wakeman and Palmer; that there was but one thing which could be done, and that was to induce Mr. Mitchell to come to Buffalo and give him half the time to answer Wakeman in public debate;

and the question is, "will you go, and we will pay you all your expenses," to which we unhesitatingly consented.

The discussion at Buffalo was in the theatre, and there was a large audience assembled, at fifty cents admission. Mr. Wakeman and myself sat behind the scenery, and just before commencing the debate, he said to us, "Mr. Palmer has gone home and left me alone;" and we may add the fact that the next day Mr. Wakeman also went home, leaving the dozen Freethinkers' conventions engaged to be held in Western and Southern cities, unheld that year. Wakeman and Palmer knew that the people of those cities had seen the newspaper reports of their failure at Rochester and Buffalo, and they went home demoralized. The conditions of the debate at Buffalo, as advertised, was that Mr. Wakeman was to speak the first hour, beginning at eight o'clock, and we the following hour. Notwithstanding this, Mr. Wakeman continued his speech until near ten o'clock, though some time before he closed, we audibly asked, why do you intrench upon our time, to which he replied, "I am going to speak until I get through." And we may add that there was no applause during his whole speech, which was simply a rehash of Herbert Spencer's speculations on protoplasm. We began by saying, you saw how Mr. Wakeman attempted to intimidate us by exalting Spencer to such an altitude in the literary world, that, as he said, no man dare question his conclusions. He has not only wrongfully taken our time, but endeavored to make it appear presumption in us to question the authority of Spencer. Of course, this was his only hope to impose atheistic schemes upon you for truth—to prevent us from speaking at all, and if we did speak, to not call in question the authority of his master Spencer. In view of the lateness of the hour we simply rise to make an apology for not attempting to make a speech. These remarks called forth loud applause from all parts of the house, mingled with cries of Go on, go on ! and we continued: We need scarcely say, that the course of Mr. Wakeman, in thus violating the rules of honest debate, had the effect of arousing our indignation to a degree that relieved us from care to use smooth words toward a man who had no more respect for himself or a public audience who had paid to hear a debate.   It also had the effect of relieving us from undue leniency in handling Spencer's atheistic science.

We continued by saying: You have listened to a long, and as we judge, a wearisome rehash of Herbert Spencer. Mr. Wakeman said: No conceivable God is imagined back of this order of nature, as Mr. Spencer has shown, and is thinkable to us; but all was unmixed with an idea of his own.   He was, however, original in his furious attempt to terrify us away from calling in question the foolish protoplasm speculation of so great an authority as Herbert Spencer; but we appeal to the audience if such an effort does not come with an ill grace and impertinence from such a man as Mr. Wakeman, who has here, to-night, called in question the authority of God Almighty and even denied his very existence.   [Loud and continued applause.]   Mr. Wakeman's long speech is a true type of his master's long written volumes, in which he asserts everything and proves nothing.   Spencer starts with the sophistical statement, that every truth has some error mixed with it.   In saying this, if he is honest, Spencer admits his inability to discover and draw the line of demarcation between truth and error, or else dishonestly attempts to hide it, so as to make his books appear as truthful as others.   The fact, however, is that truth and error are as eternal opposites, as light and darkness, and the effect of the darkness is to prevent the light from being seen, just as error hides the light of truth.   But in his superficial reasoning, Spencer adds book after book, sophism after sophism, assertion upon assertion, in vain attempts to make the foolish myth of protoplasm, which lies at the foundation of evolution, appear to be scientific truth; and he has the audacity to declare spontaneous generation to be science; and Mr. Wakeman echoes the presumption, and refers you to Prof. Haeckel as authority, making this author state as a fact of science that for which he himself declares there is no evidence in its defence.   In his " History of Creation " Haeckel says:

"Though spontaneous generation is a pure hypothesis, never having been observed, or proved by observation or experiment, yet it is essential to the non-miraculous origin of living things." Thus does Mr. Wakeman come here and, either ignorantly or dishonestly, misquote the writers on evolution, of course presuming upon your ignorance, and upon such false attempts to set aside the philosophic necessity for a miraculous creation of living things. We make the assertion, and hold ourselves able to defend it by every source of human knowledge, that there never was an author who wrote upon the problems of natural science, whose works contain so much error as those of Herbert Spencer, not excepting Thomas Paine!

We had so completely demolished the theory of protoplasm in the debate at Rochester, that we are astonished at the presumption of Mr. Wakeman in repeating the foolish thing here; but as it is the only leg upon which evolution can stand, though amputated in one place, its defenders go to another and declare it to be a good, healthy, and true leg still. Nothing is clearer than that such men both fear and hate the truth, whether revealed in philosophical science, the work of God, or in his written Word. You recollect how Mr. Wakeman told you to look up and behold the blue sky, and that this was protoplasm. Such sayings are those upon which the false science called evolution is based, such fanciful flights are its facts. According to this instruction, if you wish to experiment in order to satisfy yourself as to the truth of the science, take a peck measure and ascend high enough above the earth's surface to get it full of blue sky, and then ask yourself what have I got, and the answer will be—a peck of my protoplastic ancestors—a peck of my parental progenitors! What do you think of our orator's profound arguments and repeated facts of modern science? As soon as the applause had ceased, we said, Take another example of the wonderful protoplastic revelation, and one which has more palpability than the sky-blue phenomenon: Do you see that swamp, to which Mr. Wakeman referred you, and if you wish to demonstrate the truth of the science of evolution, go there and

measure up an exact quart of its stagnant water, and you
have a quart of our fathers and mothers.   This gives us
an insight into the magnificent science of evolution,
which, Mr. Wakeman says, has come to take the place of
all natural science.   Behold! what a thing to be of sufficient power to shut God out of his universe!   Here we
took our seat ; but still amid cries of Go on, though it was
now eleven o'clock.   We may remark that the whole of
our speech was received with every mark of interest, and
even enthusiasm.   Such was the satisfaction we had for
going to Buffalo.

Ingersoll Challenged to Public Debate, and Refused.

It was in the spring of the year of this convention that
Freethinkerism was at its zenith in the United States, and
at which time we went to Washington, D. C., and challenged Robert G. Ingersoll to a public discussion in that
city, and at his own home.   The topics were to be those
of his sceptical lectures.   The challenge was published
in the *Washington Republican*, requesting him to answer
through that paper.   The conditions were that he and I
were to speak alternately each night, and from the same
platform, equally dividing the time, and to continue the
discussion until one of the parties was vanquished.   We
waited in the city a week for a reply, but none was
made.   Not willing to let Ingersoll off in this way, we
went to his residence, and found him in his parlor with
two friends.   After introducing myself, I said, " Did you
see the challenge in the paper for a discussion ? " to which
he replied that he had, and added, " Why did you not
come to me privately? "   I said, " Did you not make a
general challenge in your answer to Dr. Talmage, in the
words :   ' No minister dare meet me in public discussion.'
This is what we have come to accept, and our object in
doing it through the press was to bring public opinion to
bear, making it more likely for you to accept."   " Well,
what do you want me to do? "   I replied, " Consent to
hold the discussion."   He said, " The platform is open
to you as well as me."   " Yes, but the same persons who

hear you will not generally hear me; and in this manner they will hear both sides of every question and be prepared to judge upon which side lies the truth." After a little hesitation he said, "Well, I will not do that." I asked, "Why will you not; have you not got the time?" "Oh, yes, I have plenty of time; but I will not do that," and he assigned no reason for refusing.

At this point he commenced his cunning tactics of making ministers appear ridiculous by asking questions and playing upon the replies, as subject matter for his public lectures, in order to make fools laugh and get their money, as is his common practice. So he said, "I suppose you have come to save my soul?" to which I replied: "Well, I would like well enough to be the means of that; but your soul is not worth much; what we want to do is to save the thousands of souls you have poisoned!" This put an end to his efforts in that direction, and more than ever confirmed the opinion that Ingersoll ranks among the lowest braggarts of the scoffing world, and with an increasing disgust for the man we left him. The year before we had published a book entitled "Cosmogony," concerning which the press of the country had said many good things, generally admitting that the arguments wrest natural science from the hands of the sceptic, and turns its powerful weapons against him, by demonstrating evolution to be false science, as well as the claim of geology, making the world older than the statements of Genesis show it to be. From its notice in the sceptical press, we could not but infer that Ingersoll had read the book, and we entertain the opinion that no man can do this and then be induced to hold a public discussion with its author, whether his atheism masquerades under the deceptive color of a scientist, or as a more honest and openly avowed atheist. We were sure of accomplishing one of two things by thus challenging Ingersoll. First, if the great scoffer accepted and the debate was held, it would have left him paralyzed for future harm in the field of infidelity. Secondly, if he refused, that would be published throughout the country, and it would be nearly as effectual in destroying his influence for evil. The result was that the secular and religious press, as well as that of the sceptics, did publish it. Even *The Truth* did this, and headed its article, "Ingersoll Challenged to Public Discussion in His Own City, and Backs down." This was nine years ago, and who has heard of Ingersoll lecturing since upon his sceptical themes, especially until very late? And we wish here to say, that the challenge remains the same for his acceptance, or for that of any other sceptic or opponent of the Bible.

At the request of a number of clergymen of Washington, we wrote the account of the interview with Ingersoll, and asked the editor of the *Republican* to publish it, which he said he would be glad to do. The article closed by saying: "It is believed by many that Ingersoll is a sincere seeker after truth. If he is, why did he not accept this challenge, so that both sides of the questions of the subjects of his public lectures might be heard by the same audiences? This refusal shows him to be conscious of his inability to defend the attacks he makes upon God and the Bible, and that he is a moral and intellectual coward, engaged in a dastardly crusade of slandering God and his laws against evil, and that too for the love of money—the worship of his mammon-god—the World."

Up to this time *The Washington Republican*, the most popular paper in the city, every few days published a reported interview with Ingersoll; these reports were copied by the press of the country, which became its most popular reading, especially by the young men. But after this cowardly refusal to hold a public discussion with the first minister who had accepted his public-defiant challenge, the conductors of the paper ceased to publish Ingersollism, in consequence of which the voice and pen of the arch scoffer for future evil was as dumb as a sphinx !

COSMOGONY.

" *Cosmogony's* " *Critic.*

To the Editor of the Merchant and Manufacturer :

In your issue of September 23d, I find an article criticising my book " Cosmogony," signed " Truth Seeker," to which, according to the common rules of journalism, I suppose you will permit me to reply. I admire the *nom-de plume*, which first struck my attention and led me to hope it would be vindicated by the spirit and letter of the article, but I must say that this expectation was not very satisfactorily realized ; but still I thank the writer, in these days of " sailing under false colors," for his courage in styling himself a " Truth Seeker."

This class of writers, especially upon the subject of " Cosmogony," generally repudiate all Scripture statements as authority, and demand the evidence. To this we cheerfully comply, but on the condition that we equally repudiate the statements of all other men, and upon all other subjects, as *authority*, and demand the evidence. What we say to the followers of Darwin, Huxley, Tyndall, Haeckel, Lyell, and Proctor, or any others, is that, as they refuse the grand embodiment of the wisdom of God contained in the Holy Scriptures, we hurl back with perfect disdain the opinions of these his creatures as authority. We despise your little tapers when you blow out our sun. So, gentlemen critics, having chosen your position and thus understanding ours, you may easily see the utter futility of intimidating us by quoting the opinions and definitions of those who *think for you* as authority for us.

The history of the past shows it to be a hopeless task to repeat the attempt to settle any question of science, philosophy, or religion upon the mere principle of authority

or opinion; for upon everyone of these, men of equal
natural and acquired talents, and furnished with the cult-
ure of any and every age, have radically differed. This
fact shuts us up to the question "What is truth?" and
refers us to the two great standards, Nature and Scripture,
as alone containing the solution of any of these problems,
and not only indicates each man's right to think for himself, but imposes it as a duty. Regardless of this principle, your critic arraigns us for calling in question Humboldt's definition of Physics, and because it suits his
theory of evolution, he thinks it quite unbecoming that
we should doubt. He attempts to bolster up that given
by Webster, seeming to forget that Webster gives the
definition of words which they have acquired by conventional usage, which has originated the words and definitions, and therefore of themselves prove nothing and
settle no question of natural science. In the estimation
of Webster, Physics commenced with the creation, or the
creation of the world gave Physics its birth, while Humboldt's idea of Physics is that the Universe brought herself into existence by the inherent properties of simple
vapory cloud—nebula. He says: "Among the wonderful things discovered by science and art, by the aid of
powerful instruments scanning the regions of space, *we
see* the remote nebulous mass resolving itself into worlds
of stars." ("Cosmos," i. 20.) If "the nebulous mass
resolves *itself into stars*," of course it leaves no work for
a Creator to do in making stars. In order to give full
credit to this opinion, we must remember that it is held
by this same scientist, as well as by all others of the
modern school, that the stars thus formed are suns, each
of which has a planetary system like our own solar system,
with its planets and satellites. Here, then, is the strongest possible expression of atheistic materialism, for which
there is not the least evidence in science. ("Cosmogony," p. 4.) Our critic says: "A better definition of
Physics could hardly be given than this of Humboldt."
Well, if such an absurdity suits him, he is welcome to it,
but is it modest to require everybody else to adopt such
folly?

Humboldt says: "Laplace has given us this nebular theory free from all processes of demonstration." He looked into space and "saw the nebula forming itself into worlds of stars." He gives us no proof other than his assertion. That this is absurd, Professor Proctor demonstrates by the time it consumed—millions of years— in the process of forming our moon, the smallest and nearest to us of all the heavenly bodies. Suppose Laplace looked through the largest telescope in the world all his life of three-score and ten years, could he see the nebula *forming itself* into worlds of stars ? He would be obliged to look a million of years for the process to have advanced far enough to produce at least a hundredth part of the moon, to be able to determine the fact. Even then, how could he know that it was the nebula *itself* doing the work, and that it was not moving and forming by the direct will-power of its Creator?

By the aid of the most powerful telescopes all that is discernible upon the face of the moon is a roughness ; the highest points or projections do not appear to be more than an inch in comparison with its whole disk. An instrument would have to be invented which would magnify millions of times more than any we have in order to discover a being the size of a man in the moon ; and yet Laplace saw the nebula—whose particles are so small that they can only be observed by the microscope—"forming *itself* into worlds of stars," and Humboldt believes it without evidence. It may well be said that it is handed down "free from all processes of demonstration," and yet the leading evolutionists adopt the absurdity as the starting-point of their machine, and "Truth Seeker" thinks Humboldt's definition of physics is the best that could be given. It would be more rational to believe that the moon is made of green cheese, for in that case it *was made* and did not make itself. The true definition of any natural phenomena must include not only the agencies involved, but the prior existence of an intelligent being who involved them, and as all natural phenomena is agency, this proprietor must be above her, and therefore supernatural.

"But," remarks our critic, "what analogy is there between the functions of an artificial construction (a steam engine) and a natural organism? The one is evolved by nature out of the particles which compose the things organized, and by their properties ; the other is the result of an extraneous combination of substances to a definite end and by the hand of man." We are sur-prised that a man could have read "Cosmogony," and then have asked this question, wherein we have demonstrated by a score of syllogisms that the solar system, as a part of the cosmos, was organized by the extraneous power of God—the great artist—endowing the particles of nature with the properties necessary to such organization, just as the machinist selects and prepares the material for the construction of his steam-engine : and that the materials of nature were no more adapted to form a plant, for example, nor was nature capable of accomplishing the work, than were the materials of which the engine was formed capable of preparing and forming themselves into it. Do you see the analogy? If you do not, it is because you are looking through the foolish eyes of evolution.

He says he will condemn where he "finds only vagaries or futilities, or such statements as he believes to be untrue." Well, we say to him that we do not in the least fear his expressions of unbelief or denunciation, and esteem the condemnations as the best and only substitute for truth in the possession of him who employs them.

In "Cosmogony" we undertake to prove by fact and fair reasoning every position we assume, and nothing can be more unfair for a seeker after truth than to quote our positions and conclusions and give them to the public, leaving out our arguments in their defence.

He says : "The Professor gives himself away by saying of the particles of matter : ' that they have no intelligence, and yet they perform intelligent purposes.' The pretence is the veriest nonsense."

In answer to this modest paragraph, we say that there is nothing more conclusively proved in "Cosmogony" than that there is not a particle of matter in the universe capable of acting by its own self-possessed qualities, and that they have not only no intelligence, as this is the result of animal organization, but that they must be endowed with affinities or substances by an intelligent being, and then they move toward and combine with each other, forming the intelligent purposes the Creator designed. In view of this we ask to whom belongs the "veriest nonsense?" and not only this, but to whom belongs the perversion of our views?

He says: "The Professor argues the existence of matter at some time, without qualities or properties, which is a mere sophistry." This is another misrepresentation, as we have said that the original matter was *cold*, and its particles had *size*, which are *properties*. In relation to it we have agreed with Huxley, from whose views upon the subject no intelligent evolutionist dissents, that the original matter was homogeneous—particles of the same nature—like each other; and, therefore, that they had no chemical or electrical properties, which, if they had, the matter would not have been homogeneous; that this endowment by the Creator gave birth to what we call the "laws of nature," so far as atomic phenomena are concerned. In view of this teaching of our book, we ask our readers to judge whether this is sophistry, and whether "Truth Seeker" does not misrepresent us?

He finds us tripping ourselves up again by denying that names of things are a part of the knowledge of natural science. He says: "Names are given as special exponents of the nature of the objects upon which they are bestowed. This is the sense of Adam's naming the animals, as the roots of the words employed, taken in their innate and symbolical import, most clearly prove." That the names Adam gave the animals indicate their peculiar disposition, is assuming that which the history does not warrant, and we suppose that, had Adam named a lamb a lion, the lamb would have always been the symbol of fierceness and power; and likewise, had the lion been called the lamb, it would ever afterward have been the symbol of harmless meekness. He says: "Webster puts the misconception at an end by giving a list of the principal names of the persons in the Old Testament, when taken with the meaning or signification of the words in their original languages.'' In answer to this we say that these persons were generally named because of some peculiar circumstance attending their birth, and not to designate their natural disposition, features, or color. We said in '' Cosmogony '' that a man might memorize the name of every object in the universe, and not understand the natural science or philosophy of any one of them, and this fact demonstrates our position, which '' Truth Seeker '' should have stated and then refuted to make out his case.

He says further : '' The acumen of Professor Mitchell is further tested by his unguardedly saying : ' In the year 248 B.C. Ptolemy Philadelphus founded a library at Alexandria of 700,000 volumes, which was totally destroyed by the Saracens, by the command of Omar, A.D. 642. A second was founded by Ptolemy's successors of 400,-000 valuable books in manuscript, which was nearly destroyed when Julius Cæsar set fire to Alexandria, 47 B.C.' '' We did not suppose any man was so deficient in intellectual comprehension as to charge us with being the author of these historic facts and figures. We will refer our learned friend to Blair's '' History and Dictionary of Dates, or World's Progress,'' p. 395, where he will find the exact words and figures. Our acumen is best tested by what we have written as author, and not by what we have quoted from others. But it is not strange that the mental vision of this evolutionist, like that of all the rest, should be so mixed up with myths, secret sciences, and occult mysteries, that he should fail to discern between these and the substantial facts of history and science.

When our '' Truth Seeker '' shall give the public more of our weak points, if the article comes under our observation we shall try to find time to attend to him. We are aware that we have a great work on hand in demolishing atheistic evolution, but its defenders have a greater in making the legless, crutchless thing stand before the common sense and common reason of the world.

THOS. MITCHELL.

BROOKLYN, N. Y.

Professor Mitchell comes Back at His Assailant.

To the Editor of the Merchant and Manufacturer :

The mail which brought us your issue of November 4th, containing "Truth Seeker's" rejoinder, also delivered us a letter from the editor of the *Detroit Evening News*, apologizing for delay in publishing a review of "Cosmogony," and promising a column in a few days. In the letter he says : "I have been delighted with the manner in which you have rattled the dry old scientists (?) about." It seemed quite coincidental immediately to read the dry, hollow article of "Truth Seeker." It would be no honor to make such an empty source as that from whence it emanated *rattle noisily*, which a mere breath of science or philosophy would do. We were perfectly aware that the first effect of the publication of "Cosmogony" would be to unmask the atheists and pantheists who have been sailing under the colors of scientists, and to a considerable extent this has been realized. It is a fact, however, that the wise and discreet among them have not made public attacks ; but we hope to hear from them, and at no distant day. Until then we shall amuse ourselves in answering such chaffy, Ingersoll echoes as those which come from "Truth Seeker," who, having the confidence of ignorance, sends forth such effusions of pride and conceit to the public. You know the adage : "The prudent man foreseeth the evil and hideth himself, but the simple pass on and are punished."

"Truth Seeker" says : "There are many independent spirits in the world that neither worship men or gods, and 'Truth Seeker' is one of them." We are glad of having compelled this sceptic to acknowledge his infidelity, so that he can no longer palm himself off on the unwary as a mere "scientist," under the pretence of which to inculcate his poisonous sentiments. By even his superficial examination of "Cosmogony," he has become conscious that the powerful weapons of even false science have been wrested from his hands by true science ; then, as if to bolster up his waning courage, he makes the above bold and defiant declaration, that he worships no man nor god. Worship means to honor another. It is a law of mind that, if a man conceives so that he mentally admits there is a being in the universe greater than himself—call him a man, angel, or god—he cannot avoid rendering him reverence—honor. He may despise his moral character, but reverence his intellectual greatness. Indeed, the very conception of the existence of such a being is worship. If he outwardly protests that he does not thus worship, it only shows him to be a hypocrite. If, therefore, a man pays no act of worship to any other being—god, angel, or man—then in his ignorant pride and conceit he, himself, is the *greatest being* in the universe. Here we lift the curtain and call on the gods, angels, and men to behold his honor, "Truth Seeker," who, by his own confession, "cannot be brought to worship men or gods."

We may also refer to another self-evident truth, namely, that a man cannot write intelligently about that of which he knows nothing ; and as "Truth Seeker" does not conceive of the existence of a being higher or greater than himself, therefore he knows nothing about God ; hence, if he writes or talks at all upon the subject, it must be incongruous twaddle, and here we introduce a specimen :

" Everywhere throughout the Bible the omnific or god-power of light is testified. Its potency is declared from Genesis to Revelation. The *primum mobile* of the universe, it was 'the Spirit of God' that moved upon the waters of primal darkness, and it is yet that power which statedly rescues and redeems our planetary world from Nature's Womb of Chaos. Can too much be said in praise of light ? Our earth floats upon it as a cork on water, and it is that principle in nature which holds the whole vast machinery of the universe in equilibrated poise. 'GOD IS LIGHT,' declared John ; 'the Father of Light,' affirmed James ; and 'Jehovah is my Light,' proclaimed David, adding elsewhere : 'Thou coverest thyself with Light as with a garment.' He, therefore, who denies Light denies God, and his words are but ' as sounding brass and tinkling cymbal.' "

" Nebula, *or light*, is the one primal source whence all things have sprung—no substance, organic or inorganic, existing that is not the incarnation of light. *In light* we live, we move, and have our being, and without it we are not."

Being equally ignorant upon the subjects of *life* and *motion*, his discourses bear the same stamp of absurdity. Here is another specimen :

" Among other unphilosophical dogmas advanced by him is "inertia" as the normal condition of matter, whereas the whole vast universe is known to be one eternal sea of *ceaseless motion*—not a particle of matter existing therein that is not in motion and which has *ever been in motion*—motion being the life of the whole. How absurd, very absurd, therefore, to argue the essentiality of an extraneous power to give matter motion in order that it might possess life, when it did not have motion and was *always alive*."

" The universe, whose circumference is everywhere and centre nowhere, brought itself into existence, when not the first particle of matter, of which it is composed, and it is *all* matter, ever began to be, but always was?"

Let us dissect this about " Truth Seeker's " God, Light, upon which he cannot bestow too much praise, and yet he says he cannot be brought to worship any god. Space is the universe—space is filled with matter —every particle of matter is in motion—motion is eternal —motion is life, therefore space is a living animal. This also : Matter is nebula ; nebula is light ; " light is the primal source whence all things have sprung." " Source " and "sprung " mean something coming out from, and in this case all things came out from light. Coming out from implies a time when the operation took place, and therefore a time also before it took place : Now, as all things in nature and the universe itself, if it is anything— nebula itself, if it is anything—matter itself, if it is anything—space itself, if it is anything—life itself, if it is anything—sprung from light, the primal (" first in order of time, original ") source, and before this all was primal darkness, light was the God-power, it was the spirit of God "that moved upon the face of the waters." "In *light* we live, and move, and have our being," and "God is Light." If this is not sound orthodoxy upon the doctrine of the creation of all things, then we do not understand what orthodoxy is. All the matter of the universe was brought into existence, whether organic or inorganic. It did not therefore have any existence before this operation.

Light is the source from whence all things sprung, and light is God, therefore God is the source from whence all things sprung. This was the power that redeemed (delivered from) chaos our planetary world ; therefore the devout "Truth Seeker" exclaims: Praise God! for he is light, and "in light we live and move and have our being."

"In the beginning God created the heaven and the earth, and the earth was without form and void ; and darkness was upon the face of the deep. And the spirit of God moved upon the face of the waters. And God said, Let there be light ; and there was light." (Gen. 1 : 1.) Do you see the agreement?

We do not for a moment suppose that "Truth Seeker" intended to speak this truth ; but if a man talks at all about a subject of which he is ignorant, he is as likely to speak truth as error. It puts us in mind of an instance of a similar character which happened a long time ago. "Balak, king of Moab, hired Balaam, a false prophet (teacher), to curse Israel, but God put words of blessing and truth into his mouth, which he spake instead." "And God came unto Balaam at night, and said unto him, if the men (servants of Balak) come to call thee, rise up and go with them ; but yet the word which I shall say unto thee, that shalt thou do." (Num. 22d.)

"Nebula, or light," says our philological and philosophical critic, confounding the terms, which he has not the least authority for doing. It would be just as proper to say nebula, or *darkness*. Nebula, in its primary sense, is *thick*, or mixed, and therefore the great chaotic deep of matter out of which God formed the solar system and what it contains. In its closer-defined modern phase, nebula means fog, cloud, a white spot, a slight opacity of the corona. In astronomy it is a name given to misty appearances which are dimly seen among the stars, resembling fog. Hence, instead of nebula being bright, or light, it is mist, fog, cloud, and can only be seen by being illuminated from other bodies. It becomes a halo or a luminous circle around the sun, moon, or stars in our atmosphere, by the light shining on it from those bodies. Nebula is, therefore, a dark body, and like any other opaque substance, could not be seen at all except thus illuminated. Here we see, by the light of scientific observation, "Truth Seeker's" god, nebula, light, quenched in darkness.

In the use of this iconoclastic club we give our friend the true light of science, and expose his bad use of words. Had he studied the facts of science, philosophy of nature, and illustrations "Cosmogony" contains, he would have learned that light is an effect of friction in the process of decomposition, setting on fire the oxygen all combustible substances contain, and therefore, instead of light being the foundation from whence all things emerged, its existence depends upon destroying or consuming things. Hence, wherever a ray of light is seen, it is the demonstration that something is burning, decomposing, dying— exactly the reverse of its being "the creative force of the universe, which brought all things into existence." He would have learned that oxygen is the foundation of all light. Make a vacuum of our atmosphere, or simply take the oxygen out of it—which is only twenty-seven parts of it to seventy-three of nitrogen in one hundred, the latter of which quenches all light—and instantly our planet would be enveloped in total darkness, every ray from the sun, moon, or stars would be quenched before reaching a human eye, and therefore upon the surface of the earth not a heavenly body could be seen. Here, then, Mr. worshipper of light as the creator of all things, you must change your god to oxygen—darkness which gives birth to every ray of light. That light redeemed nature from chaos, and that it is the principle of gravity, are other silly vagaries of this assumed scientist and philosopher.

He makes the same blunder in confounding motion and life, and that everything that moves is alive, when we defy him to explain what *motion* or *life* is.

Thus writing about things which he does not understand, how can what he says be anything else but nonsense? A man with a friction match sets fire to a city, and it is all in motion, consuming not only the buildings, but the inhabitants. In the process the city is destroyed and the inhabitants are dead. What did it? We answer the motion and the light; "Truth Seeker" answers, motion which is life, and light from which all life comes. "In *light* we live and *move* and have our being." No, sir; but in this motion and light every living thing died, and the motion and the light did it.

When "Truth Seeker" makes such blunders in his understanding of nature, the work of God, how can he be expected to do better with his revealed word contained in the Bible? We have seen how he confounds the moral, intellectual light therein brought to view with the physical light of nature, and for fear we would expose it, he attempts intimidation, firing off a cracker supposing it to be a cannon-shot of the largest calibre. Here it is: "He, therefore, who denies light denies God, and his words are but as sounding brass and tinkling cymbal."

The following is another example of his profound knowledge of Scripture:

"Turn we to Webster (list of scriptural names), and we read: 'Adam—earthy man, red.' Yes, precisely, 'the red earth'—the very chap we are looking for. The earth personified is Adam, and red its condition in our hemisphere at the spring equinox, from lack of verdure. But, instantly queries Prof. Mitchell, how do you know the earth to be Adam? We answer from Gen. 2 : 7 : 'And the Lord God (the Summer God—Aries elohistic or light dispensing—the sign of the Ram nearing the equinox of spring—the prophets saw 'the Divinity clothed in a garment white as snow, and his hair white like unto wool') formed (moulded by the power of light) man (the personified earth) of the dust (matter) of the ground (the uteric glebe—Earth in Virgo, the womb or foundation, the Sun being in Pisces with winter expiring), and breathed (infiltrated) into his nostrils (pores) the breath of life (animistic and polarized light), and man (the personified earth) became (was turned into) a living (animated) soul (existence—being).' 'There now, you execrable sinner!' ejaculates the Rev. Mr. Mitchell, forgetting his professorship, 'you have dared let the cat out the bag.' So have we, but we are obliged to do it in self-defence. It was our only alternative, and we have but employed the knowledge with which we are clothed. 'Awful,' no doubt, cogitates our learned antagonist, having relapsed into discreet silence. But so it is that on each recurring spring equinox, in our hemisphere, *Adam, or the Earth*, comes forth in renewed being, to enter upon the duties of husbandman or vine-dresser in the Edenic garden—the light or Summer Zodiac."

Again, he says we cannot understand the Scriptures unless we have penetrated the arcana of the Order of Free and Accepted Masons—taken the Blue Lodge and its higher degrees. In "Cosmogony" we have claimed that it is the right of every man to study the Bible for himself, and equally to test every religious sentiment by this standard; in answer to which "Truth Seeker" discourses thus:

"This implies that Prof. Mitchell understands the import of Scripture statements. But does he? By what token is he to be known as a Bible light? Is he a Free and Accepted Mason? Has he taken the Blue Lodge and higher degrees of the Masonic institution, and studied and penetrated its arcana? Surely, if he has not he knows little of the Bible or its statements, for the door of Masonry is a passport to the knowledge of the hidden truths embodied in the Bible, which he could not attain, one chance in a million, unless he had entered that door. A book which comprises the sublimated wisdom of the ages, and whose innate meaning could only be broached within the tiled recesses of the secret societies of antiquity that gave it form and birth, is not to be expounded by

every wiseacre that comes along, and whose only freedom
to its pages is by the lurid light that glimmers within his
own dark and especial labyrinth of uninitiated ignorance."

He also says: "The personages mentioned in both
Old and New Testaments are altogether mythological."
The word "mythological" means fabulous, feigned, a
fictitious story, not real. In reference to Bible names let
us give an example or two: "Now, in the fifteenth year
of the reign of Tiberius Cæsar, Pontius Pilate being the
governor of Judea, and Herod being Tetrarch of Galilee," etc. (Luke 3 : 1.) "And it came to pass in those
days that there went out a decree from Cæsar Augustus,
that all the world should be taxed." (Luke 2 : 1.) According to the mythological rule of interpretation of Scripture, "Truth Seeker" learned in the Blue Lodge arcana
of Masons that Tiberius and Augustus Cæsar were myths,
not real men. In a word, that they are fabricated lies.
In further illustration of the "sublimated wisdom"
taught in this arcana, he gives us the foregoing relating
to Adam not being a man, but a myth representing the
"Earth," as though a myth could represent anything—
nothing representing something. If there ever was a rig-
marole, a barbarous jargon of cant, this bears the palm.
That nothing of the like is taught in the Bible is proved
by the fact that its contriver has been obliged to make
one covering the subject—a mythical bible, which is no
Bible at all. Look at the contrast: "And the Lord God
formed man of the dust of the ground, and breathed into
his nostrils the breath of life, and *man* became a living
soul." (Gen. 2 : 7.) Here was *man*, a living soul, organized according to the laws of animal life, requiring
lungs to breathe, stomach to digest food—in a word, the
existence of every vital organ, and not admitting of a
single rudiment. His Maker breathed into his nostrils
the first breath *of life*, not life itself, and the second and
every subsequent one the man inhaled himself, in consequence of which each vital organ began to perform its
function, and the result was, "the *man* became *a living
soul*." Here was a man made out of the earth, the pro-

genitor of the human species.   The first name of this living soul was *Man*, which does not signify red earth ; his
second name was Adam, which does signify red earth,
and because this is the signification of the second name,
Adam, therefore the Man was not a man but a myth,
representing the whole red earth.   The name " animal "
as much signifies " red earth " as that of man, and because the animals were also made out of red earth they
were not animals at all, but mythical red earth.

These are the silly effusions which come from a man
who does not rank high enough in the scale of mental
conception to *know*, from the observation of nature, that
there is a personal God, and that by Him the world was
created.   In fact, this wheelbarrow load of red earth,
" Truth Seeker," has not intelligence enough to comprehend what intelligence is, or any of the conditions essential to its existence, really supposing it to be a certain
portion of all matter, and which can therefore be measured up in a bushel like any other commodity.   Hear
him : " Intelligence is in every particle of matter—pota-
toes, cabbages, corn, wheat, onions, leeks, and garlic—
you eat. All contain the elements of intelligence."
Science, however, teaches and demonstrates that intelligence is that faculty of the mind which receives or
comprehends the ideas communicated to it through the
senses—the faculty of thinking—the conditions of which
are the possession of brain and at least one of the organs
of sense, all combined in a single body, and that body
must be alive, and it must breathe to be alive, and it
must have lungs in order to breathe.   As not one of the
things " Truth Seeker " here names has any of these faculties, or possesses one of the conditions, not one of them
has the least intelligence.   Here again this man puts himself in contradiction to the science of physiology, mental
philosophy, and the universal facts of nature and observation.

He also quotes as follows from " Cosmogony," and so
dishonestly that it demands a brief notice :

" If ' seed in itself ' means anything, it means inherent
power in the seed in sufficient strength to bring forth

fruit conformable to the seed's nature, when the elements are free to act. If it have not this power, and supernatural power must intervene to effectuate the evolvement, then 'seed in itself' is not 'seed in itself,' but something else. How does this strike you, Professor?"

Here "Truth Seeker" mistakes and misstates our argument, and then asks "how it strikes us." The short answer is, it strikes us just as we have here declared. Our argument in "Cosmogony" is, that it is not necessary for the evolvement of seed after its kind that supernatural power must intervene; but that his intervention was necessary to *involve* this faculty in the first seed of each species of plant and animal kind, the work of nature being limited to the evolution—the bringing out of the seed that faculty the Creator had previously incorporated, involved, in the seed, or in the plant, the faculty which endowed it with the power to produce the seed after its kind. The first was involution, the second evolution; but the superficial mind of "Truth Seeker" is such that he does not conceive the necessity of first putting things *into* before you can bring them *out of*. But, Mr. "Truth Seeker," we will add to our answer the assertion that, if you did not pervert our ideas contained in "Cosmogony," you would have nothing to say, and if you were not conscious of this fact you would state them as they are, both positions and arguments sustaining them, which you have not done in a single instance.

He says: "God could not involve where segregation could not exist." Segregation means separation. Very well; but is not all the matter of the universe an aggregation of atoms, and could not God have involved in each of them the properties of electrical polarity and peculiar chemical affinity, forming all into classes with these differences, just as we find them? And this is the doctrine contained in "Cosmogony." His language implies that its author entertains the silly notion, which no one ever advanced before intimated by "Truth Seeker," that all original matter was a solid bulk, an impenetrable mass; and then, as though it was our idea, and in order to prove our doctrine of involution false, which demonstrates every phase of evolution such, he puts this in his article as replying to us.   Well, we would not deprive him of the empty honor of thus setting up a man of straw and knocking him down again, in order to show your readers he is capable of doing something ; but he should have been honest enough not to charge us with the work of its erection.

He says something about our syllogisms, and the view he takes of them, which is rather incoherent, but we take it for granted that it is some mythological inconception floating in the brain (" red earth ") of the mythical Adam, " Truth Seeker."   That he may have a clear view of a syllogism hereafter, we will remind him that it is a form of reasoning, or an argument, consisting of three propositions, of which the first two are called premises, and the last the conclusion.   In this argument the conclusion necessarily follows from the premises ; so that if the two first propositions are true, the conclusion must be true, and the argument amounts to demonstration. There are more than forty of these syllogisms in " Cosmogony," demonstrating the existence of a personal God —that he created the world—that it was created and could not have evolved—that it was perfect at first—that nature was incapable of the work, and it was therefore supernatural, and therefore also, miraculous, etc.   No one of these syllogisms depends upon another ; any one of them, therefore, *being a syllogism*, demonstrates our position.   If " Truth Seeker " wishes to destroy this conclusion, his task is to show they are not syllogisms, or any of them.

In conclusion, permit us to say that it seems but reasonable that we should ask our opponents to recognize the fact that a book entitled " Cosmogony " is published, of which we are the author, and in which every question of natural science of any importance has been investigated, including every other which has ever been arrayed against the direct inspiration and revelation of the Holy Scriptures, and that by the mind and will of God.   What we, therefore, demand of our opposers is, that they shall state our position in the discussion of any of these questions in our own words, giving our arguments and illustrations in its defence, and then let them show our error by producing more conclusive arguments against it.

THOS. MITCHELL.

BROOKLYN, N. Y.

Prof. Thomas Mitchell Answers Dr. Woolley.

EDITOR MERCHANT AND MANUFACTURER :

In answer to the article of Dr. Woolley, in your paper of January 20th, we may remark that, however reluctantly we may have engaged in this controversy, the dates show our position to have been defensive, and now the only possible escape is the weakness of our cause. To hide this, we hope to have the magnanimity toward our opponents that disdains the employment of mere sophistry. That Dr. Woolley made the attack on us, the following from his first letter to the editor of the *Merchant and Manufacturer* shows :

"Seeing in your valuable paper a criticism by ' Truth Seeker' of Prof. Mitchell's new work entitled ' Cosmogony,' and an answer thereunto by the author of said work, it occurred to me that neither party rightly understood his subject, ' Cosmogony.' "

Now, sir, did not such an imputation render a reply from us a necessity? This, our second reply, we introduce by asking the questions which we shall endeavor to answer, What is " Cosmogony ? " and, What is Mythology? In our book entitled " Cosmogony " we have used the word to signify the origin of the universe, limiting the word " universe " to the solar system, and as comprehending the manner of its origin, and that manner to have been the direct work of a living, personal Creator. That this modern signification of the word " Cosmogony " is correct, is proved by the fact that all the great lights in modern science discard it, as conflicting with Prof. Proctor's fiery origin of the solar system as well as with that of evolution. One of these authorities, Prof. Tyndall, in his Belfast speech, made in August, 1874, gives us the following in relation to this word : "All religious theories, schemes, and systems, which embrace notions of 'Cosmogony,' or which otherwise reach into its domain, must, in so far as they do this, submit to the control of science, and relinquish all thoughts of controlling it."

In relation to mythology and its origin, we quote the following condensed history from "The World's Progress," p. 432, under the "Mysteries" and "Mythology."

"The mysteries originated in Egypt, the land of idolatry, and were an institution of the priesthood to extend their own influence; so that all maxims in morality, tenets of theology, and dogmas in philosophy were wrapt up in a veil of allegory and mystery. From the Egyptian mysteries of Isis and Osiris, sprung those of Bacchus and Ceres among the Greeks. The Eleusinian mysteries were introduced at Athens by Eumolpus, 1356 B.C. The laws were: 1. To honor parents. 2. To honor the gods with the fruits of the earth. 3. Not to treat brutes with cruelty. The Eleusinian mysteries were abolished by the emperor Theodosius, A.D. 389. Mythology, or Fable, usurped the place of historical truth as soon as the authentic tradition concerning the creation had been lost or adulterated ; and persons who had rendered themselves renowned as kings or leaders in this life, and whose achievements had dazzled the benighted understanding of men living in a state of nature, were supposed to be more than mortal, and therefore after death the multitude were easily taught to reverence them with divine honors. The Egyptians and Babylonians, after forgetting the invisible and true God, worshipped positive objects, as the sun and moon, and then transferred their adoration to the operations of nature and the passions of their own minds, which they embodied under symbolical representations, and ultimately worshipped the symbols themselves. Thoth is supposed to have introduced mythology among the Egyptians, 1521 B.C.; and Cadmus, the worship of the Egyptian and Phœnician deities among the Greeks, 1493 B.C."

All ancient history attests the fact that Egypt was the

cradle of mythology, and the earliest date of its origin is 1521 B.C., while the chronology of the creation, as given in the Scriptures, runs back from that twenty-five hundred and eighty-six years.

This written account of the origin of the world was in the possession of a genealogical line of the oldest son of each successive generation from Adam to Noah—from Noah to Jacob, then among the Hebrews in Egypt, four hundred years, reaching to Moses, and so on down. All other branches of these families, settling other countries, depended upon tradition to hand down the cosmogony of the world, and therefore necessarily the true account became corrupted, and this corruption is mythology. They were not atheists, rejecting the idea of the existence of a personal God, or that he created the world. This degree of degradation was left to their modern type, such as Dr. Woolley and "Truth-Seeker." Everyone of their gods was a person; and dark as were their minds, they had sufficient reason not to commit so great a blunder as to make a personal image to represent an impersonality— a thing to symbolize a myth, a nothing. Having lost the knowledge of the true God, by the march of generations, but still retaining the conviction of the existence of a power above them as the life-giver and bread-giver, and that in the course of nature the sun was the most prominent source from whence these proceed, they worshipped him. Then discovering that "*heat*" was also an essential worker in the production of food and clothing, they worshipped "fire." They now had a god of light and a god of fire. But by observing the operations of nature, they saw that "Summer" was also concerned in the production of the fruits of the earth, and they added Summer to the nomenclature of their gods. Still enlarging their knowledge of natural science, they discovered rain to be one of these essentialities, and so they had a rain-god. Continuing the investigation, and discovering by the interdependence of the organic and inorganic things of the world, sun, and moon, and even supposing all the stars in some way connected in the production of the means of human life and support, they worshipped "all the host of heaven." Thus they continued to increase the number of their gods of nature until Orpheus, a Grecian philosopher, who went to Egypt to finish his education, taught that everything in nature was god and god was everything.

Thus we trace the history of mythology, from its origin to its present condition, every step of the way receding further and further from the knowledge of the one living and true God, until in its lowest form, and of course the most degrading of all, it sees no god at all, and nothing but the unknowing universe, and pays to the suns, moons, summers, rains, stocks, and stones its sordid worship. This is the religion of Dr. Woolley, his "whirl-god," or world-god, which has so blinded his mind that he is not ashamed to attempt its defence in a public journal.

And here may we not ask, if it is superstition to believe in one God, how is it increased by believing that there are as many gods as there are elements, parts, and phenomenal manifestations in nature? If it is superstition to believe that this God existed before the world, separate from it, and also that he made it, how much greater to believe that he is part and parcel of nature, and that she made herself, and therefore that God made himself?

Paul once delivered a discourse on Mar's Hill, Athens, surrounded by mythologists, in which he charged them with this mental habit thus: "Ye men of Athens, I perceive that in all things ye are too superstitious; for as I passed by, and beheld your devotions, I found an altar with this inscription: 'To the unknown God;' whom therefore ye ignorantly worship, him declare I unto you;" and he preached unto them "Jesus and the resurrection." (Acts 17: 22, 23.)

It is superstition to believe things without evidence. A philosophic mind demands evidence for its belief, and reason for its conclusions. In contrast to this is a mythological mind. It requires for its belief that which it cannot comprehend. Philosophic science is too gross for its appetite; it grows only on the marvellous—mysteries for facts, myths for gods. Feed it with hallucination and it is in its element. In the use of words such minds act as though they were the proprietors of the words, and therefore change their orthography and definition to make them express the marvellous. Dr. Woolley wishes to make it appear that the ancient mythologists believed the world and universe made one turn each year, and this is taught by the use of these two words, thus :

" Prof. Mitchell makes *Universe*, and truthfully, too, synonymous with *world*. Therefore, what the one means the other means. Now, *Universe* signifies *one-turn*, or *the year*, as does *world* or *whirled*, the latter being so called because the earth is *whirled* through space around the sun once every year, thus enabling the astronomical observer to view the whole heavens, both the upper and the lower, in his own latitude during this one turn."

That these mythologists did not know that the earth was a sphere, or that it turned or moved at all, we have the testimony of Euclid as late as about 300 B.C. And it must be remembered that Euclid was in possession of almost all the writings of the philosophers who had preceded him. This is from a discourse given to a pupil by Euclid in his library. Said the pupil :

" Euclid asked me how so ponderous a mass as the earth could maintain its equilibrium in the air. It is the same with the earth perhaps as with the planets and stars. ' But,' said he, ' precautions have been taken to hinder them falling by attaching them to spheres extremely solid, but transparent ; these spheres turn, and the heavenly bodies revolve with them, but we see nothing around us by which the earth can be suspended ; why, therefore, does it not plunge into the depth of the surrounding fluid ? Some say the reason is because it is on every side environed by air ; the earth is like a mountain, the foundations or roots of which extend themselves into the infinite profundity of space. We occupy the summit of this mountain, and may sleep in safety upon it. Others flatten the under part of it, that it may rest on a greater number of columns of air, or float upon the waters.

" ' But, in the first place, it is almost proved to be of a spherical form ; and if we make choice of air to sustain it, that is too weak; if of water, it may be asked: What does that rest upon? Our natural philosophers have lately discovered a more simple method of calming our apprehensions. By virtue of a general law, say they, all heavenly bodies tend toward one great point, which is the centre of the universe, the centre of the earth. All the constituent parts of the earth, therefore, instead of flying off from this centre, are continually pressing against each other to approach it.' "

Here is the fact that the ancients used the word " world," but they had no idea it whirled round once a year. They used the word " universe," also, but had not the least conception that the word signified to turn round once a year. We may credit this to Dr. Woolley as hallucination No. 1.

He further says:

" The Cosmogonies of all nations relate to the phenomena of the year only, and not at all to the making of something out of nothing."

The Cosmogonies of all nations do not relate to the phenomena of the year, nor to the year itself, but to the origin of the world, and that, too, connecting it with the Deity or Supreme Being. Nor does the Cosmogony of the Scriptures teach that the Creator made all things, or anything, " out of nothing." These are, therefore, Nos. 2 and 3 of the Doctor's hallucinations. Again we have the following:

" Let us examine more critically, to be quite certain, and also in self-defence, the Hebrew cosmogony as found in Gen. 1: ' In the beginning God created the heaven and the earth.' The Hebrew text, by a strict rendering, will read: ' In the head the Elohim *divided* the heavens and the earth.' Here *Elohim*, the word translated God, is a plural noun. Drop *im*, the sign of the plural, and *Eloh* remains. Eloh (the Allah of the Moslems) is a compound made up of *El*, Aries, and *oh*, *iah*, or *jah*, the short for *jahoch*, the Summer Sun. *Eloh*, then, is Aries-Sun, or the Sun in Aries and during summer. The Sun enters Aries at the spring equinox. This proves that the word rendered ' beginning ' should have been translated *head*, since at that time the Ram is exactly over the man's head."

Marvellous exegesis, pure myths.

Because a certain group of stars, the outlines of which somewhat resemble those of a ram, is exactly over the man's head in a certain season of the year, it proves that the word *beginning* should have been rendered *head;* instead of the heavens and the earth. Behold what a genius of a linguist is a mythologist? This is hallucination No. 4.

" It was before the beginning at the spring equinox, ' when the upper region was not yet called Heaven, and the lower region was not yet called earth, and the Abyss of Hades had not yet opened its arm, that the chaos of waters gave birth to all of them.' " (See Lenormant, "Chaldean Magic," p. 122.)

The word "beginning" conveys the idea of time, but "head" does not, and if it means "head," then you have no right to use it as here in the sense of time ; hence your rendering "head" in the other passage debars you from rendering it "beginning" in this, and this fact spoils the text. The passage which this lying Chaldean magician, or this modern writer on magic, thus perverts is this: "And God made the firmament and called the firmament heaven, and he said let the waters under the heaven be gathered together unto one place, and let dry land appear, and the dry land be called earth, and the waters seas." Here the heavens or upper region was created before the waters, instead of the waters giving it birth. But how can you reason against such marvellous credulity? This is hallucination No 5.

" All was then chaos. The earth was *dreary and desolate.* ' None of the gods had yet been born.' (Ibid.) ' God (*Eloh*) came from Teman ' (the south). (Hab. 3 : 3.) When we reflect that at the winter solstice Aries is on his meridian, and that from thence he makes his way day by day toward the east until the sun coming from the south joins him at the spring equinox, we can readily understand how God (*Eloh*, singular) came from the south, and why the gods (*Elohim*, plural), or the seven summer months, were not yet born. Of course, then, where there are no gods, there can be no creation, no cosmogony, no clothing and beautifying the earth; and the fool (Nabal, winter, emptiness, Abigail's husband) spake truth when he said in his heart (mid-winter) there are no Elohim.'' (Ps. 14: 1.)

At this time all was chaos, none of the gods had yet been born. All was a confused mass; there were no different kinds; all was disorder. This is Ovid's view of it. Now the disorder goes to work and makes order, no kind commences and makes kinds—these kinds are light, heat, spring, summer, etc., and these are the gods, and thus were they born, and of course Chaos was their mother that brought them to birth. These gods or this god came from the South—the South of Chaos, when Chaos had no South; the South—the equator—was one of the gods that was born, then god came from Chaos, and not from the South. Now, Doctor, as we are not blessed with mythic eyes to see how all this could have been, will you not please descend to our low reasoning faculties, and explain the scientific and philosophic principle upon which the Chaos, the confused mass of matter, the disorder, commenced and prosecuted the task of making the universal order which exists? Do not overlook the point as to how she made the gods which control her, and why the mother wished to be controlled by her children—a very unnatural occurrence.

The passage from Habakkuk which the Doctor here attempts to reduce to mythology, is a prophetic prediction of the work to be accomplished by God, the Holy One, at the end of this world, and the Holy One in Scripture is God the Creator of the world, invested with a human form precisely like that of man, which being human was crucified, from which God withdrew while he hung on the cross. This the crucified, the Holy One, was in the grave; but not long enough to "see corruption," as God again invested himself with it on the morning of the third day. (See Acts of the Apostles.) He is to come again to re-create the world into a new and endless one, and in the glory of his Father—the glory of God—the indissoluble investment—the embodiment of the God-head.''

The passage which brings to view these great events, instead of teaching the childish myth the Doctor sees in it, is as follows : '' God came from Teman, the Holy One from Mount Paran. His glory covered the heavens, and the earth was full of his praise. And his brightness was as the light ; and had horns coming out of his hands ; and there was the hiding of his power. Before him went the pestilence, and burning coals went forth at his feet. He stood and measured the earth : he beheld, and drove asunder the nations ; and the everlasting mountains were scattered ; the perpetual hills did bow : his ways are everlasting.'' (Hab. 3 : 3-6.) In contrast to this is Dr. Woolley's hallucination No. 6.

'' We may here note that *yoni*, the Hebrew for day, may denote a period of time, as well as our English word day. During the second day (April) the waters were dried from the face of the earth, as they are at this day. This was the second Hebrew month, and the very month in which Noah left the ark and became a husbandman. During the third day (May) the grass was fit for pasture. On the fourth day (June) *the Elohim erected, or set up,* two great lights, *i.e.*, they brought the sun and moon up into the highest heavens, at the summer solstice ; the one to rule the day, *i.e.*, the longest day, and the other to rule the night—the shortest night. This is the true rendering ; the common one bears upon its face the stamp of ignorance and falsehood, and gives infidels, equally ignorant with James's translators, occasion to scoff at and ridicule the true Scriptures, for which there was no need. An honest translation would have revealed the truth.''

Here the Doctor groups together, as having taken place in a single month, the events of creation and those of the deluge, which were 1,556 years apart. He also makes the days of creation months, whereas they were measured by the periods of morning and evening, and light and dark-ness ; consequently they were days of twenty-four hours, and nothing less nor more.

Another of his mental myths is, that the ignorant trans-

lators of King James's version have given men occasion to
scoff at the true Scriptures. If ever a man deserved desig-
nation of scoffer for perverting and mutilating the Word
of God, and belittling his great Creator to a myth, that
man is this same Doctor Milton Woolley, and we freely
give him credit for hallucination and blasphemy, No. 7.

"According to the ancients, whose works we are reviewing, the sun perishes and is reproduced annually at
the winter solstice. Therefore, the sun is older than the
Elohim, as proven by the facts above stated. On the fifth
day (July) the Elohim caused the animals to become fat
and fruitful. On the sixth day (August) the Elohim
made the beasts of the field (domestic animals), the creeping things, and lastly man, and to him and to the beasts
also they gave " *the seeding seed*" (see marg. reading),
i.e., the crops, and every green thing. And the Elohim
saw and pronounced everything they had made—*good*.

"Thus we have enumerated and described the days on
which the Elohim (LORD, or *bread-distributor*) *worked*,
and these six days answer to the six months during which
the sun and Aries are in conjunction and above the
equinoctial line. During the seventh day (September),
while the sun is in Libra and Aries is setting, *i.e.*, while
the earth is passing between Aries and the Sun, the Elohim " end their work," after which they (" God ") rest.
Thus have we seen that the Chaldean, the Persian, and
the Hebrew Cosmogonies run parallel in every particular."

The Doctor is reviewing the works of the ancients,
and he finds them saying that the sun perishes every winter and is reproduced every summer. According to the
Scriptural Cosmogony (and that it means simply phenomena, as the Doctor claims for it), the sun has endured the same in winter and summer ever since the creation of the world, and is so to continue until its end.
Here are two Cosmogonies totally different, and yet the
Doctor says : " They run parallel in every particular."
The universal observation of mankind pronounces the
Cosmogony of the ancient mythologists a lie, and that of
the Scriptures the truth. But why do you use the term,

"the six days answer to six months," when your description shows that they *are the six days?* Is it because you have not the moral courage to openly repudiate the book and thus sophisticate? But when a mind is so strangely mixed up with sun, moon, and stars, gods, beasts, and creeping things, as part and parcel of the same, we are disposed to credit him with honesty, and therefore in this, as in other instances, we designate what he says here as hallucination No. 8.

The Doctor calls the Scripture account of Creation the "Hebrew Cosmogony," when the fact is, both the work and we think its written account existed 2,674 years before the Hebrew nation, or before Moses.

"And the additional month is what the myth of Abraham (Summer) refers to. He attempted at the end of the sixth month to slay his son Isaac (heat), but the LORD stayed his hand, and Abraham offered a ' ram caught in a thicket (Aries setting) instead of his son.' " (Gen. 22 : 13.)

This is beautiful! Abraham is summer, and Isaac is heat. Summer attempted to slay heat at the end of six months, but the Lord (which is light, summer and heat) prevented him from doing it! Summer attempted to commit suicide, but could not accomplish the act.

This is the version of Scripture given by the man who denounces the ignorance of King James's translators, because it gives occasion to scoff at a book whose words may be so wrested. But we cloak it over with the mild phrase—hallucination No. 9.

"Ani is the Sun, Anima is the life, the soul. Animare means to animate. Our very language to-day recognizes the Sun as the source of animation or existence."

It is of no importance that we concede superior intelligence to Dr. Woolley. His articles, and especially the one we are reviewing, abundantly attest that fact. They also show him to be master of his subject, and it is fair to presume that there is no important idea or mythological interpretation of nature or its phenomena known to its ancient schools of which he is ignorant. If this be a

fact, and if we demonstrate his theory erroneous, then it
follows that all its defenders, of all ages, are equally in
error. It will be seen that the above paragraph clearly
defines and presents the fundamental principle of Mythology as the only foundation upon which the whole superstructure stands. "Ani is the Sun, Anima is the life,
the soul; Ani-mare means to animate." That the sun
is the source of animation or existence is what the Doctor has been aiming to establish in both of his articles. It will be seen that the sun existed before any of
the gods, and these are only such parts of the world or
its phenomena as the sun brought into existence; as light,
heat, summer, etc. Here then we have the position
clearly defined, that the sun existed before the first living
soul, or man, and that it animated him or gave him life.
We have no doubt that Dr. Woolley will agree with us
in the conclusion that it adds nothing to the truth of this
mythic doctrine, that thousands of intelligent people in
all ages believed and now believe it. If the sun was and
is incapable of the work here assigned to it, then it is
false and should be abandoned by every honest man.
That we may have a proper understanding of this subject,
let us inquire, What were the conditions upon which it
was possible for the first man to have been animated into
a "living soul?" and as this is the manner of expressing
the work in the Scriptures, as well as by the Doctor, it
supersedes any argument upon this point. Its precise
words are : "And the Lord God formed man of the dust
of the ground, and breathed into his nostrils the breath
of life, and the man became a living soul." (Gen. 2 : 7.)

The well-known laws of physiology, confirmed by
observation and the facts of natural science, demonstrate
that access to oxygenized air is essential to the commencement and continuance of the life of man. Prevent
any man from inhaling this air for the space of fifteen
minutes, more or less, and his living animation ceases,
though the sun-god may be shining upon him in his
strength. It is also a fact that a man will become and
remain animate in total darkness, even from birth to
maturity, as hundreds have in mines, where not a ray of

the sun-god has ever touched them. Here are two facts
which demonstrate the dark air-god to have superior
animating power to that of the sun-god. A third fact is
that the sun cannot animate the least living insect into
life, though its vital organs are perfectly formed, if the
insect is deprived of air. The conclusion is, that the sun
itself never did, and is unable now, either to animate
with life, or continue in life a single hour, any living
creature. Forgive us, Doctor, for using this iconoclastic
club in the demolition of your shining sun-god. But as
we propose to give your mythology the benefit of all that
the gods of nature can do, we will agree to throw into
your scale the "air-god," and let them co-operate with
all their separate or combined powers, and see if they are
able to cause a man to exist animate with life. For the
test we will give the two gods an infinitely better chance
than they could have had. We will suppose a man to
have been formed with all the vital organs, except lungs,
and now awaits the action of the two gods to animate
him into life. The sun pours his tropical rays, and in
the springtime of the year, upon the inanimate object,
and has tried the process all day, but has gone down in
disgust at his feebleness—the forthcoming man is still as
cold as death. He rises in the morning, beholding the
lifeless thing, and invokes the aid of his fellow air-god,
who immediately responds ; finding his nostrils and
mouth open, he at once presses into the place where the
lungs should have been, but are not, columns of air with
a force of fifteen pounds to the square inch, but he starts
back in astonishment at beholding no responsive respira-
tion ; yet the lifeless form lies stiff, inanimate, and cold.
How, now, Doctor, about your mythic gods, who ani·
mated and animate every living thing? But if it will
save you from embarrassment, and your system from
destruction, we will give the man perfect lungs ; and
though the sun-god fails to animate him into life, perhaps
the air-god can succeed ; and now he has inflated the
lungs the first time, and the machinery itself performs
the second inhalation and exhalation, and the third and
so on, and the man lives ; but he was on a sandy desert

when the operation took place, where there was no water, and in five days he famished ; or he was where there was no food, and he starved ; no sun-god could keep the animation in him.

Thus, Doctor, you see that we might go through the whole list of vital organs, and everything connected with the human body is vital, the removal of which would put out the animation. Indeed, we might carry this argument, as we have done it in " Cosmogony," and show that to keep a man alive, clothe, and feed him, exhausts the resources of the whole solar system, and that it had no power to organize the first persons so that they were susceptible of animation ; demonstrating, therefore, as such beings do live, that their organization was the work of a power superior to nature, and therefore miraculous, the definition of which is to cause that to exist of which nature is incompetent. Here we find that the manner of bringing the first man into living existence, by philosophic and scientific necessity, was the Cosmogony of the Sacred Scriptures. The man was perfectly organized first, and animated by forcing into his nostrils the first breath of life ; the second and every other he inhaled himself. No, Doctor, if you still believe in mythology, that the sun is the source of all animate life and existence, we will be obliged to credit you with the most wonderful hallucination of all, No. 10.

But he says of us :

" Professor Mitchell is greatly concerned lest the Scriptures be corrupted."

No, Doctor, you are mistaken in the supposition, as we hold that work to be impossible ; and they are uncorrupted to-day. Let us explain what we mean, and we say that there is not a version of the Scriptures, made prior to the last thirty years, that contains a single doctrine or phase of one which is not taught in every other ; nor is there one omitted in either of these. God, the author of the work, holds the copyright, and as he has ever kept it thus pure, so is he bound to do. Now, after having passed down through all the mythologies, and false religions, hatred of atheists, and " oppositions of science, falsely so-called," with its statements as to the origin of nature, demonstrated to have been scientific and philosophic necessities, how can we be afraid that men will corrupt it? It is true, men may make books, and call them versions of Scripture, such as what is now called the "New Version," and which contains ideas not in the Scriptures, but this cannot have the blessing of the author of Scripture, and it will consequently become obsolete, except as it may remain in the hands of those who hate the Word of God, and love this book because it is not his word, and because those who made it took the side of the scoffers, decrying the "Scriptures of truth" as being full of errors. And we will add that the marginal readings in the common version we also discard, as they often convey meanings in conflict with the truth as taught in the sacred text.

This is our position and opinion of the Bible, King James' version, after carefully studying it more or less every day for fifty years, without note or comment.

"Our Professor is greatly exercised over the inroads which modern science has made and is making against his old Cosmogony. He condemns, in unmeasured terms, the cultivators and abettors of such science."

Here the doctor does us injustice, conveying the impression that our book consists in denunciation of the cultivators of modern science. The fact, however, is, we have shown modern science to be false science, by contrasting it with the true; and that too at every point, demonstrating the modern astronomical, geological, and evolution theories of the origin of the solar system, the world, and its inhabitants, are without evidence, fact, or reason in their defence. On the other hand, showing that the statements of Scripture touching the origin of these, and therefore the old Cosmogony, are the most perfect science and philosophy. If the doctor wishes to show this old Cosmogony false, and he felt himself competent to the task, why did he not show, at least, some one of our positions unsound? What we have done (unless our arguments are proved defective) is this: we have wrested natural science from the grasp of the sceptics of every grade and name, and have turned the potential weapons fatally against them. If this be so, then these scientists, atheists, pantheists, and mythologists will have cause to be greatly exercised over the inroads thus made into their fallacious schemes. Instead of designating this paragraph of the doctor's hallucinatiion, we are compelled to denominate it, misrepresentation No. 1.

"But Professor Mitchell, like thousands of others, believes there is a 'personal God,' who, being everywhere present, fills all space, and yet, though invisible to the prying eye of science, guides and directs the affairs of our little planet. This is his privilege, and no one has a right to censure or call him names on account of his belief."

If Dr. Woolley had read "Cosmogony," he would not have made all these imputations. It is true we believe in a personal God. It is not true that we believe he fills all space, because he sees and knows whatever exists in space, as he made all. As an answer to this see our article in the *Merchant and Manufacturer* of January 27th, in answer to "Truth Seeker." That a personal God is invisible to the prying eye of science, is true only as to the eye of such science as the mythical and of the doctor's kind, while to the eye of true science, comprehending every fact and phenomenon of nature, a personal God is as visible in the universe as the universe itself. The absurd ridicule of the doctor's, to the effect that God should have condescended to guide the affairs of this little planet, is only equalled by the ignorance of him who made it, in reference to it. It supposes a being could have had interest enough to have made such a vast piece of complicated mechanism, the most minute thing of which answers a purpose, "as the great globe we inherit"—starting and keeping it in operation for six thousand years—teeming with successive generations of animal and plant life, to make a single inch of the simplest leaf, sets all human skill at utter defiance, and yet that he takes no interest in its affairs and guidance. This is too supercilious for serious contemplation, and can only emanate from a man whom this great God ap-

propriately describes thus: " The fool hath said in his
heart there is no God." That one of these should have
presumed to award us the right to believe in the existence
of this personal God, fully identifies him with this character. We can only appropriately designate this paragraph as an incongruous mixture of misrepresentation,
vanity, and arrogance.

We cannot close this article without noticing the following sarcastic and unjust fling:

" But he is particularly *laudative* of the times when
' men lived for many ages in a state of ignorance which
left their reason at peace ! Contented with the confused
traditions transmitted to them concerning the origin of
things, they lived happy without seeking to enlarge the
sphere of their knowledge.' O, how happy ! Doubtless
our worthy professor would be glad to lapse into the
middle ages, otherwise styled the dark ages, when the
human intellect was well nigh blotted out. He would
dispense with the printing-press, the steam-power, ships,
railroads, telegraphs, and every means of intercommuni-
cation and consequently of civilization. Above all, he
would do away with all schools, public libraries, and everything that has a tendency to enlighten the people. That
such would be the policy of the man, if in his power, who
dare at this day assert in a public journal ' that the discoveries of modern science have only degraded the mod-
erns to the level of the ancients, manifests the basest retrogression instead of progress,' who can doubt ? "

Whatever laudation there is here expressed of the ignorance of the ages, it is what was said by Callias, the high
priest of Ceres, to a student in the library of Euclid ;
and, though a mythologist himself, he refered to the mental satisfaction existing in the ages of the world before
the foolish lies of the astrologers and mythologists began
to confuse the minds of the people. See p. 45, " Cosmogony." For a man to attribute this passage to us exhibits either gross dishonesty or a want of mental acumen
to discern between the original writing and quotation.
The inference he draws, that we are a conspicuous advocate for ignorance bears the same stamp—arrogance,

if he has not read our book; and ignorance if he has. We venture the remark that there never was a book published, which discussed the subject at all, that contends more strongly and absolutely for freedom of thought and untrammelled reason, denouncing the clogs of bigotry and superstition, with greater severity than '' Cosmogony." Thus we leave Dr. Woolley in his mythical glory.

THOS. MITCHELL.

BROOKLYN.

Professor Mitchell Replies to "Truth Seeker."

EDITOR MERCHANT AND MANUFACTURER:

We thank you for a copy of your issue of January 6th, containing "Truth Seeker's" second rejoinder. It is a fortunate circumstance that our defensive article did not so far wound the refined sensitiveness of our antagonist as to prevent a reply, and that his "heroic virtue and self-command" were equal to surmounting the gravity of the offence. We presume he would not be so out of patience with us were we to adopt the silly, superstitious notions called astrology, of Chaldea, Persia, and Egypt. "Truth Seeker" cannot endure the priests of the Christian religion, but he is in full sympathy with the heathen priests of two and a half centuries ago. That the religion of "Truth Seeker" is a degradation of the ancient superstition, is proved by the fact that every one of its priests, whose real or mythological opinions have come down to us, or those of the philosophers who have expounded them, held to the personal existence of God; that there was one God supreme over all others; that he was alive, and that the images they made were but symbolic representations of the great, living Supreme. That these astrologers might convey to the common people their conception of godhead, and that he was alive, intelligent, and capable of performing acts of volition, they made them images in the shape of man, the most intelligent creature on earth, and involved in them machinery, so that their eyes would open and shut, and they would manifest other phenomena of life and volition. They also believed that this Supreme Being created the world and all it contains, and communicated to the solar system all its motions.

As these ancients were not in possession of the revelation of the Supreme Being and his work the Scriptures contain, they learned these great truths from the study of nature, and themselves, the most important part of nature. They saw from the natural interdependence of things the necessity that the world should have thus originated, and in the same degree were their minds relieved of superstition, always the daughter of ignorance, and we defy "Truth Seeker," or any of his school, or any other school of sceptics, to produce any real evidence to the contrary ; that is, that the universe did always exist, or that it brought itself into existence by an inherent principle of matter. Notwithstanding this, our antagonist says : "A God of the Mitchell type may as well, and at once, properly and forever and ignominiously be dismissed from the mind of man as the veriest chimera that ever emanated from human brain. Of this God we therefore say he has no place in the universe."

Is it not wonderful that "Truth Seeker" should stigmatize any man, angel, or devil with egotism, while he, in his infinite pride, arrogance, and conceit, ignominiously turns God out of his universe ? Sin against God is not measured by what a man does or can do, but by what he would do if he had the power ; and here we have an example of its intense malignancy and measureless turpitude. Give this specimen of man, whose feebleness is only equalled by his pride and presumption, the rule of the universe, and behold the wreck and ruin that would follow his terrible march !

He not only denies the cosmological views of the ancient astrologers, but, by the grossest violation of language, attempts to drag the Bible into the muddy pool of his silly cant and preposterous nonsense, to make it teach that God did not create the world ; indeed, that it teaches God is the dirt of the world itself, and which brought itself into existence.

We are gratified that "Truth Seeker" has now been

compelled to define his grade of scepticism to be pantheism—God is the universe and the universe is God. We might fill a number of columns in exposing the dishonest tricks of " Truth Seeker " in making us say things we never said, but we will only give one example, and that in order to expose his foolish interpretation of Scripture. We define the worship of God the Bible inculcates to be " honor and reverence," and because the word worship, outside of the Bible, has been made to mean " slavishness," to express the kind of worship the superstitious bigots in their ignorance have paid to things which are no gods, such as " Truth Seeker " pays to the universe, he says our " definition carried out would abolish the priesthood forever." He says : " Religious superstition is founded on the letter and not on the spirit of the sacred Word " (that is, " secret " word). It is fair to suppose that this parenthetical reading is an example of what " Truth Seeker " understands to be the difference between the letter and spirit of words, or between the literal and spiritual interpretation of the Bible, and he is here discoursing upon the interior teachings of the Bible —known only to Masonry. By the use he makes of the so-called spirit teaching of its words, he shows that he means its symbolisms.

If " Truth Seeker " is a correct exponent of Masonry, then we are to understand that within its marvellous inclosure words do not mean, or have the same definition, as in the outer world ; that here " sacred " things mean " secret " things. We understand " sacred " to mean holy, or that which pertains to God or to his worship ; and " secret," concealed from the notice of all persons except those concerned ; but, Masonically speaking, these words convey the same idea, and may be properly used the one for the other. Hence, the letters s a c r e d may be discarded, and the spiritual, mysterious ones s e c r e t substituted. Having adopted this rule of interpretation, it is no wonder " Truth Seeker " gives us the Babel mixture of the created with the Creator, the animate with the inanimate, the organic with the inorganic, or the living and lifeless, culminating in the monstrosity that God and the whole matter of the universe are one and the same thing.

Cut loose from the fundamental principles of language, that, conventionally, certain letters compose certain words, and that these are signs of certain things or ideas, and adopt the rule of " Truth Seeker," that " sacred " means " secret," and " secret " Masonry, and the symbolic Babel is complete, but from that moment all intelligent commerce among men is destroyed. Every man may then say that black means white, light darkness, Adam red earth, and Jehovah the matter of the universe. We are not a Mason, but we do not think they are truly represented by " Truth Seeker." It is, however, for them to make the defence. He says again :

" That the Bible is one of the most *symbolical* books in the world we have the decided opinion of Sherer, clearly expressed in his ' Masonic Ladder.' And that we may know it to be symbolical, we have only to peruse and penetrate the writings of Madame Blavatzky, as embodied in her ' Isis Unveiled,' or to examine and master the subjects so learnedly discussed by Rev. Robert Taylor, in his ' Diegesis,' ' Devil's Pulpit,' and ' Astronomical Lectures,' or to revel in the masterly production of Dr. Milton Woolley, of Streator, Ill., entitled the ' Science of the Bible.' "

Suppose this to be true, does it follow that its words are not to be understood by their letters ? or that each different word does not convey its own definite idea, or phase of it, in a sentence ? or that the symbol employed makes the sense double, dubious, or equivocal ? On the contrary, symbolic language is representative, showing the difference between things by comparison of resemblance ; hence its intelligent use is to illustrate qualities and ideas, and in the same degree it destroys mystery by the inculcation of clear conceptions. If this is not correct, then Masonry, as " Truth Seeker " tells us, is composed of almost an endless chain of symbols, but which are not understood by the fraternity, as the letters of the words, or the words themselves, are not to be construed according to the same in the description of the symbols, but different words composed of different letters may be employed at the option of any member. There is no book more highly symbolic than "Bunyan's Pilgrim's Progress," and for this very reason its ideas are easily understood, and that, too, by the composite lettering of its words. The fact is, there would be no force or spirit in words only as they are understood to convey certain ideas, and this peculiarity consists in the peculiar letters of which they are composed. Why does "Truth Seeker" give us the opinion of the above-mentioned authors in proof that the Bible abounds in symbolic language? Does he not know this fact by his own reading of the book? and, if he has read it, did he not discover that the symbol and the thing symbolized were interpreted by the words employed, composed of certain letters, and, therefore, according to the "*letter*" of the book?

For example, in the highest symbolic book of the Bible we read : "And to her was granted that she should be arrayed in fine linen, clean and white, for the fine linen is the righteousness of saints." (Rev. 19 : 8.) Let us ask, are not the fine linen and righteousness both literal things composed of certain letters, and do they not convey definite ideas of the things? Here is another : "And he saith unto me, the waters which thou sawest are peoples, and multitudes, and nations, and tongues." (Rev. 17 : 15.) Here, again, is not the symbol, "water," a literal thing, and are not the people symbolized such also? But what kind of work would we make of the intelligent ideas conveyed here, if we took the liberty of saying that the white robes, righteousness, water, people, and nations were all the same thing, just as sacred and secret mean the same.

When this same "Truth Seeker" undertakes to show that the Bible teaching confounds God and the universe, he has recourse to letters which form one of the names of God, thus :

"God and the universe are one, or his ubiquity is a misnomer. If God and the universe are one, and this is the Bible doctrine, then pantheism is unadulterated science and true religion. It is the religion of 'Truth Seeker,' and a religion of which he is very justly proud. It cannot be overturned, and never has been overturned, though Mitchell does claim to have consummated the feat. Mitchell has said that God is to be known by his names. One of these names ' Je-ho-va-h,' otherwise J-H-V-H, the tetragrammation, or ' Jod-he-vau-he.' Now what are these four latter etymons? The names of four Hebrew letters? Precisely. Which symbolize what? The four elements. How? ' Jod '—fire ; ' he'—air ; ' vau'—earth ; and ' he '—water ; out of which was made all things and without which ' was not anything made that was made.' Esoterically, the mystic philosophy correlates the fire with the oxygen, the air with the nitrogen, the earth with the carbon, and the water with the hydrogen. (*Vide*, Pancoast's *Kabbala*, Dia. Jewish Sephiroth —Adam Kadmon—opp. p. 24.) Can modern chemistry gainsay the elemental nature of oxygen, nitrogen, carbon, and hydrogen? If not, score one for the chemical knowledge of antiquity, and score one, also, for the unity of God and matter. Even Mitchell, despite his usually unbalanced ratiocination, is constrained to dedicate materiality to his sort of God."

The first that claims our attention here, is the meaning of the word "ubiquity," according to which "Truth Seeker," concludes God is the universe, and therefore the Bible teaches unadulterated pantheism. In answer to this, we say that "ubiquity" is not a Bible term, nor is "omnipresence," neither is "omniscience ; " but if they were, they only teach pantheism when defined by pantheists and seen through the distorted and sordid vision of a man that, instead of beholding the handiwork of God in his own make and in all the work nature manifests, sees nothing beyond the work itself. His mind is too unphilosophic, and in mechanics he is too much of a dunce, to comprehend the fact that a human machine (say a locomotive) must have had a maker ; that he must have been an intelligent person, and, as such, possessing volition, the power to make or not to make the machine as he pleased ; and in these qualities the mechanic himself is in contrast, and superior to all the lifeless universe besides, which, not being an intelligent person, had no power to commence or stop work. The phenomena, therefore, the universe, or inorganic matter, demanded a superior being, who first formed its whole machinery and then compelled it to work out the purposes of his will, and to arrest the work when finished.

In relation to these quantities and mental dynamics, the language of the Bible explicitly declares that God, having made the world and everything in nature, answering a purpose, had a perfect knowledge of all, involving in its nature the limit of its duration, so that, as a part of the whole, it might answer the purpose for which it was designed ; and from the moment of the creation everything, whether organic or inorganic, was in the mental presence of the Maker ; and from thenceforth the possibilities and susceptibilities of everything in its minutest detail, and during the progress of its duration, was fully known and foreknown because thus foreseen. Here are a few examples of the description of this knowledge and presence : " Known unto God are all his works from the beginning of the world." (Acts 15 : 18.) " Whither shall I flee from thy presence ? If I say, Surely darkness shall cover me ; yea, the darkness hideth not from thee, but the night shineth as the day : the darkness and the light are both alike to thee." (Ps. 139.) The Scriptures teach that the Lord Jesus Christ is God incarnate, God in human form, God with a human body. " In him dwelleth all the fulness of the Godhead bodily." (Col. 2 : 9.) That he was in the world and left it, " ascending up far above all heavens." (Eph. 4 : 10.) And that He is to come again in like manner at the end of the world, or to put an end to it, and re-create it into a new world, composed of a new heaven and a new earth. In view of such facts, what can be more preposterous than the talk about this God being the world or universe itself, and that the foolish doctrine is taught in the Bible ?

The idea that God must be in immediate local contact with everything He sees or that is in His presence, is to reduce Him below the capacity of a man. The sun, moon, and stars are in his presence, because he sees them, and yet some of them are millions of miles distant from him. A man has the mental conception of a machine he has made or directed to be made, and had before he made it, and after he had concluded to make it after a certain model ; he knew its capacity and duration of existence, and therefore the substantial facts in its coming history, though the machine and himself, at any subsequent period, may be in different continents. When we concede that God is everything, the epithets signify that men have applied to him, and for which there is no reason, he is everything and nothing ; we are bound, therefore, as a believer in the Bible, to discard all the adjectives describing him, as well as the names not found in the sacred Scriptures. These cannot be held responsible for anything but their own teachings, which must be interpreted by the same rules as any other book.

" Truth Seeker " somewhat correctly quotes us as saying that " God is to be known by his names," but he should have added, " his names the Bible contains ; " according to which (he says), " one of these names is Jehovah, otherwise J-h-v-h." But why " otherwise ? " Surely not because of the letters composing the word, " J-h-v-h " (if it be a word, having no phonetic but the letter J), nor because it any more signifies that which Jehovah does than it does " fool," or any other word of four letters. But " Truth Seeker " says : " The tetragrammation "—the name among the mythological priests which signified the mystic number *four*, and this is the Deity. This was not because of the character of the letters or their combination, but simply because of their number, being four. His effort here amounts to this : That inasmuch as the name " Jehovah " is composed of seven letters, and he wants a name formed of four only, so as to have the mystic signification and to be able therefore to weave the heathen tetragrammation into the Bible name of Jehovah, he just leaves out three of the letters ! Besides, there is no ancient tetragrammation composed of " J-h-v-h " and used to symbolize God, and if there was it would only be the first corruption of the Scriptural name of God, Jehovah, and now seconded by " Truth

Seeker." But he says " these four letters symbolize fire, air, earth, and water, the elements of which all things are composed." This was the knowledge of ancient chemistry, whereas it now teaches that there are over sixty elements entering into the composition of the earthly bodies. In view of these well-known facts of science, " Truth Seeker" ambiguously asks : " Can modern chemistry gainsay the elemental nature of oxygen, nitrogen, carbon, and hydrogen?" This, however, is not the question, but can modern chemistry gainsay the ancient ignorance which taught that all things were composed of these four elements? But he must take this position, and deny the true, natural science of our day, and adhere to that taught by the ancient priests, in order to make their sacred tetragrammation "four" teach the foolish notion that Jehovah means " J-h-v-h," and this means fire, air, earth, and water, and also that these different natural elements teach the unity of God and matter. Besides this, " Truth Seeker " scouts the idea that the Bible is to be interpreted according to the letters of its words, and then, to obtain something of a crutch upon which his pantheistic god can seem to stand, he takes the literal words of the Bible, even to the letters, and tells us J-E-H-O-V-A-H are the same as J-H-V-H. From such disgusting nonsense as this, behold the bombastic conclusion : " Score one for the chemical knowledge of antiquity, and one also for the unity of God and matter ! "

Suppose, however, that this name of God, by its orthography, does signify fire, air, earth, and water, and of course because it contains the letters J-H-V-H. But there are about a dozen other names by which he is designated in the Bible, not one of which contains these letters, and is therefore not susceptible of such violent torture. If one taught that God and the matter of the world were the same thing, then the other eleven names must also tetragrammatically symbolize the matter of the universe. Instead of this, the author of nature and the Bible employs this great number and variety of names to reveal himself to man, so that it would be impossible for any

of them, having common sense and common honesty, to
confound him with any of his works, much less with the
common matter out of which all are formed.   The names
of God, and the connection in which they stand in the
Bible, describe him as having existed before the world ;
that he took the matter and " created," " made," or
" formed " all things it contains (these words being used
interchangeably, descriptive of the work, and therefore
mean the same thing, and this use is the biblical rule of the
interpretation of its own words) ; that he cursed the world
for man's sake—and if he was the world he cursed himself ; also that he is a living person, and as such he is not
now located in the world.   In view of such facts, what
an advance in egotism and arrogance must a man have
made to teach the idea that the lifeless, senseless matter
of the world is the same thing as the living God himself,
and that this is taught in the Bible ?

He again says : " Pantheism is true religion.   It is the
religion of ' Truth Seeker,' and a religion of which he is
very proud."   He also says : " God and the universe are
one," and, as we have seen, defines the universe to be
fire, air, earth, and water ; hence the god of the religion
(for every religion must have its god) of which he is
proud is fire, air, earth, and water.   He worships fire because it warms him when cold ; but how does his patience
and reverence hold out with his god when it burns him
alive, and during the process does he then worship or
curse him ?   He worships air because it cools him when
too warm ; but how is it when it freezes him to death ?   He
also worships the air (wind) because by its inhalation it
supports his life ; but how does he feel toward this part of
his god when he gets into a fury and blows down his
house, killing his family ?   Is he so disinterested and sto-
ical that he is still proud of him ?   He is also proud of
paying devotion to earth, the third part of his god, because it grows him bread ; but how is it when he gets
lazy and sends you famine, and while you are starving, do
you still praise him for his goodness? or how is it when
he " sacredly," " secretly " mixes poison with the bread-
stuff, that kills the eater ? or when his good, merciful god

(earth) opens his horrid jaws and swallows a city with its inhabitants, men, women and little innocent children indiscriminately, how about your god and his good religion now? Do you still feel proud of him? You are proud of the fourth part of your god (water) because you can drink him to quench your thirst, and thus save your life; he is a good servant, and you rejoice in such a salvation; but how is it when you are on shipboard and he gets into one of his pranks and dashes you, ship and lifeboats against the rocks—part of your god—all to pieces, and then in his wrath he drinks you in turn with the whole helpless crew?

Here, Mr. "Truth Seeker," is the damnation part of your god, who never shows the least mercy upon his devotees who violate his commands, whether the sin is committed knowingly or ignorantly. Behold the cruelty of the quadruple god of your religion!

We are also given to understand that the fire, air, earth, and water god esoterically (privately) and correlatively (reciprocally) metamorphoses itself into the form of oxygen, nitrogen, carbon, and hydrogen, which words are composed of entirely different letters and number of letters from J-H-V-H, and yet these letters are the symbols of those other unlike words. Here we are taught that the name "Jehovah" is the symbol of J-h-v-h, that J-h-v-h is the symbol of Jod-he-vau-he; these are the symbols of fire, air, earth, and water; these are the symbols of oxygen, nitrogen, carbon, and hydrogen; these again are the symbols of the matter composing the earth and which signifies god. But is this four-quartered, gaseous god any more worthy of claiming the devotion of "Truth Seeker," on account of this change? You love oxygen, his first quarter, because he is a part of the air, another part of your god, and by inhaling him he supports your life, by creating animal heat; but he also feeds the conflagration that consumes you and your dwelling, and without him there would be no such catastrophe. He is the merciless god of these feats; do you love him still? His second quarter is nitrogen, and is the most deadly antagonist to the first quarter, creating a terrible warfare in the members of your curious god. He quenches all fire, puts out all light (another part of your god), and if you inhale him prompt death is the result. Now, how can you obey these gods which demand opposite service? One because he gives you warmth and life, and the other because he lays you in the icy arms of death? If for a few moments you inhale carbon, the third quarter of your god, he also puts out your life. Nor can he nourish a single plant for your food, until the plant is first fully organized (and this is its creation); the plant can now decompose the carbonic god, and finding him mixed with oxygen, making carbonic acid gas, can inhale him, and from that manufacture its own food, and that also upon which all animals feed, not any of which exists in nature outside of the plant itself. This great fact of natural science should lead " Truth Seeker " to worship the living God, who created—organized the first plants, in this act endowing them with the faculty of thus preparing—manufacturing—all the plant or vegetable food there is in the universe. Do you see? The last quarter of the god of your religion is hydrogen. But, standing alone, he is too ethereal for you to breathe, eat, or drink, or to furnish covering for your nakedness. What part of your religion do you dedicate to him?

In another point of view, Mr. " Truth Seeker," there is no reason or sense in making the first four quarters of your god symbolize the second four quarters; oxygen is not fire, though its presence is required to make fire ; but here even this analogy ends, for instead of air answering to nitrogen, it is itself composed of oxygen, nitrogen, carbon, and hydrogen. Nor is it possible to make carbon the symbol of the earth, as the earth itself is composed of these four gases. This is also the fact respecting hydrogen and water, as this gas constitutes but one-ninth of water, and oxygen eight-ninths; and though it is so called because it is considered the generator of water, yet it can only generate its own proportion, one-ninth, while oxygen generates its eight-ninths. Besides, it is a fact that the decomposition of nature equally generates hydrogen. Thus, when we come to analyze the gaseous god of

"Truth Seeker's" religion, he is dissipated into mythic nothingness, and the whole speculation, though it is the only foundation of pantheistic religion, is one of the most silly jumbles of nonsense ever invented, without science, philosophy, reason, logic, or fact in its defence ; and to be its originator would degrade a child of twelve years, except perhaps for its grotesque imagination.

It is a most gross violation of symbolic language to use a symbol to symbolize a symbol, or a symbol to symbolize that which is not known to exist—a real thing, an unreal. But here we have a half-dozen symbols symbolizing symbols involved and complicated in the most heterogeneous manner possible, destitute of likeness or correspondence, which absolutely forbids the intelligent employment of the word. Behold the beauties of the god of the pantheist and his religion ! Had you not, Mr. "Truth Seeker," better embrace atheism, and with Ingersoll come out frankly against all the gods at once ?

Again, "Truth Seeker" animadverts upon us in the following manner :

"To call Truth Seeker an infidel, however, is an equivocal outrage on truth, inasmuch as the charge implies an obligation or duty on the part of Truth Seeker to pander to Church sophistry and falsehoods, without stint or question of propriety, to which condition he could by no manner of means ever be brought. And neither owing nor ever having owed obligation or faith to the Church, he could by no possible contingency be infidel or false to that which has not now nor never has had right or claim to faith or allegiance from him."

No, sir ; we did not call you "infidel" because you do not "pander to Church sophistry and falsehood," or because you have assumed no obligation to such organizations, but because you are so unfaithful to the obligations imposed on you by the God and proprietor of your being, that you even deny his existence and pay all the devotion of which you are now capable, after your long, grovelling hunt among lifeless matter for the power that brought you into existence, to that sordid matter as your god, thus committing the greatest possible insult to the living God, and degrading yourself to the lowest degree of heathen idolatry, every form of which, whether ancient or modern, held or holds to the personal existencé of an intelligent God, supreme above all other gods, to whose direct hand they ascribed the creation of the world. Whether they acknowledge it or not, there does not exist a being capable of knowing the difference between right and wrong, whether he be an angel, devil, or man, who, from the moment he became possessed of such knowledge or faculty, but was, is, and must ever be, under the most sacred obligation to honor, worship, and obey his Creator, and that, too, simply because of this relation. It might as well and truly be said a man is not infidel to his earthly parent, the mere instrument of his being, to deny obligation to him because he had not openly professed owing it, or were he to deny his father was such. This duty is imposed by the nature of things as between the Creator and the created ; is sovereign, universal, and eternal, as well as by the commands of the "Scriptures of truth," thus : "Thou shalt love the Lord thy God with all thy heart, and with all thy soul, and with all thy strength, and thy neighbor as thyself." (Deut. 4: 5.) That the devil is not exempt because he is a devil, is shown by the following : "Then saith Jesus unto him, "Get thee hence, Satan ; for it is written, Thou shalt worship the Lord thy God, and him only shalt thou serve." (Matt. 4: 10.) If you will follow the written instructions of the living God it will elevate you in the present world mentally, morally, and physically, to the highest susceptibility of your nature, and in the world to come to the grandeur of immortal being and close association with the Lord Jesus Christ, the embodied Godhead.

For the third time we here take leave of our friend "Truth Seeker," hoping that he will become such indeed, and that the search shall be the revealed will of God to man, the embodiment of Sacred Truth.

THOMAS MITCHELL.

BROOKLYN, N. Y.

The Infidel and Atheist go but one step further than the Creed-Makers and their adherents in crediting the teaching of Scripture. The latter of these take the liberty of changing the meaning of its language [which they cover by calling it interpretation] to make it teach the doctrines of all creeds and all faiths, which they define them to be ; the others logically reject a book as having an all-wise Author who gives authority for such differences and contradictions. But in vindication of the Book and equal condemnation of both of these classes, two things may be said, that neither claim to take the words of the book to mean what they say, as they do those of every other book, when taking everything into the account it contains upon the subject. Of both classes the author makes the complaint, " They handle the word of God deceitfully." " They put light for darkness, and darkness for light." " They teach for doctrines the commandments of men." And scores of similar remonstrances are uttered in his book. In regard to the age of the world from its revealed chronology, we have shown that it is to be six thousand years. At the end of this period it is to be again dissolved into its elements by a universal conflagration and re-created into a world of perfection, beauty, and endless duration, as the endless dwelling-place of Christ and his immortal-resurrected people. One line of the revelation of this design as taught, running through the Scriptures of the Old and New Testaments, is, by using the seven days of the first Creation as symbols of seven thousand years : six covering the work and the seventh that of the rest from it.   Of course, these are seven millenniums, which though not a BIBLE word, means " A thousand years—*mille*, a thousand, *annus*, a year.

The seventh-thousand-year day, on which the Creator rested from the work of making the world and its inhabitants, because all were finished, is the symbol, or type, of the thousand-year-day on which the Creator is again to rest from the destined work of re-creating the world and its inhabitants into " a New Heaven and a New Earth," " The World to come."   " Wherein dwelleth righteousness," because none but righteous men and angels are citizens of that country.   As the rest of God on the seventh day from the work of the first creation had no end, his work being finished, so the seventh millennium day of the rest of God with his people will have no end—the work of the New Creation being also finished.   This is the only millennium taught in the Bible.   It seems unquestionable, that if the Scriptures are revelations of God and appoint the work for the new creation to take place at the expiration of six millenniums, and that at the very commencement of the sixth he began to give by a genealogical line of the first-born of each generation of men— the years of age between each, from Adam onward— which line added together makes the revealed chronology —then he must have continued that chronology until its figures, numbers, dates, and periods amount to six thousand years.   Of course, all these figures, numbers, periods, and dates must be found in the Scripture revelation, and a single break would destroy the whole, as in Bishop Usher's chronology, which contains numerous figures and dates taken from profane historians.   The Biblical Chronology we herewith submit to the public, everyone can see, meets all these conditions, superseding the necessity for human opinion. It will also be seen that our attitude is explained by the phrase, " What saith the Scripture?" If Ingersoll can scoff away Bishop Usher's chronology, not knowing enough about it to offer a criticism, except being printed in the margin of Bibles—which as he charges people confound with the text—what will he do with this BIBLICAL CHRONOLOGY, which makes the age of the world 6,000 years A.D. 1905? the whole of which we have found taught in the volume of the Book, by a half century of research to know the truth; which has been simply our duty, as it has been that of every other man during his life. Says the author: " Search the Scriptures: for they are they which testify of me." " I receive not testimony of men."

Biblical Chronology of the World from the Year One.

" This is the book of the generations of Adam. In the day that God created man, in the likeness of God created he him." (Gen. 5: 1.) Adam lived an hundred and thirty years and begat a son in his own likeness, after his own image, and called his name Seth. (Gen. 5: 3.) 130

Seth lived an hundred and five years, and begat Enos. (Gen. 5: 6.)......................... 105

Enos lived ninety years, and begat Cainan. (Gen. 5: 9.) 90

Cainan lived seventy years and begat Mahalaleel. (Gen. 5: 12.)........................ 70

Total 395

Brought forward...................... 395

Mahalaleel lived sixty-five years, and begat Jared.
(Gen. 5: 15.).............................. 65

Jared lived an hundred and sixty-two years, and
begat Enoch. (Gen. 5: 18.) 162

Enoch lived sixty-five years, and begat Methuselah. (Gen. 5: 21) 65

Methuselah lived an hundred and eighty and
seven years, and begat Lamech. (Gen. 5:
25.) 187

Lamech lived an hundred and eighty-two years,
and begat a son ; and called his name Noah. (Gen.
5: 28.) 182

Noah was five hundred years old, and begat Shem.
(Gen. 5: 32.) [Flood, 1556.]................. 500

Shem was an hundred years old, and begat Arphaxad. (Gen. 11: 10.)..................... 100

Arphaxad lived five and thirty years, and begat
Salah. (Gen. 11: 12.) 35

Salah lived thirty years, and begat Eber. (Gen.
11: 14.) 30

Eber lived four and thirty years, and begat Peleg.
(Gen. 11: 16.) 34

Peleg lived thirty years, and begat Reu. (Gen.
11: 18.) 30

Reu lived two and thirty years, and begat Serug.
(Gen. 11: 20.)............................. 32

Serug lived thirty years, and begat Nahor. (Gen.
11: 22.) 30

Nahor lived nine and twenty years, and begat
Terah. (Gen. 11: 24.)...................... 29

Total 1876

Brought forward......... 1876

Terah lived seventy years, and begat Abram.
(Gen. 11 : 26.) 70

Abram was an hundred years old, when his son
Isaac was born. (Gen. 21 : 5.) 100

Isaac was three-score years old, when Jacob was
born. (Gen. 25 : 26.)...................... 60

Joseph brought in Jacob his father, and set him
before Pharaoh ; and Jacob blessed Pharaoh ; and
Pharaoh said unto Jacob : How old art thou? And
Jacob said unto Pharaoh, The days of the years of my
pilgrimage are an hundred and thirty years. (Gen.
47 : 7–9.) 130

Now, the sojourning of the children of Israel in
Egypt was four hundred and thirty years, even the
self-same day it came to pass, that all the hosts of
the Lord went out from the land of Egypt. (Exo.
12 : 40, 41.) [Exodus, 2666.]............... 430

And it came to pass in the four hundred and
eightieth year after the children of Israel came out
of the land of Egypt, in the fourth year of Solomon's
reign over Israel, in the month Ziff, which is the second month, that he began to build the house of the
Lord. (1 Kings 6 : 1.) 480

This period covers the time of the journey of the
wilderness, the entire reign of the judges, the forty
years of the reign of Saul, the forty years of the
reign of David and the first four years of the reign
of Solomon, leaving thirty-six years of the reign
of Solomon to be added to the chronology. (1
Kings 11 : 42.) 36

Total 3182

Brought forward 3182

Rehoboam, the son of Solomon, was forty and one years old when he began to reign in Judah, and he reigned seventeen years in Jerusalem (1 Kings 14: 21.).............................   17

And Rehoboam slept with his fathers, and was buried with his fathers in the city of David, and Abijam his son reigned in his stead. Three years reigned he in Jerusalem. (1 Kings 14: 31, and 15: 2.)...................................   3

Abijam slept with his fathers, and they buried him in the city of David ; and Asa his son reigned in his stead. Forty-one years reigned he in Jerusalem. (1 Kings 15: 8–10, 41.)   41

Asa slept with his fathers, and was buried with his fathers in the city of David, and Jehoshaphat his son reigned in his stead. (1 Kings 15: 24.)......

Jehoshaphat was thirty and five years old when he began to reign, and he reigned twenty-five years in Jerusalem. (1 Kings 22: 42.)..............   25

Jehoshaphat slept with his fathers, and was buried with his fathers in the city of David, and Jehoram his son reigned in his stead. (1 Kings 22: 50.) Jehoram was thirty and two years old when he began to reign, and he reigned eight years in Jerusalem. (2 Chron. 21: 5.)..............................   8

And the inhabitants of Jerusalem made Ahaziah his youngest son king in his stead. Forty and two years old was Ahaziah when he began to reign ; and he reigned one year in Jerusalem. (2 Chron. 22: 1–2.)   1

Total 3277

Brought forward......................3277

And when Athaliah, the mother of Ahaziah, saw that her son was dead, she arose and destroyed all the seed royal, and she reigned six years in Jerusalem.   6

In the seventh year of Jehu [which was also the seventh year of Athaliah] Jehoash began to reign; and he reigned forty years in Jerusalem. (2 Kings 12 : 1.)..   40

And the rest of the acts of Jehoash, are they not written in the Book of the Chronicles of the kings of Judah?   And his servants smote him, and he died ; and they buried him in the city of David, and Amaziah reigned in his stead.   He was twenty and five years old when he began to reign ; and he reigned twenty and nine years in Jerusalem.   (2 Kings 14 : 1, 2.)..   29

And all the people of Judah took Azariah [who is also called Uzziah], and made him king, instead of his father Amaziah.   Azariah was sixteen years old when he began to reign, and he reigned two and fifty years in Jerusalem.   (2 Kings 15 : 1, 2.).....   52

So Azariah slept with his fathers in the city of David ; and Jotham his son reigned in his stead. Five and twenty years old was Jotham when he began to reign ; and he reigned sixteen years in Jerusalem.   (2 Kings 15 : 33.)....................   16

And Jotham slept with his fathers in the city of David ; and Ahaz his son reigned in his stead.   (2 Kings 15 : 38.)

Twenty years old was Ahaz when he began to reign ; and he reigned sixteen years in Jerusalem ..   16

Total 3436

Brought forward...........................3436

And Ahaz slept with his fathers in the city of David; and Hezekiah his son reigned in his stead. Hezekiah was twenty-five years old when he began to reign; and he reigned twenty and nine years in Jerusalem. (2 Kings 18 : 2.).................. 29

And Hezekiah slept with his fathers; and Manasseh his son reigned in his stead. (2 Kings 20 : 21.) Manasseh was twelve years old when he began to reign; and he reigned fifty and five years in Jerusalem. (2 Kings 21 : 1.) 55

And Manasseh slept with his fathers, and Amon his son reigned in his stead. (2 Kings 21 : 18.) Amon was twenty and two years old when he began to reign; and he reigned two years in Jerusalem. (2 Kings 21 : 19.)........................... 2

And the people of the land made Josiah his son king in his stead. (2 Kings 21 : 24.) Josiah was eight years old when he began to reign; and he reigned thirty and one years in Jerusalem. (2 Kings 22 : 1.)............................... 31

And the people of the land took Jehoahaz, the son of Josiah, and anointed him king in his father's stead. (2 Kings 23 : 31.) Jehoahaz was twenty and three years old when he began to reign; and he reigned three months in Jerusalem. And Pharaoh-nechoh, king of Egypt, put him in bands at Riblah, that he might not reign in Jerusalem. (2 Kings 23 : 32, 33.) And he made Eliakim, the son of Josiah, king in the room of his father, and he turned his name to Jehoiakim, and took Jehoahaz to Egypt,

Total 3553

Brought forward.......................3553
and he died there. (2 Kings 23: 33, 34.) And
Jehoiakim was twenty and five years old when he
began to reign ; and he reigned eleven years in Jerusalem. (2 Kings 23 : 36.)..................... 11

And Jehoiakim slept with his fathers ; and Jehoiachin his son reigned in his stead. (2 Kings 24:
5, 6.) Jehoiachin was eighteen years old when he
began to reign ; and he reigned in Jerusalem three
months. At that time [the end of the three months]
the servants of Nebuchadnezzar, king of Babylon,
came against Jerusalem and the city was besieged,
and Jehoiachin, king of Judah, went out to the king
of Babylon, he and his mother, and his princes, and
his officers, and the king of Babylon took him in the
eighth year of his reign. And carried out thence
all the treasures of the king's house, and cut in pieces
all the vessels of gold which Solomon, King of Israel,
had made in the temple of the Lord, as the Lord had
said. And he carried all Jerusalem, the princes, and
all the mighty men of valor, even ten thousand captives, and all the craftsmen and smiths : None remained save the poorest sort of the people of the
land, and he carried away Jehoaichin to Babylon.
(2 Kings 24: 10–16.)
The reign of the kings ends.................... 8

This event was the fulfilment of the prophecy of
Jeremiah, one passage of which is as follows : "The
word of the Lord that came to Jeremiah concerning all the people of Judah, in the fourth year of
Jehoiakim [the year the prophecy was given] the

Total 3572

Brought forward........................3572

son of Josiah, king of Judah, and that was the first year of Nebuchadnezzar, king of Babylon. Therefore thus, saith the Lord of hosts : " Because ye have not heard the words. [And all the calamities of the world come because men will not hearken and obey the words of the Lord.] Behold ! I will send Nebuchadnezzar, king of Babylon, my servant ; and will bring him against the land and against the inhabitants thereof, and will make them an astonishment, and an hissing, and perpetual desolation, and this whole land shall be a desolation and an astonishment ; and they shall serve the king of Babylon seventy years." (Jer. 25th.)

The captivity of Babylon was seventy years 70

The seventy weeks of Daniel, 490 days, fulfilled in four hundred and ninety years, ended in the year A.D. 37. Deduct 37 from 490, leaves 453. This reaches from the end of the captivity of Babylon to the beginning of the Christian Era............... 453

In our work entitled " The Latter Day Glory," we have shown that the prophetic period of the seventy weeks of Daniel's prophecy, ninth chapter, 490 days, was fulfilled in 490 years, both by biblical and profane history, and rests upon the same evidence as that this is the year A.D. 1893.

We have also shown in another work, entitled " Cosmogony," that there are no facts of geological science which prove the age of the physical globe, or

------

Total 4095

* Christ born 4095 of the world ; not 4004 as Bishop Usher has it, but 91 years later.

Brought forward...................4095
of its organic inhabitants, to be equal to that which
biblical chronology makes it, and equally, that there
is no evidence furnished by philosophical science in
defence of the hypothesis of evolution.

That the world may be considerably older than
the round numbers of the chronology make it, and
nearer its maturity of six thousand years, becomes
obvious by taking certain facts into the account.

First. There are forty-four factors, or numbers,
which make up this chronology. Second. It does
not reckon fractions of years. For example, it could
not be said that a certain king reigned fifty years if
it was anything less than that number. It is therefore obvious that no man can calculate the day,
month, or year when the six thousand years will be
complete. Add to these numbers the Christian Era
up to A.D. 1905 it makes the age of the world at
that date 6,000 years old.....................1905
                                              ‾‾‾‾
Grand Total 6000

We present these figures, facts, and reasons, but
give no opinion as to the age or end of the world.
"Let every man be fully persuaded in his own
mind."

"COSMOGONY."

PERSONAL TESTIMONIES.

This hard word is of Greek derivation, and means literally the generation of the world, or that science which treats of the origin of the material universe. It is the title of a recently published and most remarkable book by Professor Thomas Mitchell, and issued by the American News Company. No person can peruse carefully this volume of 450 pages—or fifteen chapters—without being impressed with the intellectual acumen, learning, and vast research of its author. He discusses in a masterly manner, and yet in a popular style, the most important subjects, such as creation, revelation, evolution, atheism, and all those insinuating errors that tend to undermine the very foundation of all religious belief.

His practical design is to enthrone God as the creator of all worlds—the infallible author of the two books, *Nature* and *Revelation*, and that therefore there can be no conflict between the two. He shows that the positions taken by modern scientists are both presuming and premature ; that evolution is a fallacy ; and that the averments and denials of modern scepticism have no foundation in science, philosophy, or common sense. After a careful perusal of this "Cosmogony," we must confess that our faith in Moses, if it were possible, has been strengthened ; that more than ever we regard Christianity as a fixture which cannot be moved, and that all the cavils of infidelity to its verity are as puff-balls hurled against the mighty fortress of Gibraltar.

Professor Mitchell, in our judgment, has done good service to truth and evangelical Christianity in writing this book, which is destinated to live after its author has gone to his reward.

SAMUEL D. BURCHARD, D.D.,

New York, 1881.   *President of Rutger's College.*

REV. THOMAS MITCHELL.

DEAR SIR : I have read your "Christianity Defended," and consider it an able and thorough overthrow of the vaporings of those who deny reason and degrade themselves by making matter their god.   Yours very truly,

HOWARD CROSBY.

MY DEAR BROTHER : I hope that the republication of "Christianity Defended" will have a wide circulation, for it is well worthy of the thoughtful examination both of sceptics and Christians.

Yours affectionately,
THOMAS ARMITAGE, D.D.

I have carefully read "Christianity Defended," by Rev. Thomas Mitchell, and regard it an unanswerable argument against evolution and atheism, and should it be published with other kindred matter [the kindred matter referred to is that of this book] by the same author, in book form, and widely circulated, it would in my judgment be a potent factor in counteracting the prevailing scepticism of the time.   Yours fraternally,

Office of the President,   S. D. BURCHARD.
)   Grand Central Depot.

REV. THOMAS MITCHELL.

MY DEAR SIR : I have read your pamphlet against the free-thinkers with much interest, and regard it as a very lucid and able production—indeed, the ablest work I know of upon the subject.

Yours very truly,
CHAUNCEY M. DEPEW.

DR. P. PERRY, of Massachusetts, says :

REV. THOMAS MITCHELL.

MY DEAR BROTHER : Book, "Cosmogony," and lecture, "Christianity Defended," received, and such a gift ! Beats any book, beats any lecture I have ever heard or read about ! While reading the lecture, my head was submerged at times, and then I would paddle up and go on, down again into the deep ! This is all true, and my wonder is that any man could dig so deep—go back of creation, and scoop out the planetary world with the hand. O what would I not have given to have been a listener, and to have observed how crest-fallen those dupes of unbelief looked. No wonder Ingersoll dared not meet you in public debate.

The "Cosmogony" buries modern science ! It is dead, and you killed it ; but you must have had the help of God.

Your lecture should be given in every College, Theological Seminary and High-school in the United States. Then go over the big pond and lecture in Oxford, getting two hundred dollars per lecture.   My everlasting love,
P. PERRY.

OPINIONS OF THE PRESS.

Troy Daily Times says :

" Cosmogony." The first volume of a work, to be complete in two volumes, by Prof. Thomas Mitchell, of Brooklyn, N. Y., is before us. It bears the title "Cosmogony, the Geological Antiquity of the World ; Evolution, Atheism, Pantheism, Deism, and Infidelity refuted by Science, Philosophy, and Scripture." As may be seen, the author has laid out a formidable task. The first volume is in many ways a remarkable book, and if the second is like unto it the author must be credited with profound zeal, wide and exhaustive study, and deep-seated conviction. It is unnecessary to say he contradicts most of the materialist reasoning of the day point blank at the outset. Humboldt's " Cosmos " was defective, because he was absorbed in the temporal and disregarded the infinite and the eternal ; and accepted the Laplace theory of Nebulæ, for which there

2

was no reason given. Schelling defined nature as the creative force of the universe, but failed to explain the origin of nature itself. Other scientific and materialist theories are taken up one by one, and answered in like manner. By applying the true standard—the necessity for explaining the cause, of which all things in nature are effects—Darwin appears a sophist, Huxley's and Tyndall's materialism is false science, and Proctor's nebular hypothesis entirely inadequate to the requirements of the subject. In short, the doctrine advanced is, that God, an actual personal being, is the author and creator of all things; that his purpose is the grand and beneficent one to re-create the present temporal world into one of endless duration and absolute perfection. Prof. Mitchell's book is one of the strongest and most radical rejoinders to materialist teachings that could be made. In these times of loose theological reasoning it is refreshing to read so scholarly and exhaustive a treatise on the most important topic that men can consider. THE SECOND VOLUME WILL BE AWAITED WITH DEEP INTEREST BY THE THINKING PART OF THE PUBLIC.

Toledo Evening Bee says:

"Cosmogony." This work is a most valuable accession to the literature of the world, and peculiarly applicable to these times, when the rapid spread of infidelity is noted with alarm. In this great work the Rev. Thomas Mitchell attacks with skill and spirit the positions and theories of the evolutionists, geologists, astronomers, chronologists, and the whole school of atheists who are panoplied in the garb of science. In it he reaches conclusions not only logical, but which are unanswerable. It fully meets the pretended scientific objections to the Holy Scriptures and Christianity, as well as those of the sceptical and atheistic world. He marches boldly into the enemy's country, and fights him on his own ground and with his own weapons, the truths of science. In dealing with Robert G. Ingersoll he uses no velvet words—no gloved hands. He directly charges him with untruth and misrepresentation. He also shows Humboldt's defects with irresistible argument. It is a work of great merit and displays wide research and learning, with its facts well arranged, its illustrations apt and striking, and its language clear and forcible. IT IS A WORK THAT SHOULD BE WIDELY READ.

Pittsburg Telegraph says:

"Cosmogony." Certain philosophers, at different times in the history of the world, have attempted to show that there is an unreconcilable difference between Scripture and science, and have labored to demonstrate that the world does not owe its being to an intelligent first great cause. At the present time certain scientists are putting forth the most Herculean efforts to convert the world to a belief in their infidel tenets, but the champions of the Holy Scriptures and their divine inspiration are not all asleep. On the contrary, many able pens are busily engaged in counteracting the influence of a false philosophy, and are nobly defending the bulwarks of orthodox faith.

Judge Black, in his reply to Col. Robert Ingersoll, adopts the mode of warfare formerly used by the stump speakers, and indulges in personal abuse of his adversary. His reply is all assertion, and contains no argument. There is nothing in it that would convince and convert any person whose name is enrolled in the Ingersoll school. Indeed, the denunciation and abuse which Judge Black hurls at the head of his antagonist would, in the opinion of a good many, go to show that he had no faith in the strength and impregnability of his own cause.

Prof. Mitchell does not indulge in the use of abusive language against Darwin, Lyell, Huxley, and others. His work is argumentative from the *Alpha* to the *Omega* of the first volume, and, in our opinion, his arguments are unanswerable. Besides, his work is stripped, as far as can be, of the technicalities of the scientists, which so much bewilder the common people. He presents an abstruse subject in about as popular a form as it could well be presented, and we have no doubt his work will be duly appreciated by both the learned and unlearned.

Pittsburg Daily Post says :

"Cosmogony." Prof. Thomas Mitchell, of Brooklyn, N. Y., in this work, the first volume of which has been published, aims to meet all the objections to the Scriptures and Christianity, as well as those of the scientific and atheistical world. A critic says of the work that "it displays research, learning, and thorough acquaintance with the sacred volume. The facts are well arranged, the illustrations are apt and striking—all expressed in clear and forcible language." The Professor charges on the whole battalion of materialists and infidels of the day, from Darwin to Ingersoll.

New York Herald says :

"Cosmogony." Under this title Professor Thomas Mitchell has written a very elaborate and learned work.

Syracuse Herald says :

Mitchell's "Cosmogony." As this is not a newspaper devoted to religious or scientific polemics, the most we can hope is to give the reader a general idea of what the work sets out to do ; and this we may sum up in the brief statement that it takes the Bible just as we find it in the English version of King James, and argues for the absolute truth thereof, without reservation. The first step in his method is to show by certain familiar illustrations that nature is not self-existent, and hence that the universe must have had a personal creator. The second step, which is an easy one after the first is fairly settled, is to direct the inference that it would have been quite possible for the Creator to bring the universe into being in its present state, with its strata of rock and its fossil formations placed just as we find them, for a purpose of his own, and all actually within the six solar days allotted to the work in the book of Genesis. We make space for one short extract from an argument intended to show the falsehood of the data depended on as essential by the scientists :

"Let it be conceded that the world was created with a degree of perfection capable of sustaining life—which implies a condition as high as that which now exists, everything in maturity—do we not see that all bore the marks of age? For example, a tree was made a tree, with its ripe fruit ready to sustain the life of man, and its trunk would perhaps show thirty rings or grains, one of which is formed each year by the law of nature, or of natural growth. Understanding this law, a botanist would have pronounced the tree thirty years old the day on which it was made. Adam was made a man, and not an infant to grow to one; the day after this he might have been pronounced thirty years old. The two great whales made on the fifth day might have been pronounced a hundred years old on the day of their creation. A certain stratum of granite as the foundation of others: God endowed the atoms with affinities and adhesive attractions requisite to such formation, which sent them in rapid haste toward each other, and in like manner each stratum was formed in an hour."

Boston Sunday Herald says:

"Cosmogony" is the title of a well-printed volume, in which Prof. Thomas Mitchell, from the standpoint of an orthodox believer in the Scriptures, strikes all the modern scientists with sledge-hammer blows. He argues with ability that Profs. Darwin, Lyell, Huxley, Tyndall, and Proctor, and all the other materialistic philosophers of our time are teaching false doctrines to the people. It is a very interesting volume, and the old-fashioned defenders of the divine inspiration of the Scriptures against the assaults of the modern materialists are to be congratulated that they have so learned, logical and altogether able defender.

Brooklyn Union-Argus says:

"Cosmogony." This is the first of two volumes, the second being now in press, by Prof. Thomas Mitchell, of this city. The Professor has manifestly made the topics here treated of the subject of long and earnest thought, and has been a wide and careful reader. He deals with a subject of vast importance, and one that has attracted the master minds of all ages. He boldly confronts error wherever he finds it; he shuns no investigation, and deals with the whole range of natural philosophy and science, from the grandest complication to the simplest molecules. He regards the Bible statements of creation as the most advanced science, and the spiritual narrative as true, the deluge as universal; and points out how the structural and superficial changes in the earth may be accounted for, and consistent with the destruction of the Eden world by that flood. He denies the existence of a glacial period or a carboniferous epoch, and broadly meets the speculations of Lyell, Darwin, Agassiz, Tyndall and Huxley, and the nebular hypothesis of Laplace, and advises "the star-gazers," whose telescopes pierce the interstellar spaces, to betake themselves to substantial investigation, and give us either matter of fact or logical argument. Mr. Mitchell attacks the assumed science of these men with science—its own weapons, which it has

5

self revealed. The closing section is a picture of the world with man extinct, and is a striking statement of a demonstration of the belief that all organic beings and things, plants and animals, with man at their head, came into existence simultaneously.

Sunday Baltimore News says:

"Cosmogony." By Prof. Thomas Mitchell. This is a very comprehensive and able work upon the creation of the world and all incidental themes and subjects growing therefrom. It has the commendation of several of the leading men of the country—those of most profound thought—and will do much good service in brushing away the cobwebs of sophistry woven about matters which, for good and wise purposes, have always been wrapped in mystery.

Baltimore Sunday Press says:

"Cosmogony." By Prof. Thomas Mitchell. This work is devoted to a refutation of the theories of the geological antiquity of the world, evolution, pantheism, deism, and infidelity by science, philosophy, and Scripture. The style of the author is clear and attractive, and his arguments have remarkable force and originality. The book is by no means as tedious as metaphysical works generally, but has decided points of interest for even the casual reader.

6

BOOK READY APRIL 15TH.